for
reference

HISTORICAL DICTIONARIES
OF U.S. HISTORICAL ERAS
Jon Woronoff, Series Editor

1. *From the Great War to the Great Depression,* by Neil A. Wynn, 2003.
2. *Civil War and Reconstruction,* by William L. Richter, 2004.

Historical Dictionary from the Great War to the Great Depression

Neil A. Wynn

Historical Dictionaries of
U.S. Historical Eras, No. 1

The Scarecrow Press, Inc.
Lanham, Maryland, and Oxford
2003

SCARECROW PRESS, INC.

Published in the United States of America
by Scarecrow Press, Inc.
A wholly owned subsidiary of the Rowman & Littlefield Publishing Group, Inc.
4501 Forbes Boulevard, Suite 200, Lanham, Maryland 20706
www.scarecrowpress.com

PO Box 317
Oxford
OX2 9RU, UK

Copyright © 2003 by Neil A. Wynn

All rights reserved. No part of this publication may be reproduced,
stored in a retrieval system, or transmitted in any form or by any
means, electronic, mechanical, photocopying, recording, or otherwise,
without the prior permission of the publisher.

British Library Cataloguing in Publication Information Available

Library of Congress Cataloging-in-Publication Data
Wynn, Neil A.
  Historical dictionary from the Great War to the Great Depression /
Neil A. Wynn.
    p. cm. — (Historical dictionaries of U.S. historical eras ;
no. 1)
  Includes bibliographical references.
  ISBN 0-8108-4843-0 (alk. paper)
  1. United States—History—1913—1921—Dictionaries.   2. United
States—History—1919–1933—Dictionaries.   I. Title. II. Series.
E740.7 .W96 2003
973.91'03—dc21   2003009142

⊗™ The paper used in this publication meets the minimum requirements of
American National Standard for Information Sciences—Permanence of
Paper for Printed Library Materials, ANSI/NISO Z39.48-1992.
Manufactured in the United States of America.

AUSTIN COMMUNITY COLLEGE
LIBRARY SERVICES

CONTENTS

Editor's Foreword

When writing history, there is a temptation to enliven it with such words as *crisis*, *turning point*, or *watershed*, whether they are justified or not. In the period from 1913 to 1933, roughly from the election of Woodrow Wilson to Herbert Hoover's failure to win a second term, these expressions are entirely appropriate in referring to United States history. The period opened with a moment of dramatic political change at home, followed by a major international crisis, World War I, which drastically affected in United States. It ended with another major crisis, an economic depression that gradually spread to many other countries and in its severity and duration justified the description of the Great Depression. There was also a great deal of significant social change, change in the situation of women in the workplace and in the election booths, change in the ethnic composition of the country with massive immigration and a flight of black Americans to the North, change in the attitudes and status of the working class, and also change in the attitudes of African Americans (although a change in their status lagged behind). In some cases, the change was great enough to be called a *turning point*. This is particularly true of America's position in the world, moving from peripheral to central, and shifting from isolationism to active participation in world affairs, although there was a temporary retreat after World War I.

This explains why the *Historical Dictionary from the Great War to the Great Depression* is so interesting, and also fairly large. A lot happened in these two decades, more than usually happens in such a short period. As usual, the broad view is sketched in the introduction while the details are drawn in the dictionary entries. These entries include the major events, not only political but also economic, social, and cultural, the presidents and other significant persons, organizations and institutions, movements and legal decisions, plus some of the fads and fashions that marked the times. The chronology makes it easier to see how things came together. And the bibliography directs readers who want further information to the relevant literature.

Although most of the volumes in this new series of Historical Dictionaries of U.S. Historical Eras are written by Americans, some are not. This can have definite advantages when they treat the subject carefully and objectively but from a distance. The author of this volume, Neil A. Wynn, studies and now teaches in Great Britain at the University of Gloucestershire, where he is professor of twentieth century American history. However, he has frequently visited and taught in the United States. Although his special interest is African American history, the time period he knows best is, not by coincidence, the same one that is covered here. In addition to lecturing, Dr. Wynn has written extensively on the period, including two books, *From Progressivism to Prosperity: World War I and American Society*, which he authored, and *America's Century: Perspectives on U.S. History since 1900*, which he coedited. This time he provides an excellent vantage point for surveying what can justifiably be called an "interesting" period.

Jon Woronoff
Series Editor

Chronology

1913   9–18 February: The government of Francisco Madero was overthrown by Victoriano Huerta in Mexico. The United States did not recognize the new regime. **25 February:** The Sixteenth Amendment empowering Congress to tax incomes, passed by Congress on 12 July 1909, was ratified. **4 March:** President Woodrow Wilson (Democrat) inaugurated having defeated William Howard Taft (Republican) and Theodore Roosevelt (Progressive) in the election in November 1912. In his inaugural address Wilson promised to tackle the "fearful physical and spiritual cost" of the country's industrial growth. **30 March:** The Sixteenth Amendment, providing Congress with the power to tax incomes, was ratified. **8 April:** President Wilson broke with tradition and outlined his legislative program in person to a special session of Congress. **31 May:** The Seventeenth Amendment, providing for the direct election of senators, ratified. **3 October:** The Underwood-Simmons Tariff Act was passed providing for the first significant lowering of duties since 1861. **November–April 1914:** The Wilson administration sought to achieve the removal of Huerta from power in Mexico through diplomatic means. **23 December:** Federal Reserve Act passed establishing 12 regional Federal Reserve Banks supervised by the Federal Reserve Board to regulate currency and credit operations in the United States.

1914   27 January: United States' forces landed in Port-au-Prince, Haiti, to protect American interests until order was restored following the outbreak of revolution on the island. **10 April:** United States seamen from *U.S.S. Dolphin* were arrested when they landed without permission in Tampico, Mexico. Although the men were soon released and an apology was given, the Wilson administration demanded that United States' flag be given an official salute or suffer the consequences. **21 April:** United States Marines occupied Vera Cruz, Mexico, following the

Tampico incident and the failure to salute the United States' flag, and in order to prevent the landing of a shipment of arms. **8 May:** The Smith-Lever Act providing federal funds for agricultural extension colleges and adult education was passed. **28 June:** Archduke Franz Ferdinand assassinated in Sarajevo, Bosnia, sparking the crisis that led to the outbreak of World War I. **4 August:** Following various declarations of war in Europe President Wilson announced United States' neutrality. **29 August:** 1,500 women march in silence down Fifth Avenue, New York City, in protest against the outbreak of war in Europe. **10 September:** Federal Trade Commission Act passed. It abolished the Bureau of Corporations established in 1903 and replaced it with a five-man Federal Trade Commission to supervise business in order to prevent corporations from using unfair means of competition. **15 October:** Clayton Anti-Trust Act strengthening the 1890 Sherman Anti-Trust Act passed. The Act prohibited interlocking directorates, forbade corporations from purchasing securities of other companies to eliminate competition, and held company officers personally liable for offenses. It also sought to exclude labor from antitrust legislation by declaring that the "labor of human beings is not a commodity or article of commerce."

1915 A "Preparedness" movement developed in the United States in response to the war in Europe and increasing conflict about shipping rights between the U.S. and belligerent powers. Organizations such as the National Security League (formed in December 1914) and the American Defense Society (August 1915), supported by individuals such as Theodore Roosevelt and Senator Henry Cabot Lodge, called for an increase in U.S. military and naval strength. **10 February:** Following a German declaration establishing a war zone around Great Britain, the Wilson administration announced it would hold Germany strictly accountable for the sinking of United States vessels by U-boats. **4 March:** The Seaman's Act establishing minimum standards for sailors, sponsored by Senator Robert M. La Follette, was passed. **7 May:** The Cunard passenger liner, *Lusitania*, was sunk by German U-boat off Ireland with the loss of 1,200 lives including 128 Americans. The Wilson administration warned that similar actions could be construed as "deliberately unfriendly." **7 June:** Secretary of State William Jennings Bryan resigned in protest at the strength of Wilson's statement. **28 July:** United States' forces took control of Haiti following a series of internal revolts. The United States effectively remained in control until 1934. **19 August:** The British liner *Arabic* was sunk by a German U-boat with the loss of two American lives. The German government disavowed the action and temporarily abandoned unrestricted submarine warfare. **4 November:** President Wilson announced his "Preparedness" defense program and called for its adoption in the light of growing differences with Germany. The plans included expansion of the navy and army.

1916   9 March: Mexican forces led by Pancho Villa attacked Columbus, New Mexico, killing 19 Americans. **15 March:** A "Punitive Expedition" of United States troops led by General John Pershing entered Mexico in pursuit of Pancho Villa and his forces. The expedition was withdrawn in February 1917. **18 April:** Following the sinking of the unarmed French Channel steamer *Sussex* on 24 March by a German U-boat, President Wilson issued an ultimatum to the German government threatening to sever diplomatic relations. The German government pledged to suspend unrestricted submarine attacks without warning. **15 May:** United States forces occupied and took control of Santo Domingo in the Dominican Republic following the overthrow of the government. They remained in control until 1924. **3 June:** National Defense Act, increasing the strength of the United States Army, passed as part of the "Preparedness" campaign. **8–10 June:** Republican Party convention in Chicago nominated Charles Evans Hughes as presidential candidate. The Progressive Party nominated Roosevelt who declined and urged his supporters to back Hughes. The Progressive Party disbanded shortly after, but many leading members threw their support behind Woodrow Wilson who was renominated for the Democratic Party at the convention in St. Louis. The slogan that emerged from the convention was "He kept us out of war." **11 July:** The Federal Highway Act provided $75 million over five years to match state spending on road building. When the act was renewed in 1921 it introduced the systematic numbering of highways in the United States. **17 July:** Federal Farm Loan Act passed establishing 12 Farm Land Banks supervised by a seven-man Federal Farm Loan Board to provide bank credits for farmers. **August:** A Workmen's Compensation Act for federal employees was passed. **4 August:** Treaty of Denmark confirmed the United States' purchase of the Virgin Isles. **29 August:** A Council of National Defense was established to direct industrial mobilization as a part of "military preparedness." **1 September:** The Keating-Owen Child Labor Act, prohibiting the shipping across state lines of goods manufactured by companies employing children under 14 or mines employing children under 16, was signed by President Wilson. **3 September:** Adamson Act passed introducing the eight-hour day for workers on interstate railways starting from 1 January 1917. The act was passed to avert a general railway strike after railroad presidents had refused to accept the principle voluntarily despite the pleading of President Wilson. **7 September:** United States Shipping Board created to enlarge the merchant marine. In April 1917 this became the United States Emergency Fleet Corporation. **7 November:** President Wilson was re-elected. He received over 9 million votes as against 8.5 million for Hughes. Wilson won 277 votes in the Electoral College, a majority of 23. However, the Democratic majority in the Senate was reduced from 16 to 12 while the balance between the two major parties in the House was held by a handful of Progressives, Independents, and a Socialist.

1917   22 January: In an address to the United States Senate President Wilson called for a "peace without victory" in any postwar settlement. **3 February:** Following the resumption of unrestricted submarine warfare, the United States broke off diplomatic relations with Germany. **5 February:** An Immigration Act introducing a literacy test was passed over President Wilson's veto. **1 March:** Contents of the Zimmerman telegram promising German support for territorial gains by Mexico in the event of a future war with the United States were made public having been intercepted by the British government on 16 January. **2 March:** Jones Act established Puerto Rico as a territory and conferred United States citizenship on Puerto Ricans. **19 March:** Daylight Saving introduced. The measure was repealed in 1919. **6 April:** Following the resumption of unrestricted submarine warfare the United States declared war on Germany and joined the Allied countries in World War I. **13 April:** A Committee of Public Information (CPI) chaired by George Creel was established to mobilize public opinion in support of the war. **18 May:** The Selective Service Act introducing wartime conscription was passed. **15 June:** Espionage Act providing for fines of up to $10,000 and 20 years in prison for acts of sabotage passed. **2 July:** A race riot in which at least 29 African Americans and 8 whites died broke out in East St. Louis, Illinois. **28 July:** Several thousand people marched in a silent protest in New York City organized by the National Association for the Advancement of Colored People (NAACP) to protest against race violence. **28 July:** A War Industries Board (WIB) was established to coordinate economic mobilization. Banker Bernard Baruch became head of a strengthened WIB in March 1918. **10 August:** Lever Food and Fuel Control Act passed establishing the U.S. Food Administration and U.S. Fuel Administration. **23 August:** Following several incidents of racial harassment members of the Third Battalion of the all-African American 24th Infantry fired indiscriminately on white people in Houston, Texas. Sixteen whites and four blacks were killed in the riot. Thirteen of the black soldiers were subsequently court-martialed and executed in San Antonio in December 1917. **6 October:** Penalties were introduced for anyone trading with the Central Powers under the Trading with the Enemy Act. **21 October:** The first contingents of the American Expeditionary Force entered the line in France. **26 December:** The federal government took control of the railroads under the Rail Administration headed by William Gibbs McAdoo.

1918   January: All industries east of the Mississippi were ordered to close for a week by James A. Garfield, head of the Fuel Administration, in order to break the deadlock in coal supplies. **8 January:** In a speech to Congress President Wilson outlined the "Fourteen Points" on which an armistice with the Central Powers could be signed, including provision for a League of Nations. **March:** The first outbreak in what was to become a worldwide influenza epidemic began at a military camp in Kansas. Eventually more than 650,000 Americans died as a result of the illness. **9 April:** The National War Labor Board (NWLB) was established to mediate in labor disputes affecting war production. **16 May:** Fines of up to $10,000 and prison terms of up to 20 years were established for anyone uttering, writing, printing, or publishing anything that might hinder the war effort or be deemed critical of the United States government or armed forces were introduced under the Sedition Act. **20 May:** The Overman Act, enabling the president to redistribute powers among executive agencies without consulting Congress, was passed to increase government efficiency in wartime. **3 June:** In *Hammer v. Dagenhart* the Supreme Court found by five votes to four that the 1916 Keating-Owen Act was unconstitutional. **July:** 275,000 United States troops took part in the battle of the Marne halting a German offensive. **16 August:** United States troops sent to Vladivostock, Siberia, in the Allied intervention in Russian Civil War. **26 September–11 November:** United States' troops played a leading role in the Meuse-Argonne offensive that ended with the re-capture of Sedan and negotiations for an armistice. **5 November:** The Republican Party gained majorities in both the House and Senate in the midterm elections. **8 November:** An armistice was agreed between the Allied and German forces on the western front. **11 November:** The armistice between the Allied Powers and Germany, bringing an end to fighting on the western front, was formally signed at 11 a.m.

1919 Second Child Labor Act passed introducing a tax of 10 percent on products made in businesses employing children under the age of 14. The Supreme Court declared the law unconstitutional in 1922. **18 January–28 June:** Versailles Peace Conference met to agree the terms of the settlement after World War I. **21 January–10 February:** Strike by shipyard workers in Seattle turned into a general strike, but collapsed in face of public opposition and police action called by Mayor Ole Hanson. **29 January:** The Eighteenth Amendment introducing Prohibition was ratified. **3 March:** In *Schenck v. United States* the United States Supreme Court upheld the conviction of Charles T. Schenck on the grounds that the distribution of leaflets urging draft resistance constituted a "clear and present danger" to the country during war. **July:** Two African Americans died during a race riot in Longview, Texas. **27 July:** A race riot began in Chicago. When the riot ended five days later 23 African Americans and 15 whites were dead. **9 September:** Boston police struck for union recognition. Looting and violence broke out in the city until the State Guard was called in to restore order. **22 September–8 January 1920:** A national steel strike took place in an attempt to gain union recognition and win an eight-hour day. The strike was unsuccessful. **26 September:** President Wilson suffered a stroke while on a speaking tour in support of the Versailles treaty. **30 September:** African American sharecroppers meeting to form a union in Elaine, Arkansas, were involved in a confrontation with a group of white men. After a white deputy sheriff was shot and killed in the clash, violence spread as a white mob attacked the black community. Five whites and "anywhere from 20 to 200" African Americans died in the ensuing violence between 1 and 3 October. **11 October:** The Volstead Act or National Prohibition Act was passed to implement the provisions of the Eighteenth Amendment. **6–23 October:** An Industrial Conference with representatives of employers, labor, and the public met in Washington, D.C., to try to settle the postwar industrial unrest. No agreement was reached. **7 November:** In the first raids authorized by Attorney General

A. Mitchell Palmer, 600 people were arrested as suspected revolution-aries in different cities. **10 November:** In *Abrams v. United States* the United States Supreme Court upheld the conviction under the Sedition Act of Julius Abrams for distributing leaflets denouncing American intervention in the Russian Civil War by a majority of seven to two. **11 November:** Wesley Everett, a member of the Industrial Workers of the World (IWW) was castrated and lynched following a confrontation between the IWW and members of the American Legion, aided by the Citizens' Protective League, in Centralia, Washington, in which three members of the Legion were killed.

1920   January–March: A Second Industrial Conference met to con-sider the problems of industrial relations. It proposed a 48-hour week, minimum wages, and equal pay, but had little impact amid the postwar recession and the "Red Scare." **1 January:** United States census re-ported that the United States population was 105.7 million. For the first time in United States history, the urban population exceeded rural population. **2 January:** The "Palmer Raids" continued. Under the direction of Attorney-General A. Mitchell Palmer 2,700 suspected communists were arrested. By the time the raids ended in May 6,000 people had been arrested. **5 January:** Boston Red Sox baseball star Babe Ruth was sold to the New York Yankees for $125,000, the biggest trade deal in baseball up to that time. **15 January:** The League of Na-tions first met in Paris. **17 January:** The Eighteenth Amendment to the United States Constitution went into effect, and Prohibition began with the ban on the making, selling, or the transportation of alcoholic bev-erages. **24 January:** The United States Expeditionary forces returned from Europe. **1 March:** The Railroad Transportation Act (Esch-Cummins Act) ended wartime federal control of the railroads, provided federal funds to help rail companies re-establish themselves, and es-tablished a Railway Labor Board to mediate in labor disputes. **19 March:** The United States Senate refused to join the League of Nations or rat-ify the Treaty of Versailles. **26 March:** F. Scott Fitzgerald's *This Side of Paradise*, his first novel, is published to wide acclaim. **1 April:** Five elected members of the New York state legislature were expelled for be-ing members of the Socialist Party. **19 May:** Twelve people, mostly men from the detective agency hired by coal operators to stop the or-ganization of mine workers by the United Mine Workers' union, were killed at Matewan, West Virginia. **8 June:** The Republican Party convention nominated Warren G. Harding in the convention at Chicago. **28 June:** The Democratic Party convention, divided between pro-League supporters and isolationists, antiprohibitionists and prohibitionists, nominated James M. Cox on the 44th ballot. **29 July:** First transcontinental airmail service, New York to San Francisco. **26 August:** The Nineteenth Amendment to the United States Constitution accepting women's right to vote was ratified. **16 September:** A bomb exploded near the Wall Street offices of J. P. Morgan's company, killing 30 (some accounts say 35). Suspected radicals were arrested and later released, but the perpetrator was never found. **2 November:** Republican Warren G. Harding won the presidential election when he defeated the Democratic candidate James M. Cox by 16.1 million votes to 9.1 million, and 404 Electoral College votes to 127.

1921 4 March: Warren G. Harding inaugurated as President of the United States. **10 May:** President Harding issued an executive order transferring management of the navy's emergency oil field deposits to the Department of the Interior. One of the oil fields was located at Teapot Dome, Wyoming. **19 May:** Quota Act limited immigration to no more than 3 percent annually of each nationality, based on the number of that nationality already residing in the U.S. (as of 1910). **31 May:** Trial of Sacco and Vanzetti, Italian anarchists accused of robbery and murder, began in Dedham, Massachusetts. **31 May:** Race riot in Tulsa, Oklahoma, began. It was estimated that as many as 200 blacks and 50 whites died in three days of violence. **10 June:** The Budget and Accounting Act was passed establishing the fiscal year from 1 July to 30 June and creating the General Accounting Office and Bureau of the Budget. **2 July:** First radio broadcast of heavyweight boxing title bout between Georges Carpentier and Jack Dempsey from Jersey City, N.J. This was also the first time that box office receipts for a boxing match reached $1 million. **14 July:** The case of Sacco and Vanzetti became a cause of national and international protest when they were convicted of murder and sentenced to death. Their conviction appeared to be due more to their immigrant background and political views than the weight of evidence. **9 August:** The Veterans Bureau was established. **25 August:** Peace Treaty between United States and Germany signed. **12 November–6 February 1922:** International Disarmament Conference began in Washington, D.C., to address mutual concerns about a developing postwar arms race. United States Secretary of State Charles Evans Hughes proposed that the major powers stop building large navy ships for 10 years. The United States, Britain, France, Japan, and Italy agreed to the terms by the conference's end on 6 February 1922. **23 November:** Sheppard-Towner Act providing federal funds for maternity and infant health care was passed. It remained in operation until 1929.

1922   1 April: A national coal strike began in protest of wage reductions and industrial and government labor union policies. The strike ended in September with some concessions to the miners. **7 April:** Secretary of the Interior Albert B. Fall leased the navy's Teapot Dome oil field secretly, without competitive bidding, to Harry F. Sinclair and the Mammoth Oil Co. Later, on April 25 and 11 December, Fall leased the Elk Hills Reserve to Edward L. Doheny in similar fashion. It was later found in investigations that Fall had taken bribes for these transactions. **15 May:** The Supreme Court found that the 1919 Child Labor Law was unconstitutional in that a 10 percent tax on goods produced in factories employing children was a selective penalty. **1 July:** Railway shopmen went on strike. The strike ended unsuccessfully after several weeks when Attorney General Harry Daugherty secured a court injunction severely restricting the strikers' actions. **21 September:** The Fordney-McCumber Tariff Act, raising many duties to the levels of 1909 or earlier, passed to protect new war industries. **21 November:** Rebecca Latimer Felton, appointed in Georgia to fill a deceased senator's unexpired term, became the first woman senator in the United States. **4 December:** Dyer Anti-Lynching Bill, although passed by the House of Representatives, was withdrawn from the Senate after a filibuster by southern states.

1923   1–5 January: A white mob murdered eight African Americans and forced the population of Rosewood, Florida, to flee following an unconfirmed report of an assault on a white woman by a black male. No one was prosecuted for the outrage. **3 March:** United States Senate rejected the proposal for the United States to join the International Court of Justice. **2–3 May:** First transcontinental airplane flight made in 26 hours, 50 minutes, from New York to San Diego. **2 August:** President Harding died of apoplexy (heart attack) in San Francisco. Vice president Calvin Coolidge took office the next day. **13 August:** U.S.

Steel introduced an eight-hour work day at the urging of Secretary of Commerce, Herbert Hoover. On 16 August, the Carnegie Steel Company also accepted the eight-hour work day.

1924   16 January: The first McNary-Haugen bill was introduced in Congress. Intended to raise farm prices artificially by employing a federal farm corporation to store surplus agricultural produce, the measure was defeated in 1924, passed in 1927, and vetoed by President Coolidge in February 1927 and again in May 1928. **3 February:** Former President Wilson died. **28 February:** United States troops landed in Honduras to protect American interests. **26 May:** National Origins Act, limiting immigration to 150,000 a year and further reducing quotas on certain national groups, passed. The act completely prohibited Japanese immigration, sparking diplomatic protests from Japan. **10 June:** The Republican Party convention in Cleveland nominated Calvin Coolidge and Charles G. Dawes. **24 June:** The Democratic Party nominated John W. Davis as presidential candidate and Charles W. Bryan as vice presidential candidate at the convention in New York. **4 July:** The Conference for Progressive Political Action, an alliance of Progressives, farm interests, and the American Federation of Labor, met in Cleveland to form a new Progressive Party with Robert M. La Follette as presidential candidate, and Burton K. Wheeler as the vice presidential candidate. **16 August:** The Dawes Plan reducing German reparation payments was adopted by a London conference. The plan's coauthors, United States Secretary of State, Charles G. Dawes, and the British Foreign Secretary, Sir J. Austen Chamberlain, won the Nobel Peace Prize in 1925. **June:** Congress passed the law granting citizenship to American Indians. **10 September:** Nathan Leopold, Jr., 19, and Richard Loeb, 18, who kidnapped and murdered a 14-year-old boy on 22 May for sport, were sentenced to life in prison rather than the electric chair following the successful use of the "insanity defense" by Clarence Darrow. **4 November:** Calvin Coolidge was elected president with 15.7 million votes to 8.3 million for the Democrat John W. Davis, and 4.8 million for the Progressive candidate, Robert M. La Follette.

1925   5 January: Nellie Tayloe Ross (Dem.) became first female state governor when she completed the two years remaining of her dead husband's term in Wyoming. She was defeated in the election of 1926. **10 April:** F. Scott Fitzgerald's acclaimed novel of the Twenties, *The Great*

Gatsby, was published. **10–25 July:** The "Scopes Monkey Trial" in which John T. Scopes was accused of teaching evolution in a Tennessee school in violation of state law pitted the leading lawyer, Clarence Darrow (representing Scopes), against the former politician William Jennings Bryan for the prosecution in a great debate that gripped the national media. Scopes was found guilty on July 21 and ordered to pay $100 plus court costs. His fine and the case were dismissed on a technicality on appeal in January 1927 by the Tennessee Supreme Court. **8 August:** An estimated 40,000 Ku Klux Klan members marched through Washington, D.C., as part of the organization's first national congress. **3 September:** The navy dirigible *Shenandoah* crashed in Ohio killing 14 airmen. United States Air Service General William "Billy" Mitchell, a hero of World War I and early air power advocate, criticized government administration of its air fleet as incompetent following the airship crash. He was subsequently forced to resign.

1926 Railway Labor Act (Watson-Parker Act) abolished the Railroad Labor Board established in 1920 and replaced it with a National Board of Mediation. **May:** Leading evangelist Aimee Semple McPherson mysteriously disappeared. She reappeared several weeks later claiming to have been abducted and tortured. Later speculation was that she was actually in hiding with a lover, or pulling a publicity stunt, or both. **2 May:** United States troops landed in Nicaragua to restore order following a revolt. **9 May:** United States Commander Richard E. Byrd and pilot Floyd Bennett became the first people to fly over the North Pole. **26 June:** McNary-Haugen Bill to introduce tariffs on agricultural produce was defeated in the Senate. **6 August:** Gertrude Ederle became the first woman to swim the English Channel, a feat that earned her a New York City ticker tape parade. **23 August:** Rudolph Valentino, star of *The Sheik*, and movie idol died of a perforated ulcer at age 31. **25 September:** Henry Ford instituted the five-day work week and eight-hour day to reduce overproduction.

1927 **1 March:** President Coolidge appointed the first five-man Federal Board of Radio Control to oversee radio broadcasting and issue licenses. **7 March:** The Supreme Court declared the Texas law excluding African Americans from voting in the state's primary election unconstitutional. **16 April:** The worst Mississippi River flooding (until 1937) occurred, eventually covering 4.4 million acres and causing $300 million in damage. **4 May:** United States Marines land in Nicaragua to supervise elections. American troops remained until 1932–33. **20–21 May:** Charles Lindbergh made the first one-person, nonstop transatlantic airplane flight, from New York to Paris, in his *Spirit of St. Louis* monoplane. **20 June–24 August:** An international conference called by President Coolidge met at Geneva to consider further naval limitations. Only Great Britain and Japan took part with the United States and no agreement was reached. **2 August:** President Coolidge unexpectedly announced he "did not choose to run for president in 1928." **23 August:** Sacco and Vanzetti were executed at Charlestown State Prison, Massachusetts. **30 September:** New York Yankees baseball star Babe Ruth hit his 60th home run for the season, a mark not again achieved for 34 years. **6 October:** Premiere of the movie, *The Jazz Singer*. Although only a partial "talkie" using conversational dialogue as part of a dramatic story, the film was regarded as the first sound picture. It earned more than $3 million, making it one of the biggest hits of the 1920s, and changed the film industry forever. **10 October:** The Supreme Court upheld lower court rulings that Teapot Dome oil leases with Harry Sinclair's Mammoth Oil Co. were fraudulently obtained and should be declared illegal. Earlier, on 28 February, the court ruled oil contracts and leases granted to Edward Doheny by Interior Secretary Albert Fall in 1921 to be illegal and fraudulent. **2 December:** Ford Motor Co. unveiled the Model A to replace the Model T car that had revolutionized motorcar manufacture.

1928   12 January: Ruth Snyder became only the second woman to be electrocuted when she was executed at Sing Sing prison New York for the murder of her husband. Her lover, Judd Gray, was executed the same day. **15 May:** Flood Control Act passed to provide a $325 million, 10-year program of flood control on the Mississippi River and tributaries. **June:** The Republican Party convention in Kansas City nominated Herbert Hoover as their candidate to succeed Calvin Coolidge. The Democrats, meeting in Houston, Texas, nominated Al Smith, governor of New York with Joseph T. Robinson of Arkansas as his running mate. The campaign was to focus on Smith's Catholicism, his opposition to Prohibition, and his urban, immigrant background. **17–18 June:** Amelia Earhart made the first transatlantic flight by a woman, flying with Wilmer Stultz and Louis Gordon. **27 August:** Kellogg-Briand Pact outlawing war as an instrument of foreign policy signed in Paris. **6 November:** Herbert Hoover was elected president, defeating Al Smith by

21.4 million votes to 15 million, and 444 Electoral College votes to 87. Significantly, while Hoover carried half of the states of the traditionally Democratic former Confederacy, Smith won majorities in the largest cities most of which had previously voted Republican.

1929   14 February: Seven gangsters were killed in the "St. Valentine's Day Massacre" by members of Al Capone's gang. **3 March:** Herbert Hoover was inaugurated as president of the United States. **20 May:** President Hoover appointed the National Commission on Law Observance and Enforcement (the Wickersham Commission) to examine the impact of Prohibition on crime rates. **June:** Agricultural Marketing Act or Cooperative Marketing Act passed to assist farmers' market produce. **14 September:** The United States joined the International Court. **24 October:** "Black Thursday" — 13 million shares were sold in trading on the New York Stock Exchange and began the Wall Street Crash. **29 October:** "Black Tuesday" — a further 16 million shares were sold on the stock exchange as the crash deepened. By 1 December the value of stocks listed on the New York exchange had fallen to $63.5 billion from $89.6 billion on 1 September, 1929. **1 November:** Former Secretary of the Interior Albert Fall became the first cabinet officer convicted of crime while holding office when he was found guilty of accepting bribes in the Teapot Dome scandal. **29 November:** Commander Richard Byrd and pilot Bernt Balchen became the first people to fly over the South Pole.

1930   17 January: The London Naval Conference met, with delegates from Britain, France, Italy, Japan, and the United States agreeing reductions in naval strength. **17 June:** Hawley-Smoot Tariff was passed raising import duties to some of the highest levels ever in United States history in order to protect American industry in the face of the Depression. The measure proved counterproductive and resulted in retaliatory measures from other powers.

1931   6–9 April: Trial of the "Scottsboro Boys," eight black youths accused of rape took place. Found guilty, they were sentenced to death. Their case became a cause of national and international protest and the convictions were later overturned by the Supreme Court. **1 May:** The Empire State Building in New York City opened. At the time it was the tallest building in the world. **September:** Following the Wall Street Crash a bank panic hit the United States and over 800 banks closed in September and October.

1932   7 January: Stimson Doctrine, stating opposition to Japanese aggression in Manchuria and refusal to accept any territorial gains from such an act, was set out in a note by Secretary of State Henry Stimson. **22 January:** A Reconstruction Finance Corporation was established to provide loans to banks and insurance companies to stabilize the deteriorating banking situation following the Wall Street Crash. It lent $1.5 billion up to 1933, but could not stop the collapse of banking and was widely regarded as a "rich man's dole." **2 February–July:** The United States participated in the Geneva Disarmament Conference that was to last two years. Despite the involvement of over 57 countries little agreement was achieved. **1 March:** The baby son of the aviator Charles Lindbergh was kidnapped. Despite payment of a $50,000 ransom the child was found dead several months later. Bruno Hauptmann was subsequently found guilty of the abduction and murder and executed on 3 April 1936. **3 March:** The Twentieth Amendment, ending "lame duck" congresses by introducing the completion of terms of office in January rather March, was ratified. **20 May:** Amelia Earhart became the first woman to fly across the Atlantic alone. **29 May–28 July:** The "Bonus Army" of about 3,000 World War I veterans marched on Washington, D.C., to lobby for early payment of veterans' bonuses. By July some 25,000 people had made camp in the capital. On 28 July armed troops forced the veterans out of the camp that was then destroyed. **14 June:** President Hoover was renominated at the Republican Party convention in Chicago. **21 July:** President Hoover signed the Emergency Relief and Construction Act into law to provide $300 million in relief loans to the states. **1 July:** Franklin Delano Roosevelt was nominated as the presidential candidate for the Democratic Party. The following day, having flown to Chicago to address the delegates, he promised the American people "a New Deal." **22 July:** Federal Home Loan Bank Act passed, establishing Home Loan Banks to provide credit for real estate financing to offset the impact of the Wall Street Crash and Depression. **8 November:** Roosevelt was elected president in a landslide, with 22.8 million votes to Hoover's 15.7 million. Roosevelt became the longest serving president when he was re-elected in 1936, 1940, and 1944.

1933   5 December: The Twenty-First Amendment was ratified ending Prohibition with the repeal of the Eighteenth Amendment. **15 February:** Guiseppe Zangara attempted to assassinate President-elect Roosevelt during a visit to Florida. One of the shots hit the mayor of

Chicago, Anton Cermak, who was traveling with Roosevelt. Cermak subsequently died and Zangara was executed on 21 March. **4 March:** Franklin Roosevelt was inaugurated president of the United States. Declaring that the nation had "nothing to fear but fear itself," Roosevelt called for broad powers to combat the impact of the Depression. He was to initiate a program of reform, known as the "New Deal" that established the basis of a federal welfare system and shaped American politics through to the 1960s.

Introduction

The period from 1913 to 1933 is not often seen as a coherent entity in the history of the United States. It is more often viewed in terms of two distinct periods with the prewar era of political engagement, idealism, and reform known as "progressivism" separated by World War I from the materialism, conservatism, and disengagement of the "prosperous" 1920s. To many postwar observers and later historians, the entry of the United States into the European conflict in 1917 marked not just a dramatic departure in foreign relations, but also the end of an era of reform. More than this, the war was also often perceived to have brought disruption, conflict, and the suppression of civil liberties at home with little positive benefit.

Such negative views were expressed particularly strongly in the 1930s as war clouds threatened once more. Those in favor of neutrality measures argued that the United States had entered the Great War because of the baleful influence of British propaganda or the vested interests of munitions' manufacturers. Even among those Americans who believed that World War I had been fought for the cause of democracy and freedom, there were many who felt that such aims had been sacrificed in an unjust peace settlement at Versailles. The postwar disillusionment evident in such expressions, again seemed to underline the difference between two eras and to separate the 1920s from the prewar years.

The 1920s themselves have often been characterized as a distinct and separate era in United States history, sandwiched between the end of World War I on one side and the onset of the Great Depression on the other. The decade, known variously as the "Jazz Age," "Roaring Twenties," "Prosperity Decade," and "New Era," was depicted by one of its greatest chroniclers, the author F. Scott Fitzgerald, as "an age of miracles, an age of excess," when "a whole race was going hedonistic, deciding on pleasure." The sudden growth in consumerism associated with the automobile industry, new electrical appliances, movies, radio, and sport supported Fitzgerald's view. However, this image overlooked not only some of the harsher realities, but also elements of continuity between this decade and those before and after. There were in fact several common threads running across the decades. Rather than ending them, World War I often accelerated existing political, social, and economic trends. Many of the issues and developments evident before 1914, including some of those on the reformers' agenda, either came to fruition during the war or continued after it, surviving in some instances even into the 1930s.

Whatever the debates, the years from 1913 to 1933 marked a period of enormous change in the history of the United States as the characteristics of modern America—an industrial/urban economy, an increasingly powerful and interventionist national government, a mass national popular culture, and an international role—emerged. The United States had begun to grapple with the consequences of massive industrial growth from the last quarter of the 19th century onward, but that development reached its height in the first decade of the 20th century. Among the most pressing issues was the question of how to deal with the rise of huge corporations and business monopoly, mass immigration and mass urbanization, social inequality and issues of public welfare, and increasing class divisions and social conflict. The political response to this was the movement known as "progressivism," a broad movement of reform beginning at the local and rising to the federal level. Eventually progressivism influenced both main parties, Republican and Democratic, and produced a third party, the Progressive Party, in 1912.

Although diverse, this reform movement rejected traditional notions of individualism and limited government enshrined in principles of "laissez faire" so evident in the preceding "Gilded Age." Instead the reformers demanded that government should tackle the economic and social problems facing the nation. They argued too that government itself should be more efficient and more responsive to the public will. Women were often at the fore of the call for greater social responsibility and a more representative government. Several states adopted referenda, recall, and voter initiatives between 1900 and 1914 and the direct election of senators came into force in 1913. Jane Addams, one of the founders of the settlement house movement that played a leading part in urban reform, argued that women's involvement in politics would lead to better "civic housekeeping." The demand for women's suffrage gained increasing support in the years just prior to 1914 and culminated with the passage of the 19th Amendment in 1920.

Other groups were less fortunate. A strong anti-immigrant feeling was evident before, during, and after World War I. The desire to "keep America American" revealed deep-seated ethnic and racial prejudices fueling a nativism that lasted for 50 years or more. For African Americans, most of whom lived in the former Confederate states of the South, the prewar years saw the final implementation of the system of racial segregation known as "Jim Crow." The quickening movement of the black population to northern industrial centers in search of greater social and economic opportunities saw the spread of race conflict. However, it also brought with it a growing black consciousness and the rise of new civil rights organizations.

If the domestic concerns of this period were those that were to feature for much of the 20th century, then so too were the issues in foreign relations. In the 1890s the United States had become an imperial power following the acquisition of the Philippines after the Spanish-American War. However, although increasingly active in the international arena and already becoming the world's leading economic power, the United States was not committed to any alliances and acted largely independently of other nations. Under the presidencies of Theodore Roosevelt and Woodrow Wilson the United States increasingly intervened in the affairs of Central American and Caribbean states in a "policing role." Such intervention brought a deterioration in relations with Mexico that almost led to war in 1915 and 1917. As far as Europe was concerned, however, most Americans still clung to notions of "isolationism." The outbreak of war in 1914 immediately challenged such assumptions and forced the United States to face the realities of total war in the modern age.

The attempt to insist on both neutrality and the right to trade and travel freely after 1914 failed, and America entered the war in 1917. By then her role was justified in terms of high principle, a war to make the "world safe for democracy." The involvement of the United States broke the deadlock on the western front and contributed significantly to the final victory. Sadly, the attempt to establish a liberal world order along the lines indicated by President Woodrow Wilson did not materialize in the Versailles settlement and the treaty, and with it the League of Nations, was rejected by the Senate. Although it appeared that the United States retreated once more to an isolationist position in the 1920s, in reality she was involved through economic concerns and in attempts to lessen the risk of another war. However, for some historians the failure of the United States to join international peacekeeping in the League of Nations, and also to fully accept the responsibilities that went with her now confirmed dominant economic power, contributed to the Great Depression and coming of World War II.

POLITICAL DEVELOPMENTS

The election of the Democratic presidential candidate, Woodrow Wilson, in 1912 and his inauguration on 4 March 1913 marked the culmination of the Progressive reform movement. The election had been contested by three major candidates—Wilson, William Howard Taft for the Republican Party, and former Republican president, Theodore Roosevelt for the Progressive Party—all of whom could claim to be progressive. In addition Eugene V. Debs stood for the Socialist Party and there was also a candidate for the Prohibition Party. The support of insurgent progressive Republicans, like Robert M. La Follette for Roosevelt's candidacy, divided the Republican vote and ensured victory for Wilson and the Democrats.

Initially rejecting what he saw as the paternalistic approach of Roosevelt's "New Nationalist" platform, Wilson's "New Freedom" program promised to protect the economic and political liberties that enabled ordinary people to prosper by further empowering the federal government to curb business monopoly, stabilize the financial system, and encourage competition. This was done by introducing sweeping tariff reform, creating the Federal Reserve System, and implementing and extending the antitrust principles of the Sherman Act (1890) through the Clayton Antitrust Act (1914) and the creation of a Federal Trade Commission (1914). Government itself became more responsive to the popular will through the direct election of senators in 1913. Between 1915 and 1916 Wilson also accepted a measure of social policy reform with the passage of the federal workmen's compensation law, the introduction of the eight-hour day for railroad workers, child labor restrictions, and federal farm loans. In doing so he increased the power and influence of the federal government, and particularly the president, and established a form of liberal capitalism within the existing constitutional framework.

Faced with the possibility of a second Democratic victory in 1916 and critical of Wilson's "cowardice and weakness" in foreign relation, the ever belligerent Theodore Roosevelt disbanded the Progressive Party. Although not selected as the Republican candidate, Roosevelt threw his support behind the party's choice of Charles Evans Hughes. However, Wilson successfully attracted many of the Progressive movement with his record of reform and peace and narrowly secured a historic second election victory.

Wilson's second term in the White House was dominated by foreign affairs following the outbreak of World War I in Europe in 1914. The presence of a large and diverse immigrant population, coupled with a progressive abhorrence of war as a means of settling disputes, guaranteed support for Wilson's policy of neutrality. However, when his attempts to mediate a peaceful settlement failed and the German use of unrestricted submarine warfare threatened both American trade and lives, the president who had been re-elected on the slogan "He kept us out of war" was forced to ask Congress for a declaration of war. Although the request was granted, divisions still remained within the United States and the federal government took steps to mobilize the population and silence any opposition. The creation of a propaganda agency, the Committee of Public Information, together with the passage of the Espionage and Sedition Acts, encouraged anti-German feeling and led to the suppression of antiwar groups, most notably with the arrest of leaders of the Socialist Party and Industrial Workers of the World (IWW). These actions contributed to a mood of war hysteria and xenophobia that seriously threatened civil liberties during the war and continued when the war was over.

The need for economic mobilization to wage war led to a plethora of new federal agencies, creating what some contemporaries referred to as "war socialism." The most obvious extension of government authority was in the implementation of selective service through the draft that registered more than 20 million men for service and raised an army of four million. A War Industries Board was created to direct economic mobilization, a War Labor Board was established to prevent the disruption of the war effort by labor disputes, food and fuel conservation each became the subject of separate agencies, and transportation came under the direction of the Railroad War Board. However the federal government relied a great deal on the voluntary cooperation and participation of businessmen and experts in the many war agencies. For example the Food Administration headed by Herbert Hoover, unlike its European counterparts, relied upon persuasion rather than imposing rationing and controls in its efforts to regulate supplies.

Although these many measures were dramatic and certainly confirmed the central role the federal government now played in the lives of American citizens, they were for the duration only. The end of the war brought rapid demobilization both of the American Expeditionary Force in Europe and of the war agencies at home. The election of 1920 in which the Republicans returned to power appeared to indicate a repudiation of government intervention and Wilsonian idealism. The return of former progressive Republicans to their party fold helped to secure Warren Harding's victory and suggested a return to more traditional "conservative" policies. However, politicians like Robert M. La Follette kept aspects of the reform agenda alive throughout the 1920s, and in reality the return to "laissez faire" was never as complete as it sometimes seemed.

The Republican administrations of Harding, Coolidge, and Hoover shared a number of common features, particularly of cabinet personnel. The most significant cabinet members were Charles Evans Hughes, secretary of state, Henry C. Wallace, secretary of agriculture, Andrew Mellon, secretary of the treasury, and Herbert Hoover himself who was secretary of commerce under his two presidential predecessors. While Mellon was responsible for many probusiness policies, especially with regard to taxation, Hoover believed that government had a role to encourage and lead businessmen, farmers, and others to cooperate voluntarily in a process of self-regulation to fix standards, stabilize prices, and maintain economic stability. To that end he organized meetings and conferences with the leaders in different sectors of manufacturing and business, supported the formation of trade associations, and had federal agencies compile statistical information.

If Hoover's actions belied those of the traditional conservative and reflected a degree of moral earnestness, this could not be said of some others in the new Republican administration. Warren Harding himself was chosen as the Republican presidential candidate as a compromise choice who would offend the least people. He was neither a leading thinker nor speaker and often seemed more interested in golf and poker games with his cronies than in the business of government. However, he was a popular president and was personally responsible for the early release from prison of some of the antiwar leaders, including the socialist Eugene V. Debs, appointed women to federal bureaus, and spoke out against race violence and in favor of racial equality in politics and economics. His administration, with Hoover particularly active, helped secure the introduction of the eight-hour day in the steel industry, an aim long sought after by labor. However, Harding's government was beset by corruption, most infamously in the Teapot Dome scandal that involved the secretary of the interior, Albert Fall, who received bribes in return for leasing federal oil reserves to private companies. Fall was eventually convicted and jailed for his part in these events, while the attorney general, Harry Daugherty, was forced to resign for his failure to prosecute the case with sufficient rigor.

Harding died in office in 1923 before the scandals became public, but after his death a record of poor appointments and marital infidelity obscured the few successes of his administration and ensured that he was judged harshly by historians. His successor Calvin Coolidge, elected in his own right in 1924, did not fare much better. Known as "Silent Cal," this taciturn president is remembered for his inactivity. However, Coolidge allowed his cabinet members to get on with their work, and his administration balanced the budget, reduced government debt, and began construction of a federally funded highway system. Coolidge also presided over a period of considerable economic growth. The election in 1928 of his successor, Herbert Hoover, was in many ways an expression of approval for Coolidge's policies although the fact that the Democratic candidate, Mayor Al Smith of New York City, was of Catholic Irish extraction and an opponent of Prohibition, was clearly also a factor.

Hoover reflected on his predecessor's success when he suggested in his inaugural address that poverty might soon be a thing of the past. Sadly, events quickly proved him wrong. The Wall Street Crash in October 1929, itself a product of inflated optimism and rash financial practices caused a financial panic that revealed the flaws in "Coolidge prosperity." Hoover's responses, based on his previous experiences as head of the wartime Food Administration, relied on exhortation and appeals to state and local officials and businessmen to act for the public good.

The president tried to boost morale, first by using the term "depression" rather than "panic" or "collapse," and by suggesting the crisis would soon be at an end. Although he enacted a series of measures that far exceeded anything previously done, they proved insufficient and were often undercut by other actions. Thus, Hoover initially cut federal taxes and increased spending on public works and created the President's Organization for Unemployment Relief (POUR) to mobilize private funds to aid charities and local relief agencies. More dramatic in terms of direct state intervention was the Reconstruction Finance Corporation (RFC) set up in 1932 to provide loans to businesses and banks in the hope that this would "trickle down" through companies to employees.

All of these measures proved inadequate and subsequent tax increases and the implementation of tariff barriers against foreign imports only aggravated an already serious situation. As the crisis deepened Hoover's name soon became synonymous with the Depression, the severity, duration, and spread of which led it to be known as the Great Depression.

When World War I veterans who had marched to Washington, D.C., in the "Bonus Army" to call for the early payment of their service bonuses were driven out of the capital by force, Hoover's reputation was in tatters. His defeat in the 1932 presidential election by the Democratic candidate Franklin D. Roosevelt was virtually inevitable. Although Hoover's program included elements that his successor would build upon, Roosevelt's victory and his "New Deal" marked a comprehensive return to reform and led to the creation of the modern welfare system in the United States.

ECONOMIC, SOCIAL, AND CULTURAL TRENDS

With the exception of a severe, but brief, recession after World War I, the period from 1913 to 1933 was one of unprecedented economic growth. The 30 or 40 years prior to 1910 had already witnessed the transformation of the United States from an agricultural nation into an industrial giant. The development of key basic industries producing capital goods—railways, iron, coal, steel, oil, and banking—was combined with the rise of huge business corporations and the expansion of the factory system of production. The late-19th century also saw mass immigration and the rise of the city. The years after 1910 brought a greater diversification of the economy and the rise of fully fledged systems of mass production coupled with the growth of a mass consumer society. Total national income rose from $36.5 billion in 1900 to $60.4 billion in 1920 and $82.8 billion in 1929. From the end of the postwar recession in 1922 to the Wall Street Crash in 1929 the economy grew by 5 percent a year, and the Gross National Product (GNP) rose from $70 billion to $100 billion as manufacturing output increased by 50 percent. The key industries in this phase of economic growth were automobiles, electrical appliances, chemicals, leisure industries (movies, radio, sport), and advertising itself. At the same time, the nation became more clearly urban in emphasis and gave the appearance of greater homogeneity. However, many of the social tensions and conflicts evident before 1913 were still present during the 1920s.

The basis of the consumer society that emerged in the 20th century was the system of mass marketing and national markets that had sprung up in the preceding 20 or 30 years. The expansion of agriculture to meet an ever-increasing population, swollen by the huge influx of immigrants who populated the growing cities and worked in the new factories, was coupled with the development of a national railway network and huge national corporations headed by ruthless business entrepreneurs. The exploitation of the United States' rich supply of natural resources inevitably made it one of the world's leading economic powers. By 1929 the United States produced 40 percent of the world's coal, 70 percent of its gasoline, and 50 percent of its steel. The development of new technologies, such as electricity, increased productivity; their application to the home, opened up the market for consumer production.

The nation's economic supremacy was confirmed during World War I as foreign powers such as Great Britain and France sold their investments in the United States and borrowed money to fund their war machines. By the end of the war the United States was no longer a debtor nation but a creditor, owed millions by the European powers. Moreover, the war brought a huge expansion in American industrial production with none of the physical destruction and much fewer military casualties than those experienced by other participants.

The methods of mass production already developing prior to 1914 were accelerated to meet the demands to feed, clothe, and arm Allied and, after 1917, American armed forces. The automobile manufacturer, Henry Ford, responsible for developing the moving assembly line production technique before the war, in 1916 employed 32,000 workers; by 1918 this had risen to 48,000. The workforce at General Motors rose from 10,000 to 50,000 during the same period. By the 1920s automobile manufacture was second only to steel in value. Henry Ford's model T Ford, first produced before the war led the way in developing mass produced, cheap, standardized vehicles in the 1920s. A total of more than 26 million automobiles were registered by 1929.

Business profits soared during the war, and after a brief recession from 1920 to 1921, this pattern resumed in the 1920s. Farmers were less fortunate. The war gave a considerable impetus to agricultural expansion and farm production rose by over 20 percent despite a fall in the size of the farm labor force. Increased production was achieved by increasing acreage—and increased indebtedness. When the war ended and world trade resumed, farm prices fell and with it farm incomes. Few farmers shared in the prosperity of the 1920s and the problem of agriculture led to repeated calls for assistance. The passage of a succession of McNary-Haugen farm bills to create federal price supports reflected farmers' concerns and the strength of the farm lobby in Congress. They were vetoed by President Calvin Coolidge who believed that farmers had always been poor and the government could not (and should not) do anything about it.

Like farmers many industrial workers also benefited from the war as the demand for production led to full employment, increased wages, and increasing recognition of labor unions led by the American Federation of Labor (AFL) and Samuel Gompers. The government's War Labor Board acknowledged the right to collective bargaining and incorporated the principle of the eight-hour day and a living wage in many of the cases it adjudicated during the war. While earnings in some cases rose by 50 to 100 percent, membership in labor unions rose from under three million in 1914 to over five million in 1920. However, those gains were short-lived. The withdrawal of government support with the end of wartime agencies combined with the postwar recession placed labor unions in a weak position. The outbreak of strikes to increase union representation and combat falling wages in 1919 was met with employer resistance and characterized as the work of Bolsheviks in what became known as the "Red Scare." The return of conservative Republican administrations and a less sympathetic attitude toward labor unions, coupled with the prosperity of the 1920s, saw union membership fall back to prewar levels.

While on average real wages rose between 20 and 30 percent during the "prosperity decade" of the 1920s some areas of the workforce did not share in the boom. Older industries such as steel and coal mining declined and new technology served to displace many workers, if only temporarily. Unemployment, although low, was still a constant feature in many lives, if only for a short period in any year.

The uneven distribution of wealth and income meant that domestic markets had their own limitations. Tariff barriers that limited imports also restricted the ability of foreign nations to purchase goods from the United States. The increasing reliance on credit at home to purchase consumer items was also a major weakness in the economy. These factors taken together with the conservative attitudes toward government intervention contributed significantly to the coming of the Great Depression following the Wall Street Crash in 1929.

The Wall Street Crash ended a boom in the sale of stocks and shares, the "bull market," that had been developing since the end of the postwar recession in 1921 and had quickened in 1927 and 1928. Confidence in the economy had encouraged more and more people to invest, and by 1929 about four million owned stock. As stock market prices soared, investments became more than just a reflection of the strength of the economy or consumer spending, both of which were slowing. Instead it became a business itself as speculation encouraged dubious or even illegal financial practices. While some unscrupulous entrepreneurs floated multiple investment trusts, many people purchased stock "on margin," putting down a deposit, in some cases as low as 10 percent, on the expectation that values would continue to rise. When, however, prices began to fall there was a rush to sell in order to cover outstanding debts and a rapid downward spiral began. As individuals and financial institutions lost their investments, credit shrank. Many small banks which, like the stock exchange had hardly been regulated, could not meet their obligations. Some 5,000 banks failed between 1929 and 1932 wiping out the savings of thousands of Americans in the process. Industry, no longer able to borrow, had to reduce costs and cut wages and labor forces. By 1933 industrial production had fallen to below 50 percent of the 1929 levels and unemployment had risen to 17 million or 25 percent of the labor force. This economic collapse, although it eased somewhat, was to last until well into World War II.

THE SITUATION OF WOMEN AND
ETHNIC AND RACIAL MINORITIES

The war boom brought job opportunities to groups previously largely excluded from industrial employment. The economic position of women had already been changing as the number of women in paid employment outside of the home doubled between 1870 and 1910. By then 8 million women workers made up over 20 percent of the labor force. The vast majority worked in domestic service or in industries traditionally associated with women—garment making, textiles, the needle trades. However, there was a rapid increase in female employment as telephonists, typists, and sales assistants in the decade before World War I. These new trends continued as more than a million women entered paid employment during the war. Many women found work in war industries and others were used for the first time in the uniformed branches of the armed forces. Although many of these jobs were lost after the war, women's employment was clearly more widely accepted and continued in the 1920s. By 1930 10.8 million were in paid employment. The biggest increase took place in clerical occupations—by 1930 two million women worked as typists, bookkeepers, and clerks. Significantly the number of married women who worked outside the home rose from 1.9 million to 3.1 million.

Women's war work strengthened the demand for political recognition that finally resulted in the passage of the Nineteenth Amendment in 1920. The campaign for the vote, led particularly by the National American Women's Suffrage Association (NAWSA), had been growing from 1900 on and had secured a number of victories at state level. As more states granted the vote during the war, the passage of a federal amendment became inevitable. But with victory won the women's movement divided into separate interest groups and became less conspicuous. However, continued political and economic advances combined to create the notion of the "new woman" in the 1920s. In reality, however, the percentage of women who worked remained constant, as did their proportion in the labor force. New female stereotypes in advertising and the movies that suggested a greater liberation in fact only confirmed gender difference. Similarly new household appliances made housework lighter, but rather than freeing women this only meant that more women did their own housework rather than employ domestic servants.

The extent to which women's position had advanced was revealed in the 1930s. When the Depression struck the United States, there was a widespread demand for working women to give up their jobs for men and for married women once more to stay in the home. Paradoxically, however, economic necessity often forced more women to seek work if only on a part-time basis in the traditional and poorly paid area of domestic service. It was not until World War II that really significant changes occurred in women's employment.

Like that of women, the situation of African Americans appeared to go through considerable change between 1913 and 1933, but in reality there was a considerable element of continuity. In 1900, the black population of nine million constituted 12 percent of the United States' population and 90 percent of them lived in the South, mainly employed in the agricultural pursuits of their slave ancestors. Free in name, the largely property-less African Americans were forced into a system of economic dependency in the sharecropping system under which tenant farmers worked the land owned by whites. In the late 19th century, African Americans had seen their right to vote denied through various legal devices such as the grandfather clause, poll tax, and literacy test. Laws segregating the races on railways and streetcars and in schools and all places of public accommodation were passed throughout the South from the late 1870s on. Where these measures failed, violence was used to "keep them in their place." Black leadership was long dominated by the "accommodationist" principal of Tuskegee Institute in Alabama, Booker T. Washington. However, more militant voices were being heard, particularly those of Monroe Trotter and W. E. B. Du Bois. Du Bois joined a small group of white Progressives who, shocked by increasing race violence, organized the National Association for the Advancement of Colored People (NAACP) in 1909 to protest on behalf of the black population.

Initially, the NAACP had little impact. Under Woodrow Wilson, segregation spread to the federal civil service. Black participation in the military during World War I was only reluctantly accepted and was strictly segregated. Some 400,000 African Americans served in the armed forces, but only about 40,000 in combat roles. There was more significant change on the home front, where the demand for industrial labor increased and the normal supply of immigrant labor declined. During the war, between 300,000 and 400,000 African Americans moved north in the "Great Migration" to find work in the war industries in centers such as Chicago, Detroit, Philadelphia, and Pittsburgh. This trend continued in the 1920s, and by 1930 almost one million African Americans had left the South.

Although the move north offered African Americans new job opportunities in industry and greater access to education and political influence, it also resulted in race violence as whites reacted to the competition for housing and jobs. Race riots occurred in East St. Louis in 1917 and in Chicago, Washington, D.C., and a number of other towns and cities during the "Red Summer" of 1919. However, African Americans now fought back and a less passive mood was evident in the physical resistance of the "New Negro" and in the cultural expression of the literary and artistic "Harlem Renaissance" that was a feature of the 1920s.

Despite the adoption of African American culture by some white Americans, mainly among the young or literary circles, that gave the 1920s the title "Jazz Age," racial intolerance and race violence continued intermittently throughout the decade. Riots in Tulsa, Oklahoma, 1921, and Rosewood, Florida, 1923, or the case of the Scottsboro Boys in 1931, indicated how little the plight of the majority of African Americans who still remained in the South had changed. With the onset of the Depression, black Americans once more found themselves "last hired, first fired," and unemployment rates were twice as high for African Americans as they were for whites. As in the case of women, this situation did not change until World War II.

The persistence of discrimination and prejudice against African Americans, evident in the revival of the Ku Klux Klan in 1915 and its spread into states such as Indiana and Illinois during the 1920s, was indicative of the deep-seated racism in American society. The Klan did not confine its attention just to African Americans, but instead also expressed opposition to Catholics, Jews, and those of nonwhite Anglo Saxon backgrounds. To a considerable extent this was a continuation of the nativist sentiment evident from the end of the 19th century on. Such feelings were heightened during the war with its emphasis on 100 percent Americanism, total loyalty, and the suppression of civil liberties. Anti-German feeling, fanned by war propaganda, easily became antiforeign feeling. In the instability of the immediate postwar period, this quickly translated into anti-Bolshevism and led to the "Red Scare" in which hundreds of immigrants were deported. The anti-immigrant sentiment finally culminated in the passage of the Quota Act of 1921 and National Origins Act of 1924, severely restricting immigration along ethnic lines. A hatred of foreigners combined with antiradicalism was also evident in the trial for murder of two Italian anarchists, Sacco and Vanzetti, who were executed in 1927 despite national and international campaigns on their behalf. Anti-Catholicism was also a significant factor in the defeat of the Democratic presidential candidate, Al Smith, in 1928.

CULTURAL CONFLICTS

Anti-Catholicism was evident in American society as far back as the 1840s. Religious fundamentalism stretched back even further. With the anti-immigrant sentiment, both were apparent in the late-19th century and could be seen in elements of both Populism and the Progressive movement. In the 1920s, such beliefs seemed to represent a conservative, rural-based culture in a reaction to the growing challenge of modernism. The battle between the old and the new, the rural and urban was fully illustrated in the Scopes Monkey Trial in Tennessee in 1925, which pitted the old Populist and fundamentalist William Jennings Bryan against the labor lawyer Clarence Darrow. Although Darrow lost in the sense that his client John Scopes was convicted for teaching Darwinist theories of evolution, the fundamentalist belief in the strict interpretation of the Bible upheld by Bryan was exposed to ridicule and scorn.

Nowhere was the clash of values more evident than in the battle over Prohibition. Prohibition, too, had its origins in the religious movements of the early 19th century. It gained support in the moral crusades of the 1880s and 1890s and was often seen by reformers as a means of tackling poverty, industrial accidents, and the break up of families. For many of its supporters, saloons were associated with urban immigrant ghettos and political corruption. Nineteen states had already passed Prohibition laws prior to 1914. During World War I, Prohibition was seen as a means of conserving grain; it was also aimed at brewers, many of whom were of German descent. Enacted first as a war measure, Prohibition became fully established with the ratification of the Eighteenth Amendment in 1919 and its enforcement from January 1920 on.

Prohibition was resisted from the outset and the issue divided the Democratic Party between "wets" and "dries" for much of the 1920s.

Many reformers like Jane Addams supported the conservative Republicans because of their backing for Prohibition. However, it was clear that other Americans did not believe that the law applied to them and the continued demand for alcoholic beverages led to the rise of an illegal industry with "speakeasies" supplied by gangsters led by individuals like Al Capone. The rise of gangsterism and the impossibility of enforcing the law led eventually to the repeal of the amendment in 1933.

Prohibition, religious fundamentalism, racism, anti-immigrant sentiment, and political conservatism reflected the narrow-mined parochialism of the small-town America depicted in the works of novelist Sinclair Lewis, sociologists Robert and Mary Lynd, and social critic H. L. Mencken. These movements also represented a reaction to the rapid social and cultural change that transformed the United States and threatened established values. In 1920, for the first time, the census recorded that the urban population exceeded the rural. The city and the factory with their polyglot immigrant inhabitants and industrial workforces were now dominant. Although regional, ethnic, and racial differences continued, the growth of national businesses, brand names, chain stores, and mass communication through movies and the radio helped to create a modern and more homogenous national culture. At the heart of this culture was mass consumption, entertainment, and leisure. Movie stars like Charlie Chaplin, Lillian Gish, Douglas Fairbanks, Jr., Mary Pickford, and Rudolph Valentino all became national icons. They were also stars who set fashions and created desires. The actress Clara Bow for example symbolized the liberated "flapper" both in clothing and in sex appeal. Mass circulation magazines, ranging from *True Stories* to the *Saturday Evening Post*, advertised cosmetics, soap powders, and electrical appliances. The growth of radio, too, sold goods through advertising and helped to make national heroes of sportsmen like boxer Jack Dempsey and baseball player "Babe" Ruth and turned sport into a mass industry. The media also helped to lionize Charles Lindbergh, the lone flyer who crossed the Atlantic in 1927 and demonstrated that the individual could still triumph in the modern age.

It was not just rural traditionalists however who resisted or reacted against the social and economic changes of the "new era." On the other side, a critical literary movement, first evident in the prewar Greenwich Village group of writers and artists, developed more fully after World War I. Many were either disillusioned as a consequence of the war itself or alienated by postwar materialism and political complacency. Some like Lewis, Mencken, and Edith Wharton, stayed in the United States to produce biting satire or critical observations of their modern society. Others, like Ernest Hemingway, John Dos Passos, F. Scott Fitzgerald, and T. S. Eliot became temporary or permanent exiles, a "lost generation" that adopted the new style and tones of the modernist movement and reinvigorated American arts in the process. The identification of such writers with cultural movements elsewhere was exceptional. Most of American popular culture turned its back on Europe, looked steadfastly inward, and reflected a mood often misleadingly described as "isolationist."

FOREIGN AFFAIRS

In foreign affairs, the Republican period was remarkable for the attempts to maintain a world role while at the same time not being enmeshed in international agreements or organizations like the League of Nations. This struggle between internationalism on the one hand and isolationism on the other was already evident at the end of the 19th century but increased as a consequence of World War I. For most of the 19th century, the United States could adhere to the principles enunciated by George Washington and Thomas Jefferson, and further expressed in the Monroe Doctrine—a desire to avoid "entangling alliances" and the maintenance of the independence of the nations of the New World. However, the growth of the United States as an economic power trading in, and affected by, world markets began to challenge those principles. The application of "dollar diplomacy" by the administrations of William McKinley and Theodore Roosevelt saw an increase in United States investments in the Pacific and in the Caribbean. The Spanish-American War in 1898, ostensibly against Spanish imperialism and in defense of the Monroe Doctrine, reflected United States' interests in Cuba and elsewhere. The acquisition of the Philippines and Hawaii following the war marked the United States' entry onto the world stage as an imperial power. The construction of the Panama Canal under American aegis between 1904 and 1914 and the control of the Canal Zone confirmed the United States' authority in Central America and the Caribbean.

When the Democrats gained control of the White House under Woodrow Wilson, it was widely assumed that foreign relations would change direction. Many Democrats, like the new secretary of state William Jennings Bryan, had opposed imperialist ventures overseas and the threatening use of the "big stick" in foreign affairs advocated by Roosevelt. Moves were made toward granting independence to the Philippines, reparations were agreed with Colombia for the loss of Panama (although the treaty was not approved by the Senate until 1921), and 30 conciliation agreements were signed with foreign powers to bring any possible disputes before an international commission. However, the new administration felt obliged to keep United States' troops in Nicaragua to prevent civil war and to protect U.S. financial investments. Troops were also sent to Haiti and Dominica to avert revolutions also perceived as threatening American interests.

Revolution had already occurred in Mexico when Wilson became president. Offers to mediate between the new government of Victoriano Huerta and his opponent Venustiano Carranza were rejected by the Mexicans as interference. In 1914, an incident that began with the arrest of American seamen in Tampico became a full diplomatic incident when Admiral Henry Mayo rejected the Mexican apology and demanded a salute to the American flag. Mexico's failure to respond satisfactorily was met with the seizure of Vera Cruz. The threat of war was averted by mediation under the leadership of envoys from Argentina, Brazil, and Chile and by the abdication of Huerta in favor of Carranza in July 1914.

Relations between the United States and Mexico continued to be strained and became more inflamed as a result of the actions of the Mexican military commander, Francisco ("Pancho") Villa. Determined to provoke a war, Villa killed 16 American passengers on a train near Santa Ysabel in January 1916 and then attacked Columbus, New Mexico, killing a further 19 people on 9 March 1916. A punitive expedition led by General John Pershing pursued Villa deep into Mexico. Clashes with Mexican troops led to casualties on both sides, and the two nations once again came close to war. However, the likelihood of the United States becoming involved in war in Europe forced Wilson to back down. The troops were withdrawn in January 1917 and the Carranza regime officially recognized in March.

WORLD WAR I

The outbreak of war in Europe in 1914 confirmed to many Americans the validity of the policy of isolation. There was considerable support for President Wilson's call for impartiality in thought and deed. However, the conflict was a total war that involved entire populations and their economies. Supplies were vital, and maritime trade itself was threatened. The Wilson administration's insistence on the right of United States' citizens to trade with whomever they wished and to travel freely on the high seas soon came into conflict with the reality of modern warfare. The imposition of a tight naval blockade on European ports by the British provoked several protests from the Wilson government but little more. These conflicts could be left to the courts to adjudicate. This was not the case when the German government responded to the blockade by using submarines (the U-boat) to attack merchant and passenger vessels from February 1915 on. The sinking of the passenger ship *Lusitania* with the loss of 128 American lives on 7 May led the Wilson administration to warn that further such attacks would be seen as deliberately unfriendly. William Jennings Bryan considered this response so strong that he resigned as secretary of state. A further protest following the sinking of the *Arabic* in August produced a promise that unrestricted attacks on unarmed passenger vessels would cease. However, in February 1916 the German government announced that armed merchant vessels would be sunk without warning. The Wilson administration refused to warn American citizens against traveling on armed ships and blocked the Gore-McLemore Resolution introduced in Congress to implement such warnings. When a German submarine torpedoed an unarmed ship, the *Sussex*, on 24 March 1916, President Wilson threatened to sever relations with Germany unless the unrestricted submarine campaign ceased. Although the German government acceded, it indicated that it might resume the campaign if the British naval blockade continued.

The growing realization that the war in Europe would not come to a speedy conclusion, combined with the threat it posed to the security of the United States, encouraged a "preparedness campaign" that brought the first steps toward war planning in America. It also led Wilson to initiate proposals to mediate a peace settlement. The first discussions began when Wilson's secretary Colonel Edward House went to Europe first in 1915, and again the following year. In January 1917, Wilson went before the Senate and outlined his proposals for a "peace without victory." However, as neither side was willing to give up whatever advantage they held at any given moment, or while a military victory seemed possible, the discussions came to nothing.

On 31 January 1917, the German government announced their intention to resume unrestricted submarine warfare. President Wilson broke off diplomatic relations on 3 February and on 26 February asked Congress for the power to arm American merchant ships. Opinion in the United States began to mobilize behind such measures, particularly following the publication of the Zimmerman telegram, in which the German foreign secretary proposed an alliance to the Mexican government. Mexico was promised the possibility of regaining New Mexico and Arizona in the event of a victory in a war against the United States. The change of regime in Russia with the overthrow of the Tsar also made the Allied cause seem more attractive as a defense of democracy. However, it was the sinking of several United States' ships that forced Wilson to go before Congress on 2 April 1917 to ask for a declaration of war to "make the world safe for democracy." The declaration was approved on 6 April.

About two million soldiers from the United States served in France in the American Expeditionary Force (AEF) led by General John J. Pershing between 1917 and 1918. Their arrival could not have been more timely as the submarine campaign threatened Allied supplies and the withdrawal of the Russians from the war following a second, Bolshevik, revolution in November 1917 freed German troops for the western front. American troops were first thrown into action as part of a unified Allied command in response to the German offensive along the Somme in March 1918. The intervention of additional United States' divisions in the Aisne-Marne offensive in May 1918 led to the victories at Chateau Thierry and Belleau Wood. Over a quarter of a million American soldiers then took part in the Allied counteroffensive along the Marne that opened in July 1918. Another 500,000 men of the AEF launched an attack on St. Mihiel on the River Meuse in September, and 1.2 million Americans took part in the Meuse-Argonne offensive that began later that month and concluded with the signing of the armistice that brought the war to an end on 11 November 1918. More than 60,000 soldiers from the United States died in combat during World War I. Another 60,000 died of disease, many of them victims of the worldwide influenza pandemic that took 20 million lives across the world in 1918.

VERSAILLES AND AFTER

In January 1918, President Wilson had outlined his war aims in his "Fourteen Points" speech to Congress. His speech stressed self-determination and independence for the people of the former Austro-Hungarian and Ottoman empires, free trade, arms reductions, open treaties openly arrived at, and a world organization to ensure future peace. In December 1918, the president led the American delegation to take part in the peace negotiations in Versailles, near Paris. Only one Republican was included in the group, despite the Republican victories in the congressional elections that gave them control of both houses of Congress. The peace treaty eventually drawn up did not accord with the Fourteen Points. Although independence was granted to Poland, Estonia, Latvia, Lithuania, Czechoslovakia, Hungary, and Yugoslavia, Germany was forced to accept a war guilt clause, lost all of its colonies and some of its lands in Europe, and was required to pay huge reparations. The now communist Russia was excluded from the peace negotiations and Allied (including American) troops were sent to Siberia ostensibly to protect war material but in reality to support the Bolsheviks' opponents. The newly created eastern European countries ringed Russia with a "cordon sanitaire" and the United States denied the Soviet Union recognition until 1933.

Included in the peace settlement was a covenant to establish a League of Nations on which Woodrow Wilson pinned his hopes for future peace. However, Republicans in Congress led by Senator Henry Cabot Lodge indicated that they would not accept the league as proposed. Wilson, who refused to accept any amendments, suffered a stroke campaigning in defense of the treaty in September 1919. On 19 November 1919, Democrats, instructed by Wilson to reject any reservations to the treaty, voted with the Republican "Irreconcilables" to reject the Versailles treaty and League of Nations.

FOREIGN RELATIONS DURING THE 1920S

The newly elected Republican president, Warren G. Harding, undoubtedly captured the mood of many of his fellow citizens when he evoked the tradition of isolation in his inaugural address in 1921 and declared "We do not mean to be entangled." However, certain facts could not be ignored. After World War I, the United States was a world power in terms of its naval strength and its merchant marine; it was also the world's greatest financial and economic power. If in appearance the United States might have seemed isolationist, in reality the thrust of its foreign policy in the 1920s was the preservation of peace on its own terms without becoming inextricably involved in the conflicts of other nations.

From 1922 on, the United States sent observers to the League of Nations and participated in many of the League's conferences. The Republican administrations also sought to achieve membership for the United States in the Permanent Court of International Justice established under the Covenant of the League of Nations, but separate from it. However, reservations attached to America's proposed membership by isolationists in Congress in 1926 led to the rejection of the United States by the other member countries.

The Republican administrations consistently attempted to ensure peace through arms limitations and played a leading part in the Washington Naval Conference (1921–22) that resulted in a treaty limiting the size of the navies of the United States, Britain, Japan, France, and Italy. Treaties were also agreed with regard to relations in the Pacific. A further agreement at the London Naval Conference in 1930 restricted the number of smaller ships the respective navies would have. Even more remarkable was the Kellogg-Briand Pact outlawing war as an instrument of policy. Initiated by the French foreign minister Aristide Briand and signed by Secretary of State Frank B. Kellogg in 1928, the agreement was eventually joined by 62 nations. However, lacking in any power of enforcement, the pact proved meaningless in the face of aggression from nonparticipants.

The issue that most undermined the isolation of the United States during the 1920s was that of war debts and war reparations. During and immediately after the war, the United States had lent almost $10 billion to Allied governments. Requests for these debts to be canceled or reduced were rebuffed although tariffs in the United States made it impossible to repay the loans in goods and services. The Allies in turn demanded payment in full of the huge reparations ($33 billion) imposed on Germany. This situation threatened the economic stability of nations already weakened by the war and necessitated further renegotiation. In 1924, a committee headed by Charles G. Dawes and Owen D. Young produced the Dawes Plan that scaled down the amount owed in reparations and provided for loans from the United States to Germany. A further committee led by Young reduced the reparations payments even further in 1929. Although these efforts eased the immediate financial crisis, they established a dangerous flow of capital which, if broken, could produce an economic collapse. This is precisely what happened following the Wall Street Crash in 1929.

The 1920s also witnessed an improvement in relations with Latin American nations. Charles Evans Hughes, the new secretary of state in 1921, was opposed to Woodrow Wilson's interventionist policies and initiated the process by which United States' troops were withdrawn from the Dominican Republic in 1924 and from Nicaragua in 1925. Marines returned to Nicaragua in 1927 to assist in the suppression of a revolt and were only gradually withdrawn between 1931 and 1933. Relations with Mexico were more problematic. A slight improvement occurred after Carranza had been replaced by Alvaro Obregon, but when the more radical Plutarcho Calles assumed power in 1924, relations worsened once more. They continued to be difficult until President Calvin Coolidge sent Dwight Morrow as ambassador to Mexico City in 1927. Morrow was able to establish a good working relationship with the Mexican government and set up more friendly links between the two countries. Although the United States delegation led by Hughes to the Pan-American Conference in 1932 refused to give an unequivocal undertaking not to intervene in the affairs of neighboring nations, the Clark Memorandum drawn up in 1928 by the State Department following president-elect Herbert Hoover's visit to Latin America acknowledged that this was the case. Thus, the Republican administrations helped to undo some of the policies of their predecessors and lay the groundwork for the "Good Neighbor" policy of the succeeding administration.

THE DICTIONARY

– A –

ABBOTT, EDITH (1876–1957). Edith Abbott studied at the University of Nebraska and completed a Ph.D. in political economics at Chicago in 1905. Abbott then conducted research on **women** in industry for the Carnegie Institution before undertaking a postgraduate program at the London School of Economics. From 1907 to 1908 she taught at Wellesley College and then joined her sister **Grace Abbott** at the **Hull House settlement** in Chicago where they lived for the next 12 years. Edith Abbott began to assist **Sophonisba Breckinridge** at the Chicago School of Civics and Philanthropy in a program to professionalize **social work**. Her study of *Women in Industry* was published in 1910 and, with Breckinridge, Abbott coauthored *The Delinquent Child and the Home* (1912) and *Truancy and Non-Attendance in the Chicago Schools* (1917).

Abbott became dean of the new School of Social Service Administration at the University of Chicago in 1924. In 1927 she and Breckinridge established the *Social Service Review*, a professional journal for social workers. At the same time Abbott was conducting studies of the employment and behavior of immigrants to the United States and in 1929 President **Herbert Hoover** appointed her to the Wickersham Commission on Law Observance and Enforcement. Abbott's research, published as the *Report on Crime and Criminal Justice in Relation to the Foreign Born* in 1931, demonstrated that immigrants committed proportionately less crime than the rest of the population.

Abbott's role in social work education was recognized in her election to president of the National Conference of Social Work in 1936.

Users of this volume should note that cross-references in each dictionary entry are printed in boldface type.

In 1951 she was awarded the National Conference of Social Work's Survey Award for her services.

ABBOTT, GRACE (1878–1939). Like her sister **Edith Abbott**, Grace Abbott began her career as a high school teacher. She studied law at the University of Nebraska before enrolling at the University of Chicago in 1907 and gained a master of philosophy in 1909. Abbott also lived in the **Hull House settlement** where she became involved in social reform activities. She was active in the Juvenile Protection Association, the Immigrants' Protective League, and the Women's Trade Union League, and in 1915 chaired a special committee on Penal and Correctional Institutions. In 1917 Abbott published *The Immigrant and the Community*.

In 1917, Abbott joined the **Children's Bureau** in Washington, D.C. She went briefly to Chicago to head the state commission on immigration but returned to Washington, D.C., in 1921 to replace **Julia Lathrop** as head of the Children's Bureau. Abbott led the administration of the **Sheppard-Towner Act** extending federal aid in maternity and infant childcare services. She was president of the National Conference of Social Work from 1923 to 1924.

Abbot resigned from the Children's Bureau in 1934 to take up a teaching position at the University of Chicago. She also worked on the President's Council on Economic Security, 1934–35, and helped to draft the Social Security Act. Her study of *The Child and the State* was published in 1938. *See also* SOCIAL WORK.

ABC MEDIATION, 1914. Deteriorating relations between the United States and **Mexico** following the seizure of power by Victoriano Huerta in 1913 threatened to bring the two nations to war. In an attempt to avert conflict, the "ABC" powers, Argentina, Brazil, and Chile, offered to mediate. Meetings took place between 18 May and 2 July 1914 but accomplished little. The overthrow of Huerta by Venustiano Carranza in July brought some brief improvement in relations, but war seemed possible again when the United States sent a **punitive expedition** into Mexico in response to the attacks of **Pancho Villa** in 1916.

***ABRAMS V. UNITED STATES* (1919).** In 1919, the **Supreme Court** upheld the conviction of Jacob Abrams under the **Espionage** and **Sedition** legislation by a verdict of seven to two, Justices **Oliver Wendell Holmes** and **Louis Brandeis** dissenting. Abrams, an anarchist who had recently entered the United States, had distributed pamphlets in the tenement area of New York City denouncing American military intervention in Russia.

ADAMSON ACT, 1916. Brought about by a threatened strike of railroad unions, the Adamson Act introduced the eight-hour day, with time and a half for overtime, for workers on interstate railways as of 1 January 1917. The law also established a commission to study the problems of railroad labor. *See also* TRADE UNIONS.

ADDAMS, JANE (1860–1935). Social reformer, suffragist, and pacifist, Jane Addams was a leading figure in the prewar **Progressive** reform movement. Educated at Rockford Female Seminary, Addams was one of the first-generation of college-educated **women**. Unable to continue her medical studies at Philadelphia Medical College, Addams was inspired by a visit to Toynbee Hall, a **settlement house** in London, England. In 1889, with **Ellen Starr** she founded **Hull House** in Chicago, which, as one of the first settlement houses in the United States, became an inspiration for many other reformers. Addams lived there for the rest of her life.

Addams was active in the **women's suffrage** movement, president of the National Conference of Charities and Corrections (later the National Conference of **Social Work**), a founder of the **National Association for the Advancement of Colored People**, the **National Consumers' League**, and in the formation of the National **Progressive Party** in 1912. She was also one of the founders of the **Woman's Peace Party** and became chairperson in 1915. Addams was elected president of the International Congress of Women in The Hague the same year and then president of the Women's International League for Peace and Freedom. She maintained her pacifist stance throughout the war and suffered a decline in popularity as a result. However, her activities in the cause of peace were recognized in 1931 when she became the first American woman to be awarded the Nobel Peace Prize. Addams wrote two accounts of her work, *Twenty Years at Hull House* (1910) and *The Second Twenty Years at Hull House* (1930).

ADKINS V. CHILDREN'S HOSPITAL, 1923. In 1923, the **Supreme Court** dismissed the defense of minimum wage legislation for **women** brought by **Felix Frankfurter** in the case of *Adkins v.*

Children's Hospital when they upheld the concept of "liberty of contract" to strike down a District of Columbia minimum wage law for women.

ADVISORY COMMISSION TO THE COUNCIL OF NATIONAL DEFENSE. The Advisory Commission was a committee of seven experts appointed in 1916 to assist the **Council of National Defense** in mobilizing the nation for war as part of the "Preparedness" program. The members were the chairman, Daniel Willard, president of the Baltimore & Ohio Railroad, Howard Coffin, vice president of the Hudson Motor Co., Hollis Godfrey, head of the Drexel Institute, Dr. Franklin Martin, director of the College of Surgeons, **Julius Rosenwald**, president of Sears Roebuck, **Bernard Baruch**, and **Samuel Gompers**. The use of experts drawn from business and industry on a voluntary basis was a model to be followed during the war, and the Advisory Commission created a plethora of similar sub-committees dealing with all aspects of war production.

AFRICAN AMERICANS. In many respects, the period 1913–33 was one of considerable continuity for the African American population, with racial prejudice, discrimination, poverty, and violence being the constant features. Although only 12 percent of the whole population, the majority of African Americans (90 percent) still lived in rural areas in the former slave states of the South in 1900. In 1930, the proportion was still almost 80 percent despite the **"Great Migration"** to the North that began during **World War I** and continued in the 1920s. The late-19th and early-20th centuries also witnessed the full implementation of the system of racial segregation in the South known as "Jim Crow." The process of excluding African Americans from the political system through poll taxes, grandfather clauses, literacy tests, and open intimidation occurred at the same time. Race violence increased and more than 1,000 black people were lynched between 1900 and 1914. Race riots in which white mobs attacked black communities took place in Atlanta, Georgia, in 1906 and in Springfield, Illinois, in 1908. This violence continued through the war, with 38 lynchings in 1917, 64 in 1918, and 83 in 1919. There were major riots in **East St. Louis** (1917), and in **Chicago** and other towns and cities during the **"Red Summer"** of 1919. Such outbreaks continued with the riot in **Tulsa**, Oklahoma, in 1921 and in Rosewood, Florida, in 1923. Denied a political voice, the African Americans were largely ignored at the federal level by all administrations, whether **Republican** or **Democratic**.

However, there were some significant underlying changes. The "accommodationist" leadership of the black educator, Booker T. Washington (who died in 1915), was increasingly challenged by leaders such as **W. E. B. Du Bois**. Du Bois and others demanded full equality, and with a few white **Progressives** appalled by the spread of race violence to the North, formed the **National Association for the Advancement of Colored People** (NAACP) in 1910 to campaign against discrimination. The organization grew in the aftermath of World War I and, under the leadership of **James Weldon Johnson** and **Walter White**, led the campaign against lynching and race prejudice generally.

During World War I, the issue of race was raised with the implementation of **Selective Service**. Many white southerners opposed the inclusion of African Americans in the military, while blacks demanded the right to fight for their country. African Americans were drafted into the military, but the army and navy were both segregated and blacks were excluded from the Marine Corps and the Army Air Force. Over 400,000 African Americans served in the army, but only 42,000 in combat roles. On the domestic front, the need for industrial labor encouraged the large-scale migration of African Americans to the northern manufacturing centers. Although they benefited from new job opportunities, the black workers faced discrimination from **trade unions** and conflicts over housing and transportation.

The disillusionment felt by returning black servicemen and black workers encouraged a mood of militance associated with new leaders such as **Marcus Garvey** and **A. Philip Randolph**. The willingness to fight back was expressed by the **"New Negro"** while the sense of black community and pride found a cultural voice in the **Harlem Renaissance** during the 1920s. The new black northern populations also found a political voice and began to have an influence that came to fruition in the Democratic Party and resulted in some recognition in the **New Deal**. **Eleanor Roosevelt** also conspicuously defended the rights of black Americans and reactions to the case of the **Scottsboro Boys** revealed that many white Americans were now much more sympathetic towards African Americans. Despite this, during the **Depression** African Americans were still "last hired, first fired," and there was once more a rise in race violence. *See also* HARLEM; JAZZ.

AGRICULTURAL CREDITS ACT, 1923. A law passed to provide additional credit facilities to enable farmers to purchase farm equipment and livestock through Federal Intermediate Credit **Banks** in each of the 12 districts created by the **Federal Farm Loan Act** of 1916. These **banks** could extend loans to farmers for periods of from six months to three years and were administered by the boards of directors of the Federal Land **Banks**.

AGRICULTURAL MARKETING ACT, 1929. Also known as the Cooperative Marketing Act, the Agricultural Marketing Act passed in June 1929 was intended to assist farmers in marketing their produce. It established a **Federal Farm Board** of eight members appointed by the president, plus the secretary of agriculture. The Board was provided with $500 million to lend to cooperative associations and stabilization corporations that could buy, sell, or store surpluses of the specific commodity with which each corporation dealt. The Board attempted to raise the prices of cotton and wheat by making heavy purchases, but was unable to counteract the downward trend in world prices.

AGRICULTURE. *See* FARMING.

ALEXANDER, WILL WINTON (1884–1956). The southern liberal Will Alexander was educated at Scarritt-Morrisville College, Missouri, and Vanderbilt where he received his BD in 1912. Alexander was ordained as a Methodist minister in 1911 and held a number of pastorates in Tennessee between 1911 and 1917. In 1919 Alexander established the Commission on Interracial Cooperation in Atlanta. The commission, which Alexander directed for 25 years, aimed to improve race relations in the South through programs of education and public information. Details of the activities of the **Ku Klux Klan** collected by the commission were used in press exposés in the 1920s.

Alexander also worked with the Social Science Research Council's Advisory Commission on Race Studies (1927–28) and on the

Commission on Minority Groups in Economic Recovery (1934–35). Alexander was influential in the **New Deal** and was appointed assistant administrator in the Department of Agriculture's Resettlement Administration in 1935. He was actively involved in the creation of the Farm Security Administration (FSA) in 1937 and was responsible for many of its programs benefiting poor southern farmers. He resigned from FSA in 1940 to accept the chair of the **Rosenwald** Fund where he implemented a number of programs to help African Americans in the South follow an education. *See also* AFRICAN AMERICANS.

ALIEN PROPERTY CUSTODIAN. The office of Alien Property Custodian was established under the terms of the **Trading with the Enemy Act** in 1917. The custodian held enemy property in the United States in order to prevent its use during the war and to sell it once the war was over. Many German patents and other properties were seized and disposed of. Claims were subsequently settled between the United States and Germany and Austria under the Settlement of War Claims Act, 1928.

ALLEN, FREDERICK LEWIS (1890–1954). Allen was a journalist and popular historian whose best-selling portrait of the 1920s *Only Yesterday* (1931) did much to shape views of the decade. After working at the magazines *Atlantic Monthly* and *Century*, Allen became press bureau director for the Boston Writers' Council for Patriotic Service in 1917. In 1918 he became press bureau director of the **Council of National Defense** in Washington, D.C. After the war Allen managed the publicity for Harvard University before becoming articles editor at *Harper's Magazine* in 1925. He later became assistant editor (1931), and then editor in chief (1941). *Only Yesterday* was a retrospective and journalistic view of the "roaring twenties" that tended to emphasize the frivolity of the decade. His subsequent books included *The Lords of Creation* (1935), *Since Yesterday* (1940), *I Remember Distinctly* (1947), *The Great Pierpont Morgan* (1949), and *The Big Change* (1952).

ALLIED POWERS. The term applied to the Allied and Associated Powers that fought and defeated the **Central Powers** during **World**

War I. The five leading nations were the United States, Great Britain, France, Italy, and Japan. The other Allied and Associated States were Belgium, Bolivia, Brazil, China, Cuba, Czechoslovakia, Ecuador, Greece, Guatemala, the Hejaz, Honduras, Liberia, Nicaragua, Panama, Peru, Poland, Portugal, Romania, Yugoslavia, Siam, and Uruguay.

AMERICAN CIVIL LIBERTIES UNION (ACLU). The American Civil Liberties Union was founded in 1920 by **Roger Baldwin** and other social reformers including **Jane Addams, Crystal Eastman, Clarence Darrow, John Dewey, Abraham Johannes Muste,** and **Elizabeth Gurley Flynn**. The ACLU developed out of the activities of the **American Union Against Militarism** during **World War I** and was established to preserve civil liberties guaranteed under the Bill of Rights, namely, freedom of speech, press, and religion. During the 1920s, the ACLU supported **Sacco** and **Vanzetti** and **John Scopes** and was involved in the case of the **Scottsboro Boys** in the 1930s.

AMERICAN EXPEDITIONARY FORCE (AEF). The American Expeditionary Force was the name given to the United States military contingents commanded by General **John J. Pershing** that joined the **Allied** armies during **World War I**. When war was declared, the number of men in the United States Army was 200,000, one-third of whom were National Guardsmen called into federal service along the Mexican border. By the end of the war, the total force numbered 4.5 million, half of whom actually were overseas. A small number of units were sent in 1917 but the bulk of the United States Army arrived in 1918. In total, 42 divisions served in France. Following a German spring offensive, Pershing placed the entire force at the disposal of the Allied High Command and the American First Army was not created until 24 June 1918.

AMERICAN FARM BUREAU FEDERATION (AFBF). Established in 1919, the American Farm Bureau Federation represented 36 states and developed from the farm extension programs established during **World War I** to disseminate more widely scientific and technical advances in agriculture. The AFBF established lobbies at the state and federal level to promote agricultural interests. *See also* FARM BLOC; FARMER-LABOR PARTY; FARMING.

AMERICAN FEDERATION OF LABOR (AFL). A federation of **trade unions** formed in 1886 by **Samuel Gompers** and Adolph Strasser. The AFL emerged from the Federation of Trades and Labor Unions formed in 1881, and was an organization of autonomous craft-based unions. Conservative and nonpolitical in outlook, the AFL largely excluded unskilled, immigrant, and black workers. Nonetheless by 1910 it was established as the leading union organization and had a membership of over two million. Its support for the administration of **Woodrow Wilson** during the war brought recognition in terms of the inclusion of Gompers in the **Advisory Commission to the Council of National Defense** and in the recognition of unions by the **War Labor Board.** By the end of the war AFL membership had doubled, but in a changing economic climate and without government support, the organization was unable to consolidate upon the wartime advances in the face of employer resistance. Following defeats in the **Steel Strike** of 1919 and other industrial areas, union membership declined once more and by 1924 had fallen to 2.9 million. The AFL maintained its conservative outlook with regard to unskilled and immigrant workers and this approach continued when **William Green** succeeded Gompers in 1924.

AMERICAN INDIAN CTIZENSHIP ACT, 1924. The **Supreme Court** in 1894 specifically excluded **Native Americans** from the Fourteenth Amendment ruling that "all persons born or naturalized in the United States" are citizens. However, members of the Five Civilized Tribes of Oklahoma were granted citizenship in 1901 and the Burke Act of 1906 granted citizenship to Indians who left their tribes. The Indian Citizenship Act clarified the position when it conferred citizenship on all 350,000 Indians. The act did not, however, end federal control of Indian lands nor tribal government.

AMERICAN LEGION. The American Legion was an organization of veterans established by 20 officers from the **American Expeditionary Force** (AEF) in Paris on 15 February 1919 to preserve the memory of war service and promote the welfare of former servicemen. Membership was open to all ex-servicemen on an open footing without any reference to rank. At its height in the interwar years it had one million members. Veterans of other wars were subsequently admitted to membership.

AMERICAN PLAN. The "American Plan" was a program launched in 1919 by the National Association of Manufacturers to combat the wartime gains of labor organizations and restore the "open shop." The determination of employers to resist workers' demands contributed to an outbreak of strikes in 1919 and the decline of **trade unions** in the 1920s. More moderate approaches were evident in the programs of **"welfare capitalism"** adopted by some of the larger businesses in the interwar years.

AMERICAN PROTECTIVE LEAGUE (APL). The American Protective League was formed during **World War I** by a Chicago advertising executive, A.M. Briggs, to assist the Justice Department with investigations of disloyal activity, breaking up antiwar meetings, and searching for draft evaders. By 1918 the APL boasted 250,000 operatives in over 600 towns and cities and was involved in 3 million investigations. Although there was some concern about their activities, not all of which were legal, Attorney General **Thomas Gregory** described them as "a most important auxiliary and reserve force of the Bureau of Investigation."

AMERICAN UNION AGAINST MILITARISM (AUAM). The American Union Against Militarism was founded in 1916 by **Roger Baldwin**, **Oswald Garrison Villard**, and **Lillian Wald** to lobby against American entry into the **World War I**. In April 1917, the AUAM became the National Civil Liberties Bureau, later the **American Civil Liberties Union,** which campaigned for the protection of civil liberties and the rights of conscientious objectors.

ANDERSON, SHERWOOD (1876–1941). Sherwood Anderson literally rose from rags to riches. Having started work as a laborer without completing high school, he moved from advertising to the mail order business, and by 1907 was president of his own manufacturing company in Elyria, Ohio. In 1912, he suffered a breakdown and the following year he left his job and family and established himself among the intellectuals of Chicago. His first novel, *Windy McPherson's Son*, appeared in 1916. Anderson achieved his fame as a writer with the publication in 1919 of a collection of naturalistic stories depicting small-town life entitled *Winesburg, Ohio*. He continued to illustrate the frustrations of modern life in *Poor White* (1920), *Many Marriages* (1923), and *Dark Laughter* (1925). His later writing, much of it autobiographical such as *A Story Teller's Tale* (1924) and *Tar: A Midwestern Childhood* (1926), was less successful but **H. L. Mencken** nonetheless described him as "America's most distinctive novelist" in 1926. After turning to producing newspapers in 1927, Anderson continued writing through the 1930s and published *Perhaps Women* (1931) and *Beyond Desire* (1932). He died of peritonitis while traveling in the Panama Canal Zone.

ARABIC. The *Arabic* was a British liner sunk in a German submarine attack with the loss of two American lives on 19 August 1915 while en route to New York. Following American protests the German government pledged to halt attacks on liners without warning and allowing for the safety of passengers. The *Arabic* pledge averted American entry into **World War I** until the resumption of unrestricted submarine warfare in 1917. *See also LUSITANIA, SUSSEX.*

ARBUCKLE, ROSCOE "FATTY" (1887–1933). Roscoe Arbuckle ("Fatty" because he weighed over 260 pounds) began his career at the turn of the century as a singer of illustrated songs on the vaudeville circuit. Arbuckle appeared with Walter Reed in a smash-hit play, *The Campus*, in Los Angeles in 1910 before touring Hawaii, Japan, China, and the Philippines. On returning to the United States in 1913, he began work at the Keystone Film Company and by 1914 had become the company's biggest star as a slapstick comedian. In 1916, he became Hollywood's highest earner when he joined Paramount Pictures with a contract worth more than $1 million a year. He formed his own production company, the Comique Film Company, and hired **Buster Keaton**. He and Keaton made 15 films together. In 1921, Arbuckle became the center of scandal when a young actress, Virginia Rappe, suffered convulsions during a party he held in a San Francisco hotel. She died a few days later of acute peritonitis and a ruptured bladder. The police, who believed that Arbuckle had sexually assaulted her and that his weight had caused the injury, charged him with manslaughter.

Arbuckle stood trial amid a public outcry at the Hollywood excesses revealed in the Hearst press. He denied the charges and evidence was produced to show that Rappe was seriously ill and had previously had several illegal abortions. The trial ended with a hung jury. A second trial in 1922 ended the same way, but in the third trial Arbuckle was acquitted. Shortly after the trial had ended, **Will Hays** was appointed to clean up the image of the movie industry and he immediately banned all of Arbuckle's films. The ban was lifted in 1923 but Arbuckle never really recovered. He directed several films and in the late 1920s ran a nightclub in Culver City, California. In 1932, he returned to act under his own name in several movies for Vitaphone, but died amid his comeback.

ARGONNE. A wooded area in eastern France between Toul and Mezieres where the First United States Army under General **John Pershing** went into action against German positions on 26 September 1918. The fighting continued through October. Although the American advances were initially rapid, they had difficulty establishing their supply systems and it was not until November that the Germans were eventually pushed back to Verdun. By the time the **armistice** was declared, United States and French troops had surrounded the German force near Verdun. *See also* WORLD WAR I.

ARMISTICE. The armistice was an agreement to cease fire between the belligerent powers in **World War I** pending peace negotiations. It was first requested by the German government on 4 October 1918, and was to be based on President **Woodrow Wilson**'s **Fourteen Points**. A temporary cease-fire ordered to allow truce discussions was mistaken by elements of the American press as a final agreement leading to premature celebrations in the United States on 7 November. The armistice proper was finally agreed after further negotiation on 8 November and signed at 11 a.m. on 11 November. The armistice required German forces to evacuate all territory west of the Rhine, surrender large elements of its war-making capacity, withdraw all her troops from Russia, Rumania, and Turkey, and renounce the treaties of Brest-Litovsk and Bucharest. Armistices had earlier been agreed between the Allies and Bulgaria, Turkey, and Austria-Hungary. The armistice was renewed until the signing of the **Treaty of Versailles**.

ARMORY SHOW, 1913. The Armory Show was the name given to the "International Exhibition of Modern Art," which took place in the armory of the 69th Regiment of the New York National Guard in New York City from17 February to 15 March 1913. Organized by a group of artists known as the Association of American Painters and Sculptors (1911), and including Walter Kuhn, Arthur B. Davies, and John Sloan, it was the first large exhibition of modern art in the United States. Among the work shown to the American public for the first time was that of Kandinsky, Picasso, and Duchamp. Although the subject of much criticism and ridicule, the exhibition of impressionist, postimpressionist, and cubist work had a revolutionary impact on the American art world.

ARMSTRONG, LOUIS (1901–1971). Born in New Orleans, the great **jazz** trumpeter and singer Louis Armstrong was placed in a Colored Waifs' Home for Boys at the age of 12. He began his career as a professional musician in 1918 playing the cornet in clubs and on Mississippi River paddle steamers. In 1922 Armstrong moved to Chicago to play second cornet in Joe "King" Oliver's Creole Jazz Band. Armstrong made his first recordings between 1923 and 1924 with Oliver, including "Riverside Blues," "Snake Rage," and "Dipper Mouth Blues." He moved to New York City to join **Fletcher Henderson**'s orchestra in 1924. It was this new band that developed the jazz style known as "swing." Armstrong made a number of records playing trumpet with Henderson ("One of these Days," "Copenhagen," and "Everybody Loves My Baby") and also with Clarence Williams' Blue Five, a group featuring **Sydney Bechet** and the singers Ma Rainey and **Bessie Smith**. Armstrong returned to Chicago in 1925 and began to lead his own groups, the Hot Five and the Hot Seven with whom he made some classic recordings of traditional jazz—"Cornet Chop," "Gut Bucket Blues," "Heebie Jeebies," and others.

Armstrong and his band moved to New York in 1929 and made several records on which he sang, often using his improvised "scat" singing. He achieved great success with "I Can't Give You Anything but Love" and "Ain't Misbehavin'" recorded in 1929. From 1930 through the 1940s Armstrong played with a number of big bands and returned to small combos after World War II. Between 1932 and 1965 he also appeared in almost 50 movies, including *Pennies from Heaven* (1936), *High Society* (1956), and

Hello Dolly (1969). Armstrong's song "Hello Dolly" had already reached number one in the popular music charts in 1964. Through his long and successful career from the days of the **Harlem Renaissance** through to the post-civil rights period of the 1960s, Armstrong—also known as "Satchmo" or "Pops"—was one of the most significant figures in jazz music. *See also* AFRICAN AMERICANS.

AUTOMOBILE. The rise of the automobile was rapid and dramatic. Charles E. and J. Frank Duryea built the first automobile in the United States in 1892 and sold their first vehicle in 1896. **Henry Ford** produced his first gasoline powered automobile in 1893 and introduced his Model T Ford in 1908. In 1899, 30 separate automobile companies produced 2,500 vehicles; by 1914 there were more than 70 companies producing 200,000 cars a year. **World War I** led to accelerated development as Ford's mass production and assembly line techniques spread. In the 1920s the automobile became the outstanding symbol of the new consumer society. The number of manufactures declined to 44 by 1929 and three companies, Ford, **Chrysler**, and **General Motors**, were responsible for 80 percent of production. Production peaked at 5.3 million vehicles in 1929, by which time there were 26.7 million registered vehicles on the road, one per every 4.5 people.

The impact of this revolution was enormous. Automobile manufacturing employed 750,000 people directly, but 4.5 million more worked in related industries—glass, rubber, oil. While automobile prices fell, purchase was made easier by the development of credit and encouraged by the growth of advertising. The automobile encouraged highway building, and federal funding increased with the **Federal Highway Acts** of 1916 and 1921. Gasoline taxes raised $431 million a year in revenue by 1929. The automobile encouraged the start of a motel industry, made the growth of suburbia a possibility, and encouraged a real estate boom. Some people even blamed the automobile for the decline in sexual morality. The slow down in the economy when Ford switched production to a new model in 1928 was one factor associated with the **Wall Street Crash** and **Great Depression**. *See also* CHEVROLET, LOUIS; DURANT, WILLIAM CRAPO.

– B –

BABBITT, IRVING (1865–1933). Irving Babbitt was a graduate of Harvard who rejoined the university and became a professor in the Department of Romance Languages where he taught French literature. With Paul Elmer More, Babbitt became one of the leaders of the New Humanism, a critique of Romanticism, and a call for restraint and conservatism. Babbitt's published work included *Literature and the American College* (1908), *The New Laokoön* (1910), *Masters of Modern French Criticism* (1912), *Rousseau and Romanticism* (1919), and *Democracy and Leadership* (1924). Although Babbitt influenced a number of writers including **T. S. Eliot**, **H. L. Mencken**, and **Walter Lippmann**, his views tended to find their most receptive audience among conservative intellectuals.

BAILEY V. DREXEL FURNITURE CO. The decision by the **Supreme Court** in 1922, which held that the second **Child Labor** law was unconstitutional because it attempted to regulate child labor by use of a penal tax. The Court states that the tax-raising power of Congress was limited to raising revenue, not correcting social problems that were the province of the states.

BAKER, NEWTON DIEHL (1871–1937). A graduate of Johns Hopkins University (1892) and Washington and Lee University (1894), Newton Baker first worked as secretary to the postmaster general, William L. Wilson, before moving to Cleveland, Ohio, where he was city solicitor from 1901 to 1909. Baker became mayor of Cleveland in 1911 and served from 1912 to 1916, continuing the reform program of Tom L. Johnson. Although avowedly a pacifist he became secretary of war in **Woodrow Wilson**'s administration in 1913, a post he held until 1920. Baker's calm handling of the problems with **Mexico**, and the **punitive expedition**, 1916–17, helped minimize public unease. He was also responsible for the administration of the **Selective Service Act** that introduced universal military conscription in 1917. Throughout **World War I** Baker loyally supported Wilson's policies. He returned to his law practice in 1921. He continued to support the **League of Nations** and addressed the 1924 Democratic Party convention with some force on the issue. In 1928 he was appointed to the Permanent Court of Arbitration in The Hague. The following year President **Herbert Hoover** appointed Baker to the Law Enforcement Commission and during the 1930s he also served on a number of committees in relation to the armed forces. In 1933 the National Institute of Social Sciences awarded Baker a medal for "services to humanity."

BAKER, RAY STANNARD (1870–1946). A journalist and writer, Baker joined the staff of *McClure's Magazine* in 1897 and the *American Magazine* in 1906. He became famous as one of the "muckraking" journalists of the **Progressive** Era, writing critiques of the railroads and of business and financial malpractice. Baker's famous series of articles on race relations was published as *Following the Color Line* in 1908 and his study of religious life was published as *The Spiritual Unrest* in 1910. Baker contributed to the work of the **Committee on Public Information** during **World War I** and was director of the press bureau for the American Commission to Negotiate Peace at the **Paris Peace conference** in 1919. He was one of the leading biographers of **Woodrow Wilson** after the war, publishing an eight-volume study between 1927 and 1939 for which he was awarded a Pulitzer Prize in 1940.

BALCH, EMILY GREENE (1867–1961). After graduating from Bryn Mawr in 1889, Emily Balch studied in Paris for a year and published *Public Assistance in France* in 1893. After returning to the United States, she became an active reformer and in 1892 helped to found Boston's first **settlement house**, Denison House, and served as its head. In 1895, Balch produced the *Manual for Use in Cases of Juvenile Offenders and Other Minors*. That year, she began teaching sociology at Wellesley and she rose to chair of the Department of Economics and Sociology in 1913. Balch produced *Our Slavic Fellow Citizens*, a definitive study of immigrants from the Austro-Hungarian Empire in 1912. She was also active on a variety of local boards, including Boston's City Planning Board, the Massachusetts Commission on Immigration, and the Committee on **Immigration** of the **Progressive Party** in 1912. Balch was also one of the founders of the Women's Trade Union League (WTUL) in 1903 and the Boston WTUL in 1904.

Following the outbreak of war in Europe in 1914, Balch joined the peace movement and was one of the founders of the **American Union Against Militarism**. In 1915 she and other members of the **Woman's Peace Party** attended an international peace conference at The Hague that called for a conference of neutral nations, and Balch attended the Stockholm Peace Conference in 1916. In 1918 she was dismissed from Wellesley because of her pacifism and her reform activities. With **Jane Addams**, Balch attended the founding conference of the Women's International League for Peace and Freedom in Zurich in 1919, and served as secretary treasurer until 1922. She served again as secretary in 1934 and succeeded Addams as honorary international president in 1937. Balch was one of a group of investigators from the Women's International League to visit **Haiti** and their report, *Occupied Haiti* (1927), helped to bring about the end of United States occupation of the island. In 1946 she was a corecipient of the Nobel Peace Prize.

BALDWIN, ROGER NASH (1884–1981). Described as "America's foremost libertarian," Roger Baldwin graduated with a B.A. and M.A. from Harvard in 1905. He became a social worker and taught sociology at Washington University, St. Louis, from 1906 to 1909. After becoming involved in reform politics he moved to New York City in 1911. In 1917 Baldwin and others formed the **American Union Against Militarism** to provide support for pacifists and **conscientious objectors** during **World War I**. He was jailed for nine months in 1918 for refusing to answer the draft. In 1919 Baldwin briefly joined the **Industrial Workers of the World** (IWW) and took to the road. However in 1920 he was one of the founders of the **American Civil Liberties Union** (ACLU). Baldwin became the ACLU director and served until 1950.

During the 1930s Baldwin visited the Soviet Union and wrote extolling the virtues of the Communist regime. He also supported Popular Front activities to combat the rise of fascism, but following the Nazi-Soviet Pact in 1939 he campaigned to alter the ACLU charter to exclude anyone associated with totalitarian regimes. Baldwin was instrumental in the expulsion of **Elizabeth Gurley Flynn** from the organization. After World War II Baldwin acted as a consultant on civil liberties in Japan and, following his resignation as director, became active in international affairs on similar issues.

BANKING. Historically banking in the United States was a complex political as well as economic issue. Opposition to a strong centralized government led to the demise of the National Bank in 1836. Although national banking was restored with the banking acts of 1863 and 1864, the banking system was complicated and inclined to instability. A three-tier system of national banks chartered by the federal government, state banks chartered by individual states, and local banks, all of which remained independent, and essentially local businesses, existed. Lack of regulation and the impact of local events, such as problems in **farming**, often resulted in bank collapses. Bank panics (the worst in 1907), and the 19th-century crisis in farming, had led to demands for regulation that resulted in the creation of the **Federal Reserve** in 1914. While this brought some stability, it did not solve all the problems as only about one-third of all banks registered with the Federal Reserve. Between 1921 and 1928, 5,000 banks were forced to close. With the collapse in investors' confidence following the **Wall Street Crash** a further 1,345 banks failed in 1930 alone. Banking failure contributed enormously to the coming of the **Great Depression** as credit shrank and business loans and mortgages on homes and farms were called in. While President **Herbert Hoover** attempted to tackle the problem with the **Reconstruction Finance Corporation** (RFC), **Glass-Steagall**, and **Federal Home Loan Bank Acts** of 1932, many banks remained closed on the eve of **Franklin D. Roosevelt's** inauguration. It was only with the banking reforms of the **New Deal** that some order and stability returned.

BARRYMORE, JOHN (1882–1942). Like his brother **Lionel**, John Barrymore was born John Blyth, but adopted his parent's stage name. After an education in Great Britain, Barrymore worked for a while as a cartoonist at the New York *Evening Journal* before beginning his acting career in 1901. By 1909 he was established as a leading comic actor and starred in *The Fortune Hunter*, a play that he took on tour for a year after a successful Broadway run in 1909. Barrymore made his first **movie**, *An American Citizen*, in 1914, and he made another nine films before 1919. He continued to appear on stage in *Justice* (1916), with his brother in *Peter Ibbetson* (1917), and in *Richard III* (1920). He successfully played the lead in a new interpretation of *Hamlet* in 1922 and he also took the play to London in 1925. Barrymore's film career continued with *Beau Brummel* in 1923 and in the first film with a synchronized soundtrack, *Don Juan*, in 1926. He continued to make movies and appear on stage through to the 1940s, even appearing in parodies of his own life as a failing actor (*My Dear Children* [1939–40], *Playmates* [1941]). Barrymore was one of the most influential actors of his day and he starred in over 40 theater plays, 60 films, and 100 radio shows, including Rudy Vallee's *Sealtest Show* in the 1940s.

BARRYMORE, LIONEL (1878–1954). Born Lionel Blythe, Barrymore adopted his mother and father's stage name of Barrymore and quickly joined them on the stage in the 1890s. He achieved his first success in 1902 playing a character role in *The Mummy and the Hummingbird* and then in 1903 in a central role in *The Other Girl*. In 1906, Barrymore moved to Paris, France, where he studied art for three years. Returning to the United States, he played in a variety of vaudeville roles then joined **D. W. Griffith** at the Biograph Studio in New York City and appeared in dozens of **movies** between 1912 and 1914.

Between 1917 and 1920, Barrymore appeared in a number of successful Broadway plays, including *Peter Ibbetson* in 1917 with his brother **John**. He also took part in **Liberty Loan** campaigns during **World War I**. Following a series of Broadway flops in the 1920s, Barrymore turned more and more to films and signed a contract with Metro-Goldwyn-Mayer (MGM) in 1925. He starred with **Greta Garbo** in *The Temptress* (1926) and with **Gloria Swanson** in *Sadie Thompson* (1928). His theater background enabled him to make the transition to sound film and, in 1931, he won an Academy Award for his role in *A Free Soul*. He continued to make movies through the 1930s, several with his brother, and, beginning in 1938, made 15 films in the *Dr. Kildare* series. His last memorable film performance was in *Key Largo* in 1948. In addition to his film and theater work, Barrymore also starred in a number of radio series and won recognition for his paintings and for his musical compositions.

BARTON, BRUCE FAIRCHILD (1886–1967). Bruce Barton graduated from Amherst College in 1907. After a series of jobs in newspaper and magazine journalism, he became assistant sales manager for the publisher Colliers in 1912 and then editor of *Every Week* in 1914 where he developed a skill in writing inspirational articles. He became a regular contributor of such work to the *American Magazine*, *McCall's*, *Collier's*, *Good Housekeeping*, and *Reader's Digest*. Several volumes of his writings were published between 1917 and 1924.

During the war Barton worked as publicity director for the United War Work Agencies. In 1919 he joined Roy S. Durstine and Alex F. Osborne to form an advertising agency that by 1928 was the fourth largest in the United States. In 1925 Barton published the best-selling *The Man Nobody Knows* in which he portrayed Christ as "the world's greatest salesman." He also wrote a study of the Bible in a similar vein, *The Book Nobody Knows* (1926), and a portrait of St. Paul, *He Upset the World* (1932). In 1937 Barton was elected to fill an unexpired term in Congress as a **Republican** Representative for New York. He won a full term in 1938. He campaigned against the **New Deal** and, together with Joseph Martin and Hamilton Fish, was ridiculed by **Franklin Roosevelt** as one of "Martin, Barton & Fish." He failed to win election to the Senate in 1940 and returned to his advertising company.

BARUCH, BERNARD MANNES (1870–1965). After graduating from City College in New York, Bernard Baruch became a financier and successful Wall Street investor. Baruch supported **Woodrow Wilson** in 1912 and was appointed to the **Advisory Commission** to the **Council of National Defense** in 1916. In 1918 he became chairman of the **War Industries Board** where he directed the industrial war effort. He helped to formulate the economic provisions of the **Versailles treaty**. Baruch was less in the public eye during the 1920s and 1930s but as a special adviser to the Roosevelt administration during World War II he authored a report on postwar conversion. As United States Representative to the United Nations Atomic Energy Commission Baruch drew up proposals for the international control of atomic energy in 1946. *See also* WORLD WAR I.

BEARD, CHARLES (1874–1948). Charles Beard was one of America's greatest historians. He studied at DePauw University, Indiana, and gained his Ph.D. from Columbia University in 1904 and then taught history and politics there until 1917 when he resigned in protest against the dismissal of two colleagues opposed to United States entry into the war. In 1917 he became director of the Training School for Public Service, a position he held until 1922. A prolific writer, perhaps his most significant work was the *Economic Interpretation of the Constitution* (1913) where he argued that rather than idealism, many of the Founding Fathers were motivated by economic interests. His *The Rise of American Civilization* (1927), coauthored with his wife **Mary Beard**, stressed the uniqueness of American history. In the 1930s he became increasingly isolationist in outlook.

BEARD, MARY RITTER (1876–1958). Mary Beard gained her Ph.B. from DePauw University in 1897 where she met her future husband, **Charles Beard**. Mary Beard was active in reform groups in New York City including the Women's Trade Union League and Woman Suffrage Party and the **Congressional Union**. In addition to collaborating with her husband on a number of publications, Mary Beard made a major contribution to women's history and can be classed as one of the founders of that genre. She wrote *Women's Work in Municipalities* (1915), *A Short History of the American Labor Movement* (1920), *On Understanding Women* (1931), *America through Women's Eyes* (1933), and *Women as Force in History* (1946). Beard also did much to collect material and establish an archive of women's history. With Charles Beard, she wrote *The Rise of American Civilization* (1927), *America in Midpassage* (1939), *The American Spirit* (1942), and *A Basic History of the Unites States* (1944). One of Mary Beard's last works was *The Making of Charles A. Beard* (1955).

BECHET, SIDNEY JOSEPH (1897–1959). The great **jazz** saxophonist and clarinetist Sidney Bechet was born in New Orleans, where he learned the clarinet and played in his first bands. Bechet toured various states in America and visited different European countries with bands between 1916 and the early 1920s. He played with **Bessie Smith**, **Duke Ellington**, and other **African American** leading performers in different revues. In 1925, Bechet toured again in France, Belgium, Germany, and Russia, returning to the United States in 1930. Bechet played with **Noble Sissle**'s band on several occasions and, with his own sextet and quartet, recording in different forms as the "New Orleans Feetwarmers." He also recorded with **Louis Armstrong** and

Jelly Roll Morton. Bechet continued to tour the United States and Europe through to his death of cancer in 1959.

BELLEAU WOOD. The first sizeable battle involving troops of the **American Expeditionary Force** (AEF) took place at **Chateau-Thierry** and Belleau Wood in June 1918 and helped stop the German offensive on the **Marne** prior to the **Allied** counteroffensive.

BENÉT, STEPHEN VINCENT (1898–1943). Stephen Benét began writing and publishing poetry while still at school. His first book of poetry, *Five Men and Pompey* was published in 1915. He entered Yale University that year and won a number of literary prizes. He had his *Young Adventure: A Book of Poems* published in 1918. Benét completed his masters at Yale in 1920 and his dissertation, a group of poems, was published that year. Benét's first novel, *The Beginning of Wisdom*, was published in 1921, his second, *Young People's Pride*, in 1922, and the third, *Jean Huguenot*, in 1923. More of his poetry appeared in the *New Republic* and the *Nation*. He achieved commercial and popular success in 1928 with the publication of his narrative poem, *John Brown's Body*, which was widely recited on stage and radio. Benét then went to Hollywood to write scripts but did not remain long. He was elected to the National Institute of Arts and Letters in 1929 and to the American Academy of Arts and Letters in 1938. His *Ballads and Poems* appeared in 1931 and included the popular "American Names," ending with the line "Bury my heart at Wounded Knee." More poetry and a fourth novel appeared in the 1930s and during World War II he wrote scripts for the radio series, *This is War* and *Dear Adolf*, in addition to a history of the United States commissioned by the Office of War Information. *Western Star*, published after his death in 1943, won the Pulitzer Prize for poetry in 1944.

BERGER, VICTOR LOUIS (1860–1929). An immigrant from Austria, who entered the United States in 1878, Berger joined the Socialist Labor Party in 1889. He was the editor of *Milwaukee Daily Vorwaerts* (1892–98), *Social Democratic Herald* (1900), and then of the leading United States socialist daily newspaper, the *Milwaukee Leader* in 1911. A critic of the conservatism of the **American Fed-**

eration of Labor under **Samuel Gompers**, Berger was one of the founders of the Social Democratic Party that then became the **Socialist Party of America** in 1901. He became the first socialist elected to Congress when he entered the House of Representatives in 1911. He served until 1913, and was re-elected in 1918. Following his conviction under the **Espionage Act** he was sentenced to 20 years in prison and excluded from the House in 1919. The **Supreme Court** overturned his conviction in 1921 and Berger was elected and seated in the House once more from 1923 to 1929. He succeeded **Eugene Debs** as chair of the Socialist Party's national executive committee in 1927.

BILLINGS, WARREN KNOX. *See* MOONEY, THOMAS.

BIRTH OF A NATION, **1915.** Made by director **D. W. Griffith**, *The Birth of a Nation* was a path-breaking film in terms of technique, but also significant for its racial content. The film was the story of the intertwined fortunes of two families, North and South, during the Civil War and Reconstruction. It depicted the defeated South overrun by ignorant former slaves manipulated by scheming white politicians. It also showed white womanhood threatened by rapacious black men— most of whom were played in the film by white actors in blackface. The **Ku Klux Klan** was presented as the savior of the South. The film was based on Thomas Dixon's play, *The Clansman*, and reflected many of the views held at the time. President **Woodrow Wilson** said the film was "like writing history with lightning. And my only regret is that it is all terribly true." The showing of the film prompted protest from black groups and the **National Association for the Advancement of Colored People**, but it also led to a revival of the Ku Klux Klan. Technically, the film, which lasted almost three hours, included many of the features of modern filmmaking with intercutting of stories, panoramic views of battles, fade-outs, and close ups, and in that sense it remains a masterpiece.

BLACK BOTTOM. The Black Bottom was one of the several dances, like the **Charleston**, reflecting the more uninhibited styles of the 1920s and developed from a song of the same name. It was made popular in the stage play *Dinah* in 1926.

BLATCH, HARRIOT STANTON (1856–1940). Daughter of an abolitionist and Elizabeth Cady Stanton, a leader of the early **women**'s rights movement, the **women's suffrage** leader Harriot Stanton Blatch obtained her degree from Vassar in 1878 and then assisted her mother and Susan B. Anthony in writing the *History of Woman Suffrage* (1881). After her marriage Blatch lived in London, England, and became involved in women's reform movements. She returned to the United States in 1902 and set out to revitalize the American suffrage movement by including working women. She established the Equality League of Self-Supporting Women in 1907 and three years later this became the Women's Political Union (WPU). During **World War I** Blatch concentrated on helping the war effort and was head of the **United States Food Administration**'s Speakers' Bureau and director of the Woman's Land Army.

Once New York conceded women's suffrage in 1917, Blatch combined the WPU with the **Congressional Union** to fight for a federal suffrage amendment. After the vote had been won, Blatch joined the **National Woman's Party** in campaigning for an Equal Rights Amendment. Blatch also joined the **Socialist Party** and made unsuccessful bids to be elected to public office. In addition to her political activities Blatch also campaigned on behalf of the **League of Nations**.

BOK, EDWARD WILLIAM (1863–1930). Born in the Netherlands, Edward Bok emigrated to the United States with his family in 1870. After working as an office boy and reporter Bok became head of advertising for the publisher, Charles Scribner, in 1887. In 1886 Bok established his own Syndicate Press supplying material to over 130 newspapers. In 1889 he became editor of the *Ladies' Home Journal*. Under his direction the journal, which increased its circulation from under half a million to over two million, supported reform measures including city improvements, **women's suffrage**, sex education, and the Pure Food and Drug Act (1906). The journal was used to support the war effort during **World War I** and to encourage the recruitment of women into the war effort. Bok served as vice president of the Belgian Relief Fund. He resigned the editorship of the *Ladies' Home Journal* in 1919 and established an American Peace Award in 1923 and later the American Foundation to lobby for United States' entry into the Permanent Court of International Justice. Bok's autobiography, *The Americanization of Edward Bok* (1920), was a bestseller and won the Pulitzer Prize. He published numerous other books, including a second autobiography, *Twice Thirty* (1925).

BONUS ARMY. Following the onset of the **Depression**, in the spring of 1932 veterans of **World War I** began to call for the early payment of cash bonuses for military service that were due to be paid in 1945. Starting in Portland, Oregon, some of these groups, calling themselves the "Bonus Expeditionary Force" or "Bonus Army," began to travel to Washington, D.C., to lobby Congress. By the beginning of June some 3,000 veterans and their families had established a camp on the Anacostia mud flats just outside the capital. By July almost 25,000 people were assembled there.

The bill to secure the early payment was defeated in the Senate on 17 June and many of the protestors began to leave the city. However, following confrontations with the police in July in which two protestors were shot and killed, it was decided that the veterans posed a threat to public order and President **Herbert Hoover** authorized the use of military force to remove them from the capital. On 28 July infantry and cavalry, backed by tanks, under the command of General Douglas MacArthur and Major Dwight D. Eisenhower cleared the streets. Contrary to the president's orders, the troops then went on to destroy the camp in Anacostia. The images of these incidents did much to destroy the last of Hoover's reputation and bring about his political defeat.

BOOTLEGGING. Bootlegging was the term used to describe the sale or smuggling of illegal alcohol. Although its origins were in the early history of the West when traders carried a bottle of liquor in their boots, it was widely used during the 1920s and the era of **Prohibition** that followed the passage of the **Eighteenth Amendment** in 1920. Bootleg alcohol was sold in illegal bars or clubs known as "speakeasies."

BORAH, WILLIAM EDGAR (1865–1940). After a limited education in Kansas, Borah passed the bar examinations in law in 1887 and practiced for three years before moving to Idaho. Having stood unsuccessfully for the United States House of Representatives as a **Democrat** in 1896, Borah turned to the **Republicans** as a candidate for the Senate in 1902. Unsuccessful again, he was elected in 1906. Borah served six successive terms and was known for his oratory and political independence. In domestic matters he had **progressive** tendencies, supporting antitrust legislation, income tax, popular election of senators, and Prohibition. In foreign affairs he was one of the leading opponents of the **Versailles treaty** and **League of Nations,** but he supported the **Washington Conference** (1921–22). As chairman of the Foreign Relations Committee from 1924 to 1933, he helped secure ratification of the **Kellogg-Briand Pact** in 1928. He opposed revision of the Neutrality Acts passed in the 1930s and also disapproved of many **New Deal** measures.

BOSTON POLICE STRIKE. In September 1919, 75 percent of the Boston police force went on strike when the police commissioner refused to recognize their union. When Governor **Calvin Coolidge** refused to intervene, Mayor Andrew Peters used sections of the militia to break up the strike. Coolidge then ordered the police commissioner to take charge and called out the entire state guard. The strike was broken but the commissioner refused to allow those who had taken part back into the force. **Samuel Gompers** asked Coolidge to help the policemen regain their jobs—his reply that "there is no right to strike against the public safety by anybody, anywhere, anytime" won him national prominence and led to his inclusion on the Republican ticket in 1920. The strike and disorder associated with it helped to generate the hysteria that led to the **"Red Scare."** *See also* TRADE UNIONS.

BOURNE, RANDOLPH SILLIMAN (1886–1918). Randolph Bourne was one of the group of young social and literary critics who emerged in the **Progressive** Era. He was educated at Columbia University where he was influenced by **Charles Beard, John Dewey** and **James Harvey Robinson**. Bourne published his first book *Youth and Life* in 1913 and in 1914 joined the newly formed progressive journal, *New Republic*. In addition to literary criticism, he wrote a series of articles and two books, *The Gary Schools* (1916) and *Education and Living* (1917), on progressive education. He became increasingly at odds with the other writers for the *New Republic* over **World War I** and wrote a series of articles in a new avant-garde journal, *Seven*, rejecting the notion that the war was a moral crusade and criticizing the intellectuals for their naivete. He died in the **influenza epidemic** in 1918.

BOW, CLARA GORDON (1905–1965). Known as the "It" Girl for her sensuous looks, Clara Bow was the quintessential movie **"flapper."** Bow had her first part in a movie in 1921 and signed with Schulberg's Preferred Pictures in 1923. Her reputation as a "jazz baby" was established in *The Plastic Age* and *Kiss Me Again* both in 1925. Bow moved to Paramount Pictures in 1926 and achieved enormous fame exuding sexual allure in *Mantrap*. In 1927, she appeared in *It*, and she was known as the "It" girl thereafter. Between 1922 and 1930, Bow made 52 films, but with the onset of sound movies, her career and health faltered. She was fired from Paramount in 1931 and retired. Attempted comebacks in 1932 and 1933 failed although she did have some success in 1947 on the radio program "Truth or Consequence."

BRANDEIS, LOUIS DEMBITZ (1856–1941). After graduating with the highest honors from Harvard Law School in 1877 Louis Brandeis established a law practice in Boston where he earned a reputation as the "people's lawyer" and a leading member of the **Progressive** movement. Brandeis acted without fees for Boston citizens in their fight to control the price of gas. He also acted for policyholders in an investigation of life insurance companies, and he drafted state legislation to control the companies. On several occasions Brandeis also acted as mediator on behalf of labor in disputes with employers. Brandeis came to national prominence in the 1908 case of *Muller v. Oregon* when he used sociological and economic evidence rather than legal precedent to argue in support of restricting the hours of working **women**.

Brandeis also acted as an informal adviser to both **Robert M. La Follette** and **Woodrow Wilson**. In 1916 Wilson nominated Brandeis to the **Supreme Court**, and after a fierce battle over his nomination, he became the first Jew to serve as Supreme Court justice, a position he held for 23 years. Brandeis's opinions tended to be critical of any concentration of power, and he refused to endorse the government's power to restrict freedom of speech. He did, however, uphold the Court's decision in *Schenck v. United States*, but with **Oliver Wendell Holmes** dissented in *Abrams v. United States* both in 1919. Having written a seminal article on the "Right to Privacy" in 1890, Brandeis argued against the government's use of telephone tapping in *Olmstead v. United States* (1928). He argued for judicial restraint and placed considerable emphasis on the independence of the states, and in *Erie Railroad v. Tompkins* (1938) argued that federal courts had to be bound by the decisions of state supreme courts in state matters.

Outside of the courts, Brandeis was a leader of the American Zionist movement and helped to found the American Jewish Congress, the Palestine Endowment Fund, and the Palestine Cooperative Company.

BRECKINRIDGE, SOPHONISBA PRESTON (1866–1948). Born into a prominent Kentucky family, Sophonisba Breckinridge graduated from Wellesley College in 1888 and after teaching for a while began to study law. In 1894, Breckinridge was the first woman to pass the Kentucky bar examination. However, she then joined the Political Science Department at the University of Chicago where, in 1901, she received the first Ph.D. in political science awarded to an American woman. Breckinridge taught at Chicago until her retirement in 1942 and was a close associate of **Edith Abbott**. She and Abbott founded the *Social Service Review* in 1927 and together the two women produced several books on social issues.

In addition to her academic career Breckinridge served as a Chicago city health inspector, a probation officer with the Juvenile Court, was a member of the executive committee of the Consumers' League, the Women's Trade Union League (WTUL), and of the **National Association for the Advancement of Colored People** (NAACP). Breckinridge served on the commission investigating the **Chicago Race Riot** of 1919 and in a later essay blamed prejudice for bringing housing segregation. Breckinridge attended several international conferences on behalf of the United States State Department and in 1933 was the official representative at the first Pan-American Conference. In 1934 she was elected president of the American Association of Schools of Social Work. *See also* SOCIAL WORK.

BROOKS, VAN WYCK (1886–1963). The literary critic and cultural historian Van Wyck Brooks entered Harvard University in 1904, published his own poetry in 1905, edited the *Harvard Advocate* (1905), and graduated a year early. Following his graduation he spent two years in England and published *The Wine of the Puritans* in 1908. He returned to the United States in 1909 and taught at Stanford University from 1911 to 1913. After another spell in Britain and France, Brooks returned to America in 1914 and published *John Addington Symonds: A Biographical Study* (1914), *The World of H.G. Wells* (1915), and *America's Coming-of-Age* (1915). In the latter Brooks divided American culture into "highbrow" and "lowbrow" and his criticism of American materialism was to be evident in other writings. From 1916 to 1917 Brooks coedited and published *Seven Arts*, a liberal journal. He gained a national reputation when he published his essays in *Letters and Leadership* in 1918. His studies of *The Ordeal of Mark Twain* (1920) and *the Pilgrimage of Henry James* (1925) were regarded as controversial for their criticism of the two writers. In 1932 Brooks published *The Life of Emerson* and *Sketches in Criticism*. Between 1936 and 1952 he published his five-volume study of *Makers and Finders: A History of the Writer in America*. He continued to write works of criticism and a three-volume autobiography right up until his death.

BRYAN, WILLIAM JENNINGS (1860–1925). Born and educated in Illinois, Bryan moved to Nebraska where he was elected to Congress in 1890 as a **Democrat**. After two terms he campaigned for the nomination as United States senator on a platform of free silver, tariff reform, and income tax. Following his famous "Cross of Gold" speech at the Democratic Party convention in Chicago in 1896 Bryan became the leader of the rural Populist Party as well as the candidate for the Democratic Party. He was defeated by the **Republican** William McKinley. McKinley defeated him again in 1900 when he campaigned on a largely anti-imperialist ticket. He failed to win the Democratic nomination in 1904, but was renominated again in 1908, only to be defeated by **Willliam Howard Taft**. In 1916 he supported the nomination of **Woodrow Wilson** and was rewarded with the appointment as secretary of state. Although a nationalist who expanded United States influence in Central America through the **Bryan-Chamorro Treaty**, 1914, he was steadfastly neutral with regard to the European nations involved in war. Fearing that Wilson's demand of "strict accountability" from Germany following the sinking of the *Lusitania* might lead to war, Bryan resigned in 1915.

Although his political influence quickly declined, he remained a voice of rural America and campaigned in support of the **Eighteenth Amendment** that introduced **Prohibition**. He was an increasingly vocal supporter of antievolution laws and appeared for the prosecution against the teacher **John Scopes** in the famous trial in Dayton, Tennessee. Although Scopes was found guilty of breaking the law by teaching the theories of Charles Darwin, Bryan's defense of the literal interpretation of the Bible left him subject to ridicule and criticism from both scientists and defenders of academic freedom. He died five days after the trial had concluded.

BRYAN-CHAMORRO TREATY, 1914. A treaty between the United States and Nicaragua that granted the United States the exclusive right to the option to construct a canal in Nicaragua. The treaty also gave the United States the Great and Little Corn Islands on a 99-year lease in return for $3 million. Previously rejected by the Senate in 1912 it was accepted in 1914. United States troops had been sent to Nicaragua in 1912 and remained until 1924.

BUDGET AND ACCOUNTING ACT. Passed in 1921, the act created the **General Accounting Office** and **Bureau of the Budget**. The act established the fiscal year running from 1 July to 30 June and required the president to send details of the executive budget to Congress and to recommend new taxes and expenditures.

BULLARD, WILLIAM HANNUM GRUBB (1866–1927). Bullard was a graduate of Annapolis Naval Academy (1907) who became superintendent of the Naval Radio Service in 1912 and director of naval communication from 1919 to 1921. He commanded the battleship *Arkansas* during the war and commanded the Yangtze patrol of the American Asiatic fleet from 1921 until his retirement the following year. He was a founder of the Radio Corporation of America and chair of the United States Radio Commission.

BULLITT, WILLIAM CHRISTIAN (1891–1967). Bullitt began work as a writer on the Philadelphia *Public Ledger* (1915–17) but joined the State Department in 1917. In 1919 he was sent to Moscow to report on the Bolshevik government and he recommended recognition of the Soviet regime. When this was rejected he became disaffected and spoke against acceptance of the **Versailles treaty**. He was recalled from relative obscurity and appointed ambassador to the Union of Socialist Soviet Republics (Union of Soviet Socialist Republics [USSR]) from 1933 to 1936, and to France from 1936 to 1941. He became a special assistant to the secretary of the navy in 1942 but left to serve as an officer in the Free French Army, 1944 to 1945.

BUREAU OF THE BUDGET. Established in 1921 under the **Budget and Accounting Act**, the Bureau was headed by the Director of the Budget with the primary function of preparing the annual executive budget. It was also responsible for the supervision of the administrative management of executive agencies, the improvement of federal statistical services, and the promotion of economic and efficient government running.

BURLESON, ALBERT SIDNEY (1863–1937). After an education at Texas Agricultural and Mechanical College, Baylor University, and the Law Department of the University of Texas, Austin, Albert Burleson practiced law in Austin. From 1885 to 1898 he served as assistant attorney general in Austin and then attorney general for the Twenty-sixth District. In 1898 Burleson was elected as **Democratic** congressman and served until 1913. His support for **Woodrow Wilson**, and the backing of **Edward House,** led to Burleson's appointment as postmaster general in 1913. Burleson's management of the United States Post Office was generally conservative. He introduced the segregation of black and white workers, opposed postal workers' unions, and refused mailing rights to publications he judged to be critical of American involvement in the war. Burleson also attempted to make the Post Office self-sustaining by cutting back on the rural mail service, which he regarded as too expensive. When Congress refused to accept this, he attracted considerable criticism when he altered many carriers' routes and effectively eliminated others. His high-handed management of the United States Telegraph and Telephone Administration created during the war also added to his lack of popularity. However, Burleson did establish the airmail service and the parcel post system. In 1920 he returned to Austin and concentrated on his ranching and **banking** interests.

BURNS, WILLIAM JOHN (1861–1932). William Burns began work as a detective in Columbus, Ohio. In 1889, he joined the United States Secret Service. He established the William J. Burns Detective Agency with his son in New York City in 1909 and the agency soon became a national body. He was involved in the investigations that led to the conviction of John and James McNamara for the bombing of the *Los Angeles Times* office in 1910 and in the cases of municipal corruption in Atlantic City and Detroit. In the trial of **Leo Frank** in 1914, Burns presented strong evidence of Frank's innocence. In 1921, Attorney General **Harry S. Daugherty** appointed him as chief of the **Federal Bureau of Investigation**, a position he held until 1924. He then returned to his private practice. During the trial of one of his clients, the oil producer **Harry F. Sinclair**, in 1927–28, Burns was convicted of "shadowing" the jury and sentenced to jail for contempt. He was, however, released because no deliberate act was proven on his part.

BURROUGHS, EDGAR RICE (1875–1950). Burroughs was the author who created the fictional character of Tarzan. He served in the army attached to the Seventh Cavalry in the 1890s, had a stint as a cattleman, worked for his father, and then held a variety of different jobs including gold mining, janitor, door-to-door salesman, and seller of pencil sharpeners. He published his first short story, a science fiction tale, in *All-Story*, a pulp fiction magazine in 1912. Burroughs' first Tarzan story was published later that year and *Tarzan and the Apes* appeared in book form in 1914. It was a national best-seller and was followed by a total of 25 more Tarzan novels. The first film version of *Tarzan and the Apes* appeared in 1918 and was one of the first half dozen movies to gross more than $1 million. Tarzan films continued to be made right through into the 1990s. The Tarzan stories were turned into radio shows in the late 1920s and were also syndicated in comic strip form in daily and Sunday newspapers beginning in 1931. A Tarzan television series began in 1966. In addition Burroughs wrote over 20 space novels, several Westerns and historical romances, and a number of social satires. During World War II he served as a war correspondent.

BUTLER, NICHOLAS MURRAY (1862–1947). Nicholas Butler graduated from Columbia University in 1882 and went on to gain his M.A. in 1883 and Ph.D. in 1884. After a year in Europe, Butler returned to Columbia as a teacher in 1885. His essays on educational methodology were published as *The Meaning of Education* in 1915. In 1887, Butler became president of the Industrial Education Society of New York and established the teachers college the same year. The college was affiliated with Columbia in 1890 and Butler became professor of philosophy and education. He established the journal *Educational Review* in 1891 and edited it until 1919.

Butler was involved in New York politics in matters relating to public education and was president of the National Education Association, 1894–95. In 1902 Butler became president of Columbia. Under his leadership for 46 years, the university grew in size and renown. He insisted the university be run along business lines, but insisted too that donors would not affect the university's independence. Butler was active in **Republican** politics and was adviser to successive presidents and was offered a number of political posts but declined them all. In 1925 he became president of the Carnegie Endowment for Peace and held the position until 1945. He was a sponsor of the **Kellogg-Briand Treaty** in 1929 and was awarded the Nobel Peace Prize in 1931 with **Jane Addams**.

BUTLER, PIERCE (1866–1939). Pierce Butler was admitted to the Minnesota bar in 1888. He was briefly assistant county attorney and was elected county attorney in 1892 and 1894. In 1908, he was chosen as president of the Minnesota State Bar Association. A **Democrat**, Butler narrowly lost election to the state senate in 1906, but continued to advise state governors. As a member of the Board of Regents of the University of Minnesota during **World War I**, Butler supported the dismissal of professors who expressed pacifist or radical opinions. In 1922, President **Warren Harding** nominated him to the United States **Supreme Court** and he served until 1939. He was generally conservative and opposed any expansion of the power of the federal government and voted against the majority of **New Deal** measures. Butler was also conservative on issues of civil liberties and **civil rights** and he opposed the rejection of the conviction of the **Scottsboro Boys** in 1932.

BYRD, RICHARD EVELYN (1888–1957). Richard Byrd gained his commission from the United States Naval Academy, Annapolis, in 1912. He learned to fly during **World War I** and pioneered night time and sea flight navigation. In 1918, he became commander of the United States Air Forces in Canada. In 1915, Byrd took part in an expedition to Greenland directing the aviation unit. In 1926, he and pilot Floyd Bennett became the first people to fly over the North Pole, although Byrd's diary caused some later writers to question whether they had in fact reached the Pole. Both men were awarded the Medal of Honor. Byrd led the first American expedition to the Antarctic since 1840 between 1928 and 1930. Together with pilot Bernt Balchen, Byrd became the first person to fly over the South Pole in 1929. He was appointed rear admiral in 1930 and took part in two further expeditions to the Antarctic, in 1933–35 and 1939–41. The latter was an official United States expedition. After World War II Byrd was involved in two further expeditions in 1946 and 1955. He wrote two books about his experiences, *Skyward* (1928) and *Little America* (1930).

– C –

CALLOWAY, "CAB" (CABELL) (1907–1994). The **African American** entertainer Cab Calloway began his professional career in vaudeville in Baltimore from 1924 on. He also played basketball in the black professional basketball league for the Baltimore Athenians. In 1927, Calloway joined the Plantation Days revue and traveled to Chicago where he sang in the Dreamland Café with **Louis Armstrong**'s band. After a brief and unsuccessful tour to New York in 1929 Calloway obtained a part in Connie's *Hot Chocolates*, a successful Broadway revue that also went to Boston and Philadelphia. He returned to New York in 1930 and made his first recordings with his orchestra, including "St. Louis Blues," "Some of these Days," and

"St. James Infirmary." In 1931 Calloway and his band moved to the Cotton Club in Harlem, the black area of New York City, where they alternated with **Duke Ellington**'s orchestra. Calloway performed there regularly until 1936 when the Cotton Club moved from Harlem. Calloway performed at the new location until 1940.

Radio broadcasts from the Cotton Club made Calloway a national star, renowned for his singing and "jive" talk. Having already achieved recording success, in 1931 Calloway had an enormous hit with his first of several versions of "Minnie the Moocher" in 1931. Calloway's scat singing made him the "King of Hi-de-ho" and provided the inspiration for **George Gershwin**'s character Sportin' Life in *Porgy and Bess* (1935). A number of Calloway's performances figured in cartoons starring Betty Boop in the 1930s and he made several short films, *Cab Calloway's Jitterbug Party* (1935), *Hi De Ho* (1937), and *Manhattan Merry-go-round* (1937). In addition, Calloway also published a *Hepsters Dictionary* in 1938, and the sixth edition, *The New Cab Calloway's Hepsters Dictionary: Language of Jive* (1944), sold over one million copies. In 1941, Calloway's band played in the movie *Roadshow* and in 1943 Calloway costarred with Lena Horne in *Stormy Weather.* He continued to perform on stage and in film through to the 1980s. In addition to roles in *The Blues Brothers* (1980) and *The Cotton Club* (1984), Calloway also made regular appearances in the children's television show, "Sesame Street." In 1989, he appeared with Janet Jackson in her music video "Alright." Calloway's career as a performer and bandleader places him amongst the great showmen of the 20th century. *See also* HARLEM RENAISSANCE.

CANNON, JOSEPH GURNEY (1836–1926). After qualifying as a lawyer in North Carolina, Cannon moved to Illinois to practice law. He was elected to the House of Representatives 1873–91, 1893–1913, and 1915–23. He became leader of the "Old Guard" (conservative) **Republicans**, and as speaker he used his power to appoint legislative committees in a dictatorial manner until the speaker's powers were restricted in 1910 by **progressive** Republicans and **Democrats**. Cannon continued to serve in the House until his retirement at the age of 87 in 1923. Cannon's 46-year long tenure in Congress was the longest of any member before World War II.

CANTOR, EDDIE (1892–1964). The singer and actor Eddie Cantor was born Israel Iskowitz in New York City. He later changed his name when he began performing as a comedian and singer in music hall in 1907. Cantor played in a number of musicals and revues in London, New York, and Los Angeles between 1911 and 1916. He made a successful appearance in the Ziegfeld *Follies* in 1917, 1918, and 1919. He also led the strike that established the Actor's Equity Association and later he was to become president of the Screen Actors' Guild, the American Federation of Radio Artists, and the American Guild of Variety Artists. Cantor continued to appear in musical revues in the early 1920s, and he achieved a major success in one of the decade's longest running Broadway musicals, *Kid Boots*. He appeared in a silent film version of this in 1926 and in *Special Delivery* in 1927.

Cantor returned as the central performer in the Ziegfeld *Follies* in 1927 followed by *Whoopee*, which opened in 1928. Despite losing his personal fortune in the **Wall Street Crash**, Cantor achieved greater success in the 1930s and was a leading star in film and radio. From 1931 to 1934 he starred in the radio "Chase and Sanborn Hour," and with other sponsors through to 1940. He made several films with **Samuel Goldwyn** including *Palmy Days* (1931), *The Kid from Spain* (1932), *Roman Scandals* (1933). During World War II Cantor performed for wounded GIs in hospitals and also continued making movies — *Thank Your Lucky Stars* (1943), *Show Business* (1944), and *If You Knew Susie* (1948). He recorded the soundtrack to the *Eddie Cantor Story* in 1953 and appeared on television programs including "The Eddie Cantor Comedy Theater." He retired due to ill health in 1957. One of the first stars to succeed in stage, film, and radio, Cantor was also active in social causes among them the March of Dimes established to fight polio. In 1964 President Lyndon Johnson awarded Cantor the Medal of Freedom in recognition of his achievements.

CAPONE, AL (ALPHONSE) (1899–1947). Al Capone, the man who achieved fame as a gangster during the 1920s, was born in Brooklyn where he grew up among the street gangs. In 1917, he was scarred in a knife fight and earned the nickname "Scarface." Capone moved to Chicago around 1920 to work with John Torrio, who had taken over leadership of organized crime in the city. With the onset of **Prohibition**, the sale and distribution of **bootleg** liquor provided new opportunities for criminal activity. In 1924, Capone organized gunmen to determine the election in Cicero, just west of Chicago. In 1925, Capone took over the Torrio operation and rose to fame through a number of acts of violence. An assistant state attorney was assassinated in 1926, bombings occurred to influence the election of Mayor **William Thompson**'s candidates in 1928, and in 1929 Capone's rivals were eliminated in the St. Valentine's Day Massacre. In 1927 Capone was forced to move out of Chicago by police pressure and he established a base in Florida. He was arrested in 1929 and jailed for a year for carrying a concealed weapon. Released in 1930, Capone was indicted for income tax fraud in 1931. Found guilty, he was sentenced to 11 years in prison. Diagnosed with fatal syphilis of the brain, Capone was released from Alcatraz in 1939 and retired to his home.

CAPPER, ARTHUR (1865–1951). Arthur Capper was the first native-born Kansan to serve his state as governor and United States senator. Capper began his career as a journalist and newspaper owner. A **Republican**, Capper narrowly failed to win the gubernatorial election in 1912, but won it in 1914 and was re-elected in 1916. In 1918 Capper was elected to the United States Senate where he served until 1949. He voted for the **League of Nations** with reservations but tended to be isolationist until World War II. Capper was a leader of the **Farm Bloc** and supported measures to aid farm cooperatives. During the Depression Capper supported many of the **New Deal** reforms.

CARAWAY, HATTIE OPHELIA WYATT (1878–1950). Hattie Caraway graduated from Dickson Normal College in Tennessee in 1896. She married Thaddeus Caraway in 1902 and they settled in Arkansas where she raised three children. Thaddeus Caraway served first in the United States House of Representatives from 1912 and then in the United States Senate from 1921. When he died in 1931, Hattie Caraway was appointed to fill his vacant seat. She then became the first woman ever elected to the Senate when, supported by the Arkansas **Democratic Party** she won a special election. In 1932, Hattie Caraway defeated six challengers in the Democratic primary and was re-elected in her own right in 1932. Caraway won election again in 1938 and went on to become the first woman to preside over the Senate, first to conduct a Senate committee hearing, first to chair a committee, and first senior senator. She cosponsored the Equal Rights Amendment in 1943. She was defeated in the Democratic primary in 1944 by J. William Fulbright who went on to win her seat. Caraway subsequently served on the Employees' Compensation Commission and Employees' Compensation Appeals Board.

CARDOZO, BENJAMIN NATHAN (1870–1938). After graduating from Columbia Law School in 1889 and practicing law in New York City, Cardozo served as a justice of the Supreme Court of New York from 1913 to 1914 when he moved to the New York court of appeals. In 1932, President **Hoover** appointed him to the Supreme Court to succeed **Oliver Wendell Holmes.** Cardozo demonstrated a liberal inclination in generally supporting **New Deal** legislation and arguing strongly in favor of sociological jurisprudence. Cardozo was also active in a number of Jewish organizations.

CATHER, WILLA SILBERT (1876–1947). The novelist Willa Cather was born in Virginia but brought up in Nebraska. After graduating from the University of Nebraska (1895) she became a staff writer for the Pittsburgh *Daily Leader*, (1898–1901), and then associate editor of *McClure's Magazine.* (1906–12). She began publishing poetry and short stories and her first novel, A*lexander's Bridge*, appeared in 1912. She became established with *O Pioneers!* (1913) and then the classic *My Antonia* (1918), both of which focused on the role of immigrants, particularly women, in the West. Her novel about **World War I**, *One of Ours* (1922), was awarded the Pulitzer Prize and she continued to produce novels through the 1920s, including *A Lost Lady* (1923) and *Death Comes for the Archbishop* (1927). Several more novels and collections of Cather's stories appeared in the 1930s. She is widely regarded as one of the leading American writers of the 20th century.

CATT, CARRIE CLINTON CHAPMAN (1859–1947). Educated at Iowa State Agricultural College, the **women's suffrage** leader, formerly a school teacher and principal, Carrie Catt became an organizer and campaigner for the Iowa Woman Suffrage Association in 1890 and for the **National American Woman Suffrage Association** (NAWSA) from 1892. She was president of NAWSA from 1900 to 1904 and again from 1915 until her death, leading the campaign that resulted in women gaining the vote with the **Nineteenth Amendment** in 1920. Catt also founded the International Woman Suffrage Alliance (IWSA) in 1902 and was also president of the organization from 1904 to 1923. Following the passage of the amendment, Catt participated in forming the **League of Women Voters**. She was a supporter of the **League of Nations** and was head of the National Committee on the Cause and Cure of War from 1925 to 1932. Catt continued to support the committee until it ended in 1941.

CENTRAL POWERS. Originally a term used to describe Germany, Austria-Hungary, and Italy following the Triple Alliance of 1882, the name was given to the group of nations that opposed the **Allied Powers** during **World War I**, comprising Germany, Austria-Hungary, Turkey, and Bulgaria. The alliance disintegrated as each nation sought an armistice in 1918.

CERMAK, ANTON JOSEPH (1873–1933). Born in Austria-Hungary (now the Czech Republic), Anton Cermak came to the United States with his family in 1874. After working in the coal mines Cermak began a hauling business in Chicago. He joined the **Democratic Party** and rose from precinct captain to win a seat in the Illinois state legislature in 1902. In 1909, he became a Chicago City alderman, and then bailiff of the municipal court before returning to the city council once more in 1919. In 1922, Cermak was elected to the Cook County Board of Commissioners and he was soon the leader of the Chicago Democratic machine. In 1931 Cermak defeated the **Republican** incumbent, **Bill Thompson**, to become mayor. In February 1933 he traveled to Miami to meet president-elect **Franklin D. Roosevelt**. On 15 February Cermak was seriously wounded when **Guiseppe Zangara** fired several shots intended for Roosevelt. Cermak died on 8 March and Zangara was executed 13 days later.

CHAMBERLAIN, GEORGE EARLE (1854–1928). Admitted to the bar in Oregon (1878), Chamberlain served in the state legislature as a **Democrat**, 1880–82, was attorney general of Oregon, 1891–94, and governor of Oregon, 1902–09. He was United States senator from 1909 to 1921, where he chaired the Public Lands Committee. As chair of the Military Affairs Committee from 1913 to 1921 Chamberlain was responsible for such legislation as Selective Service, food controls, and war finances. He was appointed to the United States Shipping Board in 1920.

CHANEY, LON (1883–1930). Born Leonidas, Lon Chaney dropped out of school and began work in the theater in 1895. He joined a vaudeville group and moved to California where he began his film career in slapstick comedies in 1913. In 1915, Chaney joined the Universal film company and made numerous films with them before moving to Paramount in 1919. Chaney made a name for himself by using contortion and make-up in films such as *The Miracle Man* (1919) in which he played a frog, *The Hunchback of Notre Dame* (1923) as Quasimodo, the phantom in *The Phantom of the Opera* (1925), and the lead role in *Mr. Wu* (1927). Altogether Chaney made over 150 films and earned the name "The Man of a Thousand Faces." His son was also successful as an actor under the name Lon Chaney, Jr.

CHAPLIN, CHARLES (SPENCER) (1889–1977). One of the greatest performers in silent films, Charlie Chaplin was born in London, England, where he performed in music hall and plays in his early teens. In 1913, while on tour in America, Chaplin signed a contract with **Mack Sennett** at the Keystone film studios. He first appeared in a motion picture in 1914 and he made 35 films with Keystone and then 14 with Essanay before moving to the Mutual Film Corporation in 1916. He quickly established his film persona in movies such as *The Tramp* (1915), *The Vagabond* (1917), and *The Immigrant* (1917). As the little tramp with his distinctive walk, little moustache, bowler hat, and large shoes, Chaplin effectively combined slapstick with pathos. By 1917, he was a huge star and had signed a one million-dollar contract with the First National Exhibitors' Circuit to make eight films. In 1919, Chaplin joined with **Mary Pickford**, **Douglas Fairbanks**, and **D. W. Griffith** to establish United Artists to produce their own films.

Chaplin scored critical and box office successes with *The Kid* (1921) and *The Gold Rush* (1925). His first sound film was *City Lights* (1931), which had a musical score but no dialogue. Chaplin turned to social comment in the 1930s again without dialogue in *Modern Times* (1936), and in his first real dialogue film *The Great Dictator* (1940) in which Chaplin parodied Hitler. During the 1940s, Chaplin's reputation was damaged by revelations concerning his personal life and charges of immorality. His marriage to the 18-year-old Oona O'Neill in 1943 further tarnished his name. Chaplin's support for the Soviet Union during and immediately after World War II also led to criticism from conservative groups. His next two films, *Monsieur Verdoux* (1947) and *Limelight* (1952) did badly. In 1952, Chaplin, still a resident alien, applied for a re-entry permit to the United States prior to a visit to Europe. Shortly after he had set sail, his permit was revoked and it was announced that he would not be readmitted before he answered questions about his political views and moral behavior. Chaplin then took up permanent residence in Switzerland. Subsequently, he made only two more films. He visited the United States again in 1972 and was granted a special Oscar for his contribution to film. Queen Elizabeth II knighted him in 1975.

CHARLESTON. The Charleston became a popular dance of the 1920s following its inclusion in the Ziegfeld *Follies* in 1923. It was associated with the new spirit of the "Jazz Age" and the liberated **women** known as **"flappers."**

CHATEAU-THIERRY. Chateau-Thierry was a French town about 40 miles east of Paris where troops of the **American Expeditionary Force** (AEF) first played a significant part in **World War I** in June 1918. In helping to push back the German offensive on the Marne here and the nearby **Belleau Wood**, the American forces gave the **Allies** an enormous military and psychological boost.

CHEVROLET, LOUIS (1878–1841). The racing driver and **automobile** designer Louis Chevrolet was born in Switzerland. His family moved to France in 1884 and Chevrolet began work there as a mechanic. In 1900, he was sent to Canada to work and shortly after he moved to New York to work for another French car dealership.

Chevrolet began racing cars in 1905 and, by 1907, was regarded as one of the best drivers in the world. He joined the Buick Motor Car Company under **William Durant** that year. Durant later asked Chevrolet to design a mass-produced car with his six-cylinder engine and the Chevrolet Motor Company was established in Detroit in 1910. Differences over the decision to switch production from high-performance cars to cheaper, mass-produced vehicles led Chevrolet to sell his interests in the company in 1915. He and his brother, Arthur, established their own Frontenac Motor Company in 1916 and continued their career in motor racing. While the Chevrolets continued their success on the racing track, their business ventures were less successful. In 1928, Glenn Martin helped them establish the Chevrolet Aircraft Corporation, but the company was a failure. By 1933, Louis Chevrolet had liquidated all of his investments and he was forced to find work as a mechanic in the Chevrolet Division of General Motors in Detroit until ill health forced his retirement in 1938.

CHICAGO RACE RIOT, 1919. On 27 July 1919, a black youth swimming at the Chicago lakeside drowned after being stoned for crossing into a white area. When police failed to arrest the perpetrator, scuffles broke out between black and white onlookers. The violence spread and developed into a full riot lasting five days in which white crowds stopped streetcars and pulled off black passengers and beat them. Other black workers were pursued and beaten or stoned to death. A total of 23 **African Americans** and 15 whites died, and more than 300 were injured in the violence in the worst riot of the **"Red Summer."** The Chicago riot had been preceded by friction over housing and jobs following the influx of thousands of African Americans who had moved North in the **"Great Migration"** to find work in war industries. Between 1917 and 1919, more than 24 bombings of black homes occurred and there was a history of considerable conflict in the workplace, particularly between unionized white labor and nonunion black workers. An unstable political situation also added to the wartime tensions.

CHICAGO WHITE SOX. *See* WORLD SERIES 1919.

CHILD LABOR. The employment of children in industrial, mining, and agricultural occupations was widespread in late-19th early-20th-century America. In 1900, it was estimated that 1.7 million children, 20 percent of all those under the age of 16, were in employment. By 1930, the figure was less than 5 percent, although attempts to get a federal child labor law on the statute books had twice failed to meet the **Supreme Court**'s objections. This was finally accomplished with the Fair Labor Standards Act in 1938.

CHILD LABOR LAWS. One of the major concerns of prewar **Progressives** was to limit the employment of children. Although almost all states had introduced some legislation to control **child labor** by 1914, there were many variations and loopholes. The first federal Child Labor Law, the Keating-Owen Act, was passed in 1916. It prohibited the shipping across state lines of products made in factories that employed children under 14 years of age, or mines that employed children under 16, or any producer that employed children at night or for more than eight hours. The law was declared unconstitutional by the **Supreme Court** in *Hammer v. Dagenhart* on the grounds that regulation of interstate commerce could not be applied to conditions of labor. A **second Child Labor Law** passed in 1919, imposed a 10 percent tax on the products of factories or mines employing children, but this too was declared unconstitutional in 1922 in *Bailey v. Drexel Furniture Co*. A Child Labor Amendment was introduced following this decision and passed both houses of Congress in 1924 but failed to win ratification in the states. Child labor was not effectively prohibited until **New Deal** legislation in the 1930s.

CHILDREN'S BUREAU. Established in 1912 as an agency of the **Department of Labor**, the Children's Bureau was to investigate and report upon problems of child welfare. Its first head was **Julia Lathrop**.

CHRYSLER, WALTER PERRY (1875–1940). The influential automobile manufacturer Walter Chrysler began work as a mechanical engineer in the railroad industry in the 1890s. He constantly moved to new positions—from general foreman with the Colorado & Southern

Railroad in 1902, master mechanic with Fort Worth & Denver City Railroad in 1903, supervisor with Chicago Great Western Railroad in 1905, and works manager of the American Locomotive Company, Allegheny, in 1910. In 1912, Chrysler took over the management of the Buick Motor Company in Flint, Michigan, as part of **General Motors**. Chrysler introduced a considerable number of innovations and created new production processes at the plant, making it one of the most efficient of its day. Chrysler stayed with the company when **William C. Durant** regained control in 1916, but resigned in 1919 after disagreements about construction projects. In 1920, he became executive vice president of the Willys-Overland truck manufacturer, a position he held until the company was liquidated in 1921. In 1923, Chrysler became president of the reorganized Maxwell Motor Company and in 1924 Maxwell produced the successful Chrysler Six automobile. The Maxwell Company was renamed "Chrysler" in 1925. By 1928, when Chrysler incorporated the Dodge Motor Company and developed the Plymouth motor car, it was the third largest motor manufacturer in the United States. The company also built the 77-story Chrysler Building in New York City in 1930. Despite the **Depression**, the Chrysler Company became the second largest car company ahead of **Ford** in the mid-1930s when Walter Chrysler handed over the presidency to K. T. Keller.

CIVIL RIGHTS. *See* AFRICAN AMERICANS.

CLARK MEMORANDUM. A statement of foreign policy prepared in December 1928, following President-elect **Herbert Hoover**'s visit to Latin America, released by undersecretary of state, J. Reuben Clark in 1930. The memorandum declared the 1904 Roosevelt Corollary to the Monroe Doctrine invalid and that the United States did not have the right to intervene in the affairs of Latin American countries. This statement was written into the Declaration of the Montevideo Conference in 1933 and formally ratified by the Senate in 1934.

CLARKE, JOHN HESSIN (1857–1945). John Clarke graduated from Ohio Western Reserve College in 1877 and qualified in law in 1878. He practiced law and became part-owner of the Democratic newspaper, the Youngston *Vindicator*, but eventually became partner in a leading Cleveland law firm. Clarke failed to win election to the United States Senate in 1904, and failed to gain the **Democratic Party**'s nomination for the seat in 1916. **Woodrow Wilson** nominated him for a federal judgeship that year and shortly after he replaced **Charles Evans Hughes** on the **Supreme Court**. Clarke concentrated his work on patent and antitrust law and took a liberal position in enforcing the Sherman Antitrust Act. He supported **child labor laws** in dissenting decisions in *Hammer v. Dagenhart* (1918) and *Bailey v. Drexel Furniture Co.* (1922). However, he wrote the majority opinion that upheld the convictions of the six Russians in *Abrams v. United States* (1919). He resigned from the court in 1922 and became a leading advocate of United States entry to the **League of Nations** and **Permanent Court of International Justice**.

CLAYTON ANTITRUST ACT, 1914. Legislation introduced by Henry De Lamar Clayton, the **Democratic** chair of the House Judiciary Committee in 1914. The act was a supplement to the 1890 Sherman Antitrust Act and it was an attempt to exempt organized labor from the restrictions of the Sherman Act on the grounds that it was not an item of commerce. Regarded as "Labor's Magna Carta," many mistakenly believed the Clayton Act would allow peaceful strikes and boycotts without the threat of injunctions. The law also forbade interlocking directorates in the same industry and ruled that corporation officers could be held personally liable for violations of the antitrust laws. *See also* TRADE UNIONS.

COBB, TYRUS RAYMOND (1886–1961). Baseball player and manager Ty Cobb grew up in Georgia. He left home in 1904 to become a professional baseball player. In 1905, he was the South Atlantic League's outstanding player and the Detroit Tigers of the American League signed him that year. In 1907, Cobb became the league's outstanding performer, leading in batting average, base hits, runs batted in, and stolen bases. The Tigers won three consecutive pennants with Cobb (known as the "Georgia Peach") and he was probably the best-known player at the time. From 1919 on, however, the big-hitting of **Babe Ruth** challenged Cobb's domination.

From 1922 until 1926, Cobb also managed the Detroit team. He resigned following accusations that in 1919 he and others had been involved in fixing games. The baseball commissioner **Kenesaw Mountain Landis** subsequently exonerated Cobb, and he signed as a player with the Philadelphia Athletics. Cobb played successfully for two seasons before he retired, having made his fortune in the game and through shrewd investments. He was the first man elected to the National Baseball Hall of Fame when it opened in Cooperstown, New York, in 1939.

COFFIN, CHARLES ALBERT (1844–1926). Charles Coffin began a shoe manufacturing company in Lynn, Massachusetts, in the 1870s and as part of a syndicate purchased the American Electric Company of Connecticut in 1883. In 1892, the company consolidated with Edison General of New York and took the name of General Electric with Coffin as president. From 1913 to 1922, Coffin was chair of the board of directors, and he contributed to the expansion that made General Electric Company into one of the major companies in the country. During **World War I**, Coffin established the War Relief Clearing House in 1915, later taken over by the Red Cross. His war work was recognized by a number of foreign awards including the French Legion of Honor.

COLUMBUS, NEW MEXICO. In 1916, the Mexican bandit **Francisco (Pancho) Villa** attacked Columbus. Nineteen Americans were killed and the town was set on fire. As a consequence, the United States Army pursued Villa in a **punitive expedition** into **Mexico** that almost brought the two countries to war.

COMMERCE, DEPARTMENT OF. *See* DEPARTMENT OF COMMERCE.

COMMITTEE OF FORTY-EIGHT. In 1919, **Amos Pinchot** established a committee across the 48 states to unite **Progressives** and to ensure their election to Congress. However, the committee failed to agree upon candidates or establish the hoped for unity with representatives of labor at the two conventions held in 1919 and 1920. It was succeeded in 1922 by the **Conference for Progressive Political Action**.

COMMITTEE ON PUBLIC INFORMATION (CPI). The Committee on Public Information was established on 13 April 1917 to mobilize public opinion in support of the American war effort and to carry out a program of propaganda abroad to win over neutrals and undermine the morale of the enemy during **World War I**. The committee, which became one of the most important of wartime agencies, consisted of the secretaries of war, navy, and state departments but was dominated by its civilian chairman, **George Creel**. Initially, the CPI's main function was to act as a conduit for news stories for the press and to provide information through an *Official Bulletin*. However, in the face of criticism from the press and Congress, and as censorship was increasingly handled by the Postmaster General's office or Censorship Board, the CPI concentrated more on selling the war.

Drawing upon the participation of well-known writers, journalists, academics, artists, actors, and other celebrities, the CPI bombarded the country with over 100 million pieces of literature in the form of pamphlets, leaflets, and posters. It made films and enlisted movie stars such as **Douglas Fairbanks, Jr.**, **Charlie Chaplin**, and **Mary Pickford** to help "sell" the war and outline America's war aims. Over 75,000 volunteer "Four Minute Men" were used to address theater and movie audiences on themes indicated by the CPI. At the time the CPI was often criticized for acting as an agency of **Woodrow Wilson's** administration and for limiting free expression. After the war it became increasingly associated with the mood of war hysteria and "one hundred per cent Americanism" that had swept the nation in a wave of intolerance.

COMMUNICATIONS ACT, 1927. *See* FEDERAL RADIO COMMISSION.

COMMUNIST PARTY. Communism was established in America in 1919 with the creation of the Communist and Communist Labor Parties, which had been formed by elements of the **Socialist Party** and others, following the 1917 Bolshevik revolution and the launching of the Third International or Comintern in March 1919. The two groups merged in 1921 and shortly after assumed the title of Workers' Party of America. In 1928 it was renamed again as the

Communist Party. The party always remained a minority party with a large foreign-language and immigrant membership. Its greatest electoral support came during the Depression when it secured 102,991 votes in the 1932 presidential election.

CONFERENCE FOR PROGRESSIVE POLITICAL ACTION, 1922. Following World War I, **Robert M. La Follette** organized a loose alliance of **Progressive** groups, including the **Nonpartisan League**, the **Farmer-Labor Party**, and a number of labor organizations including the 16 railroad brotherhoods to try to ensure the election of Progressives to Congress and promote liberal legislation. At a national convention in Cleveland, from July 4–6, 1924, the group nominated La Follette as presidential candidate with **Burton K. Wheeler** as his running mate under the banner of the **Progressive Party**. The party polled nearly five million votes, 17 percent of the votes cast. The party carried only the state of Wisconsin. The Progressive Party faded away thereafter, and many supporters voted for **Herbert Hoover** in 1928. *See also* COMMITTEE OF FORTY-EIGHT.

CONGRESSIONAL UNION. A militant **women's suffrage** organization formed in 1913 by **Alice Paul** and Lucy Burns, and forerunner of the **National Woman's Party**.

CONSCIENTIOUS OBJECTORS. When **Selective Service** was introduced in the United States in 1917, the act provided for the right to conscientious objection for those members of "well-recognized religious sects or organizations whose creed forbids participation." In December 1917, Secretary of War **Newton Baker** extended this to include those who objected on grounds of "moral scruple." However, those exempted from armed service were expected to accept noncombatant duties and to join other servicemen at military camps, subject to military discipline and the "persuasion" of the other men in the camps. Out of 20 million men who were registered for military service, 65,000 claimed conscientious objector status and 20,813 were inducted. Of these, 16,000 gave up their claims at the camps, 1,300 accepted noncombatant roles, 1,200 were furloughed out to farms, and 99 assisted with Quaker relief. Only

1,390 "absolutists" refused to accept any form of war-related service and faced courts martial. By the time the war had ended, 500 had been tried. Of these, 17 were sentenced to death, 142 to life imprisonment, and the rest to terms from 10 to 99 years. All death sentences were commuted, and most of those jailed were released shortly after the **armistice**. Some, however, experienced very harsh treatment in prison and several died during their incarceration. *See also* AMERICAN UNION AGAINST MILITARISM; PEACE MOVEMENTS.

COOLIDGE, CALVIN (1872–1933). Thirtieth president of the United States. Born in Plymouth, Vermont, Coolidge was an Amherst graduate, a qualified lawyer, who served in town politics in Northampton, Massachusetts, where he became mayor, 1910–11. A member of the Massachusetts senate, 1912–15, and lieutenant-governor of Massachusetts, 1916–18, Coolidge became governor of Massachusetts, 1919–20. As governor, Coolidge supported the **Nineteenth Amendment** and regulation of child and female labor. He gained national prominence when he spoke out against striking **Boston** police saying "There is no right to strike against public safety by anybody, anywhere, anytime." In 1920 he was selected as **Warren Harding**'s running mate, and on Harding's death in 1923 Coolidge became president. He was elected in his own right in 1924 when he defeated Democrat **John W. Davis** by 15,718,211 votes to 8,385,283 and 382 Electoral College votes to 136. The third candidate, the Progressive **Robert M. La Follette**, received 4,831,289 votes and 13 Electoral College votes. The **Republican Party** slogan, "Keep Cool with Coolidge" was an implicit reference to the apparent prosperity that contributed to his victory.

Coolidge was a sharp contrast to Harding in that he was rather stiff, shy, sober, abstemious, cautious, and famously laconic. He quickly demanded Attorney General **Harry Daugherty**'s resignation for his failure to comply with Senate investigators looking into the Harding scandals. Coolidge also appointed special counselors to investigate the **Teapot Dome** scandal. Coolidge was often dismissed by contemporary writers and historians as "Silent Cal," a "do nothing" president who slept most in the White House. Contrary to that image, recent historians have painted a more sympathetic view of Coolidge.

The president entertained more visitors than his predecessor in the White House and established regular press conferences, although his remarks had to be attributed to a "White House spokesman," and he received the questions in advance. Coolidge kept on several members of Harding's cabinet, most notably **Herbert Hoover**, **Charles Hughes**, and **Andrew Mellon**, and he left his cabinet officers alone to do their jobs.

Coolidge continued many of the policies of his predecessor, particularly with regard to business, which he described as "the chief business of America." His administration cut taxes, including surtax and estates tax, in 1926 and 1928, and failed to pursue **Federal Trade Commission** investigations of illegal corporate activity. Coolidge acted to block two important measures passed by Congress, namely plans to take over Muscle Shoals in a government-operated project that he stopped by pocket veto in 1928, and two **McNary-Haugen Bills** that he vetoed in 1927 and 1928. He also blocked the payment of a bonus to veterans. However, Coolidge also achieved a balanced budget every year and used the surplus to reduce the national debt by one-third. The president also supported the promotion and regulation of aviation, the establishment of the **Federal Radio Commission** in 1927, and a federal building program in 1926 that included the National Archives and Federal Triangle. Coolidge believed that America should be "kept American" and supported the passage of the **Immigration Act** of 1924.

In foreign affairs, Coolidge continued the cautious policies of limited involvement established by his predecessor. He refused to cancel Allied war debts, but did accept the renegotiations of German war reparations in the **Dawes** and **Young Plans**. Coolidge recommended American membership of the **Permanent Court of International Justice** (or World Court) to the Senate, but failed to push the measure when the **League of Nations** asked for clarification of Senate reservations. The Coolidge administration supported attempts at naval reduction and called the **Geneva Naval Conference** in 1927. Coolidge also supported the **Kellogg-Briand** Pact in 1928. Relations with Latin America improved following negotiations with Nicaragua and **Mexico** and participation in the fifth and sixth Pan-American conferences in 1923 and 1928 that paved the way for the **Clark Memorandum**.

While vacationing in the Black Hills of South Dakota in August 1927, unexpectedly and without further elaboration Coolidge issued the statement "I do not choose to run for President in nineteen twenty-eight" and so left the way open for the nomination of Herbert Hoover as the Republican candidate. His enigmatic statement encouraged some historians to believe that Coolidge had foreseen the coming **Crash** and **Depression**. Although there is some evidence to support this, it seems more likely that he wished to retire after almost 10 years in Washington, D.C. After he left office, he took a position as director of the New York Life Insurance Company, wrote for various journals and in a syndicated daily newspaper column, and published *The Autobiography of Calvin Coolidge* (1929). The only public office he held was as a member of the National Transportation Committee set up to advise on the nation's transportation systems. *See also* COOLIDGE, GRACE ANNA GOODHUE.

COOLIDGE, GRACE ANNA GOODHUE (1879–1957). Born Grace Goodhue in Burlington, Vermont, the future wife of President **Calvin Coolidge** graduated from the University of Vermont in 1902 and took up a teaching position at Clark Institute for the Deaf. She married Coolidge in 1905 and they had two sons, John and Calvin, Jr. Mrs. Coolidge was an attractive and vivacious individual, much respected as a hostess at the White House. After the death of Calvin, Jr., of blood poisoning in 1924, she devoted herself to renovating the White House. Mrs. Coolidge also supported projects related to the deaf and became a trustee of the Clark Institute and was an active member of the college sorority, Pi Beta Phi.

COPLAND, AARON (1900–1990). The son of Russian Jewish immigrants, Copland was to become one of America's greatest modern composers. His work combined the influences of Stravinsky with that of jazz and American folk melodies. He wrote for radio, theater, and movies, and his first major piece was *Symphony for Organ and Orchestra*, composed in 1924. During the 1920s Copland was very much part of the avant-garde and contributed articles to the new journal *Modern Music*. He established the American Festivals of contemporary Music at Saratoga Springs in 1932. His *El Salon Mexico* (1936) was influenced by visits to South and Central America. He is best known for his later ballets *Billy the Kid* (1938), *Rodeo* (1942), and *Appalachian Spring* (1944), and for the patriotic pieces written in 1942, *A Lincoln Portrait* and *Fanfare for a Common Man*. In 1949 Copland won an Oscar for his music for the movie *The Heiress*.

COSTIGAN, EDWARD PRENTISS (1874–1939). After studying law and graduating from Harvard Law School in 1899, Edward Costigan established a law practice in Denver. Costigan was a progressive **Republican** committed to municipal reform and was founder and attorney to Denver's Honest Election League (1903–06) and the Law Enforcement League (1906–08). He was also president of the Civil Service Reform Association and chairman of the Dry Denver Campaign Committee. Costigan was a founding member of the Citizen's Party that carried Denver in 1912.

Costigan was one of the leaders of the Colorado Progressive Republican League that opposed **William Howard Taft** in 1912. Costigan first backed **Robert M. La Follettte** and then **Theodore Roosevelt** in the presidential campaign. Costigan himself stood unsuccessfully for governor of Colorado on the **Progressive** ticket in 1912 and 1914. The Colorado mining strike of 1914 divided the state's Progressive Party. Costigan served as legal counsel to the miners. In 1916 he endorsed **Woodrow Wilson**'s election on the basis of his reform program and in 1917 was appointed to the Tariff Commission. He was increasingly critical of the Republican appointments to the commission and in 1928 resigned.

Costigan supported La Follette in 1924 and **Alfred E. Smith** in 1928. He became a **Democrat** in 1930 and was elected to the United States Senate from Colorado. He supported the **New Deal** program and measures to open the sugar trade and antilynching bills. He retired from politics due to ill health in 1936.

COUNCIL OF NATIONAL DEFENSE (CND). The Council of National Defense was established under the Army Appropriations Act of 1916 as part of the program of "Preparedness." Consisting of the secretaries of War, Navy, Interior, Agriculture, Commerce, and Labor, the CND was authorized to "supervise and direct investigations and make recommendations" relating to the railroads, the mobilization of military and naval resources, and domestic industrial production in order to effect "the immediate concentration and utilization of the resources of the Nation." It was assisted by an **Advisory Commission of the Council of National Defense** and a network of subcommittees.

COX, JAMES MIDDLETON (1870–1957). Formerly a newspaper owner, Cox served in the House of Representatives as **Democratic Party** congressman from Ohio from 1909 to 1913. He was governor of Ohio from 1913 to 1915 and again from 1917 to 1921. In 1920, he was chosen as the Democratic presidential candidate on the 44th ballot with **Franklin Delano Roosevelt** as his running mate. Cox, a committed supporter of **Woodrow Wilson** and the **League of Nations**, was defeated by the **Republican Warren G. Harding**. Cox received just over 9 million votes, 34 percent of the vote, and 127 electoral college votes to Harding's 16 million votes and 404 electoral college votes.

After the election Cox completed his term as governor of Ohio and then returned to the newspaper business. He acquired several more newspapers in the 1920s and established Dayton's first radio station. In 1933, Roosevelt sent Cox as vice chairman of the United States delegation to the world economic conference in London. Cox's autobiography, *Journey through My Life,* was published in 1946.

CREEL, GEORGE (1876–1953). George Creel was a newspaperman and publicist who rose to national prominence as chairman of the **Committee on Public Information** (CPI) during **World War I**. He was editor of the Kansas City *Independent* (1899–1909), the Denver *Post* (1909–10), and the *Rocky Mountain News* (1911–13). A committed reformer, Creel served as police commissioner in Denver from 1912–13. He wrote several muckraking articles for *Harper's Weekly* and other journals and was responsible for the **Democratic Party's** publicity in 1916 and became a personal friend of President **Woodrow Wilson**. He was often accused of producing propaganda on behalf of the president while chair of the CPI and he made enemies with his acerbic comments about Congress and critics of the war effort. He accompanied the president to the Paris Peace Conference in 1919 and visited various European countries on the president's behalf. In 1920 he began work as a feature writer at *Colliers*. In 1933, he chaired the Regional Labor Board for California, Utah, and Nevada and directed the West Coast office of the National Recovery Administration. Unsuccessful in his attempt to win the Democratic nomination for governor of California in 1934 he returned to *Colliers*. After the World War II he supported Senator Joseph McCarthy's anti-Communist campaign.

CROLY, HERBERT DAVID (1869–1930). Although he failed to complete his academic studies at Harvard University, Herbert Croly was to gain enormous influence as a political philosopher and editor during the **Progressive** period. He began writing in his father's journals, *Real Estate Record and Builders' Guide* and the *Architectural Record*, in 1889, and later coauthored books on architectural style and urban planning. In 1909, his influential work of political philosophy, *The Promise of American Life*, was published. Calling for an abandonment of laissez faire principles and simple individualism, Croly advocated federal regulation and reform to tackle the problems of industrialism. **Theodore Roosevelt** incorporated aspects of Croly's philosophy, including the phrase "new nationalism," into his **Progressive Party** campaign in 1912.

In 1914, Croly became editor of a new journal, *New Republic*, which quickly became the mouthpiece of the reform movement. Increasingly the journal supported preparedness and **Woodrow Wilson's** administration. However, Croly and other writers viewed the **Versailles peace** settlement as a great betrayal of wartime idealism and turned against Wilson. The *New Republic* continued to espouse Progressive ideals during the 1920s and supported **Robert M. La Follette** in the 1924 presidential campaign. In 1928, it backed **Democrat Al Smith**. Frustrated by the conservative politics of the decade Croly began to show more interest in literary, religious, and philosophical issues. He suffered a massive stroke in 1928 that left him incapacitated until his death.

CROWDER, ENOCH HERBERT (1859–1932). An army officer and graduate of West Point, Crowder served as judge advocate of the expeditionary forces and the Department of the Pacific in the Spanish-American War (1898) and associate justice of the Philippines supreme court, 1899–1901. In 1911, he was appointed judge-advocate general of the U.S Army and became provost-marshal-general to administer the **Selective Service Act** in 1917. From 1923 to 1927, he was the first United States ambassador to Cuba.

CUMMINGS, EDWARD ESTLIN (1894–1962). Later known as e. e. cummings, the poet and artist Edward Cummings was educated at Cambridge Latin School and Harvard University, where he graduated in 1916. His first book of poems appeared with those of **John Dos Passos** in *Eight Harvard Poets* in 1917. That same year, Cummings volunteered for the ambulance corps in France. After five months, he and a colleague were detained in a French prison camp for expressing antiwar views. Sent back to the United States, Cummings was drafted and served in the army in Massachusetts in 1918. After the war, Cummings moved to New York, where his cubist paintings and avant-garde poetry won him recognition in literary circles. His novel based on his experience of prison appeared as *The Enormous Room* in 1922. Cummings's presentation of poems in a visual form on the page, and his usage of language and absence of capitalization and punctuation, appeared in print in various journals before publication as *Tulips and Chimneys* (1923), *XLI Poems* (1925), and *Is 5* (1926).

Cummings visited Europe on several occasions during the 1920s and was influenced by the Dada movement and Surrealism. Some of this was evident in his play *Him* (1927). A visit to the Soviet Union in 1931 led him to record his experiences (and disappointment) in literary form in *Eimi* in 1933. In 1935, Cummings authored *Tom*, a satirical ballet based on *Uncle Tom's Cabin*. Cummings continued to publish through the 1950s and received recognition as one of leaders of the group of postwar literary writers known as the "lost generation."

CUMMINGS, HOMER STILLÉ (1870–1956). Homer Cummings graduated from Yale Law School in 1893 and began to practice law in Stamford, Connecticut. In 1900 he was elected mayor of Stamford where he carried out a moderate program of reform during his three terms. In 1914 Cummings became state's attorney in Fairfield County, a post he held until 1924. Throughout this time Cummings was active in the national **Democratic Party** organization, and he was national chairman from 1914 to 1920. Cummings supported

Franklin D. Roosevelt in 1932 and as a reward he was initially offered the post of governor-general of the Philippines. However, when **Thomas Walsh** the attorney-general designate died en route to the inaugural, Roosevelt offered the post to Cummings. Cummings held the position until 1939 and was responsible for extending the federal role in fighting crime. He also drafted the so-called "court packing" measure, the 1936 Judicial Reorganization Act, that would have enabled Roosevelt to appoint new justices to the **Supreme Court**. The measure became the center of political controversy and was never enacted. Cummings retired in 1939 and practiced law in Washington, D.C.

CUMMINS, ALBERT BAIRD (1850–1926). Admitted to the bar in Illinois in 1875, Cummins practiced law in Des Moines, Iowa, where he won recognition as attorney for the Farmers' Protective Association against the "barbed wire trusts." Cummins was active in state **Republican Party** politics as a leader of the Progressive faction of the party. He failed to win election to the United States Senate in 1894 and again in 1900, but was elected governor of Iowa in 1901 and served three terms until 1908. Cummins was selected to fill a vacant Senate seat in 1908 and he held the position until his death. He sided with **Robert M. La Follette** in the insurgent reform movement of the Republican Party in 1912 and joined the National Progressive Republican League. Cummins supported **Theodore Roosevelt** rather than La Follette, but remained within the Republican Party.

Although he supported much of **Woodrow Wilson's New Freedom** program, Cummins opposed intervention in **World War I** and was one of the "little group of willful men" who filibustered against the arming of merchant ships in 1917. Cummins was an **"Irreconcilable"** in his opposition to the **League of Nations**. As chair of the Committee on Interstate Commerce he helped to prepare the Esch-Cummins **Railroad Transportation Act** of 1920 that returned the railroads to private ownership. Increasingly conservative in the 1920s, Cummins lost the 1926 primary to a supporter of La Follette.

CURLEY, JAMES MICHAEL (1874–1958). Curley dominated Boston politics for much of the first half of the 20th century as mayor. Born of Irish immigrant stock, he grew up in an Irish tenement neighborhood in Boston. He served as a Boston councilman and in the United States House of Representatives; he was first elected mayor in 1914, lost in 1918, re-elected in 1922, lost in 1926, and won again in 1930. He was subsequently governor of Massachusetts (1935–37), United States congressman (1942–46), and mayor of Boston (1947–50).

CURTIS, CHARLES (1860–1936). Thirty-first vice-president, 1929–33. Admitted to the Kansas bar in 1881, Curtis practiced law in Topeka, Kansas. He was elected county attorney in 1884 and was elected as a **Republican** to the House of Representatives in 1892. A mixed-blood Kaw Indian, Curtis sponsored the Curtis Act, which abolished tribal courts and the Five Civilized Tribes in Oklahoma in 1898. He also fought for the rights of Indian women and mixed-blood children, but served as an attorney for energy companies taking natural resources from Indian reservations. In 1907, he became a senator and served until 1913 and again from 1915–29. He was cosponsor of the **Dyer Anti-lynching Bill**. In 1924, Curtis was chosen majority leader in the Senate. In 1928, he was chosen as the vice-presidential candidate to appease the farm interests. His contributions as vice president were limited and he retired from politics to return to his law practice in 1932. *See also* NATIVE AMERICANS.

– D –

DANIELS, JOSEPHUS (1862–1941). Daniels began his career as a reform journalist and publisher in his home state of North Carolina where he owned and edited several newspapers including the *Raleigh State Chronicle* and the *North Carolinian*. In 1893 he became chief clerk in the Department of the Interior in the administration of Grover Cleveland, but returned to Raleigh in 1895 as owner/editor of the Raleigh *News and Observer*. He supported causes such as **child-labor** laws, **trades unionism**, better hospital provision, and regulation of the railroads. Having previously supported **William Jennings Bryan**, Daniels backed **Woodrow Wilson** in 1912 and was rewarded with the appointment of secretary of the navy in 1913. He instituted a number of reforms to open access to the navy and promotions and in 1914 banned alcohol on all naval vessels. During **World War I** Daniels was seen as responsible for the "Bridge of Ships'" that safely transported the U.S. Army to Europe. After the war he returned to his role at the *News and Observer*, but returned to political life when **Franklin D. Roosevelt** appointed him ambassador to Mexico in 1933. In this post until 1942, he was an upholder of Roosevelt's "Good Neighbor" policy. Daniels spent the rest of his life at his newspaper and completing his five-volume autobiography.

DARROW, CLARENCE SEWARD (1857–1938). Leading labor and criminal lawyer, Clarence Darrow was educated at Allegheny College and the University of Michigan Law School. He became a member of the Ohio bar in 1878. In 1887, Darrow moved to Chicago and in 1890 became general attorney to the Chicago and North Western Railway. However, he became famous for his defense of **Eugene V. Debs** in the railroad conspiracy case (1894) and of **William D. Haywood** in 1907. Increasingly associated with labor and with the disadvantaged, Darrow defended several of those people charged under the wartime **Espionage** and **Sedition Acts**. In 1924, Darrow saved **Leopold** and **Loeb** from the death penalty by using expert witnesses to argue that they were not responsible for their actions. Perhaps Darrow's most famous case was his defense of **John Scopes** in the **Scopes Monkey Trial** in 1925. In 1926, he also defended Ossian Sweet, a black man who had used violence to defend himself against a mob who attacked his home in Detroit. Darrow also worked on the case of the **Scottsboro Boys** in 1932.

DAUGHERTY, HARRY MICAJAH (1860–1941). Harry Daugherty practiced law in Washington Court House, Ohio, before he entered city and then state politics. After serving as prosecuting attorney for Fayette County, he was elected as a **Republican** to the Ohio House of Representatives where he served from 1891–95. His electoral career was effectively ended after he had been accused of accepting $3,500 to vote for a senatorial candidate. However, he continued to be active in Ohio politics and was chair of **William Howard Taft**'s election campaign in 1912. He played a part in securing the Republican presidential nomination for **Warren Harding** and managed Harding's campaign in 1920 and in return was appointed attorney general.

As attorney general, Daugherty appointed several Republican Party cronies to the Justice Department and was chief among the "Ohio Gang" of poker players and whisky drinkers who socialized with President Harding. Daugherty's role in the series of scandals that came to light in 1923 forever tarnished the Harding administration's legacy. As the scandal began to emerge, Daugherty's assistant Jess Smith committed suicide in 1923. It transpired that he had acted as go-between in arranging payments from the office of the **Alien Property Custodian** to claimants in return for a payment of **Liberty Loans**. The bonds were then sold and monies were paid into a bank run by the attorney general's brother Mal S. Daugherty. Ledgers relating to bank accounts held jointly by Smith and Harry Daugherty were destroyed. Daugherty also refused to hand over Justice Department files to the committees investigating **Teapot Dome** and when the attorney general failed to prosecute the guilty parties, **Calvin Coolidge** forced him to resign in 1924. Daugherty was twice indicted for fraud by a grand jury on corruption charges but was acquitted due to lack of evidence. He returned to Ohio to practice law.

DAVIDSON, DONALD (1893–1968). The southern poet, historian, and literary critic Donald Davidson studied at Vanderbilt University, Nashville. He served in the army during World War I and returned to complete his M.A. in 1922. He later became professor of English at Vanderbilt. Davidson was part of the Nashville literary group, the Fugitives, that included **John Crowe Ransom, Allen Tate,** and Robert Penn Warren. Davidson's own writing included *An Outland Piper* (1926), *The Tall Men* (1927), and *Lee in the Mountains* (1927). Like the other Fugitives Davidson was a defender of the South and contributed to the collection of essays presenting their case, *I'll Take My Stand* (1930). Davidson also wrote *The Attack on the Leviathan: Regionalism and Nationalism in the Unites States* (1938).

DAVIS, DWIGHT FILLEY (1879–1945). Dwight Davis graduated from Harvard in 1900. While he was at university, Davis was twice runner-up in the national men's tennis singles championship and three times winner of the doubles championship with Holcombe Ward. In 1900, he donated a trophy for the International Lawn Tennis Challenge Trophy which became known as the Davis Cup. Davis captained the victorious United States team in 1900 and played on the 1902 team that also won. Davis graduated in law from Washington University in 1903 but devoted himself to a life of public service, locally and nationally. During **World War I**, Davis became involved in military training and then enlisted in the Missouri National Guard. He served in France and won the Distinguished Service Cross for heroism during the **St. Mihiel** and **Meuse-Argonne** offensives.

In 1920, Davis failed to gain the **Republican** nomination for the United States Senate but was appointed to the **War Finance Corporation** by **Warren Harding**. In 1923, he was appointed as assistant secretary of war and in 1925 **Calvin Coolidge** chose him to succeed John Weeks as secretary of war. Davis served until 1929 and was responsible for developing plans for a comprehensive industrial mobilization. He opposed General William Mitchell's advocacy of air power, but backed the recommendations of the President's Aircraft Board for developing military air power but not a separate air force. Davis also encouraged the development of a tank force.

In 1929 **Herbert Hoover** appointed Davis governor general of the Philippines where he did much to further internal improvements. He resigned in 1932. Although a critic of the **New Deal**, **Franklin D. Roosevelt** appointed Davis as director general of the Army Specialist Corps in 1942. When the Corps, which provided commissions for highly skilled individuals that did not meet the army's physical standards, was incorporated in the Army Service Forces, Davis remained in an advisory role until the end of the war.

DAVIS, JAMES JOHN (1873–1947). Born in Wales, Davis emigrated to the United States in 1891 and was employed as a puddler in the Pennsylvania steel mills. Davis was active in the Amalgamated Association of Iron, Steel, and Tin Plate Makers. He served as secretary of labor 1921–29 and subsequently was elected to the Senate. As secretary of labor Davis established the Border Patrol to limit the influx of illegal immigrants. Although he served under **Warren Harding**, **Calvin Coolidge**, and **Herbert Hoover**, Davis was perhaps best-known for his leading role in the Loyal Order of the Moose, a fraternal order. In the Senate he cosponsored the Davis-Bacon Act that set wage levels at local rates on federal construction projects in order to stop cut-throat wage slashing in bid.

DAVIS, JOHN WILLIAM (1873–1955). John W. Davis was a lawyer who served as a **Democrat** in the House of Representatives for Virginia from 1911 to 1913 and was responsible for drafting parts of the **Clayton Antitrust Act.** As U.S solicitor general from 1913 to 1918, he argued a number of important constitutional cases. These included successfully defending the federal government's right to regulate interstate oil pipelines and to regulate railroad wages under the **Adamson Act**, a ruling against Oklahoma's "grandfather clause" denying **African Americans** the vote, and against Alabama's use of leased convict labor. In 1918 he was appointed ambassador to Great Britain, a post he held until 1921. He then became head of a Wall Street law company.

In 1924, Davis became the Democratic presidential candidate on the 103rd ballot when the convention was deadlocked between supporters of **Alfred E. Smith** and **William Gibbs McAdoo.** He lost support through his criticism of the **Ku Klux Klan** and his advocacy for American participation in the **League of Nations.** In the election he was easily defeated by **Calvin Coolidge**, winning only 8.3 million popular votes and 136 Electoral College votes to Coolidge's 15.7 million and 382 votes respectively. Davis supported **Al Smith** in 1928 and initially backed **Franklin D. Roosevelt** in 1932. However, as a believer in states' rights and the strict interpretation of the constitution Davis was critical of much of the **New Deal** and was one of the organizers of the conservative Liberty League. He was later a critic of Harry S. Truman's Fair Deal. His greatest legal victory came in 1952 in the ruling in *Youngston Sheet & Tube Co.* against Truman's seizure of the steel industry. Davis also argued in favor of the "separate but equal" doctrine in the *Brown v. Topeka Board of Education* school segregation case in 1954, but he acted as counsel for J. Robert Oppenheimer, the atomic scientist accused of being a security risk, the same year.

DAVIS, NORMAN HEZEKIAH (1878–1944). Norman Davis was a financier and diplomat who organized the Trust Company of Cuba (1905–17) and became United States Treasury representative to Great Britain and France in 1918 and served as chair of the finance section of the Supreme Economic Council. **Woodrow Wilson** appointed him assistant secretary of the Treasury, 1919–20 and he was undersecretary of state, 1920–21. He served as a delegate to the International Economic Council in Geneva, 1927, and to the **Geneva Disarmament Conference** in 1932. He headed the United States delegation to the International Sugar Conference in 1937.

DAWES, CHARLES GATES (1865–1951). Thirtieth vice president, 1925–29. Dawes was a financier who was United States comptroller of the currency, 1897–1901. In 1902, he organized the Central Union Trust Company of Chicago and served as president and later chairman of the board. During the war he was chief of supply procurement of the **American Expeditionary Force**. From 1921 to 1922, he was the first director of the **Bureau of the Budget**. As chairman of the Allied Reparations Commission (1923–24), he was instrumental in drawing up the **Dawes Plan**. He was elected vice president on the **Republican** ticket in 1924. In 1925, he won the Nobel Peace Prize (with Austen Chamberlain of Great Britain), and from 1929 to 1932 he was United States ambassador to Britain. He was appointed chairman of the **Reconstruction Finance Corporation** (RFC) in 1932. His own bank in Chicago received a loan from the RFC, but only after he had left office.

DAWES PLAN 1924. The Dawes plan was drawn up by various European representatives under the direction of **Charles G. Dawes** to solve the problem of the collection of reparations for war losses from Germany. The plan stabilized the German currency with a loan raised by mortgaging German railways and other industries and set reparations at one billion gold marks rising to 2.5 billion by 1928. The plan was replaced by the **Young Plan** in 1929.

DAYLIGHT SAVING. Daylight saving, achieved by advancing clocks forward by one hour on the first Sunday of April, was introduced as part of the Standard Time Act of 19 March 1918, that established the continental time zones introduced by the railways in 1883 as part of federal law. Daylight saving was repealed in 1919 and reintroduced in 1942. It was repealed with the end of World War II and reintroduced again in 1966.

DEBS, EUGENE VICTOR (1855–1926). Debs was a **trade union** activist who began his career as a railroad fireman and served as an official of the Brotherhood of Railway Firemen. He was elected city clerk of Terre Haute as a **Democrat** in 1879 and in 1884 was elected to the Indiana General Assembly. Debs founded the first industrial union in the United States, the American Railway Union (1893), and was jailed for contempt of court as leader of the Pullman strike in 1894. He helped organize the Social Democrat Party in 1897 and was a founder member of the **Socialist Party of America** and ran as the party's presidential candidate in 1900, 1904, 1908, 1912, and 1920. In June 1918 in Canton, Ohio, Debs spoke out publicly against **World War I** and compared the American businessmen with the Kaiser's Junkers in Germany. As a result he was convicted under the **Espionage Act**. He was sentenced to 10 years in prison. He campaigned for the presidency from prison and won almost one million votes. President **Warren Harding** commuted his sentence and he was released on Christmas Day 1921 and returned home to Terre Haute.

DeFOREST, LEE (1873–1961). Lee was a pioneer inventor who patented hundreds of inventions in the areas of wireless telegraphy, motion picture sound, radio, telephone, and television. He added a third electrode to the electron tube, designed and installed the United States Navy's first high-power radio stations, broadcast the first radio news in 1916, and developed sound-on-film motion pictures shown in New York City in 1923.

DELL, FLOYD JAMES (1887–1969). The novelist and critic Floyd Dell moved from Davenport, Iowa, to Chicago in 1908 and in 1909 became an associate editor with the *Chicago Evening Post's* "Friday Literary Review." Dell became editor in 1911 and he encouraged a number of writers such as **Theodore Dreiser** and Upton Sinclair. In 1913, Dell moved to **Greenwich Village**, New York, where he became an associate editor on the radical magazine *The Masses*. In 1918, Dell and **Max Eastman** were tried twice for attempting to obstruct the draft. After two hung juries the charges were dropped.

Dell's first novel, *Moon-Calf*, was published to critical acclaim in 1920. His second novel, *The Briary Bush*, appeared in 1921. His third novel, *Janet March* (1923), was withdrawn by the publishers because of its treatment of sex and abortion. Dell's other writing did not have the success of his earlier work. In 1935, he assumed an editorial role in the Works Progress Administration (WPA) and continued to write for the government until 1947. He continued to write after his retirement but published little.

DE MILLE, CECIL BLOUNT (1881–1959). The pioneer motion picture director-producer Cecil B. De Mille trained as an actor at the American Academy of Dramatic Art in New York and worked in the theater from 1900 to 1912. In 1913, he entered into partnership with Jesse Lasky and Samuel Goldfish (**Samuel Goldwyn**) to produce films in the Jesse L. Lasky Feature Play Company. Their first film, *The Squaw Man*, was successfully released in 1914. The energetic, dictatorial De Mille quickly made a reputation as a successful producer, particularly of films dealing with moral issues of sex, sin, and high society, often starring **Gloria Swanson** in sensual roles. However, in 1923, De Mille scored a huge success with the epic *The Ten Commandments*. In 1925, he established his own studio and had another success with the life of Jesus, *King of Kings* (1927). However, later films were less successful and De Mille was forced to join Metro-Goldwyn-Mayer (MGM) in 1928. In 1931, he joined Paramount. He achieved success once more with historical and biblical epics: *The Sign of the Cross* (1932), *Cleopatra* (1934), *Samson and Delilah* (1949). *The Greatest Show on Earth* (1952) won De Mille an Oscar for best film and his last film, a remake of *The Ten Commandments* (1956) was a huge commercial success. De Mille was planning a new film when he died in Hollywood. His legacy was 70 films, many of which set pathbreaking precedents and broke box-office records. *See also* MOVIES.

DEMOBILIZATION. When **World War I** ended on 11 November 1918, little preparation had been made to return the United States armed forces home. Plans to return soldiers gradually on the basis of their skills and occupations were quickly abandoned in favor of a unit-by-unit demobilization that was carried out at the rate of 15,000 a day. The returning forces were carried in converted cargo vessels and U.S. warships. The United States Navy also discharged 400,000 men in a year and the United States Marine Corps discharged 50,000. By August 1919, only a force of 40,000 Americans remained in occupied Germany and the United States military presence continued until 1923. During the 1920s, the United States armed forces were reduced to little more than a token force.

DEMOCRATIC PARTY. Excluded from the White House and the minority party in Congress since 1892, the Democratic Party benefited from divisions in the **Republican Party** to gradually gain control first of Congress and then of the White House with the election of **Woodrow Wilson** in 1912. The Democrats held a majority in both the Senate and the House of Representatives during the 63rd (1913–15) and 64th Congress and maintained a majority in the Senate during the 65th Congress (1917–19). After 1919, the Democrats were divided on the issues of **Prohibition**, the **League of Nations**, and on race. The divisions often reflected the difference between rural and urban areas and the South and North. They were not able to unite again until the election of 1932 when, in the face of the **Depression**, they united behind **Franklin D. Roosevelt** and recaptured control of both the House and the Senate.

DEMPSEY, JACK (1895–1983). The future world heavyweight boxing champion Jack Dempsey was born William Harrison Dempsey and grew up in a poor family in the West. He traveled as a hobo from 1911 to 1916 and built a reputation as a boxer. In 1919, Dempsey defeated the reigning heavyweight champion, Jess Willard, in three rounds. The following year Dempsey, who had not seen military service during World War I, faced trial having been accused of draft evasion. He was acquitted as sole supporter of his wife and mother, but his reputation was damaged. In 1921, Dempsey successfully defended his title in a match with the Frenchman Georges Carpentier in front of a crowd of 80,000.

Dempsey's popularity was enhanced by his appearances in movies: in a serial, *Daredevil Jack* in 1920, and in the series *Fight and Win* in 1924. His tough fighting style earned him the title of "Manassa Mauler." In 1926, after a long absence from the ring, Dempsey unsuccessfully defended his title against **Gene Tunney**. In the rematch in 1927, Dempsey knocked Tunney down but failed to retreat to a neutral ring and Tunney benefited from the "long count" to go on to win. Dempsey did not fight again. Having lost much of his wealth following the **Wall Street Crash** in 1929, Dempsey earned a living in boxing exhibitions and wrestling. During World War II, he served in the Coast Guard and directed the physical fitness program. He was inducted into the International Boxing Hall of Fame in 1990.

DENBY, EDWIN L. (1870–1929). Denby, son of the United States minister to China where he was educated, qualified as a lawyer in 1896 and practiced in Detroit until 1898. He enlisted in the navy during the Spanish-American War in 1898, then returned to his practice. He served as a **Republican** congressman from Michigan in the United States House of Representatives from 1905 to 1911. Following his political defeat Denby founded the Hupp Motor Company and was involved in the Federal Motor Truck Company and the Detroit Motor Bus Company. He was president of the Detroit Board of Commerce from 1916 to 1917. In 1917, he re-enlisted in the U.S. Marines and rose to rank of major. At the end of the war he became chief probation officer in the Detroit recorder's court and chief probation officer in Wayne County.

In 1921, Denby was **Warren Harding**'s surprise choice as secretary of the navy. His career ended when he became implicated in the **Teapot Dome** scandal. It was Denby who transferred the naval oil reserves to the Department of the Interior because, he believed, he had been instructed to do so by the president and because the Department of Interior would be better able to handle the oil reserves. In the light of the investigation into the affair Denby resigned in 1924. In 1927, the **Supreme Court** found that Denby had taken "no active part" in the negotiations, and the head of the Senate investigating committee, Senator **Thomas Walsh**, also acquitted Denby of any wrongdoing. Denby successfully returned to his law practice in Detroit and his work in the **automobile** manufacturing and **banking** businesses.

DEPARTMENT OF COMMERCE. The Department of Commerce was established under the administration of **William Howard Taft** in 1913 with the reorganization of the Department of Commerce and

Labor (established 1903). The function of the Department was to promote domestic and foreign commerce, collect, analyze and disseminate information relating to commerce, carry out the census, and establish weights and measures.

DEPARTMENT OF LABOR. Established as an executive department under the administration of **William Howard Taft** in 1913 following the division of the Department of Commerce and Labor, originally set up in 1903, and the creation of a separate **Department of Commerce**. The function of the Department of Labor was to "foster, promote and develop the welfare of wage earners" which it did primarily through the investigation of, and publication of information relating to, labor conditions and problems. It contained divisions dealing with children, women, wages and hours, and labor statistics.

DEPRESSION. *See* GREAT DEPRESSION.

DE PRIEST, OSCAR STANTON (1871–1951). Born in Alabama, the son of a former slave, Oscar De Priest migrated first to Salina, Kansas, and then to Chicago, where he established a successful real estate business. He entered local politics and with a power base of **African American** votes, he became Cook County commissioner in 1904 and 1906. In 1915, he was elected to the city council, where he introduced a civil rights ordinance and campaigned against job discrimination. In 1917, he was accused of taking a bribe from a gambling house, but was successfully defended by **Clarence Darrow**.

De Priest was elected a ward committeeman in 1924 and 1928; in return for his support for Mayor **William Hale Thompson**, he was appointed assistant Illinois commerce commissioner in 1927. In 1928, he won the **Republican** nomination for Congress and was elected despite facing an indictment for gambling connections and vote fraud. The case against him was eventually dropped and De Priest was the first African American congressman for 28 years, and the first from a northern state. He was re-elected in 1930 and 1932. He campaigned against lynching, fought to defend the **Scottsboro Boys,** and in 1933 obtained the inclusion of an amendment prohibiting discrimination in the bill creating the Civilian Conservation Corps. In 1934, he was defeated by the first black **Democrat** elected to Congress, Arthur W. Miller, and returned to local politics and his real estate business.

DEWEY, JOHN (1859–1952). Perhaps America's greatest philosopher, John Dewey was educated at the University of Vermont and Johns Hopkins University. Dewey taught at the universities of Minnesota, 1885–89, Michigan, 1889–94, Chicago, 1894–1904, and Columbia, 1904–39. He wrote on education, psychology, and philosophy and became president of the American Psychological Association, 1899–1900, president of the American Philosophical Association, 1905–06, and vice president of the American Association for the Advancement of Science in 1909. Involved in the **settlement houses** at Hull House and Henry Street, his work showed the influence of William James' notions of pragmatism. Dewey referred to the "instrumentalism" of ideas, meaning that ideas were instruments that could be used in social reform to tackle the problems that were created by society not nature. He viewed education as a means to improving society and he established an experimental school at the University of Chicago. Over the years Dewey developed and modified his theories and shifted emphasis from biology and psychology to anthropology and history as determinants of human nature. Increasingly, too, Dewey argued that the value of ideas was measured by their outcome and this could only be ascertained by continuous testing. His work ranged over ethics, logic, education and pedagogy, art, and religion.

Dewey supported American participation in **World War I** as a means of securing a lasting peace, but he defended the right to dissent and principles of academic freedom. He was one of the founders of the **American Civil Liberties Union**. After the war, Dewey visited Japan, Mexico, and later the Union of Soviet Socialist Republics (USSR). He called upon the United States to recognize the communist regime. In 1937, he chaired an unofficial commission to examine the charges brought against the Russian revolutionary, Leon Trotsky, in the Moscow show trials of 1936. After several meetings with Trotsky, the commission found him not guilty.

During the 1930s, Dewey was an advocate of American neutrality, but he abandoned this position following the German invasion of Poland in 1939. He was one of the organizers of the Committee for

Cultural Freedom that criticized the "repression of intellectual freedom" in Germany, Italy, Spain, and the Soviet Union. After World War II, Dewey spoke out against the activities of the House Un-American Affairs Committee and the exclusion by some universities of staff accused of communist sympathies. Dewey's many publications included: *Psychology* (1887), *The Study of Ethics* (1894), *School and Society* (1899), *How We Think* (1910), *Democracy and Education* (1916), *Human Nature and Conduct* (1922), *Experience and Nature* (1925), *The Quest for Certainty* (1929), *Art as Experience* (1934), *Liberalism and Social Action* (1935), *Logic: The Theory of Inquiry* (1938).

DEWSON, MOLLY (MARY WILLIAMS) (1874–1962). Molly Dewson graduated from Wellesley College in 1897 and joined the Women's Educational and Industrial Union in Boston. In 1900, Dewson became the superintendent of the parole department of the Massachusetts State Industrial School for Girls in Lancaster. She resigned in 1912 to take part in the campaign to establish a minimum wage for **women** workers in Massachusetts, the first in the United States.

In 1917, Dewson and her partner Mary G. Porter volunteered for service in France with the American Red Cross and then settled in New York City in 1919. From 1919 to 1924, Dewson was the research secretary of the National Consumers' League, and she became president of the New York Consumers' League until 1931. An active campaigner on behalf of the **Democratic Party**, Dewson ran the Women's Division of the Democratic National Committee from 1933 to 1937, and she worked closely with both **Eleanor** and **Franklin D. Roosevelt**. She was a member of the Committee on Economic Security in 1934 that helped to draw up the Social Security legislation, and in 1937 Dewson became a member of the Social Security Board. She retired from government service in 1938 and spent the rest of her life with Porter.

DOHENY, EDWARD LAURENCE (1856–1935). Edward Doheny began his business career in 1892 when he opened the Los Angeles oil fields. He went on to develop the Tampico oilfield in Mexico and organized the Mexican Petroleum Company of California. In 1922 he secured a contract from the United States government to build a naval fuel station at Pearl Harbor, Hawaii, and also obtained drilling rights in the naval oil reserves at Elk Hills, California. However, a Senate investigation into the **Teapot Dome** scandal revealed that Doheny had given Secretary of the Interior **Albert Fall** $100,000 in cash. Doheny claimed this was a loan, but he and Fall were indicted in 1925 for bribery and conspiracy. In 1926, both were acquitted of conspiracy and in 1930 the judge instructed the jury that they could acquit Doheny of giving a bribe but convict Fall of receiving it. Nonetheless, the government canceled Doheny's oil leases and he was required to repay profits made from them.

DOMINICAN REPUBLIC. In 1916, United States troops were sent to the Dominican Republic, in the West Indies, when internal unrest threatened American business interests on the island. The troops remained until 1924.

DORR, RHETA CHILDE (1866–1948). Rheta Dorr began her career as a journalist reporting on the Klondike gold rush for the New York *Sun* from her vantage point in Seattle. She left her husband in 1898 and moved to New York where she became a full-time reporter for the *Evening Post*. Having reported on **women** in work, she became an activist campaigning for **women's suffrage**, minimum wage laws, and better working conditions for women. In 1906, Dorr left her job, visited Europe, and subsequently worked in department stores and garment industries. Her accounts of these experiences were published in *Harper's Weekly, Everybody's Magazine,* and *Hampton's Magazine*, and formed the basis of her book *What Eight Million Women Want* in 1910. After spending time with Emmeline Pankhurst in England, Dorr founded and edited the *Suffragist* for the Congressional Union of Woman in 1914. Dorr reported on the Russian Revolution in 1917 and was a war correspondent for the New York *Evening Mail* for three months. After the war she spent time in Europe and served as a foreign correspondent for the New York *Herald Tribune* from 1920 to 1923. In 1928, she published a *Biography of Susan B. Anthony*, one of the leading American suffragists.

DOS PASSOS, JOHN RODERIGO (1896–1970). John Dos Passos's first poems were published with those of **E. E. Cummings** in *Eight*

Harvard Poets in 1917. After graduating from Harvard University that year, Dos Passos served through **World War I** as an ambulance man in Italy. He won recognition for his books, *One Man's Initiation* (1919) and *Three Soldiers* (1921), based on his war experiences. In 1925, *Manhattan Transfer*, his first book written in the style mixing fact and fiction ("faction") that was to become his trademark, appeared.

In addition to poetry and travel writing, Dos Passos wrote three plays during the 1920s: *The Garbage Man* (1926), *Airways, Inc.* (1928), and *Fortune Heights* (1933). His *United States* trilogy consisting of *The 42nd Parallel* (1930), *Nineteen Nineteen* (1931), *The Big Money* (1936) continued in the realist vein and offered a radical critique of American capitalism through the eyes of various fictional and real characters and a commentary by the narrator acting as the "Camera Eye." Dos Passos defended **Sacco** and **Vanzetti** in 1927 in *Facing the Chair: Story of the Americanization of Two Foreignborn Workmen*. Dos Passos also reported on strikes and covered the trials of the **Scottsboro Boys**. During the 1930s, he spent time in and reported on events in Spain. His political concerns were reflected in his *District of Columbia* trilogy: *Adventures of a Young Man* (1939), *Number One* (1943), and *Year of Decision* (1943). He also wrote books on Thomas Jefferson and Tom Paine. During World War II, Dos Passos was a war correspondent for *Life* magazine in the Pacific. After the war, he wrote a number of historical works focusing on the founding years of the American republic and continued to write books on travel. He is mainly remembered with **E. E. Cummings**, **Ernest Hemingway**, and **William Faulkner** for his writings in the interwar years and for his use of new styles.

DREIER, MARY ELIZABETH (1875–1963). Like her sister **Margaret Dreier Robins**, Mary Dreier attended the New York School of Philanthropy and was involved in Asacog House, a **settlement house** in Brooklyn. Both sisters joined the Women's Trade Union League (WTUL) and Mary Dreier succeeded Margaret as president in 1906 and served until 1914. As a wealthy middle-class woman, her arrest in support of strikers in the Triangle Shirtwaist Company in 1909 brought considerable publicity to the **women's** cause. In 1911, Dreier was the only woman appointed to the New York State Factory Investigating

Commission established following the Triangle Shirtwaist Company fire in which 146 women had died. Dreier served until 1915 when she joined the New York City Board of Education.

Dreier resigned from the WTUL in 1915 and became chair of the New York City Woman Suffrage party's industrial section and concentrated on the **women's suffrage** campaign. During **World War I**, she headed the New York State Women in Industry Committee. After the war, Dreier campaigned for protective legislation for women and in 1924 was elected to the WTUL's executive. In 1935, Dreier was appointed vice president of the WTUL and served until the organization ended in 1950. *See also* SOCIAL WORK.

DREISER, THEODORE (1871–1945). The son of German immigrants, Theodore Dreiser became one of the leading figures in the prewar literary naturalism movement that depicted characters as victims of their internal drives or social environment. He wrote as a journalist for several years for the Chicago *Globe*, St. Louis *Globe-Democrat* and *Republic,* and the Pittsburgh *Dispatch*. He edited *Smith's Magazine* (1905–06), *Broadway Magazine* (1906–07), and *American Spectator* (1907–34). In 1900 he published *Sister Carrie* showing a woman driven by her desire for material success above all moral values. *Jennie Gerhardt* (1911) focused on an immigrant girl disowned by her family when she becomes pregnant out of wedlock. In *The Financier* (1912) and *The Titan* (1914) he focused on the rise to power and influence of an amoral businessman, based on the life of businessman, Charles Yerkes. The final volume in the trilogy, *The Stoic*, was published in 1947.

In 1919, Dreiser moved to Hollywood where he worked on film scripts. His great postwar novel, *An American Tragedy* (1925), was widely regarded as his masterpiece. In it, the main protagonist was a young man, who, driven by sexual desire and greed, murdered his pregnant mistress to marry a wealthy woman, but was discovered, convicted, and executed. Like a number of his works, this attracted the attention of some censors for its supposedly immoral content, but the book was a commercial success. In 1927, Dreiser visited the Soviet Union and he subsequently wrote positively of communism during the **Depression**. He became a political activist in the thirties as a member of the League of American Writers and chair of the National

Committee for the Defense of Political Prisoners. His *Tragic America* (1932) was a critique of large corporations, **banks**, and railroads. In 1938, he attended an international peace conference and campaigned in America on behalf of the Spanish Republican forces. He argued against United States involvement in the war in Europe in 1941. In 1945, he very publicly joined the Communist Party. In addition to his novels, Dreiser published several collections of poetry, short stories, travel books and works of journalism, but he is remembered as perhaps America's greatest writer of naturalist fiction.

DUBINSKY, DAVID (1892–1982). Born in Poland, Dubinsky was imprisoned in Siberia for his early **trade union** activities. He emigrated to the United States in 1911, found work as a cutter in the garment industry, and joined the International Ladies Garment Workers Union (ILGWU) and the **Socialist Party**. He became secretary-treasurer of the union in 1929 and president in 1932. He held the position until 1966. In 1934, he became vice president of the **American Federation of Labor** (AFL) but left to help form the Congress of Industrial Organizations (CIO) in 1936. He was one of the leading trade union supporters of **Franklin D. Roosevelt** and the **New Deal** and in 1936 he left the Socialist Party to help found the American Labor Party (ALP). He left the CIO in 1938 and the ILGWU was independent until 1945 when it rejoined the AFL. Dubinsky left the ALP in 1944 and was one of the founders of the Liberal Party. He was also active in Americans for Democratic Action formed in 1947 to oppose communism. After the war Dubinsky was involved in combating racketeering in the unions and was a member of the AFL-CIO Committee on Ethical Practices.

Du BOIS, WILLIAM EDWARD BURGHARDT (1868–1963). W. E. B. Du Bois was an **African American** scholar—historian, sociologist, poet—and **civil rights** leader. From Great Barrington, Massachusetts, he was educated at Fisk, Harvard, and Berlin, and gained his Ph.D. from Harvard in 1895. Professor of economics and history at Atlanta University, his influential collection of essays *The Souls of Black Folk* (1903) included an attack on the "accommodationist" leadership of Booker T. Washington. In 1905, Du Bois was one of the African Americans who called together black leaders in the Niagara Movement to challenge segregation. In 1909, a number of white liberals joined with African Americans to form the **National Association for the Advancement of Colored People** (NAACP) and Du Bois was appointed editor of the journal *The Crisis*. Under his editorship, *The Crisis* became a major outlet for the expression of black culture and opinion. Du Bois's own writings on subjects such as lynching, support for the American war effort, and postwar race relations, were of major influence.

After **World War I**, Du Bois was active in the Pan African movement and attended congresses in Paris (1919), London, Brussels, and Paris (all in 1921), and London and Lisbon (1923). Du Bois increasingly questioned the gradualist approach of the NAACP and he resigned in 1934 and concentrated on teaching and writing as professor at Atlanta University. In 1935, Du Bois published *Black Reconstruction in America*, a work that still stands as a major study of the post-Civil War period. After World War II, he was an advocate of world peace and nuclear disarmament and as such was seen as a communist sympathizer. Du Bois prepared *An Appeal to the World*, a petition to the United Nations protesting the plight of African Americans tabled by the Union of Soviet Socialist Republics (USSR) in 1947. His membership of the Peace Information Center led to his indictment under anticommunist legislation. He was acquitted, but denied a passport until 1958. Du Bois left the United States to live in Ghana in 1961 and renounced his U.S. citizenship a year later.

DURANT, WILLIAM CRAPO (1861–1947). The **automobile** manufacturer and financier, William Durant began his working career as a patent medicine and cigar salesman in the 1880s. In 1886, he and J. D. Dort bought a company making horse-drawn carriages, which they moved to Flint, Michigan. By 1900, the Durant-Dort Company was the largest of its type in the United States. In 1904, Durant moved into automobile manufacturing when he took over the struggling Buick Motor Company and in 1908 he established the **General Motors Corporation** (GM) and added Oldsmobile and Cadillac in addition to another 20 companies to the new organization.

Durant lost managerial control of General Motors in 1910. The following year, he financed the production of a touring car by **Louis Chevrolet** and in 1913 created the Chevrolet Motor Company. By 1915, Chevrolet was the country's second largest automobile manufacturer. Using Chevrolet shares, Durant regained control of GM in 1916. Another financial crisis in 1920 forced Durant to give up the presidency of the company once more. In 1921, he established Durant Motors and in two years the new company had captured a fifth of the automobile market. The shaky foundations of the company were exposed by the **Wall Street Crash** in 1929 and Durant was forced to declare bankruptcy in 1936. He opened a supermarket in New Jersey in 1936 and a chain of bowling alleys in Flint in 1940, but he was never able to regain the heights he had formerly held. *Also see* FORD, HENRY.

DYER ANTILYNCH BILL. A bill to outlaw illegal lynching by penalizing mob violence introduced in Congress by Indiana **Republican** Senator, Leonidas Dyer, and Republican Congressman, **Charles Curtis**, of Kansas in 1919. It passed in the House of Representatives but was rejected by the Senate in 1921 and again in 1923.

– E –

EARHART, AMELIA (1898–1937). Amelia Earhart learned to fly in 1921 and became an exhibition flyer. She became the first woman to fly across the Atlantic when she flew in a plane piloted by two men from Newfoundland to Wales on 17 June 1928. She was feted in London and New York. Earhart toured the United States promoting aviation and the new airmail service with **Charles Lindbergh** and speaking on behalf of equal rights for women. In 1932, she flew single-handed from Newfoundland to Londonderry, Ireland, and was awarded the United States Distinguished Flying Cross for her achievements. In 1935, Earhart flew across the Pacific from Honolulu to California. In 1937, she went missing over the Pacific with navigator Fred Noonan while trying to fly around the world from east to west.

EAST SAINT LOUIS RACE RIOT, 1917. On 2 July, a race riot broke out in East St. Louis, Illinois, in which 39 **African Americans** and 8 whites died. Unofficial estimates put the figure for black deaths much higher. East St. Louis had seen an increase in black population of about 5,000 because of the increased job opportunities in defense industries. The city was also a terminus through which many African Americans passed on their way to other towns and cities. This influx created conflict over housing and employment.

In response to the riot and the general increase in racial violence, the **National Association for the Advancement of Colored People** (NAACP) organized a silent protest march on 28 July in which several thousand African Americans marched down Fifth Avenue, New York. Further race violence erupted in the **"Red Summer"** of 1919.

EASTMAN, CRYSTAL (1881–1928). A law graduate, Eastman investigated labor conditions as part of the Russell Sage Foundation's Pittsburgh Survey and published a report on *Work, Accidents, and the Law* in 1910. She was the first woman to serve on New York State's Commission on Employers' Liability and Causes of Industrial Accidents and was responsible for drafting the state's workmen's compensation law, the first in the country. Between 1913 and 1914, she was an investigating attorney for the United States Commission on Industrial Relations. A committed suffragist, she was one of the founders of the militant **Congressional Union**. In 1915, she founded the **Woman's Peace Party** and led the New York branch. She became an executive director of the **American Union Against Militarism** that attempted to keep the United States out of the war and then became an advocate for conscientious objectors in the National Civil Liberties Bureau in April 1917. When the war ended, she organized the First Feminist Congress in 1919 and with her brother **Max Eastman** became copublisher of the radical journal, *The Liberator*. As labor lawyer, social worker, suffragist, pacifist, and defender of civil liberties, Crystal Eastman was an example of the new women's activism during and after the **Progressive** Era.

EASTMAN, MAX FORRESTER (1883–1969). The radical editor, Max Eastman, was educated at Williams College and Columbia University. Influenced by his sister **Crystal Eastman**, he joined the literary circles in **Greenwich Village** in 1910 and in 1912 became editor of *The Masses*. Eastman revitalized the left-wing journal and attracted some of the leading writers of the day to contribute. During **World War I**, Eastman and six others associated with *The Masses* were indicted for sedition and conspiracy to obstruct military enlistment, but they were acquitted when two juries failed to reach a verdict. *The Masses* collapsed in 1917 after being denied its mailing privileges under wartime legislation. In 1918, Eastman established *The Liberator*, which survived until 1924. In 1922, Eastman traveled to the Soviet Union and after two years, to Europe. He returned to the United States in 1927 and for a while was Leon Trotsky's literary agent. Eastman increasingly wrote critical studies of Stalin's Soviet policies and renounced socialism in *Marxism: Is It Science?* in 1940. In 1941, he became an editor with the *Reader's Digest* and in the 1950s he even supported Senator Joseph McCarthy's anti-Communist crusades. Eastman's memoirs *Enjoyment of Living* (1948) and *Love and Revolution* 1964), plus his many essays, provide a detailed insight into the "lyrical left."

EDERLE, GERTRUDE (1906–). Gertrude Ederle began swimming as a child and was already a world record holder by the age of 12. By the time she was 17, she held 18 world swimming records. In 1924, at the Paris Olympics Ederle won one gold and two bronze medals. After failing to swim the English Channel in 1925, she turned professional in order to finance a second attempt. In 1926, Ederle broke the record for the channel swim and became the first woman to complete the challenge when she swam the distance in 14 hours 31 minutes. This time was soon beaten by men, but remained the record time for **women** until 1964. Ederle swam in exhibitions for a time after her success, but increasingly suffered from hearing loss due to the aggravation of an existing problem by the salt water. In 1933, she fell and damaged her spine and was in casts for four years. During World War II, Ederle worked in aircraft factories. After the war, she became a swimming instructor for deaf children. She was inducted to the Swimming Hall of Fame in 1965.

EIGHTEENTH AMENDMENT. The Eighteenth Amendment to the constitution prohibiting the manufacture, sale, or transportation of alcohol was adopted by both houses of Congress in December 1917 and ratified by the necessary two-thirds of the states in January 1919. It was put into force by the **National Prohibition Act** in October 1919. (*See* appendix II.)

ELAINE, ARKANSAS. Elaine was the location of one of the race riots that swept America during the **"Red Summer"** of 1919. On 30 September 1919, **African American** sharecroppers meeting to form a union were involved in a confrontation with a group of white men. After a white deputy sheriff was shot and killed in the clash, violence spread as a white mob attacked the black community. Five whites and "anywhere from 20 to 200" African Americans died in the ensuing violence between 1 and 3 October.

ELIOT, T. S. (THOMAS STEARNS) (1888–1965). The poet T. S. Eliot was born in St. Louis, Missouri, but he settled in England in 1915 and became a British subject in 1927. Eliot was educated at Smith Academy, Harvard, the Sorbonne in Paris, and Oxford University. In England, Eliot was introduced to the literary circles by **Ezra Pound**. Eliot's first collection of poems, *Prufrock and Other Observations* was published in 1917, and the second collection, *Poems*, in 1919. Eliot's poem *The Waste Land* was published in 1922 and became one of the major works of the "lost generation" of postwar disillusioned writers and the modernist school. The poem first appeared in the *Criterion*, which Eliot edited for 17 years. When the journal was taken over by the publishers Faber and Faber, Eliot became a director with the company and helped to publish the work of major English writers such as W. H. Auden and Stephen Spender. Eliot also became one of the leading literary critics on the interwar period.

Eliot's later work such as "Journey of the Magi" (1927), "Ash Wednesday" (1930), and the essays for *Lancelot Andrewes* (1928), reflected his conversion to the Anglican Church in 1927. The subject of Christianity was also evident in his plays, the history of the Church in *The Rock* (1934), *Murder in the Cathedral* (1935), and *The Family Reunion* (1939). Eliot's last work of nondramatic poetry, regarded by many critics as his greatest work, was published as *Four Quartets* in 1943. After World War II he continued to write chiefly for the theater and *The Cocktail Party* (1949) was one of his most successful plays.

ELLINGTON, "DUKE" (EDWARD KENNEDY) (1899–1974). The **jazz** musician and composer was born Edward Kennedy Ellington, but acquired the nickname "Duke" as a schoolboy in Washington,

D.C. Ellington did not have professional musical training, but learned how to play from other black musicians. He formed his first group in 1917 and in 1923 he and several band members moved to **Harlem**, New York, where they found work in clubs. In 1924, Ellington became the bandleader and developed an improvisational style of composition. In 1926, the Ellington band recorded "East St. Louis Toodle-Oo," followed in 1927 by "Birmingham Breakdown" and "Black and Tan Fantasy." It was in 1927 that the band became the resident band at Harlem's famous Cotton Club. Over the coming years Ellington and his band composed and recorded what were to become jazz classics: "Creole Love Call" (1927), "Mood Indigo," "Sophisticated Lady" (1932), "Solitude" (1934), and many more. With successful recording and live broadcasts from the Cotton Club from 1931 on, Ellington became a major figure in popular music.

Ellington continued to produce great jazz hits through band and record label changes. In 1940, the band recorded "Take the 'A' Train," "Cotton Tail," and "Ko Ko." After a brief lull in their success, the Ellington band had a revival of fortunes following a performance at the Newport Jazz Festival in 1956. Before he died, Ellington had been awarded honorary degrees, membership in the American Institute of Arts and Letters, the French Legion of Honor, and the Presidential Medal of Freedom.

ELLSWORTH, LINCOLN (1880–1951). Lincoln Ellsworth was an explorer who led a geological expedition to the Andes in 1924, went with Amundsen from Spitsbergen to Alaska by seaplane in 1925, and made a transarctic submarine expedition in 1931. In 1935, he flew 2,300 miles across the Antarctic claiming the new land for the United States. He was the author, with Amundsen, of *First Crossing of the Polar Sea* (1927), and sole author of *Beyond Horizons* (1938).

EMERGENCY QUOTA ACT. *See* QUOTA ACT OF 1921.

EMERGENCY RELIEF AND CONSTRUCTION ACT, 1932. Signed by President **Herbert Hoover** on 21 July 1932 in response to the deepening **Depression**, the Emergency Relief and Construction Act provided $300 million for the **Reconstruction Finance Corporation** to make relief loans available to states. It also authorized funds for federal, state, and local public works. These relief programs were to be far exceeded during the **New Deal**.

EMPIRE STATE BUILDING. When it opened on 1 May 1931, the Empire State Building on Fifth Avenue, between 33rd and 34th Streets in New York City, was, at an original height of 1,250 feet, for a time the tallest building in the world. Ironically, much of the new office space provided was not initially used because of the onset of the **Depression**.

ESCH, JOHN JACOB (1861–1941). John Esch graduated from the University of Wisconsin in 1882. He took a law degree in 1887, was admitted to the bar, and began to practice law in La Crosse, Wisconsin. Active in the state guard, from 1894 to 1896 Esch served as judge advocate general with the rank of colonel. He was a delegate to the **Republican Party** convention in 1894 and 1896 and in 1898 was elected to the United States House of Representatives. He served for 22 years. Esch's major contribution was on the Committee on Interstate and Foreign Commerce where he supported measures to increase the power of the Interstate Commerce Commission. Esch opposed United States involvement in **World War I** and voted against the declaration of war in 1917.

As chair of the House Commerce Committee after the war, Esch was cosponsor of the **Esch-Cummins Act**. Criticism from Senator **Robert La Follette**, who argued that the act would increase rail costs and consumer prices, led to Esch's defeat in the Republican primary in 1920. President **Warren Harding** appointed Esch to the Interstate Commerce Commission in 1921, and he served as chairman in 1927. Southern politicians voted against confirming his renomination in 1928, and Esch then established a law practice in Washington, D.C. He also served as president of the American Peace Society from 1930 to 1938.

ESCH-CUMMINS ACT. *See* RAILROAD TRANSPORTATION ACT.

ESPIONAGE ACT, 1917. Passed in June 1917, the Espionage Act established a $10,000 fine and up to 20 years' imprisonment for acts of sabotage, promoting the success of the enemy, or obstructing military recruitment and operations in wartime. Anyone using the mail in violation of the statute was liable to a $5,000 fine and up to five years' imprisonment. By May 1918, 45 newspapers or journals had had their mailing rights suspended under the legislation. The act was further amended in 1918 under the **Sedition Act** to give even greater powers of suppression to the government.

EVANS, HIRAM WESLEY (1881–1966). Evans was a dentist from Texas who rose through the ranks of the **Ku Klux Klan** to become imperial wizard from 1922 to 1939. The Klan expanded and became a significant force in several northern states under his leadership in the mid-1920s. Evans wrote several books, including *The Menace of Modern Immigration* (1923), *The Klan Tomorrow* (1924), and *The Rising Storm* (1929).

EXCESS PROFITS TAX. First levied by Congress in 1916 to deal with high war profits and raise money for the war effort, the excess profits tax was a graduated tax on business profits in excess of a fixed percentage of capital investment or of average profits. In its first year it yielded approximately $2 billion. The law was repealed in 1921 but reintroduced in 1933.

– F –

FAIRBANKS, DOUGLAS (1883–1939). Born Douglas Elton Ulman, Fairbanks changed his name in 1900. In 1902, he made his acting debut in New York and he became a leading Broadway star and was one of New York's best-paid leading men by 1914. In 1915, he joined Triangle Film Productions and he had appeared in 23 films by 1918. By 1916, he was writing his own scripts and producing his own films. By 1919, Fairbanks was America's leading movie star and he had also authored three books *Laugh and Live* (1917), *Assuming Responsibilities* (1918), and *Making Life Worth While* (1918). That year he joined with director **D. W. Griffith** and two other stars, **Charlie Chaplin** and **Mary Pickford**, to form the United Artists Film Corporation. In 1920, Fairbanks married Pickford and they became an internationally known "couple."

Starting with *The Mark of Zorro* in 1920, Fairbanks turned to the swashbuckling costume dramas with which he was forever associated. The enormously successful *Robin Hood* (1922) followed the *Three Musketeers* (1921). *The Thief of Baghdad* (1924), *Don Q. Son of Zorro* (1925), and *The Black Pirate* (1926) crowned Fairbanks' success. Several other silent movies followed, but Fairbanks' style seemed increasingly dated as the talkies took over and later as the **Depression** undercut the optimism and exuberance central to his movies. In 1935, he and Pickford were divorced and by 1938 **Samuel Goldwyn** had acquired major control of United Artists, which was renamed Samuel Goldwyn Studios. In 1939, Fairbanks won a posthumous Academy Award for his contribution to the development of motion pictures.

FALL, ALBERT BACON (1861–1944). Albert Fall grew up in Tennessee where he later began teaching and studying law. He moved to Kansas and then Texas in 1881 before prospecting in New Mexico where he settled in 1887. Initially a **Democrat**, Grover Cleveland appointed him judge on the territorial bench in 1893 and he served until 1895. He subsequently established a law practice in El Paso, Texas, and became involved in a variety of business activities in Mexico and New Mexico. Fall served in New Mexico's legislature from 1891 to 1895, 1897, and 1903 to 1905. He changed political allegiance in 1904 when he supported the **Republican** platform and was Republican senator for New Mexico from 1912 until **Warren Harding** appointed him secretary of the interior in 1921. He resigned in 1923 and in 1924 a Senate investigation revealed he had accepted large bribes from his friends in the oil business, **Edward Doheny** and **Harry Sinclair**, in return for leasing naval oil reserves in **Teapot Dome**, Wyoming, and California. Fall was convicted of bribery in 1929 and served nine months of a one-year prison sentence, the first cabinet officer to be convicted of a felony committed while in office.

FARM BLOC. The Farm Bloc was a congressional coalition of western **Republicans** and southern **Democrats** led by **Arthur Capper** that fought for legislation to improve the plight of farmers during the 1920s. The 25 senators and approximately 100 representatives supported the **Agricultural Credits** and **Agricultural Marketing Acts**

and the **McNary-Haugen Bills**. The Bloc also managed to obtain the passage of legislation in 1922 exempting farmers' cooperatives from antitrust legislation.

FARMER-LABOR PARTY. A third party formed in 1919 by members of the **Committee of Forty-eight** in an attempt to unite farmers and the labor movement under a reform program. The party first nominated **Robert M. La Follette** as their presidential candidate, but when he rejected the nomination the party turned instead to Parley P. Christensen of Utah. In the 1920 election he received 260,000 votes. In 1924 the Farmer-Labor Party supported La Follette's **Progressive Party**. *See also* FARM BLOC; FARMING.

FARMING. For much of its history, the United States was a predominantly agrarian economy. The industrial revolution in the early-19th century stimulated the expansion of agriculture and the move westward after the Civil War (1861–65) led to growth in machine technology with the use of threshers, reapers, and combined harvesters. The new large-scale farming, linked to eastern cities by the **railroads**, provided the food for growing industrial, urban populations. But by the 1890s, manufacturing output began to exceed agricultural production and as the farmers were displaced socially and politically, they also experienced increasing economic problems due to overproduction and worldwide competition that resulted in falling prices. Angry farmers blamed their indebtedness on the high interest charged by **banks**, the rates levied by the railroads, and **tariffs** that protected industry, but raised consumers' costs. In the 1880s and 1890s, this anger saw the rise of a farmers' movement and the creation of the Populist Party in 1892. A depression in 1893 only worsened their situation and in 1896 the Populist Party supported the **Democratic Party**'s candidate, **William Jennings Bryan**. Bryan's defeat signaled the demise of Populism and the domination of the political system by the **Republicans** until 1912.

Many of the Populists' demands for railroad and bank regulation were incorporated in the agenda of the **Progressives** and rising prices saw some improvement in the farmers' situation. **World War I** brought a boom in agriculture, as world trade was limited. The demand for grain and food to feed both the United States' and **Allied** armies brought an expansion in farm acreage and output. Mechanization and the use of tractors contributed further to farm efficiency. After the war, however, world competition resumed and the artificially high commodity prices fell. American farmers once again struggled to pay off the debts they had incurred, and 453,000 farmers lost their property in the immediate postwar crash. The farm population, over 32 million in 1910, was 31.9 million in 1920, and had fallen to 30.5 million by 1930. As a proportion of the total population, this represented a drop from over 30 percent to just under 25 percent.

Despite falling numbers, this vital sector in the economy failed to share in the prosperity of the 1920s. In 1919, gross farm income accounted for 16 percent of the national income; by 1929 it was 8 percent and average per capita farm income was 25 percent of the national average as the value of farm products fell by half. Farmers in the Midwest organized in the **Nonpartisan League** echoed Populist demands for federal action to control prices on their behalf, but had limited success. The **American Farm Bureau Federation** (AFBF) established a lobby in Washington, D.C., and a **Farm Bloc** of Western Republicans and Southern Democrats struggled to achieve the passage of legislation to protect farmers, but with little effect.

The **Great Depression** only worsened the situation of farmers as agricultural prices collapsed after 1929. By 1932, average farm income had dropped by two-thirds. With many farmers unable to meet mortgage repayments almost a million farms were repossessed between 1930 and 1934. The drought and dust storms of the 1930s only added to the misery. Desperate farmers declared "farm holidays" in which they withheld their produce from the market or dumped it in the roads. Farm sales following evictions were often blocked and farmers demonstrated in their neighboring towns. President **Herbert Hoover** responded by signing the **Agricultural Marketing Act** and attempted to stabilize prices through **Federal Farm Boards**. However, this had little immediate effect and it was not until the coming of the **New Deal** that farming began to experience a recovery. *See also* CAPPER, ARTHUR; FORDNEY-McCUMBER ACT; McNARY-HAUGEN BILL; TOWNLEY, CHARLES ARTHUR; WALLACE, HENRY.

FAULKNER, WILLIAM HARRISON (1897–1962). William Faulkner was one of the greatest Southern writers of the 20th century. Born William Cuthbert Falkner in Mississippi, he had a desultory education, worked in the family bank, and spent some time at the University of Mississippi. Rejected by the United States Army, Faulkner joined the British Royal Air Force in Canada in 1918. After the war, he studied at the University of Mississippi from 1919 to 1921 and published various poems and reviews. Faulkner earned a living as postmaster at the university until 1924. His first book, *The Marble Faun*, was published that year to be followed by many others including *Soldier's Pay* (1926), *Sartoris* (1929), *The Sound and the Fury* (1929), *As I Lay Dying* (1930), *Sanctuary* (1931), *Light in August* (1932), *Absalom, Absalom!* (1936), *Intruder in the Dust* (1948), *Requiem for a Nun* (1951), and *The Reivers* (1962). In many of these novels, Faulkner traced the decline of the Old South through the stories of fictional families in "Jefferson," a composite Mississippi town in the mythical county of Yoknapatawpha. He was the winner of the Nobel Prize for literature in 1950.

FAUSET, JESSIE REDMON (1882–1961). Jessie Fauset was the first black woman admitted to Cornell University. She graduated in 1905 and completed an M.A. at the University of Pennsylvania. After a period of study in France, Fauset taught in high schools in Baltimore, Washington, D.C., and New York City. From 1919 until 1926 she was literary editor of the **National Association for the Advancement of Colored People** (NAACP) journal, the *Crisis*. Fauset was a part of the **Harlem Renaissance** and her books, *There Is Confusion* (1924), *Plum Bun* (1928), *The Chinaberry Tree* (1931), and *Comedy: American Style* (1933), deal with black middle-class society and issues of "passing," miscegenation, lynching, and race pride.

FEDERAL BUREAU OF INVESTIGATION (FBI). The FBI began when Attorney General Charles J. Bonaparte created a corps of special agents within the Department of Justice in 1908 to investigate crime at a federal level. In 1909 it was named the Bureau of Investigation. Following America's entry into **World War I**, the Bureau became responsible for investigating violations of the **Selective Service Act**, **Espionage Act**, and **Sabotage Acts**. Headed by A. Bruce Bielaski the Bureau grew in size and influence. This growth continued during the

Red Scare of 1919 and under the new leadership of William J. Flynn who assumed the title of director that year. The Justice Department widened its brief with the creation of a General Intelligence Division headed by **J. Edgar Hoover**. The Federal Bureau was created in 1924 to investigate violations of federal law with Hoover as its head.

FEDERAL FARM BOARD. The Federal Farm Board was a nine-man agency, eight appointed by the president, plus the secretary of agriculture, created by the **Agricultural Marketing Act** in 1929. Provided with a fund of $500 million, the Board was empowered to establish stabilization corporations to make purchases in agricultural commodities in order to support price levels. Two such corporations, for grain and cotton, were established but achieved very little. Having used all of its appropriation to little effect, it was abolished in 1933. *See also* FARMING.

FEDERAL FARM LOAN ACT, 1916. Passed on 17 July 1916, the Farm Loan Act established 12 Federal Land **Banks** along similar lines to the Federal Reserve Banks (*see* **Federal Reserve Act**) in order to provide more accessible credit to farmers through farm loan associations. The Federal Land Banks were under the control of a Federal Farm Labor Board consisting of the secretary of treasury and six members appointed by the president. The Land Banks were funded initially with a minimum capital of $750,000. Mortgages of up to 50 percent of land value and 20 per cent of improvements were issued to run from 5 to 40 years.

FEDERAL FOOD ADMINISTRATION. *See* UNITED STATES FOOD ADMINISTRATION.

FEDERAL HIGHWAY ACT, 1916. The first Federal Highway Act provided matching federal funds to states and local authorities for highway building. The planned program was overtaken by the outbreak of World War I, necessitating further legislation in 1921.

FEDERAL HIGHWAY ACT, 1921. Under the second Highway Act, additional federal funds were provided for highway building, increasing spending from $19.5 million in 1920 to $88 million in 1923.

FEDERAL HOME LOAN BANK ACT, 1932. Passed in July 1932, following the **Wall Street Crash**, the Federal Home Loan Bank Act established a series of discount **banks** for home mortgages, similar to the service provided by the **Federal Reserve** System. The failure of banks to cooperate limited the act's success.

FEDERAL RADIO COMMISSION (FRC). The Federal Radio Commission (FRC) was a five-man regulatory body established under the Communications Act of 1927 that took over the regulation of radio from the Department of Commerce. The commission had authority to grant licenses to broadcasting stations and approve their locations. It could also prescribe wavelengths and hours of operation, but did not control program content other than to forbid the use of "obscene, indecent or profane language." A Federal Communications Commission established in 1934 replaced the FRC.

FEDERAL RAILROAD ADMINISTRATION. *See* UNITED STATES RAILROAD ADMINISTRATION.

FEDERAL RESERVE ACT, 1913. Passed on 23 December 1913, the Federal Reserve Act, or Glass-Owen Act, was the first major **banking** and currency reform since the Civil War. It was intended to stabilize banking, limit the power of the bank trusts, and make access to credit easier. However, rather than create one central institution, the act established a Federal Reserve that consisted of 12 regional bodies, each one acting as a central bank run by local bankers. These banks were depositories for all national banks and for state banks and trust companies that wished to join. Each member bank subscribed 6 percent of its capital to the Federal Reserve and deposited a portion of its reserve there. The Reserve Banks were able to rediscount member banks' loans, i.e., take over loans in return for Federal Reserve Notes that could then be used to make further loans. A Federal Reserve Board consisting of seven members appointed by the president was established to supervise the system and to review the rediscount rates as necessary.

FEDERAL TRADE COMMISSION ACT, 1914. The Federal Trade Commission Act established a Federal Trade Commission consisting of five members appointed by the president to prevent unfair methods of competition. The Commission replaced the Bureau of Corporations established in 1903 and had new powers to define unfair trade practices and to issue, cease, and desist orders. In practice the commission proved sympathetic to business offering advice on how to avoid antitrust prosecutions.

FEDERAL WATER POWER ACT, 1920. The Federal Water Power Act established a five-man Federal Power Commission to license the use of navigable rivers for power and set rates for power used in interstate commerce. The licenses enabled the construction of hydroelectric power stations.

FELTON, REBECCA LATIMER (1835–1930). Rebecca Felton, a campaigner for prison reform, temperance, and **woman suffrage**, was an influence on Georgia politics through her regular contributions to the *Atlanta Journal* and her book, *My Memoirs of Georgia Politics* (1911). She became the first female senator when she was symbolically appointed by the governor of Georgia in October 1922 to fill a temporary vacancy caused by the death of the incumbent. Her tenure lasted an hour until the regularly elected male was sworn in.

FERGUSON, MIRIAM AMANDA WALLACE ("MA") (1875–1961). When Miriam Ferguson's husband, the twice-**Democratic** governor of Texas, James Ferguson, was impeached and convicted of misusing state funds in 1917, she entered the gubernatorial campaign in 1924 to clear his name. Campaigning with her husband, she appealed to "the mothers, sisters, and wives of Texas to help clear her family's name" and earned the nickname "Ma." She defeated the **Ku Klux Klan** candidate Felix Robertson to become the second woman governor (the first was **Nellie Tayloe Ross**). As governor, she secured passage of a law prohibiting the wearing of masks in public (aimed at the Klan), and an amnesty for her husband, whom she appointed as a commissioner to the State Highways Commission. Ferguson granted a total of 3,595 pardons while governor, leading to suggestions that pardons were being sold by her husband. She failed to gain the nominations in 1926 and 1930 but was re-elected in 1932. Ferguson supported the **New Deal** and approved a "bread bond" to raise money for the poor. Her attempts to raise taxes on the oil industry and on corporate business were unsuccessful. She later supported pensions for those over 65 and federal and state aid for farmers but failed to regain the Democratic nomination in 1940.

FIELDS, W. C. (WILLIAM CLAUDE) (1880–1946). The vaudeville, film, and radio comedian, W. C. Fields was born William Claude Dukenfield. His early theatrical career began as a juggler and in the 1890s through to 1915 he toured America and Europe. In 1915, Fields joined the Ziegfeld *Follies* on Broadway and appeared in a successful Broadway musical, *Poppy* from 1923 to 1924. The film version of *Poppy, Sally of the Sawdust* appeared in 1925 and Fields also appeared in numerous other silent movies in the 1920s developing his comic persona as the con man or harassed husband, both with a strong dislike of children. In the 1930s, he moved to Hollywood, where he wrote scripts and starred in several films, including *It's a Gift* (1934), *David Copperfield* (1935) and *The Bank Dick* (1940). Other successful films included *You Can't Cheat an Honest Man* (1939), *Never Give a Sucker an Even Break* (1941), and *My Little Chickadee* (1940), which also starred Mae West. Fields also had a successful radio career on *The Chase & Sanborn Hour* starting in 1937.

FITZGERALD, F. (FRANCIS) SCOTT (1896–1940). F. Scott Fitzgerald was the writer who perhaps more than any other captured the spirit of the 1920s in America. He even named the period "The Jazz Age." Born in St. Paul, Minnesota, Fitzgerald went to Princeton in 1913. In 1917, he left to take up a commission in the infantry but the war ended before Fitzgerald could see action. While serving in Alabama, he met his future wife, **Zelda Sayre Fitzgerald**. She agreed to marry him following the publication of his first book, *This Side of Paradise*, in 1920. The book, which seemed to capture the new postwar morality of the young, was a great success. His second book, *The Beautiful and the Damned* (1922) was less successful, but the Fitzgeralds were able to support their extravagant lifestyle, much of it spent in Europe, with earnings from short stories published in magazines and in collections such as *Flappers and Philosophers* (1920) and *Tales of the Jazz Age* (1922).

Fitzgerald's reputation was assured with the publication of *The Great Gatsby* (1925). The book, which caught many of the elements of moral and material corruption of the decade, stood as a lasting commentary on the American Dream itself. Despite this success Fitzgerald's life was not easy. Financial worries, tensions in his marriage, and Zelda's nervous breakdown delayed the publication of his next book, *Tender Is the Night*, until 1934. In 1937, Fitzgerald began work as a scriptwriter for Metro-Goldwyn-Mayer and his last book *The Last Tycoon* was based on his observations inside the studios. Incomplete when he died, the novel was published in 1993.

FITZGERALD, ZELDA SAYRE (1900–1948). The wife of **F. Scott Fitzgerald** and one of the celebrities of the 1920s, Zelda Fitzgerald was a writer and artist in her own right. Sadly, she suffered several nervous breakdowns requiring institutional care. In 1948, she died in a fire in Highland Hospital in Asheville, North Carolina.

FIVE POWER TREATY. *See* WASHINGTON NAVAL TREATY.

FLAPPER. The term "flapper" was used in the 1920s to describe the "new **woman**," liberated politically with the vote, economically by new work opportunities, and socially with new fashions. With her bobbed hair, straight dresses that stopped just below the knee, the flapper smoked and drank in public and discussed sexual matters in a manner inconceivable to older generations of women. However, the extent of this "revolution in manners and morals" was probably exaggerated by images in the **movies**, magazines, and advertising.

FLYNN, ELIZABETH GURLEY (1890–1964). Socialist labor organizer Elizabeth Gurley Flynn became a full-time organizer for the **Industrial Workers of the World** in 1907 and was involved in so many strikes that she became known as the "Rebel Girl." After the war, she helped to found the **American Civil Liberties Union** and was a leading campaigner in defense of **Sacco** and **Vanzetti**. She also spoke on behalf of **women**'s rights and birth control. In 1936, Flynn joined the **Communist Party**. In 1952, she was convicted of advocating the overthrow of the United States government and jailed for two years. She became national chairperson of the Communist Party in 1961. Flynn died during a visit to the Soviet Union, where she was given a state funeral before being flown back to the United States for burial.

FORD, HENRY (1863–1947). Henry Ford's name became synonymous with the 1920s with the development and sale of his mass-produced **Model T Ford**. Ford began work as a mechanic in Detroit in 1879. In 1891, he found employment with the Edison Illuminating Company and was chief engineer from 1887 to 1889. Ford built his first car in 1896 and in 1899 established the Detroit Automobile Company. For a time, Ford concentrated on building racing cars and his company became the Cadillac Motor Car Company in 1902.

Ford returned to **automobile** manufacture when he established the Ford Motor Company in 1903. He first began production of the Model T Ford in 1909 using the concept of mass-produced standardized parts and developed it further at his new Highland Park factory in 1910. In 1913, Ford developed the moving assembly line method of production enabling an enormous increase in production and a reduction in price that made motor car ownership a possibility for masses of ordinary people. In 1914, he introduced a profit-sharing scheme and a five-dollar eight-hour day for his workers and later introduced the five-day week. However, he also attempted to control workers through a personnel department that implemented mandatory English lessons for immigrant workers and a no-smoking, no-drinking, and nonunion policy. Ford also established a museum at Dearborn dedicated to preserving the rural past, complete with one-roomed schoolhouse and McGuffey readers.

Ford was a pacifist and he personally funded an attempt to bring peace when he purchased a "peace ship," *Oscar II*, in 1915 that went with delegates to Oslo, where a conference of neutral powers was held. Once America entered the war, the Ford Company turned to producing engines, tractors, and vehicles for the government. Ford opened the world's largest single manufacturing plant at River Rouge, Detroit, in 1916. Such was Ford's public stature that in 1916, he won the **Republican** presidential primary in Michigan without campaigning. In 1918, Ford was persuaded to run for election to the Senate by **Woodrow Wilson**, but a Republican opponent defeated him. There were attempts to persuade him to stand for the presidency in 1920 and 1923, but Ford supported **Warren Harding** and **Calvin Coolidge**. During the early 1920s, Ford's magazine, the *Dearborn Independent*, published a series of anti-Semitic articles and in 1938, the German Nazi government honored Ford.

After **World War I**, Ford expanded his operation to develop luxury cars (the Lincoln) and airplanes. In 1927, he ceased production of the now out-of-date Model T and began producing the Model A. This did not match up to other cars, particularly the **Chevrolet**. In 1932, Ford introduced the new V-8 engine, but the Ford Company did not recover its early domination of the market. By 1936, Ford ran third behind **General Motors** and **Chrysler** in terms of its market share. The Ford Company held out against the **trade union** drives of the 1930s, despite some bitter struggles on the part of workers. Union recognition was only granted in 1941.

During World War II, the Ford Company converted entirely to war production and built a huge aircraft production plant at Willow Run outside Detroit. Ford himself was increasingly unwell and in 1945 he was forced to yield control to his grandson, Henry Ford II. Despite this, Ford's name remained synonymous with modern car production.

FORDNEY, JOSEPH WARREN (1853–1932). Joseph Fordney began work from an early age in the lumber industry in Michigan. He became a prominent businessman and entered politics in 1895 as a **Republican** alderman in Saginaw, Michigan. In 1898, he was elected to the United States House of Representatives where he became an advocate of timber and sugar tariffs. In 1920, he became chair of the Ways and Means Committee and in 1922 achieved his protectionist objectives with the **Fordney-McCumber Act**. Fordney retired the following year to concentrate on his business interests.

FORDNEY-McCUMBER ACT, 1922. The Fordney-McCumber Act raised **tariffs** to levels higher than any previously in American history in an attempt to bolster the postwar economy, protect new war industries, and aid **farmers**. Duties on chinaware, pig iron, textiles, sugar, and rails were restored to the high levels of 1907 and increases ranging from 60 to 400 percent were established on dyes, chemicals, silk and rayon textiles, and hardware. Tariffs on a variety of agricultural produce were raised. Although the tariffs encouraged the growth of monopoly in the United States, they also made it difficult for European powers to earn sufficient dollars to repay war debts. Other nations responded by increasing their tariffs thus limiting United States exports and constricting the market. These factors helped to create the weaknesses that produced the Depression.

FOREIGN POLICY. For much of its history the United States was content to look inward and concentrate on westward expansion and settlement rather than concern itself with affairs beyond its borders. Traditionally the main feature of the country's foreign policy was **isolationism**. However, as the nation grew and as it became increasingly a world economic power, it began to look outward. The Spanish-American War (1898) resulted in the acquisition of an empire (the Philippines, Hawaii, and Puerto Rico) and concern for trade saw a widening interest in Asia and the growth of the U.S. Navy. The building of the Panama Canal (1904–14) was funded by the United States and carried out under the supervision of **George W. Goethals**. Increasingly, too, the notion of separate spheres with the United States dominant in the new world found a more aggressive expression in **Theodore Roosevelt**'s "Roosevelt Corollary" (1904) justifying an interventionist policing and protectorate policy in Central and Latin America. This was also linked to the "dollar diplomacy" that witnessed a growth of the United States' economic interests in this area. This new role lay behind the interventions in Panama (1903), Cuba (1906, 1912, 1917), the **Dominican Republic** (1905, 1916), **Haiti** (1915), and Nicaragua (1912, 1927). It also affected relations with **Mexico** and almost brought the two countries to war during **Woodrow Wilson**'s presidency. Relations with Latin America began to improve under the presidencies of **Warren Harding**, **Calvin Coolidge**, and particularly **Herbert Hoover** who began the "Good Neighbor" policy that was to continue under **Franklin D. Roosevelt**. The Roosevelt Corollary was repudiated under the **Clark Memorandum** in 1928.

Wilson's moralistic and idealist approach to foreign affairs, evident in his relations with Mexico, was also apparent during **World War I**. The outbreak of war in Europe demonstrated how difficult it was for a world power with a large immigrant population and growing trading links to remain unaffected by the conflict. The United

States' entry into the war in 1917, justified as a war to "make the world safe for democracy," seemed to mark an end to the policy of isolationism. Wilson's **Fourteen Points** and his commitment to the **League of Nations** appeared to confirm this. However, the rejection of the **Versailles treaty** and the League by the Senate in 1919, demonstrated the strength of traditional views, particularly in the **Republican Party**. The defeat of the **Democratic Party** in the presidential election of 1920 and the Republican domination through the 1920s suggested a return to isolationism, but in reality the war had underlined America's position as a leading world power.

During the 1920s, the Republican administrations were involved in disarmament plans at the **Washington** and **London Naval Conferences**, and in initiating attempts to outlaw war in the **Kellogg-Briand Pact**. Moreover, the country was vitally involved in the world's economy. In 1920, the United States produced one-sixth of all world exports and received one-eighth of all imports. Before the war, the United States was a debtor nation, owing $4 billion in foreign investments; after the war she was a creditor nation, owed $12.5 billion in war debts by nations like France and Great Britain. In addition, American financiers lent money to Germany throughout the 1920s, enabling the payment of reparations. The United States also took a lead in renegotiating reparations through the **Dawes** and **Young Plans**. Thus the raising of **tariffs** and the withdrawal of credit to foreign powers following the **Wall Street Crash** contributed to the **Great Depression** becoming a worldwide phenomena. Although isolationist tendencies reappeared as world conflict spread during the 1930s, Franklin D. Roosevelt took a much more interventionist position than his predecessors, and entry into World War II in 1941 revolutionized the United States' foreign policy. *See also* BRYAN, WILLIAM JENNINGS; HUGHES, CHARLES EVANS; KELLOGG, CHARLES B.; STIMSON, HENRY L.

FOSDICK, RAYMOND BLAINE (1883–1972). A graduate of Princeton University (1905, 1906) and New York Law School (1908), Raymond Fosdick became assistant corporation counsel for the City of New York and established a reputation as a reformer during investigations of motion picture theaters, prostitution, and loan sharking. In 1912, Fosdick became comptroller and auditor of the national **Dem-**

ocratic **Party**. In 1916, he was appointed assistant to the Secretary of War **Newton D. Baker** and during **World War I** was chair of the Commission on Training Camp Activities. In that role Fosdick encouraged the development of educational and other programs for United States servicemen.

In 1919, **Woodrow Wilson** appointed Fosdick first undersecretary to the **League of Nations** but he resigned when the Senate refused to ratify the League of Nations Covenant. He continued to support the League through the League of Nations Association that he founded. Fosdick established a legal practice in New York City and was involved on the boards of a variety of organizations associated with **Rockefeller** family philanthropies. In 1936, he became President of the Rockefeller Foundation and Rockefeller Education Board. Fosdick continued to advocate United States involvement in international affairs and supported the world court and the United Nations.

FOSTER, WILLIAM Z. (1881–1961). Having traveled the country as an itinerant worker Foster joined the **Socialist Party** in 1901 but later left to join the **Industrial Workers of the World** (IWW). Foster gradually moved away from the IWW in favor of converting existing **trade unions** to syndicalism. In 1912, he established the Syndicalist League of North America that became the Independent Trade Union League in 1914. As an organizer for the Chicago Federation of Labor during World War I, Foster helped to mobilize the meat-packing workers. The **American Federation of Labor** then appointed Foster to lead the drive to unionize the steel industry in 1919. The resultant strike ended in defeat, partially because Foster's past affiliations were used to brand the strikers as revolutionaries. Foster converted to communism in the early 1920s and was the **Communist** candidate in the 1924, 1928, and 1932 presidential elections. In 1932, he won more than 100,000 votes.

Foster resumed the leadership of the American Communist Party following the ideological differences between the established executive and Moscow in 1945. In 1948, Foster was one of 11 Communist leaders indicted by the government under the 1940 Smith Act. He was not jailed because of his ill health but his codefendants were. Foster died in Moscow in 1961 and received a state funeral there before his ashes were flown back to the United States.

FOUR MINUTE MEN. The Four Minute Men were volunteers mobilized by the **Committee of Public Information** during **World War I** to address audiences at theaters, movie halls, and public places on issues relating to the war. Some 75,000 people took part in this propaganda exercise, and there were also Junior Four Minute Men who spoke on patriotic themes in school competitions.

FOUR POWER TREATY, 1921. One of the several agreements made during the **Washington Naval Conference** in 1921, the Four Power Treaty was between the United States, France, Great Britain, and Japan. The signatories agreed to recognize each other's possessions in the Pacific and approved joint action in the event of any aggression in the Pacific by a nonsignatory power.

FOURTEEN POINTS. In a speech to Congress in January 1918 President **Woodrow Wilson** laid out the basis for an armistice with the **Central Powers**. This program, a list of fourteen points, included such principles as freedom of the seas, open covenants openly arrived at, removal of trade barriers, equal adjustment of colonial claims, and the establishment of a **League of Nations** to prevent further wars.

FOX, WILLIAM (1879–1952). The **movie** executive and producer William Fox was born Wilhelm Fuchs in Tulchva, Hungary. His family emigrated to the United States in 1880 and took the name "Fox." Fox built up a clothing company, which he sold in 1903 and bought a nickleodeon theater. Fox gradually built this into a network of theaters and he moved into the area of film production. In 1911, Fox successfully challenged the Edison Motion Picture Patents Company's (MPPC) monopolistic control of film equipment and opened the way for independent film producers and distributors. By 1927, Fox owned more than 1,000 movie theaters and he invested money in developing sound pictures and also Fox Movietone News. In 1929, he bought a controlling interest in Loews Corporation, the parent company of Metro-Goldwyn-Mayer (MGM), but was forced to sell the stock back when the Justice Department launched an antitrust suit against him. His financial dealings forced him to sell Fox Films in 1930 and the company merged with **Darryl F. Zanuck**'s Twentieth Century Pictures to become Twentieth Century-Fox in 1935. Accused of financial malpractice, Fox was first of all forced into bankruptcy in 1936 and in 1942 was jailed for bribing a judge in his bankruptcy hearings.

FRANK, LEO (1884–1915). Leo Frank graduated in mechanical engineering from Columbia University in 1906. He moved to Atlanta, Georgia, and became superintendent of the National Pencil Factory. A Jew, Frank became president of the Atlanta B'nai B'rith in 1912. On 27 April 1913, a night watchman at the National Pencil Factory found the body of 13-year-old Mary Phagan who had been brutally murdered. Two days later, Frank was arrested and charged with the murder. The Atlanta press created a mood of hysteria by focusing on Frank's religion and printing lurid and false tales about his personal and religious life. In this climate, Frank was convicted in August and sentenced to death despite clear doubts about his guilt. A national outcry developed and the case was covered in a number of northern journals, including *Collier's* and *Everybody's*. After reviewing the case, the governor of Georgia, John M. Slaton, commuted the death sentence. There was considerable public anger in Georgia orchestrated particularly by the political leader Tom Watson, and on 15 August 1915 a mob broke into the jail abducted Frank and hanged him outside the town of Marietta. No one was ever charged for the murder. Tom Watson was elected to the United States Senate in 1920. Mary Phagan's killing was said to have encouraged the revival of the **Ku Klux Klan** and Leo Frank's murder was clearly indicative of the racial and religious tensions evident in this period.

FRANKFURTER, FELIX (1882–1965). Born in Austria, Felix Frankfurter's family emigrated to America in 1894. Frankfurter gained a law degree at the College of New York and went on to Harvard University where he graduated in 1906. Frankfurter practiced briefly in New York and then became an assistant to **Henry Stimson**, a United States attorney in New York. Frankfurter became a professor in the Harvard Law School in 1914, a position he held until 1939. Influenced by **Louis Brandeis**, Frankfurter was a close associate of the editors of the *New Republic* and a part of the **Progressive** movement. During **World War I** he became assistant secretary of labor and served as secretary for the President's Mediation Commission that investigated the labor unrest in the West in 1917. In the light of protests from **trade**

unions and others, in 1916 President **Wilson** asked Frankfurter to investigate the convictions of **Tom Mooney** and **Warren Billings**, the labor leaders sentenced to death for a bombing in San Francisco in which 10 people had died. Frankfurter reported that there were several grounds for a retrial, and as a consequence the death sentences were commuted. In 1918, Frankfurter was appointed to chair the War Labor Policies Board to unify labor standards used by federal agencies.

After the war, Frankfurter called for recognition of the Bolshevik regime in Russia, defended immigrant members of left-wing groups against deportation, and called for a retrial in the case of **Sacco** and **Vanzetti**. Frankfurter and his proteges were influential in drawing up various pieces of **New Deal** legislation and in 1938 **Franklin D. Roosevelt** nominated him to the **Supreme Court** where he served until 1962. Frankfurter was not consistently "liberal" as a justice and is most remembered for his dissents in *West Virginia State Board of Education v. Barnette* in 1943 and *Baker v. Carr* in 1962. In the first, he rejected the argument that the First Amendment barred mandatory flag salutes; in the second, he rejected any judicial remedy for malapportioned legislatures. Frankfurter was, however, conspicuous in his support of **African Americans** and he wholeheartedly supported the decision against segregated schools in *Brown v. Topeka Board of Education* in 1954. He did not, though, support picketing by African Americans to secure employment in supermarkets (*Hughes v. Superior Court of California* 1950), nor did he approve of sit-ins or other militant tactics.

FROST, ROBERT LEE (1875–1963). Perhaps the greatest American poet of the 20th century, Robert Frost did not complete his university education, but for a while divided his time between farming, teaching, and writing poetry. In 1912, he sold his farm and moved to England and in 1913 published his first collection of verse, *A Boy's Will*. His second collection, *North of Boston*, was published in 1914. Having achieved some critical success, Frost and his family returned to the United States in 1915. *Mountain Interval* was published in 1916 and Frost was appointed to a teaching post at Amherst. He left his post in 1920, established a summer study program at Middlebury College, and was "poet in residence" at Ann Arbor. In 1923, *Selected Poems* and *New Hampshire* appeared; *New Hampshire* won the first of four Pulitzer Prizes that Frost was awarded. For the rest of his career, Frost divided his time between teaching appointments at different colleges.

Frost produced several more volumes of poetry. His *Collected Poems* (1930), *A Further Range* (1936), and *The Witness Tree* (1942) were awarded Pulitzers, and *In the Clearing* (1962) was well received. In 1961, Frost read one of his poems "The Gift Outright" at President John F. Kennedy's inaugural and was awarded the Congressional Medal. Frost is remembered above all for his variations on blank verse and the use of rural images and references to New England in a language easily accessible to the ordinary person.

– G –

GARBO, GRETA (1905–1990). The **movie** star Greta Garbo was born Greta Lovisa Gustafsson in Stockholm, Sweden. Her work as an advertising model in a department store led to a career in film beginning with *Peter the Tramp* (1920). From 1922 to 1924, Garbo studied at the Royal Swedish Dramatic Theater, and she acquired her stage name and reputation as an actress in *The Story of Gosta Berling* (1924). Following her success in Sweden, she moved to Hollywood in 1925 where her beauty and her husky voice perfectly enabled her to play roles of sexual passion. Garbo made a total of 24 films in Hollywood. Her films, in which she often played the part of the tragic heroine, included *Flesh and the Devil* (1927), *Love* (1927), *Anna Christie* (1930), *Mata Hari* (1932), *Grand Hotel* (1932), *Anna Karenina* (1935), *Camille* (1936), and *Ninotchka* (1939). Garbo received four Academy Award nominations for best actress. She retired aged 36 in 1941 and moved to New York City to live a secluded life. Famous for the "Garbo mystique" that she deliberately fostered, she was given a special Oscar in 1954 for unforgettable performances.

GARFIELD, HARRY AUGUSTUS (1863–1942). The son of President James A. Garfield, Harry Garfield studied law at Columbia University and practiced in Cleveland from 1888 to 1903. He taught law at Western Reserve University and then politics at Princeton University from 1903 to 1908, before becoming president of Williams College from

1908 to 1934. During **World War I** Garfield headed the **United States Fuel Administration** and was responsible for bringing some stability to the coal industry. However, faced with competing demands for fuel from industry and the railroads, he ordered a temporary closure of all industry east of the Mississippi. This led to such criticism of **Woodrow Wilson's** administration that it then asserted greater centralized control of the war economy. After the war Garfield resumed his position at Williams College. He was elected president of the American Political Science Association in 1923.

GARNER, JOHN NANCE (1868–1967). The thirty-second vice president of the United States, John Nance Garner was born in a log cabin in Texas. After limited schooling he attended Vanderbilt University briefly, studied law, and qualified for the bar in 1890. Garner practiced law in Uvalde where he became county judge, 1893–96. He was elected as a **Democrat** to the state House of Representatives in 1898 and to the United States House of Representatives in 1903. Garner served until 1933. He was not conspicuous in legislation (it was eight years before he made his first speech) but he gained power by virtue of seniority. Garner eventually became Speaker of the House from 1931 to 1933 when he was elected vice president to **Franklin D. Roosevelt**. His experience gave him a crucial role as liaison with Congress and the Texas connection gave him influence with a number of key figures and he was re-elected in 1936. He has been described as the "most powerful vice president in history." Initially a supporter of the **New Deal**, Garner was increasingly unhappy with the social welfare and prolabor aspects of Roosevelt's program. He became openly hostile when Roosevelt attempted to alter the composition of the **Supreme Court** in 1937 and stood against FDR for the nomination in 1940. When he was unsuccessful, Garner retired to his ranch in Uvalde and took no further part in politics.

GARVEY, MARCUS MOZIAH (1887–1940). Marcus Garvey was the Jamaican-born leader of the **Universal Negro Improvement Association** (UNIA), the black nationalist organization he first established in Jamaica in 1914 and then brought to the United States in 1916. Garvey's brand of nationalism with its call to people of African origin to unite under "One Aim, One God, One Destiny," had a particular appeal to disillusioned **African Americans** after **World War I**. He encouraged black economic self-determination and established a Negro Factories Corporation and a Black Cross as well as a Black Star Shipping Line to assist the movement back to Africa. The UNIA paper, the *Negro World*, was published in several languages and reached an international audience. Garvey claimed over two million supporters, but actual members were probably more in the thousands, with chapters in 30 cities. He outraged many black Americans by meeting the leader of the **Ku Klux Klan** in Georgia and suggesting that their policies of racial separation had much in common. As a consequence of financial irregularities in the running of the Black Star Line he was convicted of mail fraud in 1922 and went to jail in 1925. His sentence was commuted after two years and he was deported to Jamaica. The UNIA failed to recover from this turn of events and Garvey died in relative obscurity in London where he had moved in 1935.

GARY, ELBERT HENRY (1846–1927). Elbert Gary served briefly in the Civil War (1861–65), qualified in law, and eventually established his own law firm. Gary served as a county judge (1882–90) and was president of the Chicago Bar Association (1893–94). In 1898, he became president of the Federal Steel Company and moved to New York City. In 1901, the banker J. P. Morgan gave Gary the responsibility of organizing the U.S. Steel Corporation. Gary became a dominant figure in the corporation for the next 25 years. The steel town of Gary, Indiana, was named after him when it was created in 1913. Gary was also known for his advocacy of the open shop, and his refusal to negotiate with **trade unions** provoked the **steel strike of 1919**.

GEHRIG, LOU (HEINRICH LUDWIG) (1903–1941). Born Heinrich Ludwig Gehrig, Lou Gehrig was outstanding at football and baseball at school. He went to Columbia University in 1921, but was not able to take part in sport until the 1922–23 season because of earlier professional appearances. His performances in baseball led to his signing for the New York Yankees in 1923. He opened the season with the Yankees in 1925 and played every season until 1940. Gehrig hit 41 or more home runs, set the major league record for grand slams

(23), in 1932 was the first American League player to hit four home runs in a single game. His career batting average of .340 ranked him close to **Babe Ruth** and he earned the Most Valuable Player award in 1927, 1934, and 1936. Gehrig removed himself from the Yankees' lineup in 1939 and shortly after was diagnosed with a rare, crippling, and incurable neuromuscular disease. Gehrig was elected to the Baseball Hall of Fame in 1939. Mayor **Fiorello La Guardia** appointed him to the New York City Parole Commission and he continued working in that role until his death.

GENERAL ACCOUNTING OFFICE (GAO). The General Accounting Office was established in the Budget and Accounting Act of 1929 to supervise accounting procedures in the executive departments and agencies of the federal government and to audit federal expenditures.

GENERAL MOTORS CORPORATION. General Motors (GM), now one of the largest automobile manufacturers in the world, was founded in Michigan in 1908 by **William C. Durant** when he brought together the Buick, Oakland, and Oldsmobile companies.

GENEVA DISARMAMENT CONFERENCE, 1932. A conference of 57 nations convened by the **League of Nations** to discuss worldwide disarmament. Although not a member of the League, the United States sent a delegation. Among the many proposals was that of President **Herbert Hoover** who called for an immediate one-third reduction in existing national armaments and the outlawing of chemical warfare, bomber planes, heavy artillery, and tanks. On 27 May 1933, the United States delegation announced that the American government would be prepared to consult with other nations in the face of a threat to peace. The conference proved powerless and collapsed following the withdrawal of Germany in October 1933.

GENEVA NAVAL CONFERENCE, 1927. The Geneva Conference, which took place in Switzerland from 20 June to 24 August 1927, was called by President **Calvin Coolidge** to consider further naval limitations following on from the earlier **Washington Naval Conference**. France and Italy did not accept the invitation, but representatives of Great Britain and Japan took part in discussions with the

Americans. The United States proposals to extend the previously agreed ratios to cover other vessels were rejected by the British and the conference ended without agreement.

GERARD, JAMES WATSON (1867–1952). Gerard was a lawyer and diplomat who had qualified in law at Columbia University and practiced law in New York City from 1892 to 1908 when he became an associate justice of New York Supreme Court. In 1913 he was appointed ambassador to Germany by **Woodrow Wilson** and served until 1917. Gerard was central in representing the United States government's responses to the use of submarines by the Germans. Although he did express some sympathy for the German position, Gerard made it known publicly that unless some peace settlement was reached in 1916, unrestricted submarine warfare would resume. When this occurred in 1917, the United States government broke off diplomatic relations and Gerard was recalled. Gerard published two accounts of his experiences, *My Four Years in Germany* (1917) and *Face to Face with Kaiserism* (1918). During the war, he addressed numerous **Liberty Loans** rallies.

In 1920, Gerard declared himself a candidate for the **Democratic** presidential nomination. He failed to win that or the vice presidential nomination but became chairman of the campaign finance committee. He continued in this or a similar capacity for the next 30 years. When World War II broke out, Gerard advocated United States intervention and spoke out in favor of Lend-Lease in 1941. In 1950, President Harry S. Truman appointed Gerard to the Advisory Board on International Development. The following year Gerard published his memoirs, *My First Eighty-Three Years in America. See also* WORLD WAR I.

GERSHWIN, GEORGE (1898–1937). George Gershwin, born Jacob Gershvin, became one of America's most famous composers of orchestral works, popular songs, jazz, and musical comedies. He worked as a pianist for a music publisher from 1914 to 1917 when he became a theater pianist. In 1919 he achieved his first hit with "Swanee," later recorded by **Al Jolson.** From 1920 on Gershwin composed musical reviews, Broadway plays, and orchestral pieces. His best known works were *Rhapsody in Blue* (1923), *Piano Concerto in F*

(1925), *An American in Paris* (1928), and the opera *Porgy and Bess* (1935), all notable for their combination of jazz and orchestral music.

Together with his brother **Ira Gershwin**, George Gershwin composed many hit songs for musicals. Among the best-known songs in these were "Fascinating Rhythm," "Someone to Watch Over Me," "'S Wonderful," "Embraceable You," and "I Got Rhythm." In 1936, the Gershwins went to Hollywood, where they wrote the music for *Shall We Dance?* in 1937. Starring Fred Astaire and Ginger Rogers, the **movie** included such hits as "Let's Call the Whole Thing Off" and "They Can't Take That Away from Me." The Gershwins provided the music for two more movies, *A Damsel in Distress* (1937) and *The Goldwyn Follies* (1937), before George's death. Gershwin's music was incorporated into a number of films after his death—*Rhapsody in Blue* (1945), *An American in Paris* (1951), and *Manhattan* (1979).

GERSHWIN, IRA (1896–1983). Born Israel Gershvin, Ira was the brother of **George Gershwin**. Ira provided the lyrics for many of George's compositions including the songs for the musicals *Lady Be Good* (1924), *Tip-toes* (1925), *Oh Kay!* (1926), *Funny Face* (1927), *Strike up the Band* (1927), and the Pulitzer Prize-winning *Of Thee I Sing* (1931). From 1936, Ira provided the lyrics for George's music in a number of Hollywood **movies**. Following George's death Ira wrote the lyrics for *Lady in the Dark* (1940), *Cover Girl* (1944), *Firebrand of Florence* (1945), *Park Avenue* (1946), *The Barkleys of Broadway* (1949), *A Star Is Born* (1954), and *The Country Girl* (1954). He was involved in the making of *An American in Paris* (1951), which incorporated some of his and George's earlier work and which won an Academy Award.

GIFFORD, WALTER SHERMAN (1885–1966). Walter Gifford graduated from Harvard University in 1905. He had already begun work for the Western Electric Telegraph Company and in 1905 he became the company's assistant secretary and treasurer in New York City. In 1908, Gifford joined the parent company, American Telephone & Telegraph (AT&T), as a statistician, and, after a brief break to manage a copper mine, in 1911 he became the company's chief statistician. In 1916 Gifford was appointed supervising director of the

Committee on Industrial Preparedness of the Naval Consulting Board and later director of the **Council of National Defense**. After the war Gifford was involved in the **Paris Peace Conference** as a member of the Inter-Allied Munitions Committee.

Gifford returned to AT&T as its comptroller in 1918. He became vice president of finance in 1920, was elected to the board of directors in 1922, and executive vice president in 1923. Gifford sold AT&T's 17 radio stations to the National Broadcasting Corporation (NBC) in order to avoid prosecution of the company under the antitrust laws. In 1925, he sold foreign telephone operations to International Telephone & Telegraph Company (IT&T). During the 1930s, AT&T automated its operations and also marketed telephones to middle-class families. Under Gifford's leadership, AT&T had become the largest corporation in America by the 1930s. During World War II, Gifford was a member of the War Resources Board and chair of the Industry Advisory Committee of the Board of War Communications. In 1948, he gave up his leading role at AT&T and in 1949 became honorary chairman of the board. In 1950, President Harry S. Truman appointed Gifford as ambassador to Great Britain. He retired in 1953.

GILLETT, FREDERICK HUNTINGTON (1851–1935). The future congressman and senator for Massachusetts, Frederick Gillett graduated from Amherst in 1874 and Harvard Law School in 1877. He began a law practice in Springfield the same year and became assistant attorney general for Massachusetts in 1879. Gillett served in the state house of representatives from 1890 to 1891 and then was elected as a **Republican** to the United States House of Representatives in 1893, serving until 1925. Gillett made a name for himself as an able orator, and he spoke in defense of **African American** voting rights in the South and in favor of civil service reform. During **World War I** Gillett was a member of the Appropriations Subcommittee responsible for reviewing the details of military spending bills. He became speaker of the House in 1919 and held the position until 1924 when he was elected to the Senate. Gillett had opposed the **League of Nations**, but supported the **Permanent Court of International Justice**. He endorsed **Prohibition** and the **Volstead Act**. Gillett retired from public office in 1931.

GILMAN, CHARLOTTE PERKINS (1860–1935). The great-niece of Harriet Beecher Stowe, writer, economist, and **women**'s rights theorist Charlotte Perkins Gilman grew up in a poor family in Connecticut. She had little formal schooling but studied art for a brief period at Rhode Island School of Design and began work designing greetings cards, teaching art, and offering private tuition. Following her marriage and the birth of her daughter in 1885, Gilman suffered from acute depression and was advised by a well-known neurologist, Dr. Silas Weir Mitchell, to give up all work, never touch a pen or brush, and devote herself to family life. Gilman rejected this remedy, moved to California, and in 1894 divorced her husband with whom she left her daughter. Gilman supported herself thereafter through her prolific writing and lecturing.

Gilman wrote some 200 short stories, 10 novels, plus various works of theory. Between 1909 and 1916, she produced her own journal, *Forerunner*. In much of her writing, she argued that women's oppression began in the home. Gilman urged women to find their own identity and stressed particularly the need for economic independence. Her famous short story "Yellow Wallpaper" (1892), was based on her own experience of illness and response to the medical diagnosis. Her international reputation was established with the publication of *Women and Economics: A Study of the Economic Relation between Men and Women* (1898). Gilman's other work included *Concerning Children* (1903), *The Man-Made World* (1911), *His Religion and Hers* (1923), and the novels *What Diantha Did* (1910), *The Crux* (1911), and *Herland: A Feminist Utopian Novel*, published in serial form in 1915. That year, Gilman cofounded the **Woman's Peace Party** with **Jane Addams**. In 1935, Gilman, suffering from inoperable cancer, took her own life.

GISH, DOROTHY (1898–1968). The younger sister of **Lillian Gish**, Dorothy Gish appeared on the stage in touring melodramas in 1902. In 1912, with Lillian, she began work in film under the direction of **D. W. Griffith**. She made over 20 **movies** in the next few years and in 1917 rose to stardom in Griffith's *Hearts of the World*. Gish made a name as the "female **Chaplin**" playing comic roles, and in 1918 she was signed by Paramount. After playing comic roles in several films, she scored another success in serious parts in *Orphans of the Storm*

(1922) and *Nell Gwyn* (1926). The latter was an English-made film. After several more movies with British director Herbert Wilcox, Gish returned to Broadway in 1928 and spent the next 30 years in theater. She appeared to some acclaim in *The Inspector General, Getting Married*, and *The Pillars of Society* in 1931. She retired from the stage finally in 1956. Gish also made appearances on television in the 1950s and made her final film appearance in *The Cardinal* (1964).

GISH, LILLIAN (1893–1993). Along with **Clara Bow** and **Mary Pickford**, Lillian Gish was one of the great stars of early silent movies. However, her career on both stage and screen continued successfully well beyond the silent era. Her stage career began in 1902 but in 1912 she and her sister **Dorothy** met the film director **D. W. Griffith**, who cast them in *An Unseen Enemy* (1912). Gish worked with Griffith for 10 years and starred in his classic film *The **Birth of a Nation*** (1915) and *Intolerance* (1916). In these and other **movies**, she developed the role of the pure, virgin heroine. During **World War I**, she starred in several of Griffith's propaganda films, including *Hearts of the World* (1918). In the early 1920s, Gish and Griffith parted company and she worked first with Inspiration Films and then Metro-Goldwyn-Mayer. After making several more movies, including *La Boheme* (1926), *The Scarlet Letter* (1926), and *The Wind* (1928), she returned to the stage and won critical acclaim in *Uncle Vanya, Hamlet, The Star Maker*, and other productions.

In the mid-1940s Gish returned to Hollywood in supporting roles in several films including *Duel in the Sun* (1947)—for which she was nominated for an Academy Award—and *Night of the Hunter* (1955). Gish also worked in television and starred in several dramas and television films, including *Arsenic and Old Lace* (1969) and *Hobson's Choice* (1983). In 1971 Gish was awarded an honorary Oscar and in 1984 the American Film Institute's Lifetime Achievement Award. Her last film role was in *Whales of August* (1987).

GLASGOW, ELLEN ANDERSON GHOLSON (1873–1945). Ellen Glasgow was born and bred into a wealthy family in Virginia. Educated at home, she began writing as a teenager. Her novels presented a fictional social history of Virginia since 1850 that rejected the romantic stereotypes of southern life and showed instead the class conflicts of the region. Her first novel, *The Descendant*, was published anonymously in 1897. Her later works included *The Voice of the People* (1900) and *The Deliverance* (1904). In *Virginia* (1913), *Life and Gabriella* (1916), and *Barren Ground* (1925), Glasgow concentrated on **women** and their responses to the patriarchal code of the South. Female characters were also central in her comedies, *The Romantic Comedians* (1926), *They Stooped to Folly* (1929), and *The Sheltered Life* (1932). Several of Glasgow's novels were on the best-seller's list in the 1920s and in 1942 she was awarded the Pulitzer Prize for *In This Our Life* (1941). Her autobiography, *The Woman Within*, was published posthumously in 1954.

GLASS, CARTER (1858–1946). After holding various types of employment, Carter Glass began work as a reporter in Virginia in 1880 and eventually became a newspaper editor and owner. He served in the state senate from 1899 to 1903 as a **Democrat** and then represented Virginia in the House of Representatives from 1902 to 1919 and in the Senate from 1920 until his death. An advocate of **banking** reform, he sponsored the **Federal Reserve Act** in 1913 and was secretary of the Treasury between 1918 and 1920. Glass was a member of the Democratic National Committee from 1916 to 1928 and, unusually for a southerner, he supported **Al Smith** in 1928. In 1932, with Representative Henry Steagall, he cosponsored the act that kept the United States on the Gold Standard; in 1933 he cosponsored the **Glass-Steagall Banking Act** that established the Federal Deposit Insurance Corporation. Increasingly, however, as an advocate of states' rights Glass opposed the **New Deal**. He did support **Roosevelt**'s foreign policy and opposed isolationism.

GLASS-OWEN ACT. *See* FEDERAL RESERVE ACT.

GLASS-STEAGALL BANKING ACT, 1932. A measure passed to stop gold withdrawals and stabilize **banking** during the **Depression** by providing government securities to guarantee Federal Reserve notes.

GOETHALS, GEORGE WASHINGTON (1858–1928). A graduate of West Point military academy Goethals served in the Army Corps of Engineers. He worked on a number of navigational improvements of United States rivers and in 1907 was appointed chief engineer on the Panama construction project by **Theodore Roosevelt**. The canal was opened ahead of schedule in 1914. He was appointed governor of the Panama Canal Zone in 1914. He was briefly general manager of the **United States Shipping Board's Emergency Fleet Corporation** in 1917 but resigned in opposition to the expansion of the merchant fleet with wooden vessels. In 1918, Goethals became head of the War Department's Division of Purchase and supplies. He retired in 1919 and established his own firm of consulting engineers.

GOLDMAN, EMMA (1869–1940). Born in Lithuania, Goldman emigrated to the United States in 1885. Together with the Polish-born Alexander Berkman, she became a leader in the American Anarchist Movement and editor from 1906 to 1917 of *Mother Earth*. A campaigner for sexual equality, birth control, and the right of free speech, Goldman also denounced **World War I** as an imperialist conflict. Together with Berkman, she was tried and convicted for violation of the draft laws. Sentenced to two years in prison in 1918, she was deported to the Union of Soviet Socialist Republics (USSR) on her release after 20 months as a part of the **Palmer Raids** in 1919. She was expelled from the Soviet Union in 1921 and lived in Great Britain and Canada. Goldman visited Spain in the 1930s and campaigned on behalf of anarchists involved in the Spanish Civil War. Her autobiography, *Living My Life*, was published in 1931.

GOLDWYN, SAMUEL (1882–1974). The pioneer Hollywood film producer Samuel Goldwyn was born Schmuel Gelbfisz in Warsaw, Poland. He fled Poland in 1894 and made his way first to England and then in 1898 to the United States, where he took the name Samuel Goldfish. Goldwyn found work as a glove-cutter in New York and then became a traveling salesman. In 1912, Goldwyn established a film company with his brother-in-law, Jesse L. Lasky. In 1916, the company merged with Adolph Zukor's Famous Players to become the Famous Players-Lasky company that later became Paramount Pictures. Goldwyn left the company in 1915 and established Goldwyn Pictures Corporation—and changed his name. The company in turn became Metro-Goldwyn-Mayer in 1924, but Goldwyn again left to establish his own Samuel Goldwyn Presents and in 1925 he joined United Artists. In 1941, he signed with RKO, where he remained until the end of his career. From 1923 to 1959, Goldwyn produced 80 motion pictures, many of high quality. Among his films were *Bulldog Drummond* (1929), *Dodsworth* (1936), *Wuthering Heights* (1939), *The Best Years of Our Lives* (1946), *Guys and Dolls* (1955), *Porgy and Bess* (1959). In his long career, Goldwyn helped establish the studio system in Hollywood and discovered many **movie** stars.

GOMPERS, SAMUEL (1850–1924). The American labor leader was born of Dutch-Jewish parents in London. Gompers' family emigrated to New York, where he worked as a cigar maker. A leading member of the Cigarmakers International Union, he became a founder and the first president of the Federation of Organized Trades and Labor Unions of the United States and Canada in 1881, which became the **American Federation of Labor** (AFL) in 1886. He was elected first president of the AFL, a position he held until his death apart from 1894–95. Under his leadership, the AFL adopted a conservative position, representing skilled craft workers, rejecting state intervention in the workplace or welfare, and was essentially apolitical. However, in the face of **Republican** antipathy, Gompers actively supported **Woodrow Wilson** in the 1912 election. He strongly backed Wilson's war policies, became a member of the **Advisory Commission to the Council of National Defense**, and discouraged strikes or other "disloyal" activity. He was part of the United States delegation to the **Versailles Peace Conference** at the end of war and served as chair of the Commission on International Labor Legislation in 1919. Gompers' significance declined with that of the labor movement after the war and the return of a Republican administration. By the time of his death, the AFL was little stronger than it had been before the war. *See also* TRADE UNIONS.

GORE, THOMAS PRYOR (1870–1949). Although blind from childhood, Thomas Gore qualified as a lawyer in Tennessee and established a practice in Texas. In 1901, he moved to Oklahoma territory, where he was elected as a **Democrat** to the territorial council in 1902. He became one of the state's first two senators in 1907 and was the first totally blind person to become a U.S. senator. He supported **Woodrow Wilson**'s program, but opposed entry into **World War I**. In 1916 he drew up a resolution warning Americans against traveling on the ships of belligerent powers. During the war he spoke against the introduction of selective service and government controls. He also opposed the **League of Nations**. He failed to regain the Democratic nomination in 1920 and practiced law until he returned to the Senate until 1930. He failed to be re-elected in 1936 because of his opposition to the **New Deal**. Gore remained in Washington, D.C., to practice law and added Indian affairs to his areas of expertise.

GRANGE, "RED" (HAROLD EDWARD) (1903–1991). The famous 1920s football player, coach and broadcaster, Red Grange was born Harold Edward Grange, but was nicknamed "Red" because of his hair color. Grange was a gifted athlete from school age on and when he went to the University of Illinois in 1922 he immediately became a successful football player. In 1924, Grange became a national hero when he amassed 480 yards against Michigan. Three weeks later, he scored three touchdowns and amassed another 450 yards against the University of Chicago. He continued to perform at that level the following season and then announced that he was turning professional. In 1925, Grange made his first appearance for the Chicago Bears and his performances were to give a considerable boost to the fledgling National Football League (NFL). The following year, Grange played for the new American Football League team the New York Yankees, later re-admitted to the NFL. Grange was injured in 1927, returned to the Chicago Bears in 1929 and played until 1934.

After leaving football, Grange worked for a soft drink company and then became an insurance broker in 1942. In 1942, he became the first athlete to become a sportscaster when he began part-time radio broadcasting. He was to cover more than 480 games before he retired in 1969. Grange was named to the College Football Hall of Fame in 1951 and the Pro Football Hall of Fame in 1963.

GRANT, MADISON (1865–1937). Although qualified in law, Madison Grant's chief interests were in natural history and ethnology. He was one of the founders of the New York Zoological Society in 1895 and served first as its secretary until 1924 and as president from 1925 until his death. He was, however, better known for his writing on theories of racial superiority and his support of **immigration** control. His writings included *The Passing of the Great Race* (1916), *The Conquest of a Continent* (1933), and, with C. S. Davison, *The Founders of the Republic on Immigration, Naturalization, and Aliens* (1928), and *The Alien in Our Midst* (1930). From 1922 until 1937 Grant was vice president of the Immigration Restriction League and he helped to frame the **Quota Act of 1924** that further restricted immigration to the United States.

GREAT DEPRESSION. The "Great Depression" was the worldwide economic crisis that followed the **Wall Street Crash** and the Depression that began in the United States in 1929. The calling in or cessation of foreign loans and the imposition of high tariffs led to a shrinking in international trade. As prices fell and trade shrank, the number of unemployed workers worldwide was estimated to be more than 30 million by 1933, with two-thirds of those in Germany, Great Britain, and the United States.

The Wall Street Crash was not the cause of the collapse, merely the trigger that revealed the underlying weaknesses of international markets and the United States' economy in particular. The apparent prosperity of the **"Roaring Twenties"** masked a number of flaws, including the maldistribution of incomes, overproduction and the build up of inventories, the problems of **farming**, the instability of **banks**, and imbalances in the international economy. The breakdown of financial institutions in the United States led to the failure of more than 5,000 banks between 1929 and 1932, and as money and credit dried up, businesses also reduced output or failed completely. Workers found their wages or hours of work cut and many were laid off altogether. By 1933, industrial production had fallen to less than 50 percent of its 1929 levels. The **automobile** industry that had played such a part in the prosperity of the 1920s was operating on 20 percent of its capacity.

Unemployment had reached an estimated 17 million, or 25 percent of the labor force. Farmers, already suffering in the 1920s, saw their situation deteriorate further as commodity prices fell by 55 percent between 1929 and 1932. Almost a quarter of farmers lost their property through foreclosures, and others were driven out by drought and dust storms in the early 1930s, joining the thousands of migrants, the "Okies" and "Arkies," heading West. Urban workers too took to the road as 250,000 families lost their homes in addition to their jobs. Many men abandoned their families and the number of female-headed households increased. Although many **women** were now forced to seek work, gender-based discrimination increased as priority was often given to men. Similarly, **African Americans** found themselves "last hired, first fired" and black unemployment rates were twice as high as those of whites. Prejudice against Hispanic Americans forced half a million to return to Mexico in the 1930s.

Many Americans began to protest as their economic plight worsened. Farmers destroyed produce or poured milk into the road; foreclosures were prevented by mob action; unemployed workers marched in protest sometimes organized by **Socialists** or **Communists**. In 1932, veterans of **World War I** marched on Washington, D.C., as part of a **Bonus Army** calling for payment of war bonuses. Their forcible removal from the capital was the last nail in the political coffin of President **Herbert Hoover**, whose name had become synonymous with the Depression. Hoover's inability to abandon a commitment to limited federal action and his reliance on "voluntarism," led to his political defeat by **Franklin D. Roosevelt** in the election of 1932. Roosevelt promised the nation a **"New Deal"** and the 1930s were to witness a whole series of programs aimed at bringing "relief, recovery, and reform." The result of this political change was the transformation of American politics and the beginning of a welfare state. However, although the situation was considerably alleviated by the New Deal, it was the expansion of industry that came with World War II that finally ended the Depression. That conflict was itself in part a result of the economic and political problems caused by the Great Depression in Europe and elsewhere.

GREAT MIGRATION. During **World War I**, **African Americans** found new employment opportunities as war industries boomed and **immigration**, the traditional source of factory labor, declined. As a consequence labor agents from northern industries set out to recruit black workers from the South. The black press, particularly the

Chicago Defender and the *Crisis* (the journal of the **National Association for the Advancement of Colored People** [NAACP]), also called upon the black population to escape discrimination and segregation for a better life in the North. As a result approximately 400,000 African Americans migrated to northern industrial centers between 1915 and 1920. Over 65,000 African Americans moved to Chicago alone. New York City and Philadelphia also attracted huge numbers. The new workers crowded into already congested ghettos such as **Harlem** in New York, leading to problems of overcrowding. Competition for housing and jobs created tensions that led to riots in **East St. Louis** in 1917, and Chicago, Washington, D.C., and other towns in the **"Red Summer"** of 1919. However, out of the violence and the new urban centers grew a mood of defiance articulated by **"New Negro"** and a celebration of blackness in the **Harlem Renaissance**.

GREAT WAR. *See* WORLD WAR I.

GREEN, WILLIAM (1870–1952). The labor leader William Green was an Ohio coal miner who rose through the ranks of the United Mine Workers of America (UMWA) to become president of the Ohio district in 1906. In 1910, he was elected to the Ohio State Senate as a **Democrat** and served two terms. As the Democratic Party floor leader he helped secure the passage of Ohio's Workmen's Compensation Act, a law restricting **women**'s working hours, and the introduction of income tax. In 1911, he returned to the UMWA as union statistician, and in 1913 was elected UMWA secretary-treasurer, a post he held until 1924. In 1913, **Samuel Gompers** appointed him vice president of the **American Federation of Labor** (AFL). He succeeded Gompers in 1924 and continued his predecessor's conservative policies. He opposed strikes and although he personally believed in industrial rather than craft unionism, he did not actively campaign for it. Green resisted those in the AFL Committee of Industrial Organizations and he continued his opposition after the formation of the Congress of Industrial Organizations (CIO) in 1938. The AFL's conservative policy remained largely unchanged and the two labor organizations stayed divided until after his death. *See also* TRADE UNIONS.

GREENWICH VILLAGE. Greenwich Village is a residential area of Manhattan, New York City, centered on Washington Square Park. In the decade or so before World War I, it became the focus for a literary and artistic community.

GREGORY, THOMAS WATT (1861–1933). Thomas Gregory qualified in law from the University of Texas in 1885 and established a law practice in Austin until 1913. Gregory was a leading Texas **Democrat** and became Austin's assistant city attorney from 1891 to 1894. He supported **Woodrow Wilson**'s nomination in 1912 and in 1913 was appointed special assistant to the attorney general. In 1914, Gregory became attorney general and after America had entered **World War I** was responsible for enforcing the **Espionage** and **Sedition Acts**. Gregory also encouraged citizens to report disloyal acts and he enlisted the aid of voluntary vigilante organizations like the **American Protective League**. Gregory resigned in 1919 and took part in the **Paris Peace Conference** as an adviser. From October 1919 to January 1920, Gregory was involved in President Wilson's Second Industrial Conference convened to improve postwar labor relations. He then returned to a law practice in Washington, D.C. He supported the election of **Franklin D. Roosevelt** in 1932.

GREY, (PEARL) ZANE (1872–1939). The famous writer of Western fiction, Zane Grey, was born in Ohio and christened Pearl Zane Gray but later changed his name. Grey trained in dentistry but published his first novel, *Betty Zane*, in 1903. In 1907, he visited the West and produced his first Western, *The Last of the Plainsmen*, in 1908. His first popular success was achieved with *Riders of the Purple Sage* in 1912. *The Lone Star Ranger* (1915) reached the best-seller list and Grey was one of the most widely read authors of his day. Many of his stories first appeared in serial form but altogether he wrote more than 80 Western adventure stories that formed the basis for almost 100 movies. Grey was also a keen fisherman and wrote many books on the subject, including *Tales of Swordfish and Tuna* (1927) and *Tales of Tahitian Waters* (1931). Grey died practicing deep-sea fishing in California.

GRIFFITH, DAVID WARK (1875–1948). D. W. Griffith was one of the great pioneers of motion pictures. After working in theater, he became first an actor and then a director with the American Mutoscope and Biograph Company in 1908. He developed a group of new **movie** stars, including **Mary Pickford** and **Lillian Gish**, but also with cameraman Billy Bitzer, established new techniques with location filming, long shots, and close-ups. He left Biograph in 1913, after making almost 500 films, to become an independent producer and established his reputation with the first four-reel film, *Judith of Bethulia* (1914), *The Birth of a Nation* (1915), and *Intolerance* (1916). His *Hearts of the World* (1918) was an enormously successful propaganda epic about the war.

In 1920, Griffith joined with **Charlie Chaplin**, **Douglas Fairbanks**, and Pickford, to form their own production company, the United Artists Corporation. He directed *Broken Blossoms* (1919), *Way Down East* (1920), *The Orphans of the Storm* (1922), *America* (1924), *Battle of the Sexes* (1928), and *The Lady of the Pavements* (1929). Griffith also made two talkies: *Abraham Lincoln* (1930) and *The Struggle* (1931). However, his later films in the 1920s did not match his earlier successes and he sold his interests in United Artists in 1933.

– H –

HAITI. After **Philander Knox** had persuaded United States financiers to invest in the national bank of the Caribbean republic of Haiti in 1910, there was considerable concern for those interests when a revolution broke out the following year. After further disturbances United States Marines were sent to the island in 1915 and American officials were placed in control of customs, policing, and other aspects of government. The marines were not withdrawn until 1934.

HAMMER V. DAGENHART. In 1918, the United States **Supreme Court** ruled by 5–4 in *Hammer v. Dagenhart* that the **Child Labor Law** of 1916 was unconstitutional on the grounds that the regulation of interstate commerce could not extend to the conditions of labor.

HAND, (BILLINGS) LEARNED (1872–1961). Educated at Albany Academy and Harvard, Learned Hand graduated from Harvard Law School in 1896. From 1897 to 1902 he practiced law in Albany then moved to New York City. President **Taft** named Hand a district judge in New York in 1909. Hand was a supporter of civic reform and an acquaintance of **Theodore Roosevelt, Herbert Croly**, and **Walter Lippmann**. He supported Roosevelt's **Progressive Party** campaign in 1912 and was involved in the founding of the *New Republic* in 1914. In 1924 Hand was named to the Court of Appeals for the Second Circuit, covering New York, Connecticut, and Vermont. He became chief judge of that court in 1939 and served until he retired in 1951.

In the course of his 52 years on the federal bench, Hand wrote more than 2,000 opinions and established a reputation as one of the leading jurists of his day. During **World War I** Hand's rulings did much to protect the publication of antiwar sentiments during a period of hysteria. Regarded as "the best judge never to become a Supreme Court justice," Hand was the author of *Spirit of Liberty* (1952) and *The Bill of Rights* (1958).

HANSON, OLE (1874–1940). Ole Hanson was born to Norwegian parents in Wisconsin where he grew up and studied law. Hanson went to Chicago where he was briefly a mining broker before he set off on travels of the South and Midwest before settling in Seattle in 1902. Hanson was fairly successful in the real estate business and in 1908 was elected to the Washington state legislature. In 1918, he was elected mayor of Seattle on a nonpartisan ticket, and he rose to national prominence during the **Seattle General Strike** in 1919. Hanson characterized the strike as the work of anarchists and Bolsheviks, and in a reference to the Russian Revolution of 1917, warned that Seattle could become the "Petrograd of America." He strengthened the police force and threatened to use violence against the strikers if necessary, but the strike collapsed of its own accord. Hanson then criss-crossed the country speaking about the Bolshevik threat and adding to the mood that fueled the **"Red Scare."** He indicated that he would be a candidate for the **Republican** presidential nomination, but to little effect. Having resigned as mayor, Hanson gave up politics and moved to California, where he again established a successful real estate business.

HAPGOOD, NORMAN (1868–1937). The journalist and political reformer Norman Hapgood graduated from Harvard University in 1890 and from Harvard Law School in 1893. After a year in a law firm he became a newspaper reporter and worked at the *Chicago Evening Post*, the *Milwaukee Sentinel*, *New York Evening Post*, and *New York Commercial Advertiser*. Hapgood also published a number of historical biographies: *Abraham Lincoln* (1899), *George Washington* (1901), and *The Stage in America, 1897–1900* (1901). In 1902 he became editor of *Collier's Weekly* and contributed to **Progressive** campaigns in favor of pure food and drug legislation and conservation. Hapgood continued to produce books with a study of *Theodore Roosevelt* (1905) and *Industry and Progress* (1911). In 1912, he resigned from *Collier's* because of its support for **Theodore Roosevelt** rather than **Woodrow Wilson**.

In 1913, Hapgood became editor of *Harper's Weekly*, which was strongly pro-Wilson. He left the journal in 1913. In 1916, he was appointed United States minister to Denmark, but he resigned in the face of Senate opposition to his appointment. From 1923 to 1925, Hapgood took over *Hearst's International Magazine* and used it to criticize conservative groups including the **Ku Klux Klan**. Hapgood supported **Robert M. La Follette** in 1924 and governor **Al Smith** throughout the 1920s. When Smith lost the **Democratic** presidential nomination to **Franklin Roosevelt** in 1932, Hapgood became a supporter of elements of the **New Deal**. He also spoke out against the dangers of fascism and Nazism on Europe. From 1936 until his death, Hapgood edited the *Christian Register*.

HARDING, FLORENCE MABEL KLING DeWOLFE (1860–1924). The future wife of President **Warren Harding** was born Florence Kling in Marion, Ohio. She studied music at the Cincinnati Conservatory, but in 1879 eloped with Henry DeWolfe by whom she had a son. She divorced DeWolfe in 1886 and married Harding in 1891. Florence Harding assisted her husband with the production of his newspaper, the *Marion Star*, and supported his political ambitions. Referred to by her husband as "the duchess," Mrs. Harding was a hard-working first lady. She was involved in veterans' causes, began public tours of the White House, entertained a large number of visitors to the White House, and reinstated the Easter egg roll on the

White House lawns. She also read her husband's speeches and apparently made suggestions as to their content. Mrs. Harding supported **women's suffrage** and accepted an honorary membership in the national **Women's Party.** Following President Harding's death in 1923, some observers suggested that Mrs. Harding had poisoned her husband either because she discovered he had a mistress or because of the scandals surrounding his administration. Most historians discount such claims.

HARDING, WARREN GAMALIEL (1865–1923). Twenty-ninth president of the United States. Harding was a **Republican** politician often depicted as a political nonentity by historians. Born in Blooming Grove, Ohio, he was a successful small-town newspaper owner-editor, who had served as Ohio State senator, 1900–04, lieutenant governor of Ohio, 1904–06, and United States senator, 1915–21. Harding was a supporter of **William Howard Taft** in 1912 and became chairman of the Republican National Convention in 1916. As a senator he supported **women's suffrage** and national **Prohibition** but was one of those who opposed the **League of Nations** and Versailles settlement. When the 1920 Republican convention in Chicago became deadlocked between **Leonard Wood** and **Frank O. Lowden,** the affable and convivial Harding was recognized as the most available candidate by a group of senators meeting in the famous "smoke-filled room" in the Blackstone Hotel. He was nominated on the 10th ballot. Described as "the best of the second-raters," whose only qualification was his looks, Harding was in fact quite a popular president. In an election with a low turnout, he defeated the **Democratic** candidate **James M. Cox** by 16,143,407 votes to 9,130,328 and by 404 Electoral College votes to 127. His success was seen as a repudiation of the idealism of **Woodrow Wilson** and a reflection of the mood of postwar reaction, which Harding captured in a speech promising "a return to normalcy."

In his first address to Congress, Harding called for a reduction in the size of government, the lowering of taxes, a reduction of **railroad** rates, the promotion of agricultural interests, a national budget system, and a department of public welfare. However, the president did little to push these measures through and his most significant accomplishment was the creation of the **Bureau of the Budget** with **Charles G.**

Dawes as director. Harding vetoed the soldiers' bonus bill and supported the passage of the **Fordney-McCumber Tariff Act** of 1922. He did speak out against discrimination against black Americans and he reversed Wilson's policies of excluding **African Americans** from federal appointments. Harding also approved the **Sheppard-Towner Act** in 1921 and called for the creation of a federal department of public welfare. Significantly Harding also personally approved the pardon of **Eugene Debs**. Little was done to counter the postwar recession and rising unemployment, and mounting farm distress in the first year of the Harding administration was reflected in the setbacks for the Republicans in the 1922 congressional elections. President Harding also allowed Attorney General **Harry S. Daugherty** to use injunctions in suppressing the national miners' strike in 1922. However, he supported **Herbert Hoover** in bringing pressure on the steel industry to accept the eight-hour day for workers.

In general, Harding allowed his cabinet officers to get on with their own business, and the key cabinet officers were Secretary of Commerce Hoover, Secretary of the Treasury **Andrew Mellon**, Secretary of Agriculture **Henry C. Wallace**, and Secretary of State **Charles Evan Hughes**. It was the latter who was responsible for improving relations with Latin American countries, sending observers to the League of Nations, and calling the **Washington Naval Conference** to limit armaments.

Although the Harding administration clearly included several distinguished individuals, it would be remembered most of all for scandal and corruption. Harding himself has been judged a failure, who although personally honest, appointed more venal friends and cronies to government office. While the president seemed more concerned with his golf game and poker evenings, his former campaign manager Harry S. Daugherty, now attorney general, turned a blind eye to failures within the Justice Department and was probably personally involved in other major scandals. The director of the newly created Veterans' Bureau, Charles R. Forbes, sold off government surplus and accepted bribes. Secretary of the Interior **Albert Fall** was eventually convicted and jailed for taking bribes from oilmen **Harry Sinclair** and **Edward Doheny** in return for leases of naval oil reserves in California and at **Teapot Dome**, Wyoming.

As some of these developments began to surface and in response to his declining popularity, in June 1923 Harding began a "Voyage of Understanding," a national tour that started in Alaska. En route from there to California, he collapsed and died suddenly as a result of a thrombosis. How much he knew of the scandals that quickly emerged following his death is not clear, but his own reputation was damaged by the later claims by Nan Britton that she had an affair with the president and that he had fathered her daughter. A former security man confirmed these claims in his own memoirs and also suggested that Harding might have been poisoned. Historians have largely discounted such stories, although it does now appear that Harding had an extra-marital relationship with another woman, Cary Phillips.

HARLEM. The area a few blocks north of 125th Street, bounded by Seventh and Lenox Avenue in New York City became the center of the city's **African American** population from the early 1900s on when a black realtor Philip Payton began to rent property. As white families moved out and property prices fell, more African Americans moved in. In 1914, the black population was estimated to be 50,000. This number increased dramatically following the **Great Migration** of African Americans from the South during **World War I**. By 1930, Harlem was almost entirely a black community numbering more than 200,000, and it had become the cultural capital for African Americans. *See also* HARLEM RENAISSANCE; JAZZ.

HARLEM RENAISSANCE, c. 1920–c. 1933. The **Harlem** Renaissance was the sudden growth in **African American** cultural expression following **World War I** that centered on the black community in New York City. The African American urban population in the North had grown during the **Great Migration** and was to provide a base for new movements and ideas such as **Marcus Garvey's** Universal Negro Improvement Association. The remarkable literary and artistic development in many ways reflected the mood of the **"New Negro"** in its demonstration of black consciousness and celebration of the African heritage. African American writers like **Claude McKay**, **Jean Toomer**, Countee Cullen, **Zora Neale Hurston,**

Nella Larsen, and **Langston Hughes** were encouraged by editors such as **Charles S. Johnson** of the **National Urban League**'s *Opportunity*, **W. E. B. Du Bois** and **Jessie Fauset** of the **National Association for the Advancement of Colored People**'s (NAACP) *Crisis*, and by white critics such as **Carl Van Vechten**. Some of their work was also published in *The New Negro* (1925) edited by **Alain Locke**. Black artists such as Aaron Douglas, Richmond Barthe, and Nancy Prophet produced African-inspired sculptures and paintings while Archibald J. Motley, and later Jacob Lawrence, depicted scenes of black life in the United States. It could be said that black music came of age during the 1920s with the development and acceptance in white culture of **jazz**. Bandleaders and musicians like **Duke Ellington**, **Fletcher Henderson**, and **Louis Armstrong** became major performers and recording stars during the period. To some extent the Renaissance ended with the onset of the **Depression** but also with the sense of increasing pessimism that followed the Harlem race riot of 1935.

HARVEY, GEORGE BRINTON McCLELLAN (1864–1928). George Harvey was a journalist who became the owner and editor of the *North American Review* (1899–1926), the president with a controlling interest in the publisher Harper & Bros. (1900–15), and editor of *Harper's Weekly* (1918–21) and *Harvey's Weekly* (1918–21). He supported **Woodrow Wilson** for governor of New Jersey and for the presidency, but opposed the **League of Nations**. It was in Harvey's room in the Blackstone Hotel, Chicago, later famously known as the "smoke-filled room," that the deadlock over the **Republican** nomination was broken in favor of **Warren Harding**. Harvey's support for Harding in 1920 was rewarded with his appointment as ambassador to Great Britain, 1921–23. In 1924, he described the choice in the election as "Coolidge or chaos."

HAUGEN, GILBERT NELSON (1859–1933). Gilbert Haugen studied at Decorah Institute and Janesville Business College, Iowa, before establishing his own farm and farm service businesses in Kensett in 1877. He was elected as justice of the peace in 1880 and county treasurer in 1887. In 1893, Haugen, a **Republican**, was elected to the lower house of the Iowa General Assembly but failed to regain the nomination in 1897. In 1898, he was elected to the United States House of Representatives. He was to serve for 17 terms, a total of 34 years, before losing his seat in 1932.

Haugen increasingly moved into the progressive Republican camp and he later supported much of **Woodrow Wilson**'s domestic program. However, he opposed United States entry into **World War I** and tried to protect farmers' interests during the war. After the war, Haugen was instrumental in the repeal of the **Daylight Savings Act** in 1919. His main concern, however, was farm prices and he was co-sponsor of the several **McNary-Haugen** Bills introduced and passed by Congress in 1927 and 1928 but vetoed by **Calvin Coolidge**.

HAWLEY-SMOOT TARIFF ACT, 1930. Approved by President **Herbert Hoover** despite the appeals of over a thousand leading economists to reject it, the Hawley-Smoot Tariff raised the tariffs of the **Fordney-McCumber Act** and set import duties at some of the highest levels in American history. Proposed by Representative Willis Hawley of Oregon and Senator **Reed Smoot** of Utah, the tariff was intended to help particularly agriculture in the face of falling prices. However, it was extended to cover many aspects of manufacturing industry. Its effects were disastrous as foreign nations introduced their own retaliatory duties leading to a further fall in American and world trade and only increasing the impact of the **Depression**.

HAYS, WILLIAM HARRISON (1879–1954). Will Hays qualified in law in Indiana and established a practice in Sullivan where he became the city attorney. He became chair of the Republican National Committee in 1918 and was credited with helping to reunite the **Republican Party** in 1920. President **Warren Harding** appointed Hays postmaster general and during his year in that position he established the Post Office Welfare Department, extended rural free mail deliveries, restored second-class mailing for newspapers, and reduced the Post Office expenses. Following a number of scandals in Hollywood (including the case of **"Fatty" Arbuckle**), Hays was appointed as head of the newly created Motion Picture Producers and Distributors of America (MPPDA). Under his leadership, the MPPDA established a code of practice to censor movies and to control material of a violent, sexual, or otherwise immoral nature. Hays claimed that "good taste is good business," but his taste often reflected that of small-town rural America. In 1945, Hays resigned his post but continued in the role as adviser to the Motion Picture Association of America. The censorship code survived until the 1960s.

HAYWOOD, WILLIAM DUDLEY (1869–1928). Known as "Big Bill," Haywood was a miner from the age of 15 and rose to become a militant leader of the Western Miners' Federation and one of the organizers of the **Industrial Workers of the World** (IWW) in 1905. In 1907, he was tried for conspiring to murder the governor of Idaho in 1905. Haywood was defended by **Clarence Darrow** and found not guilty. He stood unsuccessfully as a **Socialist** candidate in the election for governor of Colorado in 1906 but was removed from the party's executive for his militant language in 1913. Haywood returned to the IWW and led the Lawrence and Paterson textile workers' strikes in 1912 and 1913. He supported uncompromising militant mass action and opposed United States entry into the war in 1917. Arrested in 1917, he was convicted of sedition in 1919 and sentenced to 20 years in prison, but in 1921 he jumped bail and fled to the Soviet Union, where he spent the rest of his life.

HEARST, WILLIAM RANDOLPH (1863–1951). After studying at Harvard University (1882–85), William Hearst began a career as a journalist and gradually built up a newspaper empire, acquiring ownership of the San Francisco *Examiner*, Chicago *American*, New York *Journal-American*, and *Daily Mirror*. Hearst also owned several magazines including *International-Cosmopolitan*, *Harper's Bazaar*, and *Good Housekeeping*, and he created nationwide news syndicates. His papers became known for their sensationalism that earned the description "yellow journalism." They were also known for their nationalism—he was reported to have said to the artist Frederic Remington who was in Cuba in 1898, "You furnish the pictures and I'll furnish the war."

Hearst entered politics as a **Democrat** becoming a member of the United States House of Representatives from 1903 to 1907. He failed in his bid to become mayor of New York City in 1905 and 1909, and also in his attempt to become governor of New York in 1906. In 1908, he created his own Independence League in another attempt to win the gubernatorial race but failed again.

During **World War I**, Hearst's press adopted a passionately anti-British line that was abandoned once America entered the conflict. Hearst strongly opposed the **League of Nations** and United States' participation in the **Permanent Court of International Justice**. He continued to be an influential voice during the 1920s, supporting **Calvin Coolidge** and **Andrew Mellon**. However, in 1932 the Hearst press backed the Democrat **John Nance Garner** for the presidency, but was persuaded to switch support to **Franklin D. Roosevelt**. Hearst gradually turned against the **New Deal** because of its regulation of business. The Hearst empire was badly hit by the Depression and he was forced to surrender control in 1937. Nonetheless, the company emerged from the crisis as the biggest publishing organization in the United States. Hearst's great wealth was evident in the huge art collection he amassed at his home in San Simeon, California, and Hearst provided the model for the fictional character in Orson Welles' movie *Citizen Kane* (1941).

HELD, JOHN (1889–1958). The cartoonist and illustrator John Held began publishing his work at the age of 14 in the *Salt Lake City Tribune*. In 1910, he moved to New York City and found work designing posters and as a display designer. In 1917, he spent a year as the artist attached to the Carnegie Institute's archeological expedition to Central America. When he returned in 1918, he began selling illustrations, covers, and cartoons to *Judge, Puck, Vanity Fair*, and *Life* magazines. His ironic cartoons of young people, particularly the college students and the **flappers**, seemed to capture the mood of the 1920s and were enormously successful. In 1924, Held began producing a comic strip called *Oh! Margy!* That later became *Merely Margy* and then *Rah Rah Rosalie*. Held suffered an economic and a nervous collapse in the 1930s, and the popularity of his work also declined. In the 1940s, Held worked for the Signal Corps as an illustrator.

HEMINGWAY, ERNEST MILLER (1899–1961). If **F. Scott Fitzgerald** captured the mood of 1920s America, Ernest Hemingway was probably the most significant voice of the "lost generation" of alienated Americans after **World War I**. In 1917, he began work as a reporter for the Kansas City *Star*, but in 1918 he went to Italy as a volunteer ambulance driver for the American Red Cross. He was wounded and hospitalized shortly after his arrival. In 1920, he found work with the Toronto *Star* and he continued to submit articles first from Chicago and then after 1922, from Paris, France.

Hemingway published a number of short stories while he was in Paris where he became one of a group of expatriate writers and artists. His first collection of stories, *In Our Time* (1925), was followed by *The Sun Also Rises* (1926), *Men Without Women* (1927), and *A Farewell to Arms* (1929). It was in the latter that he wrote famously that after the war "all gods were dead."

Hemingway returned to America in 1928 and settled in Key West, where he wrote a study of bullfighting, *Death in the Afternoon* (1932), followed by *Winner Take Nothing* (1933) and *Green Hills of Africa* (1935). He also published short stories and magazine articles. In 1937 Hemingway went to Spain to report on the civil war. His book *To Have and Have Not* was published the same year.

In 1939, Hemingway went to Havana, where he wrote his novel of the Spanish civil war, *For Whom the Bell Tolls*, published in 1940. Hemingway was to write little of substance after this point, but he went to Europe as a war reporter for *Collier's* in 1944. In 1952, *The Old Man and the Sea* was published to considerable acclaim and Hemingway was awarded the Pulitzer Prize for fiction in 1953. In 1954, he was awarded the Nobel Prize for literature. Despite these successes, Hemingway suffered increasingly from depression and in 1961 he committed suicide.

HENDERSON, (JAMES) FLETCHER (1898–1952). Fletcher Henderson studied the piano from the age of six and although he later obtained a degree in science from Atlanta University in 1920, he began playing the piano professionally in New York City. From 1920 to 1924, he worked in W. C. Handy's music company and a phonograph company. Henderson formed his own big band in 1924 and toured widely. Henderson's band, believed to be the first organized by a jazzman, was the first **African American** band broadcast regularly on the radio and one of the most commercially successful. Many influential musicians, including **Louis Armstrong** and saxophonist

Coleman Hawkins, played with Henderson who some commentators believe was the "King of Swing." In 1939, Henderson joined the Benny Goodman orchestra. He left Goodman between 1943 and 1947 and formed several smaller groups himself before rejoining Goodman in 1947. Ill health forced him into retirement in 1950. *See also* HARLEM RENAISSANCE; JAZZ.

HEYWARD, (EDWIN) DUBOSE (1885–1940). DuBose Heyward grew up in Charleston, South Carolina, where he became a business-man before turning to writing. His first collection of poetry, *Carolina Chansons*, was published in 1922. His greatest success, however, was with the novel of black life, *Porgy* (1925), which Heyward and his wife, Dorothy, successfully converted to a play of the same name in 1927. Heyward then wrote the libretto for **George Gershwin**'s folk-opera masterpiece, *Porgy and Bess* (1935). Another novel, *Mamba's Daughters*, also based on the black community of Charleston ap-peared in 1929 and was dramatized by the Heywards in 1939. Du-Bose Heyward wrote several novels and children's stories, was the cofounder of the Poetry Society of South Carolina, and was a con-tributor to the renaissance of southern literature and culture in the in-terwar years.

HILLMAN, SIDNEY (1887–1946). Sidney Hillman was born in Lithuania. He came to the United States in 1907 and found work in the clothing industry. In 1915, he became president of the newly cre-ated Amalgamated Clothing Workers Union. During the 1920s, Hill-man espoused a New Unionism that stressed cooperation with em-ployers and workers' educational, social, and welfare programs. Hillman supported **Franklin D. Roosevelt**'s **New Deal** during the **Depression** and worked with other unionists to secure Roosevelt's re-election in 1936. In 1935, he was one of the founders of the Con-gress of Industrial Organizations (CIO) and became one of its vice presidents. In 1936, he helped to found the American Labor Party, a left-wing group in New York. During World War II, Hillman headed the labor section of the Office of Production Management and then was vice chairman of the War Production Board. He established the political action committee in the CIO to support Roosevelt. *See also* TRADE UNIONS.

HILLQUIT, MORRIS (1869–1933). Morris Hillquit was born in Riga, Russia (now Latvia), and emigrated to the United States in 1886. He worked for the *Arbeiter Zeitung*, the first American-Yiddish newspaper. Hillquit joined the Socialist Labor Party in 1886 and then later the Social Democratic Party and became a leading policymaker in the emergence of the **Socialist Party of America** (SPA). Hillquit drew up the peace platform adopted by the party in 1917. He stood unsuccessfully as a Socialist candidate in the elections for the mayor of New York City in 1917 and also stood unsuccessfully five times as a candidate for the House of Representatives. After the war, Hillquit was involved in the various factional debates involving socialists and communists that led to the SPA joining the Union of Socialist Parties rather than the Communist International in 1920. In 1922, Hillquit and **Victor Berger** were active in supporting the **Conference for Progressive Political Action** and the call for an independent Labor Party. When this failed, Hillquit supported **Robert M. La Follette** and the **Progressive Party** in 1924. Hillquit last ran for office himself when he stood again as a candidate for the mayor of New York. Although unsuccessful, he did win 250,000 votes. In addition to his organizational activities, Hillquit wrote several works on socialism and was the author of the *History of Socialism in the United States* (1903).

HINES, WALKER DOWNER (1879–1934). Hines was a successful lawyer who worked as an attorney for **railroad** companies. During World War I, he became assistant director to the **United States Railroad Administration** and then succeeded his chief, **William Gibbs McAdoo**, as director-general of the railroads from 1919 to 1920. He returned to his law practice in New York City after the war, but was also a director of a railroad company. Hines wrote *The War History of the American Railroads* (1929) and in 1925 he wrote a report on Danube Navigation for the **League of Nations**. In 1926, Hines became president of the Cotton-Textile Institute formed to promote the development of the cotton industry. He was vice president of the New York City Bar Association from 1932 until his death.

HOLMES, OLIVER WENDELL (1841–1935). After graduating from Harvard University in 1861, Oliver Wendell Holmes served in the Union Army during the Civil War and was wounded three times.

He graduated from Harvard Law School in 1866 and practiced in Boston. Following the publication of *The Common Law* (1881) in which he declared "The life of the law has not been logic, but experience," Holmes became a professor of law at Harvard Law School in 1882, and associate justice to the Massachusetts Supreme Court the same year. He served as the chief justice in the Massachusetts court from 1899 to 1902 when he was appointed associate justice to the United States **Supreme Court**. Holmes served on the Court until 1932 and was famous for his liberal dissent from majority decisions against social welfare and labor legislation, most famously in *Lochner v. New York* (1905). For Holmes, the law had to reflect social realities, rather than simply legal principle. However, in *Schenck v. United States* he authored the decision that upheld the wartime **Espionage Act** on the grounds that in wartime there was "a clear and present danger" that justified restricting free speech that was not absolute. In *Abrams v. United States*, he dissented from the decision upholding the conviction for the distribution of pamphlets denouncing United States involvement in Russia on the grounds that it presented no clear threat to the prosecution of the war.

HOME LOAN BANK ACT, 1932. The Home Loan Bank Act was passed to establish credit facilities for urban real estate financing. It created a system similar to the **Federal Reserve** System with 12 Federal Home Loan Banks that could offer credit to member banks and savings and loan associations to assist banks in financing real estate development. The act was supplemented by the **Home Owners' Loan Act, 1933**.

HOME OWNERS' LOAN ACT, 1933. Passed as a supplement to the **Home Loan Bank Act, 1932**, the Home Owners' Loan Act established a Home Owners' Loan Corporation with $200 million capital to refinance first mortgages on homes valued up to $20,000 at lower interest rates. Over a three-year period the HOLC helped to save the homes of hundreds of thousands of people. When it ceased its operations in 1936, it had refinanced more than one million mortgages.

HOOVER, HERBERT CLARK (1874–1964). Thirty-first president of the United States. Born in West Branch, Iowa, Herbert Hoover was orphaned at the age of nine. He grew up with relatives and went on to qualify in geology at Stanford University, California, in 1895. Hoover became a millionaire working as a mining engineer in various Western states and in Australia and China between 1895 and 1913. In 1914, he became chair of the American Relief Commission in London and from 1915 to 1919 chair of the Commission for Relief in Belgium. In 1917, Hoover rose to national prominence when **Woodrow Wilson** appointed him to head the **United States Food Administration**. He launched a massive national effort to maximize production and minimize private consumption through a program of propaganda that encouraged voluntary controls. Such was his public appeal that both political parties considered him as a potential presidential candidate in 1920, but he declined to run. **Warren Harding** appointed Hoover as secretary of commerce in 1921 and he was reappointed by **Calvin Coolidge** in 1924.

As secretary of commerce, and as one commentator said, "undersecretary of every thing else," Hoover modernized the department and made it one of the most important federal agencies of its day. He used his position to encourage efficiency and the reduction of waste in industry. He fostered trade associations, mergers, and standardization of production through private agreements. Although historians have regarded both the Harding and Coolidge administrations as conservative, Hoover was in many ways "progressive" in that he hoped to bring about economic and social improvement through programs of education and "voluntarism." He chaired the **unemployment conference** in 1921 to encourage business and local voluntary initiatives to counter the postwar recession. In 1921, he helped to persuade United States Steel to accept the eight-hour day. Hoover also backed the postwar "Own Your Own Homes" campaign and the Better Homes of America organization. Hoover also supported children's concerns and was president of the American Child Health Association from 1923 to 1935. He is generally credited with drawing up the Children's Bill of Rights in 1923 that was later incorporated in the 19-point Children's Charter drawn up at the White House Conference on Child Health and Protection in 1930.

In 1927, Hoover led the mobilization of relief following the **Mississippi flood**. Again relying on voluntary and charitable relief, he raised $17 million to provide assistance for the thousands affected, and further enhanced his reputation. When Coolidge declined to stand for re-election in 1928 Hoover won the **Republican Party**'s nomination and defeated **Democrat Al Smith** by a massive margin of 58 percent to 41 percent of the vote, carrying forty states to Smith's eight. While awaiting his inauguration, Hoover embarked on a six-week "good will" tour of Latin America and laid some of the foundations for **Franklin D. Roosevelt**'s "Good Neighbor policy."

On taking office, Hoover's activity contrasted with his predecessor's inertia. He supported labor legislation that resulted in the Norris-La Guardia Anti-Injunction Act (1932), set limits on oil drilling and withdrew all federally held oil lands from further leasing, and ordered all large government rebates on income, estate, and gift taxes to be made public. The new president took action against corrupt patronage practices, supported land conservation, and made some attempt to win the support of black voters with his "Southern strategy." However, Hoover's administration fell victim to the **Wall Street Crash** of 1929 and was quickly overwhelmed by the **Depression** that followed.

Hoover attempted to address some of the economic problems facing America early in his administration. In an effort to deal with the problems of agriculture, he called a special session of Congress that passed his **Agricultural Marketing Act** in 1929. A second special session was called to revise the 1922 tariff in order to help farmers. After 14 months deliberation, the result was the **Hawley-Smoot Tariff** that in the end proved counterproductive.

Following the Wall Street Crash, Hoover held a series of conferences at the White House with industrialists, representatives of agriculture, and union leaders to try to ensure the maintenance of production, employment, and wage levels by voluntary action. The president called upon state and city officials to increase public works expenditure, and in 1930 he secured federal appropriations of $150 million for river and harbor improvement, new public buildings, and the building of the Boulder Dam. In all, the federal government would spend an unprecedented $700 million on public works, but Hoover was insistent that there would be no direct federal relief. Publicly, Hoover tried to restore confidence with comments, such as the forecast in March 1930 that "the worst effects on unemployment will have passed in the next 60 days." In May, he observed "we have now passed the worst," and later remarked "at least no one has starved." All of these would come back to haunt him when the Depression continued to deepen.

In 1931, Hoover recognized that the Depression was a worldwide problem and attempted to ease the international economic crisis by declaring a moratorium on the payment of reparations and Allied debts. At home, the earlier President's Emergency Committee for Unemployment in 1931 became the **President's Organization for Unemployment Relief** headed by **Walter Gifford**. The aim of this committee was to provide direction and coordination of state and local activity, but this proved increasingly ineffectual given the lack of resources at that level. More effective were the **Home Loan Banks** and the passage of the **Glass-Steagall Banking Act** to stabilize credit and banking passed with Hoover's support in 1932. Equally significant was his approval of the Emergency and Relief Construction Act in 1932, which appropriated $2 billion for public works and $300 million for direct loans to states for relief purposes. However, he also called for increased taxation in order to balance the budget and the 1932 Revenue Act, which raised taxes by one-third, further restricted consumption.

In 1932, Hoover established the **Reconstruction Finance Corporation** to lend money to banks, industries, and **railroads** to get the economy going again, but this had a limited effect and was seen by many Americans as a "rich man's dole." As discontent increased across the country, Hoover's name became synonymous with the Depression. Tramps lived in "Hoovervilles" and the newspapers they covered themselves with for warmth were "Hoover blankets." When the **Bonus Army** was driven out of Washington, D.C., in 1932 Hoover's popularity fell even further. Despite this, an unenthusiastic Republican Party renominated him for the presidency. The outcome of the election in 1932 confirmed the voters' disapproval. **Franklin D. Roosevelt** gained 22.8 million votes to Hoover's 15.7 million and Hoover won only 59 Electoral College votes from six states.

After his defeat, Hoover dropped from the public's view. He was critical of the **New Deal** and later of America's Cold War policies. He opposed the formation of the North Atlantic Treaty Organization (NATO) in 1949 and the Korean War, 1950–53. In 1949, he was appointed chair of the Commission on Organization of the Executive

Branch of Government, and many of his recommendations were implemented by Harry S. Truman's administration. *See also* HOOVER, LOU HENRY.

HOOVER, JOHN EDGAR (1895–1972). J. Edgar Hoover was a lawyer and criminologist who joined the staff of the Alien Enemy Bureau in the Justice Department in 1917 and was active in the campaign against radicals during and after the war. As head of a newly created Radical Division, Hoover's encouragement of **A. Mitchell Palmer** did much to bring about the **Red Scare** of 1919. Hoover planned and directed the **Palmer Raids** of November 1919 and January 1920. In 1921, Hoover became assistant director of the Bureau of Investigation, which later became the **Federal Bureau of Investigation** (FBI).

As director of the Federal Bureau of Investigation from 1924 until his death, Hoover was to achieve enormous power. During the 1930s, he became a national figure in leading the attack on organized crime and against infamous criminals such as John Dillinger. Hoover was also involved in the investigation and trial of American Nazis after 1938 and of German saboteurs in 1942. He took a key role in the postwar anticommunist campaigns and provided evidence for the prosecution of leaders of the American Communist Party in 1948 and was also involved in the spy investigations that led to the trial and execution of Julius and Ethel Rosenberg in 1953. In the late 1950s, Hoover developed a Counter Intelligence Program (COINTELPRO) that was used successively against communist groups, the **Ku Klux Klan**, and, in the 1960s, against black organizations. Hoover personally led investigations to undermine the position of the civil rights leader, Dr. Martin Luther King, and even threatened him with blackmail. Later, Senate investigations produced a report highly critical of Hoover and many of the FBI's domestic activities, but such was his power that no president was able to remove him from office.

HOOVER, LOU HENRY (1874–1944). The future wife of President **Herbert Hoover** was born Lou Henry in Waterloo, Iowa. She moved to Whittier, California, in 1887 and became fascinated by the outdoors. She studied geology at Stanford University where she met Herbert Hoover. They married in 1899 and Lou traveled with her husband to China where they were caught in the Boxer Rebellion. Lou Hoover accompanied her husband with their two children to Australia, Burma, Japan, and Siberia. In 1914 she and her husband were in London when **World War I** broke out and they assisted stranded American tourists. Lou Hoover became president of the American Women's War Relief Fund while Herbert directed the commission for Relief in Belgium. The Hoovers returned to the United States in 1917 and Lou spoke at **United States Food Administration** and other events.

Mrs. Hoover was not a prominent first lady and was more private than her predecessor, **Grace Coolidge**. While she encouraged emerging artists through cultural gatherings in the White House, there is no evidence that she had any influence on her husband's speeches or policies. Mrs. Hoover also initiated a history of the White House. However, she did become the center of controversy when she invited the wife of the black congressman, **Oscar De Priest**, to a White House tea for congressional wives, an action she and her husband both stood by. After the Crash, Mrs. Hoover often privately provided relief to needy families and she arranged for food and bedding to be sent to the **Bonus Army**'s camp. In 1930, a school the Hoovers had built for the children of the area was opened in the Blue Ridge Mountains.

In 1917, Lou Hoover began a lifelong involvement with the Girl Scouts when she became a troop leader and a national Girl Scout commissioner the same year. Mrs. Hoover became vice president of the Girl Scouts in 1921 and president in 1922 until 1925. Her work for the organization became one of her main activities until her death and she was president again from 1935 to 1937. Mrs. Hoover also served as president of the women's section of the Amateur Athletics Association from 1923 to 1941.

HOPKINS, HARRY LLOYD (1890–1946). The famous **New Deal** administrator Harry Hopkins was educated at Grinnell College, Iowa. In 1912, he moved to New York City where he became a social worker. He became executive secretary of New York's Board of Child Welfare and during **World War I** was involved in civilian relief for the families of servicemen for the Red Cross. In 1923, Hopkins became president of the American Association of Social Workers and in 1924 the director of the New York Tuberculosis Association. In 1931, Hopkins was appointed by Governor **Franklin**

D. Roosevelt to direct New York's Temporary Emergency Relief Administration and then in 1933 to head the Federal Emergency Relief Administration, which spent $1 billion in two years providing jobs for the unemployed.

When initial relief measures proved too slow, Roosevelt put Hopkins in charge of the Civil Works Administration (CWA), which employed four million people in six months working on public building projects. From 1935 to 1940, Hopkins directed the Works Progress Administration (WPA), which put more than eight million workers on the federal payroll and spent $10.5 billion dollars. He became secretary of commerce in 1938 and considered running for the presidential nomination in 1940. However, ill health forced him to abandon such ambitions and he supported Roosevelt before resigning from the administration.

During World War II, Hopkins became a diplomat. He was first sent as a special envoy to Great Britain in 1941 and then to the Soviet Union. He organized Lend-Lease to the Allies before America entered the war and after 1941 headed the Munitions Assignments Board to allocate war material to different Allied powers. Hopkins continued to work in the war administration despite his own poor health and the death of a son in combat. He was an influential figure at the Teheran Conference in 1943 and at Yalta in 1945 and played a part in ensuring Soviet participation in the United Nations conference in San Francisco in 1945. That year, Hopkins resigned from government and was awarded the Distinguished Service Medal.

HOUSE, EDWARD MANDELL (1858–1938). Edward House was drawn into politics in Texas, where he ran his family's properties. His work in mobilizing support for the **Democratic** governor James Hogg in 1892 was rewarded with the title of "colonel." In 1911, House met and formed a friendship with **Woodrow Wilson** and he became his adviser and confidante. Following the election of 1912, House advised Wilson on cabinet appointments and other issues. During **World War I** in Europe, House was involved in negotiations in 1916 with Sir Edward Grey, the British foreign secretary, that resulted in an agreement for the Wilson administration to call a peace conference when the Allies indicated. The agreement was not invoked but it indicated the administration's move toward the **Allied**

cause. House was involved in preparing the constitution of the proposed **League of Nations** in 1918 and with negotiating the armistice with Germany. House continued to support the League and American participation through the 1920s. He also continued to work within the Democratic Party and supported the nomination of **Franklin D. Roosevelt** in 1932.

HOUSTON, DAVID FRANKLIN (1866–1940). After graduating from Carolina College and Harvard University, David Houston became president of Texas A&M from 1902 to 1905 and then of the University of Texas, 1905–08. In 1908, he was chancellor of Washington University in St. Louis. In 1913, **Woodrow Wilson** appointed Houston secretary of agriculture and he held that post until 1919 when he became secretary of the United States Treasury, a position he held until 1921. In 1926 he wrote *Eight Year's with Wilson's Cabinet*.

HOUSTON MUTINY, 1917. After a series of incidents of racial harassment and provocation African American troops of the 3rd Battalion of the 24th Infantry stationed at Camp Logan, near Houston, Texas, seized weapons and marched into the city, where they fired upon white townspeople. Sixteen whites and four blacks were killed in the violence. Following a court-martial in which 63 African American soldiers were tried, 13 were executed in San Antonio on 22 December without review or opportunity to appeal.

HOWE, FREDERIC CLEMSON (1867–1940). Frederic Howe was typical of many **Progressive** reformers. He obtained a Ph.D. from Johns Hopkins University in 1892 with a dissertation on "The History of the Internal Revenue System" and later qualified in law and moved to Cleveland, Ohio, where he specialized on tax issues. Howe worked in the **settlement houses** in Cleveland and was secretary to the reform organization, the Municipal Association. In 1901, Howe was elected to the city council and served two years. In 1906 he was elected to the Ohio State Senate and then became a member of the Cleveland Board of Tax Assessors until 1910. He moved to New York City in 1910 and became director of the People's Institute, an educational organization for the poor.

In 1911, Howe became secretary of the National Progressive Republican League supporting **Robert M. La Follette** and wrote a study entitled *Wisconsin, an Experiment in Democracy* (1912). When La Follette failed to win the nomination, Howe switched support to **Woodrow Wilson** who appointed Howe commissioner of **immigration** for the Port of New York. Howe's humane approach to immigrants led him to resign during the 1919 **Red Scare** rather than deport alien radicals. He campaigned in support of the **Plumb Plan** to continue government control of the **railroads** and in 1922 was involved in the **Conference for Progressive Political Action**. Howe supported La Follette once more in the election of 1924. In 1932, he supported **Franklin D. Roosevelt** and was appointed consumers' counsel on the Agricultural Adjustment Board in 1933. In 1937, Howe became adviser to the Philippine government on farm tenancy and cooperatives and the following year was a consultant on agricultural commodities for the National Economic Committee investigating monopolies.

HOWE, LOUIS McHENRY (1871–1936). Louis Howe began his career as a salesman and reporter working for his father before moving to the New York *Herald* in 1906. He then became involved in politics working first as a personal assistant to Mayor Thomas Osborne and then for **Franklin D. Roosevelt**, managing his re-election to the New York senate in 1912. Howe continued as Roosevelt's assistant, speechwriter, and publicist through to the election of 1932 after which he became the president's secretary.

HUDSON, MANLEY OTTMER (1886–1960). Manley Hudson graduated from Harvard Law School in 1910. He was a member of the American commission at the **Paris Peace Conference** in 1919. In 1923, Hudson became professor of international law at Harvard and wrote several books on international law and international affairs. In 1936, he became a judge on the **Permanent Court of International Justice**.

HUGHES, CHARLES EVANS (1862–1948). Associate justice of the United States Supreme Court 1910–16, secretary of state 1921–25, eleventh chief justice of the United States Supreme Court 1930–41.

A graduate of Columbia Law School, Hughes practiced law in New York City and served as counsel for the New York state legislature's committee investigating gas companies in 1906. He achieved national prominence when, as counsel for a similar committee investigating insurance companies (1905–06), he exposed corrupt practices. As **Republican** governor of New York from 1907 to 1910, Hughes established the public service commission, and introduced insurance law reforms and several pieces of labor legislation. He then served as associate justice to the United States **Supreme Court** until 1916, when he stood as the Republican presidential candidate. He lost the election to **Democrat Woodrow Wilson** by one of the narrowest margins.

Hughes was appointed secretary of state by Presidents **Warren Harding** and **Calvin Coolidge** from 1921 to 1925. In 1926, he became a member of The Hague Tribunal and also a judge on the **Permanent Court of Internal Justice** (1928–30). He was appointed chief justice to the United States Supreme Court by **Herbert Hoover** in 1930 and served until 1941. As chief justice, Hughes generally held a moderately conservative position. Although he wrote the opinion in *Schechter Poultry Corp. v. United States* that found the National Recovery Administration (NRA) unconstitutional in 1935, he generally voted in favor of upholding **New Deal** legislation. He vigorously opposed **Franklin D. Roosevelt**'s attempts to reorganize the Court in 1937.

HUGHES, (JAMES) LANGSTON (1902–1967). One of the major figures of the **Harlem Renaissance**, the black poet Langston Hughes published his first significant poem, "The Negro Speaks of Rivers" in *Crisis* magazine in 1921, a year after he left high school. He spent a year at Columbia University in New York City before becoming a seaman, visiting West Africa, and spending time in France and Italy. Two books of verse drawing upon the black folk idiom, *The Weary Blues* and *Fine Clothes to the Jew*, appeared in 1926 and 1927 respectively. Hughes enrolled at Lincoln University in 1926 and graduated in 1929. Supported by a wealthy white patron, Charlotte Osgood Mason, from 1927 until 1931, Hughes produced his first novel, *Not Without Laughter*, in 1930.

After traveling to Haiti, the USSR, and Mexico, Hughes wrote *Mulatto*, a play that enjoyed a long run on Broadway following its opening in 1935. Hughes's autobiography *The Big Sea* appeared in 1940 and another volume of poems, *Shakespeare in Harlem*, in 1942. Later collections such as *Fields of Wonder* (1947), *One-Way Ticket* (1949), and *Montage of a Dream Deferred* (1951) combined the blues idiom with **jazz** rhythms. Hughes also published regularly in journals and the press, and wrote a regular newspaper column featuring a humorous character called Jesse B. Semple, or Simple. These stories were published in the 1950s. Criticized for his earlier left-wing sympathies, Hughes toured Africa and other countries for the State Department. The second volume of his autobiography, *I Wonder as I Wander*, was published in 1956. He continued to publish poetry, essays, and works of history through to his death. Such was his reputation that he was known as the "Shakespeare of Harlem." He was admitted to the National Institute of Arts and Letters in 1961.

HULL, CORDELL (1871–1955). A graduate of Cumberland University, Hull practiced law in Tennessee, where he became a judge on the 5th judicial circuit, 1903–07. In 1907, he was elected to the United States House of Representatives and served until 1921. He was re-elected in 1923 and served until 1931. Hull drew up the federal income tax law in 1913 and the federal estate and inheritance laws in 1916. In 1931, Hull was elected to the Senate, but in 1933 became **Franklin D. Roosevelt**'s secretary of state, a position he held until 1944. He worked particularly in improving relations with Latin American nations and in fostering the "Good Neighbor Policy." In 1945 he was awarded the Nobel Peace Prize.

HULL HOUSE. Founded in Chicago in 1889 by **Jane Addams** and **Ellen Starr**, Hull House was one of the first **settlement houses** in the United States. Hull House was modeled on the example of Toynbee Hall in London's East End, and acted as a welfare agency for the **immigrant** population. Funded entirely by voluntary contributions from individuals and social agencies, Hull House became one of the largest settlement houses in the United States, and an example that was copied across the country in the **Progressive Era**. *See also* SOCIAL WORK.

HURLEY, EDWARD NASH (1864–1933). Edward Hurley rose from being a railway worker to become a Chicago machine tool and appliance manufacturer and a prominent supporter of scientific management and industrial rationalization before the war. In 1896, Hurley established the Standard Pneumatic Tool Company. Having become a millionaire, he retired from the company. In 1908, he established the Hurley Machine Company producing electrical home labor-saving devices and was president of the First National Bank of Wheaton.

Hurley was a supporter of **Woodrow Wilson** who appointed him vice chairman of the **Federal Trade Commission** and in 1917 chair of the **United States Shipping Board** where he energetically supported the expansion of the U.S. Merchant Marine. Hurley also took part in the peace negotiations in Paris as a shipping adviser and was awarded the Distinguished Service Medal for his work. Following his retirement from public service in 1919, Hurley served as director of a number of companies and wrote the case for a large merchant marine in *The New Merchant Marine* (1920). He also wrote an account of his war experience in *The Bridge to France* (1927). In 1924 President **Calvin Coolidge** appointed Hurley to the World War Funding Commission. He was also a member of President **Herbert Hoover**'s Advisory Shipping Commission.

HURLEY, PATRICK JAY (1883–1963). After an education at Indian University, Muskogee, and National University Law School, Patrick Hurley practiced law in Tulsa, Oklahoma, before becoming a lieutenant colonel in **World War I**. He was appointed secretary of war by President **Herbert Hoover** in 1929. It was Hurley who, in 1932, issued the orders for the expulsion of the **Bonus Army** from Washington, D.C. During World War II, Hurley served as minister to New Zealand and then as **Franklin D. Roosevelt**'s personal representative in the Near and Middle East and went on missions to Afghanistan and China. He became the United States ambassador to China in 1944, but resigned in protest over the administration's China policy in 1945. In 1946, Hurley was awarded the Medal of Merit for his services to China. Hurley ran unsuccessfully for election to the United States Senate from New Mexico in 1946, 1948, and 1952.

HURSTON, ZORA NEALE (1891–1960). Born in Alabama, the **African American** novelist, folklorist, and anthropologist Zora Neale Hurston grew up in Florida in a community she was to later turn into a subject of study. Hurston studied at Howard University from 1919 to 1923 and then at Barnard College in New York City where she studied with Franz Boas. She later began but did not complete a Ph.D. at Columbia. Joining the growing literary movement of the **Harlem Renaissance**, Hurston published a number of short stories in magazines such as *Opportunity* and several pieces on southern folklore based on her fieldwork in Florida and other parts of the South. Her first novel, *Jonah's Gourd Vine*, was published in 1934. Her second book, *Mules and Men* (1935), was based on her fieldtrips. Hurston's most acclaimed novel, *Their Eyes Were Watching God*, appeared in 1937 and focuses particularly on the plight of black **women**. *Moses, Man of the Mountains* (1939) was a version of the book of Exodus written in black vernacular. Although Hurston continued to publish in newspapers and journals through the 1950s, her career declined from the 1940s on and she died in relative obscurity. The author Alice Walker, who did much to inspire a revival in interest in Hurston's work in the 1970s, subsequently found and marked her grave.

– I –

ICKES, HAROLD LECLAIR (1874–1952). A graduate of the University of Chicago, Ickes began work as a newspaper reporter then gained his degree in law from University of Chicago in 1904. Ickes practiced law in that city and was active in **Republican Party** politics. During **World War I** Ickes served in Europe with the Young Men's Christian Association (YMCA). Despite the political climate, he continued to be active in Republican Party politics and, as a reformer, he supported **Hiram Johnson**'s presidential nomination in 1924. With the onset of the **Depression**, Ickes worked for **Franklin D. Roosevelt** and was appointed secretary of the interior in 1933, a post he held until 1946 becoming in the process one of the greatest public administrators of all time. Under his leadership, the Department of Interior expanded conservation policies and established several new national parks. Ickes was appointed head of the Public Works Administration (PWA) in 1933, but his cautious approach led to the creation of the Civil Works Administration (CWA) under **Harry Hopkins**. During World War II, Ickes was petroleum and solid fuels administrator. After the war, he retired from politics and spent most of his time writing his memoirs and columns for various newspapers.

IMMIGRATION. The movement of people from one country or land to another was central to American history. The United States was "a nation of immigrants." Until about 1890 most immigrants came from northern and western Europe: England, Scotland, Ireland, France, the Netherlands, Germany, and Scandinavia. These "old immigrants" were predominantly (the Irish being the largest and most notable exception) white Anglo Saxon protestants. This changed in the late 19th century, and the "new immigrants" were increasingly from central, southern, and eastern Europe, and were Catholics, Jews, or Russian and Greek Orthodox in religion. The scale of immigration also reached new heights with 8.7 million new arrivals entering the United States between 1900 and 1910 and another 5.7 million between 1910 and 1920. The majority of the last group in fact came before **World War I**. A million immigrants entered the country in 1913 alone.

The majority of the "new immigrants" found work in the growing industries of the North and Northeast and settled in the growing urban centers such as New York, Chicago, and Pittsburgh. Many Americans associated immigrants with urban squalor, industrial unrest, and a threat to traditional values. A powerful nativist movement calling for immigration controls developed as a consequence and eventually achieved success with the passage of the **Quota Acts** of 1921 and 1924.

INDUSTRIAL CONFERENCES. In 1919, President **Woodrow Wilson** called an Industrial Conference in order to reach "a meeting of minds" and find a settlement to the postwar strikes and lockouts. The conference of 61 representatives of labor, management, and the public, chaired by Secretary of the Interior **Franklin Lane**, met from 6–23 October. The conference ended having achieved nothing. A second conference, chaired by **Herbert Hoover**, met from January to March 1920. The conference produced a report with various recommendations such as the 48-hour week, minimum wages, and equal pay, but it had no power or authority to implement these proposals.

INDUSTRIAL WORKERS OF THE WORLD (IWW). Often known as the "Wobblies" or IWW, the Industrial Workers of the World was a radical industrial union formed in Chicago in 1905 by **William ("Big Bill") Haywood** and Daniel Deleon. The object of the IWW was to organize all workers into "One Big Union" in order to achieve a revolutionary overthrow of capitalism. It concentrated on organizing the unskilled workers on an industry-wide basis utilizing direct action methods of strike and sabotage. It was particularly successful in organizing migrant workers and miners in the West and **immigrant** groups, such as the textile workers in the East. Faced with suppression under the syndicalist laws in various western states, the IWW launched free speech campaigns in western states and led the Lawrence, Massachusetts, textile strike in 1912 and the silk workers' strike in Paterson, New Jersey, in 1913. The IWW espoused direct action tactics that included "striking on the job" (sabotage). An unofficial policy of opposition to involvement in **World War I**, plus its continued involvement in strikes, particularly in western lumber and mining industries, led to suppression under the **Espionage** laws. Following raids on its offices in 1918, 173 IWW leaders were convicted. Seriously weakened, the organization went into decline in the postwar years. *See also* TRADE UNIONS.

INFLUENZA EPIDEMIC, 1918. In March 1918, United States troops at a military camp in Kansas became ill with influenza, sometimes known as Spanish influenza or the three-day fever. Within days, several of the soldiers were dead, and the virus spread across the United States and to Europe. A second wave of the illness hit in August, and a final wave in the winter. Eventually, more than 650,000 Americans and between 20- to 40-million people worldwide died in the epidemic. When the illness reached its height in the United States, 195,000 died in October alone. Unusually, 20- to 40-year-olds seemed particularly vulnerable to the virus, and the deaths had a considerable impact on long-term birth rates.

IRRECONCILABLES. A group of 16 western and midwestern senators led by **William Borah** of Idaho and **Robert M. La Follette** of Wisconsin. They were unalterably opposed to the **Versailles Peace Treaty** because of the harsh terms imposed on Germany and because of the potentially permanent United States participation in world affairs through the **League of Nations**. Their opposition and **Woodrow Wilson**'s unwillingness to compromise led to the Senate's failure to ratify the peace settlement and join the League.

ISOLATIONISM. The traditional foreign policy of the United States of noninvolvement and independence was established with George Washington's famous recommendation in his Farewell Address (1796) to avoid "permanent alliances." This was further confirmed in the Monroe Doctrine in 1823 that also established the principle of "separate spheres" of interest between the old world and the new. These positions were seriously challenged following the outbreak of **World War I**, and the United States' entry into the war marked a major departure in **foreign policy**. However, isolationist sentiment reasserted itself after the war and led to the rejection of the **Versailles treaty** and American involvement in the **League of Nations**. However, the United States remained active in foreign affairs and took a lead in disarmament conferences and the attempt to prevent future outbreaks of war through the **Kellogg-Briand Pact**. While attempts were made to maintain an isolated position from the growing conflict in Europe in the 1930s, ultimately these failed and the United States' participation in World War II marked the end of isolationism as accepted policy. *See also* LONDON NAVAL CONFERENCE; WASHINGTON NAVAL CONFERENCE; WASHINGTON NAVAL TREATY.

IVES, CHARLES EDWARD (1874–1954). One of America's greatest composers, Charles Ives studied at Yale University and then entered the insurance business. His business was very successful and he retired a wealthy man in 1930. Ives sold insurance by day, and composed at night. Strongly influenced by his bandleader father and by church and folk music, Ives wrote complicated pieces combining hymns, gospel, folk, and other influences in a variety of pieces ranging from music for piano or organ, string quartets, and full symphonies. He published his "Concord Sonata" and a collection of 114 other pieces in 1922. Ives wrote little after that and it was only in the later 1930s that he gained recognition for his "Second Piano Sonata." In 1947, his "Third Symphony" was awarded the Pulitzer Prize.

– J –

JADWIN, EDGAR (1865–1931). Edgar Jadwin graduated from West Point in 1890 and received a commission in the Army Corps of Engineers. He worked on various river and harbor improvements and commanded a battalion in Cuba from 1898 to 1899. After holding a number of different appointments in the United States, Jadwin worked as an assistant to General **George Goethals** on the construction of the Panama Canal, from 1907 to 1911 when he returned to the United States to work in Tennessee and Pittsburgh. During **World War I** Jadwin served in France organizing and directing the construction of railways, roads, docks, and barracks. In 1919, he went first to Poland as a part of the American Mission and then to the Ukraine as an observer. Resuming his rank as a colonel Jadwin then returned to the United States and worked on different projects. In 1926, he was promoted to chief of engineers with the rank of major general. Following the **Mississippi flood** in 1927, Jadwin ordered a complete investigation of flood control methods, and his proposals formed the basis of all subsequent flood control work on the lower Mississippi. After his retirement in 1929 Jadwin served as a delegate to the World Engineering Congress and later became chairman of the Interoceanic Canal Board that examined the possibilities of increasing the capacity of the Panama Canal.

JARDINE, WILLIAM MARION (1879–1955). After working in forestry and farming in Idaho, William Jardine studied at Utah Agricultural College and graduated with a degree in agronomy in 1904. In 1907, Jardine joined the Department of Agriculture in Washington, D.C. Three years later, he was appointed at Kansas State Agricultural College and became dean of agriculture in 1913. During **World War I**, he organized the planning of agricultural production in Kansas. In 1918, Jardine became president of the Agricultural College but in

1925 **Calvin Coolidge** appointed him as secretary of agriculture. Jardine placed considerable emphasis on the marketing rather than production side of farming. He was an outspoken opponent of the **McNary-Haugen** Bill and suggested instead that farmers use cooperatives to increase efficiency. In 1929, **Herbert Hoover** appointed Jardine as minister to Egypt. He returned to the United States in 1933 and became state treasurer of Kansas for a year. In 1934 Jardine became president of the Municipal University of Wichita (now Wichita State University). He retired in 1949.

JAZZ. Jazz was the name given to the form of popular music that emerged from the **African American** community and became widely popular in the 1920s. The music had its origins in slave songs, chants, and hollers that developed into blues songs. Jazz was the instrumental form, which relied on simple rhythms and improvisation around a recurring melody line. The term was first reported being used among the black community of New Orleans in the 1870s to refer to fast, syncopated music, and jazz music was said to have originated in New Orleans at the end of the 19th century. It found expression in marching songs and in ragtime. As a result of the **Great Migration** of African Americans from the South during **World War I**, jazz moved into northern cities such as Chicago with bands like that of Joe "King" Oliver. Oliver made some of the first significant jazz recordings in the 1920s and introduced **Louis Armstrong** to a wider audience. As jazz spread it began to appeal to a white audience, and its new, uninhibited aspects seemed to capture the sense of liberation that followed the war, particularly among the young. The writer **F. Scott Fitzgerald** used the term to describe the 1920s in his *Tales of the Jazz Age* (1922), and the phrase has stuck ever since. *See also* CALLOWAY, "CAB"; ELLINGTON, "DUKE"; HARLEM; HARLEM RENAISSANCE; HENDERSON, FLETCHER.

***THE JAZZ SINGER*, 1927.** Starring **Al Jolson**, the *Jazz Singer* is normally credited as being the first sound motion picture. *See also* JAZZ; MOVIES.

JEFFERSON, ("BLIND") LEMON (1897–1929). The blues singer and guitarist Lemon Jefferson was born in Texas but traveled the

South as an itinerant musician through the 1920s before being recorded by Paramount Records in their "Race Artists" series. In 1927, Jefferson's records were released at a rate of about one a month and his 43 records sold more than one million copies. His influence on other blues and jazz musicians was considerable and his "Match Box Blues" was recorded by Larry Hensely (1934), Carl Perkins (1955), and the Beatles (1964) among others.

JOHNSON, CHARLES SPURGEON (1893–1956). The black sociologist Charles Johnson graduated from Virginia Union University and in 1917 moved to Chicago where he obtained his Ph.D. Johnson served briefly in France during World War I. On his return to the United States, he was a researcher for the **National Urban League** (NUL) and the principal author of the study of the **Chicago Race Riot** of 1919, commissioned by the Chicago Commission on Race Relations, *The Negro in Chicago* (1922). Two years later Johnson moved to New York City where he edited the NUL's publication *Opportunity: A Journal of Negro Life* from 1922 to 1928. Under Johnson's guidance, *Opportunity* became a forum for the writers and artists of the **Harlem Renaissance**.

In 1926, Johnson became professor of sociology at Fisk University. He was the first **African American** appointed to the board of trustees of the **Julius Rosenwald** Fund in 1934 and in 1937 became vice president of the American Sociological Society. In 1942, Johnson established the Institute of Race Relations at Fisk. Johnson was the author of 17 books including *The Negro in American Civilization* (1930), *The Collapse of Cotton Tenancy* (1935), *Growing Up in the Black Belt* (1941), and *Patterns of Negro Segregation* (1943).

JOHNSON, HIRAM WARREN (1866–1945). Hiram Johnson qualified in law in 1888 and practiced in Sacramento and San Francisco. He made a name in cases against political corruption in San Francisco and was elected **Republican** governor of California in 1910 and initiated a program of reform. The various measures included **railroad** and public utility regulation, the initiative, referendum and recall, workmen's compensation and child labor laws, the eight-hour day for women workers, and state commissions on industrial welfare, industrial accidents, **immigration** and housing. In 1912 he was

Theodore Roosevelt's running mate for the unsuccessful **Progressive Party** and returned as governor of California in 1914. He was elected United States senator for the state in 1916 as a Republican and Progressive. Johnson supported the declaration of war on Germany in 1917 but opposed some of **Woodrow Wilson**'s war measures such as the **Sedition Act**. In 1919 Johnson, as a strict isolationist, took a prominent part as one of the "**Irreconcilables**" in opposing the **League of Nations** in any form. In 1920 he became a leading contender for the Republican presidential nomination but lost to **Warren Harding**. He declined the vice presidential nomination, failed to gain the Republican presidential nomination in 1924, and continued to serve as U.S. senator until his death.

Johnson's biggest achievement as senator was to see through approval of the Boulder (later renamed Hoover) Dam in 1928. In 1932, he declared his support for **Franklin D. Roosevelt** and actively campaigned on his behalf. He subsequently declined the offer to become secretary of the interior, but continued to support most **New Deal** measures until 1937. In 1934, Johnson won both the Republican and **Democratic** nominations for re-election. He maintained his opposition to American foreign involvement and during the 1930s supported the neutrality acts. Johnson was re-elected again in 1940 but then supported Republican Wendell Willkie's presidential campaign. In 1941, Johnson led the unsuccessful opposition to Roosevelt's Lend-Lease measures. Ill health limited his further participation in the Senate, but in 1945 Johnson voted against the United Nations Charter. Johnson's long political character in various ways charted the path followed by many Progressives.

JOHNSON, HUGH SAMUEL (1882–1942). Hugh Johnson grew up in Oklahoma, graduated from West Point in 1903, and served with the First Cavalry in the Philippines and on national park duties. He wrote popular stories about military life for magazines such as *Colliers*, *Century*, and *Scribners*. Johnson qualified in law in 1916 and served briefly as judge advocate with General **John Pershing** in the **punitive expedition** in **Mexico**. During **World War I**, Johnson was involved in the development of the **Selective Service** system and became army representative to the **War Industries Board**. He rose to the rank of brigadier general.

Following his resignation from the army in 1919, Johnson became an executive with the Moline Plow Company. He also became an investigator for **Bernard Baruch** in 1927 and in 1933 became part of **Franklin D. Roosevelt**'s team of advisors known as the "Brain Trust." In this role, Johnson helped to write the National Industrial Recovery Act and was then appointed as administrator of the National Recovery Administration (NRA). Johnson's rather volatile leadership of the NRA attracted considerable criticism and he was replaced in 1934. He then served briefly as head of the Works Progress Administration (WPA) in New York City but became increasingly critical of the **New Deal**. In 1940, he supported the Republican presidential candidate, Wendell Willkie, and also helped found the America First Committee to preserve United States neutrality.

JOHNSON, JAMES WELDON (1871–1938). James Weldon Johnson graduated from Atlanta University in 1894, taught briefly, and was admitted to the Florida bar in 1897. He practiced law in Florida from 1897 to 1901. In 1900, with his brother Rosamond, Johnson wrote, "Lift Every Voice and Sing," a song commemorating Lincoln's birth. The song was to become known as the "Negro National Anthem." With Bob Cole, the Johnsons were to write a number of other successful songs.

In 1906, Johnson was appointed United States consul to Venezuela and in 1909 to Nicaragua where he served until 1912. In 1917, Johnson became field secretary for the **National Association for the Advancement of Colored People** (NAACP) and in 1920 became the organization's first **African American** secretary. He was awarded the Spingarn Medal for services to black Americans in 1925. It was Johnson who coined the phrase **"Red Summer"** to describe the wave of violence directed against African Americans after World War I and he actively led the campaign to secure the passage of antilynching bills in the 1920s. Johnson actively encouraged the new wave of black writers that emerged during the **Harlem Renaissance**. From 1930, Johnson was the professor of creative literature at Fisk University. He was the author of *The Autobiography of an Ex-Colored Man* (1912), *Fifty Years and Other Poems* (1917), *God's Trombones* (1927), and editor of *The Book of Negro Poetry* (1922).

He also published collections of Negro Spirituals. Johnson died in an automobile accident in 1938.

JOHNSON-REED ACT. *See* QUOTA ACT.

JOLSON, AL (1886–1950). Born Asa Yoelson in Lithuania, Jolson's family emigrated to the United States about 1894 or 1895. Jolson left home with his brother and began a career as a song and dance man on the stage. He was particularly known for his black-face minstrel performances and achieved his first Broadway success in 1911 with *La Belle Paree*. Jolson became nationally known as a musical comedy performer in a series of successful stage performances, including *The Honeymoon Express* (1913), *Dancing Around* (1914), *Robinson Crusoe Jr.* (1916), and *Sinbad* (1918). It was in the latter that Jolson introduced **George Gershwin**'s songs "Swannee" and "My Mammy." He is best known for his appearance in the first sound motion picture, *The Jazz Singer*, 1927, in which he sang "Swanee," "Mammy," and "April Showers." Jolson made a number of **movies** with Warner Bros. including *Mammy's Boy* and *Singing Fool*, both in 1928. Jolson's last Broadway show was *Hold on to Your Hats* in 1941, but his career declined after the 1930s, although he entertained the troops during the World War II and provided the voice to the *Jolson Story* made in 1946.

JONES, JESSE HOLMAN (1874–1956). Jesse Jones was a successful Texas businessman who contributed to the development of Houston as a center of commerce and banking. In 1917, he was appointed director general of military relief for the Red Cross. Jones was a **Democratic Party** activist and he accompanied **Woodrow Wilson** to the **Versailles Peace Conference** in 1918. In 1924, he acted as finance chairman for the Democratic presidential campaign. In 1932, **Herbert Hoover** appointed Jones to the **Reconstruction Finance Corporation** (RFC). **Franklin D. Roosevelt** made him chairman of the RFC in 1933, a position he held until 1939 when he became federal loan administrator. In 1940, he became secretary of commerce but he resigned all his political offices in 1945 following a disagreement with Vice President Harry S. Truman.

JONES, WESLEY LIVSEY (1863–1932). After qualifying and practicing law in Illinois, Wesley Jones moved to Washington State where he entered **Republican** politics. He was elected to the House of Representatives in 1898 and to the Senate in 1909. He served until 1932. A "conservative Progressive," Jones supported **William Howard Taft** and backed Secretary of Interior Richard Ballinger in the dispute over conservation policy with chief forester **Gifford Pinchot.** Jones did agree with reform measures such as the **Adamson Act, Clayton Antitrust Act,** and a **child labor** law. Although in favor of a **League of Nations,** he voted for the **Lodge amendments** in 1918. In 1920, Jones sponsored the **Merchant Marine Act** and a further amendment in 1928 authorizing the sale of vessels not already disposed of. Throughout the 1920s, Jones supported measures to protect the lumber industry and the enforcement of **Prohibition.** From 1929 until 1932, Jones chaired the Senate Appropriation Committee. His backing for **Herbert Hoover** cost him re-election in 1932 and he died shortly after his defeat.

JONES ACT. *See* ORGANIC ACT OF PUERTO RICO 1917.

JONES ACT, 1916. An act passed in 1916 that provided civil government for the Philippines and conferred Philippine citizenship upon all inhabitants of the islands on 11 April 1899. It granted the vote to all literate adult males and established an elected legislature consisting of a Senate and House of Representatives.

JORDAN, DAVID STARR (1851–1931). David Starr Jordan was a graduate of Cornell University and of Indiana Medical School. After holding a number of teaching positions he was appointed professor of natural history at Indiana University in 1879 and became president of that institution in 1885. Jordan's skill as an administrator contributed considerably to the growth of Indiana University and in 1891 he was invited to become president of the newly created Stanford University. He was president of Stanford until 1913 and then chancellor until 1916. Jordan became well known for dismissing the sociologist **Edward Ross** in 1900 because of his political views, an incident that did much to define academic freedom in the United States. Despite this, under Jordan's guidance

Stanford became one of the country's leading educational institutions.

As well as being an administrator Jordan published numerous books and articles, but became increasingly well known as an advocate for world peace and in 1909 became head of the World Peace Foundation. He campaigned against America's entry into **World War I**, but supported the war effort after 1917. Jordan was awarded the Raphael Herman Prize for his writings on "International Justice and Friendship."

– K –

KAISER, HENRY JOHN (1882–1967). Henry Kaiser began his career as a photographer in Lake Placid, New York, but moved to Spokane, Washington, in 1906 where he worked first as a salesman and then in highway construction. In 1914, he established his own construction company in Vancouver. As his company expanded on the West Coast, Kaiser moved his base to Oakland, California, in 1921. In 1931, he joined a consortium that won the bid to build the Hoover Dam and later for the Bonneville and Grand Coulee Dams.

In 1940, Kaiser won a contract to build cargo ships for Great Britain and, following America's entry into World War II, established new yards to produce "Liberty ships" for the United States. His company became famous for producing one third of the nation's wartime cargo vessels. In 1945, Kaiser established the Kaiser-Frazer **automobile** manufacturing company that was successful for a time in the immediate postwar period. However, faced with competition from Ford, General Motors, and Chrysler, the company ceased production in 1955. The Kaiser Steel and Aluminum companies, however, continued to be successful. Equally successful was the Kaiser health and hospital program that had begun in 1938—with 1.5 million members by 1967, it was the country's largest health insurance program. Kaiser retired to Hawaii in 1954 and devoted his time to developing the island of Oahu and sponsoring television programs.

KALLEN, HORACE MEYER (1882–1974). Horace Kallen was born in Germany. His family emigrated to the United States in 1888 and Kallen grew up in Boston. He graduated from Harvard University in 1903 and completed his Ph.D. there in 1908 having specialized in philosophy. He remained at Harvard as a lecturer but in 1911 joined the University of Wisconsin as a lecturer in psychology and philosophy. Kallen was forced to resign in 1918 because he spoke in defense of pacifists during **World War I**. In 1919, he helped to establish the New School of Social Research in New York City and he remained associated with it even in retirement. Kallen's considerable output of writing covered a broad area. His first book was *William James and Henri Bergson: A Study in Contrasting Theories of Life* (1914), while his second was *The Book of Job as a Greek Tragedy* (1918). However, perhaps his most significant contribution was in propounding the philosophy of cultural pluralism in preference to ideas of a "melting pot" in his *Culture and Democracy in the United States* (1924). Kallen also wrote extensively about Judaism and was a leader of the American Jewish Congress (1922) and a member of the executive of the World Jewish Congress. Among his other works were *Individualism: An American Way of Life* (1933), *The Decline and Rise of the Consumer* (1936), *Art and Freedom* (1942), and *Americanism and its Makers* (1945).

KEATING-OWEN ACT. *See* CHILD LABOR LAWS.

KEATON, BUSTER (1895–1966). Born Joseph Francis Keaton, Buster Keaton was born into a theater family and began work in vaudeville at three. In 1917, he joined the Comique Film Company with "Fatty" **Arbuckle**. Keaton established his trademark "stone face" in a number of silent comedies and later in a series of full-length features built in acrobatic comedy with melodramatic narratives. He achieved considerable success with *The Navigator* (1924) and *Battling Butler* (1926), but his epic *The General* (1927) was a commercial failure. In 1928, Keaton moved to Metro-Goldwyn-Mayer (MGM) and made two more silent **movies** and then appeared in a number of sound films, starting with *The Hollywood Revue of 1929*. Keaton was fired from MGM in 1933 and starred in a number of lesser-known productions for Educational Films and Columbia

Pictures. He returned to MGM in 1937 as a gagman and technical adviser and played minor roles in films such as *Hollywood Cavalcade* (1939). In the late 1940s and early 1950s, he appeared in European circuses and variety shows and also made appearances on popular television shows. It was during these later years that Keaton was increasingly recognized as one of the greats of the silent movie era.

KELLER, HELEN (1880–1968). Helen Keller was struck deaf and blind as a baby but learned to communicate through Braille and sign language. She was able to gain a full education and attended Radcliffe College and graduated with honors in English and German in 1904. Keller achieved considerable fame through her writing including *The Story of My Life* (1902) and *The World I Live In* (1908). Prior to **World War I**, Keller worked on behalf of the American Foundation for the Blind, joined the **Socialist Party**, supported **women's suffrage**, and defended the **Industrial Workers of the World**. During the 1920s, Keller appeared in a **movie** of her life and toured the vaudeville circuit to raise money for the blind. Keller's writing continued to attract public acclaim with *My Religion* (1927), *Midstream— My Later Life* (1929), and *Helen Keller's Journal* (1938). Her life, which demonstrated the triumph of potential over disability, was celebrated in two films, *The Miracle Worker* (1962), and a documentary, *The Unconquered* (1953). In 1964, Keller was awarded the Presidential Medal of Freedom.

KELLEY, FLORENCE (1859–1932). Kelley was one of the many **women** who played a leading part in the **Progressive** movement. Following her degree from Cornell University, she studied in Zurich where she translated Engels' *The Condition of the Working-Class in England* (1887) and became a socialist. In 1891, she worked with **Jane Addams** at **Hull House** and then became the first chief factory inspector in Illinois in 1893 and secretary of the **National Consumers' League** in 1899. She assisted **Louis Brandeis** in the preparation of the brief in the **Supreme Court** case *Muller v. Oregon* establishing the legality of restricting the working hours of women. She was also a suffragist, a founder of the **National Association for the Advancement of Colored People** (NAACP), and a member of peace organizations. She campaigned in support of the establishment of a federal **Children's Bureau**, created in 1912, and later to secure the passage of the **Sheppard-Towner Act** in 1921.

KELLOGG, CHARLES BILLINGS (1856–1937). Charles Kellogg practiced law in St. Paul, Minnesota, and gained a reputation as special counsel in antitrust prosecutions and in investigations of the **railroads**. He served as senator from 1917 to 1923 and was one of the few **Republicans** to support the **League of Nations**. He was ambassador to Great Britain from 1924 to 1925 before succeeding **Charles E. Hughes** as secretary of state. In 1928, he negotiated the **Kellogg-Briand Pact** with Aristide Briand, foreign minister for France. He was awarded the Nobel Peace Prize in 1929 and served as a judge of the **Permanent Court of International Justice**, 1930–35.

KELLOGG, PAUL (1879–1958). After graduating from the New York School of Social Work in 1902, Kellogg began work as a writer for *The Survey* (formerly *Charities Magazine*), a journal focused on social issues and conditions that became the leading journal of **social work** in the United States. In 1912, he became editor. He conducted a detailed study of social conditions in Pittsburgh that was published as the *Pittsburgh Survey* between 1910 and 1914 and became a model of research to aid social reform. Like many **Progressives**, Kellogg opposed United States entry into **World War I** and was one of those who persuaded **Henry Ford** to organize the peace conference in Stockholm in 1916. He was also one of the founders of the **American Civil Liberties Union**.

KELLOGG-BRIAND PACT. Also known as the Pact of Paris and the Pact of Peace, the Kellogg-Briand Pact began as a bilateral agreement between **Charles Kellogg** and the French foreign minister, Aristide Briand, in 1928 to renounce war as an instrument of national policy. Thirteen other countries signed that year and ultimately 62 countries were to ratify it. However, its effectiveness was limited due to the lack of any powers of enforcement.

KELLOR, FRANCES ALICE (1873–1952). A graduate of Cornell Law School (1897) and the University of Chicago (1901), Frances Kellor became a leading social reformer and specialist in arbitration.

In 1904, she published *Out of Work*, a study of employment agencies in New York and helped to draft the state legislation to control employment agencies. In 1906, Kellor founded the National League for the Protection of Colored Women to help southern **African American** migrant **women**. In 1910, Kellor was appointed head of the New York State Bureau of Industries and Immigration. In 1912, Kellor supported **Theodore Roosevelt** and the National **Progressive Party**. She continued after the election defeat to work to implement reform at state level.

In 1915, Kellor organized "National Americanization Day" and was an active campaigner for Americanization during **World War I**. She continued these activities through the Inter-Racial Council formed in 1918. During the 1920s, Kellor focused more on the resolution of industrial disputes and in 1926 was one of the founders of the American Arbitration Association.

KENNEDY, JOSEPH PATRICK (1888–1969). The father of the future president, John F. Kennedy, Joseph Kennedy was educated at the Boston Latin School and Harvard University. He began work in 1912 as a state bank examiner and by 1914 had become president of a bank founded by his father. In 1914, he married Rose Fitzgerald, daughter of one of the first Irish Catholic Americans to be mayor of Boston. In 1917, Kennedy became assistant general manager of the Bethlehem Steel shipyards at Quincy and after the war he became manager of an investment banking company. From 1926 until 1930, Kennedy was part of a syndicate that bought a chain of movie theaters in the Northeast and was also involved in the merger that created RKO pictures. By the 1930s, he was a multimillionaire.

Kennedy made significant financial contributions to the election campaign of **Franklin D. Roosevelt** and held a number of positions under the **New Deal**. From 1934 to 1935, he was chair of the Securities Exchange Commission and in 1937 was chair of the United States Maritime Commission. Kennedy was appointed ambassador to Great Britain in 1938 but increasingly seemed to support appeasement and he returned home in 1940. In the 1950s, Kennedy was a supporter of Senator Joseph McCarthy and other conservatives. He transferred his political ambitions to his sons, and when Joseph Sr. was killed during World War II, the focus passed to John. While his great wealth helped secure the election of John F. Kennedy as president in 1960, his previous support for right-wingers was something of a handicap. Nonetheless, Joseph Kennedy will be remembered for creating a political dynasty.

KITCHIN, CLAUDE (1869–1923). Claude Kitchin graduated from Wake Forest College in 1888, studied law, and was admitted to the bar. In 1900, he was elected to the United States House of Representatives as a **Democrat** from North Carolina and was to serve for 12 terms. Kitchin was an effective speaker and by 1915 was majority leader in the House. A supporter of **Woodrow Wilson** particularly on the **tariff** issue, Kitchin nonetheless opposed the "Preparedness" campaign and entry into **World War I** in 1917. However, he actively supported the administration's war measures and helped secure passage of the finance bills. He was incapacitated by a cerebral hemorrhage in 1920.

KNOX, PHILANDER CHASE (1853–1921). Knox was a qualified lawyer who served as assistant United States district attorney for western Pennsylvania from 1876 to 1877. A corporation lawyer, Knox was involved in the formation of the Carnegie Steel Company in 1900. In 1901, President William McKinley appointed Knox attorney general, and he continued in that position under **Theodore Roosevelt**. Knox initiated the famous suit against the Northern Securities Company that marked the beginning of Roosevelt's "trust busting." He also drafted the legislation establishing the Department of Commerce and Labor in 1903. In 1904, the governor of Pennsylvania appointed Knox to the United States Senate to complete the term of a deceased senator. He was elected in his own right as a **Republican** in 1905.

In 1908, **William Howard Taft** appointed Knox as secretary of state. Knox promoted the policy of "dollar diplomacy" encouraging United States corporations to invest in Latin America and Asia. He declined an appointment to the **Supreme Court** in 1911 and resumed his law practice in 1913. In 1916, he was again elected as a senator for Pennsylvania. Knox was one of the leading opponents of the **Versailles treaty** in 1919, and he drafted the "round robin" against the league signed by 37 Republicans. It was Knox who proposed the resolutions rescinding the declarations of war against Austria and Germany in lieu of a peace treaty that **Woodrow Wilson** vetoed. The resolution was passed after Wilson left office in 1921.

KU KLUX KLAN. Originally formed in the aftermath of the Civil War, the Ku Klux Klan was revived in 1915 at Stone Mountain, Georgia, by **William J. Simmons**, apparently inspired by **D. W. Griffith's** movie, *The Birth of a Nation*. The Klan represented the White Anglo Saxon Protestant and older rural values. During the 1920s, it was anti-black, anti-immigrant, anti-Catholic, and anti-Jewish. In 1920, Simmons enlisted the assistance of Edward Young Clark and Elizabeth Tyler and their Southern Publicity Association to help build up Klan membership. Although strongest in southern states, the Klan spread beyond the South and gained political influence in Colorado, Indiana, Illinois, Ohio, and Pennsylvania. Reports in the press, particularly coverage in the *New York World* in 1921 of 152 acts of violence, only seemed to encourage the growth.

Under the leadership of **Hiram Wesley Evans** from 1922, the Klan grew in number and influence and by 1924 was estimated to have over four million members. In 1925, 40,000 Klansmen took part in a march in Washington, D.C. The Klan's influence was evident particularly in the **Democratic Party** and affected the nominations in 1924. However, scandals and reactions against violence led to its decline. In March 1925, David C. Stephenson, Grand Dragon of the Indiana Klan, was convicted of the murder and rape of his secretary and sentenced to life imprisonment. A lawsuit against a breakaway group of Klansmen in 1927 also exposed much of the Klan's activities. In 1939, Evans sold his interest in the Klan and in 1944 the official organization was dissolved. Various unofficial versions of the organization appeared in the 1950s and 1960s.

– **L** –

LABOR, DEPARTMENT OF. *See* DEPARTMENT OF LABOR.

LADD, EDWIN FREMONT (1859–1925). A graduate of the University of Maine, Ladd worked as an agricultural chemist at the New York Agricultural Experiment Station from 1884 until 1890.

That year, he was appointed as agricultural chemist at the North Dakota Agricultural College in Fargo. He also became editor of the *North Dakota Farmer and Sanitary Home* newspaper. In addition to his teaching duties, Ladd was responsible for enforcing state pure food legislation and inspecting paint products. In 1909, the state courts and the United States Department of Agriculture upheld Ladd's argument that bleached flower was unfit for human consumption. His studies were instrumental in securing the passage of a federal Grain Standards Act in 1916. In 1920 the **Nonpartisan League** nominated Ladd for the United States Senate and he defeated the incumbent **Republican** and **Democratic** opposition. He was part of the **Farm Bloc** in Congress and supported measures to bring economic cooperation. He also called for diplomatic recognition of the USSR.

LA FOLLETTE, ROBERT MARION (1855–1925). The Republican/Progressive politician, La Follette was elected to the House of Representatives as a **Republican** from Wisconsin in 1885 and served until 1891. He became governor of Wisconsin in 1901 and quickly turned the state into what **Theodore Roosevelt** described as "the laboratory of democracy." He was responsible for the introduction of regulation of the **railroad** rates, civil service reform, the use of specialist advisors in government, public health and pure food laws, conservation legislation, workmen's compensation laws, and the nation's first state income tax. The "Wisconsin Idea" also included the democratization of the political process through the use of referenda, initiatives, and the direct primary.

La Follette was elected Senator in 1905 and served until his death. He sponsored the Seaman's Act of 1915 that introduced regulation of working conditions and wages on river, lake, and seagoing vessels. In 1911, La Follette was one of the founders of the National Progressive Republican League critical of **William Howard Taft**'s administration, and La Follette contested the Republican presidential nomination in 1912. When Taft was renominated La Follette joined Theodore Roosevelt in the **Progressive Party**. He opposed American entry into **World War I** and subsequently the **League of Nations**. He led the call for investigation into the **Tea Pot Dome** scandal. In 1924, he won almost five million votes and 13 Electoral College votes as the Progressive Party candidate in the election.

LA GUARDIA, FIORELLO HENRY (1882–1947). Fiorello La Guardia was born in New York City and raised in Arizona. His family went to Trieste in 1898 and La Guardia worked for the United States consular service and from 1904 to 1906 was acting consular agent at Fiume (now Croatia). He returned to the United States in 1907, graduated from New York University Law School in 1910, and practiced law in New York City. He served as a major in the U.S. Air Force during **World War I**. La Guardia served in the United States House of Representatives from 1917 to 1921 and from 1923 to 1933 as a **Republican**. He was president of the New York City Board of Aldermen, 1920–21. While in Congress La Guardia was cosponsor of the **Norris-La Guardia Act**. He lost his seat in Congress in the **Democratic** landslide of 1932, but in 1933 he was elected mayor of New York on a Fusion ticket, supported by Republicans and reform groups.

The diminutive mayor, known as "the Little Flower," established a reputation for honesty and for reforming the city government. La Guardia's administration witnessed slum clearance and public housing development, the building of hospitals and childcare facilities, and the construction of roads and bridges (including the Triborough Bridge and the airport that bears his name). He held the office until 1945 and was president of the United States Conference of Mayors from 1936 until 1945. During World War II, La Guardia was appointed head of the United States Office of Civilian Defense until 1942. In 1946 he became director of the United Nations Relief and Rehabilitation Administration (UNRRA).

LAMONT, THOMAS WILLIAM (1870–1948). Following his graduation from Harvard University in 1892, Thomas Lamont started work as a reporter on the New York *Tribune*. After two years he moved into marketing and established his own company in 1898. He joined the Bankers Trust in 1903, became vice president of the First National Bank in 1909, and a partner in J. P. Morgan and Co. in 1911. He became chairman of the board in 1943.

In 1917, Lamont joined the **Liberty Loan** committee to aid the Treasury selling war bonds. He was also appointed as an unofficial adviser to the **Allies** and served as a Treasury representative at the **Versailles Peace Conference** in 1918. In 1924, Lamont was involved in drafting the **Dawes Plan** and in 1929 the **Young Plan** to deal with German reparations. Lamont also headed a commission to deal with the problem of Mexico's debts, and he took part in a consortium established to lend money to China and Japan. Lamont's other role was to liaise with the press and government bodies on behalf of J. P. Morgan and Company.

A generous benefactor, Lamont donated funds to assist in the rebuilding of Canterbury Cathedral, in England, after World War II, and he left a sizeable bequest to the Metropolitan Museum of Art.

LANDES, BERTHA KNIGHT (1868–1943). After graduating from the University of Indiana, Bertha Knight Landes moved to Seattle in 1895. She became a leading member of the Women's University Club, the League of Women Voters, and president of the Seattle Federation of Women's Club. She was elected to the Seattle City Council in 1922 and became president of the council. In 1926, Landes challenged the incumbent mayor, Dr. Edwin Brown and defeated him on an anticorruption platform to become the first female mayor of a major city in the United States. As part of her campaign to clean up the city, she dismissed the chief of police. Despite some success, Landes was defeated in 1928 and concentrated on **social work** activities and writing articles advocating greater participation of **women** in politics.

LANDIS, KENESAW MOUNTAIN (1866–1944). Qualified as a lawyer, Landis briefly worked as a personal assistant to Walter Gresham, secretary of state in the 1890s. He served as United States district judge in the Northern District of Illinois from 1905 to 1922. In the course of his term, he imposed a fine of $29 million on the Standard Oil Company, attempted to bring a murder indictment against Kaiser Wilhelm II following the sinking of the *Lusitania*, and presided over the trial of 113 members of the **Industrial Workers of the World** in 1918. He imposed heavy fines and prison sentences on those convicted, including **"Big Bill" Haywood**. Landis was equally severe during the subsequent trial under the **Espionage Act** of the Socialist leader **Victor Berger**, on whom he imposed a 20-year sentence, but wished he could have been shot. His intemperate remarks led to the overturn of the conviction. In 1920, following the scandal of the **Chicago White Sox** in 1919, he was appointed commissioner for the American and National Leagues of Baseball Clubs. He claimed to have "cleaned up" the national sport by taking a tough moral stand.

LANE, FRANKLIN KNIGHT (1864–1921). Franklin Lane was born in Canada. His family migrated to San Francisco in 1871. Lane went to University of California at Berkeley and Hastings Law School and passed the California bar examinations in 1888. However, he made his career initially as a journalist working for the *San Francisco Chronicle*, *Arthur McEwen's Letter*, and the *Tacoma Daily News,* which he owned. He became a partner in his brother's law firm in San Francisco in 1895. In 1897, Lane joined the committee responsible for drawing up San Francisco's new charter and he subsequently held the office of city attorney for three terms, beginning in 1898. In 1902, Lane was unsuccessful in the Californian gubernatorial election. Although a **Democrat**, he supported **Theodore Roosevelt** who appointed him to the Interstate Commerce Commission in 1906. **William Howard Taft** reappointed him for a second term in 1911.

In 1913, **Woodrow Wilson** appointed Lane as secretary of the interior. He supported several measures to further the development of natural resources on federal lands: the Reclamation Extension Act, the Alaskan **Railroad** Act, the Alaskan Coal Leasing Act, the Federal Water Power Act, and the General Leasing Act. In addition Lane endorsed the National Park Service Act (1916) that established the National Park system.

Lane supported Wilson's wartime policies and served on the **Council of National Defense**. He supported Americanization programs through the department's Bureau of Education and proposed a land reclamation scheme to provide farms for returning veterans as part of postwar reconstruction. In 1919, he chaired the **Industrial Conference** established to try to end the postwar labor conflicts. In 1920, he resigned from the cabinet and became vice president of a petroleum company.

LANGDON, HARRY PHILMORE (1884–1944). Harry Langdon joined a traveling medicine-show company at the age of 12 and toured as a vaudeville comedian in the years before **World War I**. From 1923 on, he worked with the film producer **Mack Sennett** and he made over two dozen silent movies between 1924 and 1926. He later joined director Frank Capra and made *Tramp, Tramp, Tramp* (1926), *The Strong Man* (1926), and *Long Pants* (1927). With **Charlie Chaplin**, Langdon was one of the most popular comedians of the silent film era. Langdon did not make the transition to sound film very well and his last significant role was in *Hallelujah, I'm a Bum* (1933). He made some films in the 1930s with Laurel and Hardy and appeared on stage during World War II.

LANSING, ROBERT (1864–1928). Lansing was admitted to the New York bar in 1889 and worked in his father's law firm. He became a specialist in international law. He was the founder and editor of the *American Journal of International Law* and acted in various capacities in the Bering Sea Arbitration (1892), the Alaskan Boundary Tribunal (1903), and United States and British Claims Arbitration. In 1914, Lansing was appointed as counselor in the State Department and the following year he succeeded **William Jennings Bryan** as secretary of state. Lansing supported the dispatch of United States troops to **Haiti** and the **Dominican Republic** in 1915–16, and he had a considerable influence in shaping the policies of **Woodrow Wilson**'s administration toward Germany after the outbreak of **World War I** in 1914. In 1917, Lansing negotiated the **Lansing-Ishii Agreement** with Japan, and at the end of the war he was one of the five United States delegates to attend the **Versailles Peace Conference** in 1919. However, he disagreed with Wilson about aspects of the peace treaty and the proposals for a **League of Nations**. When Lansing began to chair the cabinet meetings after the president's stroke in October 1919, Wilson called for his resignation. From 1920 until 1925, he practiced law in Washington, D.C., and acted as counsel to several foreign governments.

LANSING-ISHII AGREEMENT. Negotiated in November 1917, the agreement between the United States and Japan pledged to uphold the "Open Door" policy and respect the territorial integrity of China. Further negotiations during the **Washington Naval Conference** abrogated this agreement.

LARSEN, NELLA (1891–1964). The **African American** writer Nella Larsen was born of a Danish mother and African American father. Her mother subsequently married Peter Larson, from whom Nella took her surname. Larsen studied science at Fisk University from 1907 to 1910, when she moved to Copenhagen. She returned to New York City in 1912 and trained as a nurse. From 1915, she worked as a nurse. **Jessie Fauset** published Larsen's first stories in 1926 and Larsen became part of the **Harlem Renaissance**. Her first novel, *Quicksand*, was published to some acclaim in 1928; her second and last, *Passing* appeared in 1929. In 1930, Larsen became the first black woman to receive a Guggenheim Fellowship, but that year she was accused of plagiarism in one of her short stories. Although she proved her innocence, she was not published again in her lifetime. Following a sensational divorce in 1933, Larsen faded into obscurity and lived the rest of her life as a nurse.

LATHROP, JULIA CLIFFORD (1858–1932). The **social worker** Julia Lathrop was educated at Rockford Seminary and Vassar. In 1890 she went to Chicago where she worked at **Hull House** until 1912. Lathrop was a member of the Illinois State Board of Charities (1893–1901; 1905–09). In 1899, Lathrop was one of the campaigners who helped bring about the creation of the first juvenile court in America. She also helped to establish the Chicago School of Civics and Philanthropy. In 1912 President **William Howard Taft** appointed her head of the Children's Bureau in the U.S. **Department of Labor**. She held the position until 1921. Lathrop was president of the Illinois League of Women Voters from 1922 to 1924 and from 1925 to 1932 she was a member of the advisory committee on child welfare to the **League of Nations**.

LAWRENCE, ERNEST ORLANDO (1901–1958). The physicist Ernest Lawrence was educated at St. Olaf College, Northfield, Minnesota, the University of South Dakota, and the University of Minnesota. He completed his studies at Yale University, where he gained a Ph.D. in 1925. Lawrence remained at Yale as a National Research Council fellow and assistant professor until 1928, and he established a reputation as a brilliant experimentalist in the field of photoelectricity. Lawrence conducted a considerable amount of research in the area of television and he was to obtain a number of patents in the field in his later years.

In 1928, Lawrence accepted a position at the University of California, Berkeley. In 1931, he developed the cyclotron, or particle accelerator, which accelerated protons to initiate nuclear reactions. In 1936, Lawrence became director of the university's Radiation Laboratory. He was awarded the 1939 Nobel Prize in physics for the invention of the cyclotron. During World War II, he was involved in research connected with the development of radar and in the Manhattan Project to develop the atomic bomb. Lawrence's work won him numerous awards and medals.

LEAGUE OF NATIONS. The first major world organization established to prevent further outbreaks of war following **World War I**. The League was initially proposed in **Woodrow Wilson**'s **Fourteen Points** speech in 1918 and its constitution, the Covenant, was formally included in the **Treaty of Versailles** in 1919. Although many Americans supported the idea of a League and were prepared to agree to the Versailles settlement in some form, it faced unshakeable opposition from 14 Republican senators, known as the **"Irreconcilables"** led by **Henry Cabot Lodge**. More moderate politicians in both parties sought compromise, but Wilson's refusal to allow any concession led to failure to ratify the peace treaty in the Senate in 1920.

Established in Geneva, the League was to be fatally weakened by the absence of the United States. Germany was only a member from 1926 to 1933 and the Soviet Union from 1933. Japan withdrew from the League in 1933 and Italy did the same in 1937. Although it achieved some success in research and refugee work, and in settling disputes between smaller nations, the League had no force to back up its decisions and relied upon sanctions to enforce its will. It was unable to prevent the aggression by Japan in Manchuria and China from 1931 on, by Italy in Abyssinia, 1935–36, or by Russia against Finland in 1939. The League proved powerless to prevent the sequence of events that eventually led to World War II in 1939 despite holding various disarmament conferences. In 1946, the League of Nations was formally dissolved. It was succeeded by the United Nations Organization.

LEAGUE OF WOMEN VOTERS. After the passage of the **Nineteenth Amendment**, the **National American Woman Suffrage Association** became the League of Women Voters in 1920 to educate **women** as citizens and to mobilize them on women's issues.

LEGGE, ALEXANDER (1866–1933). After working for a time as a cowboy in Wyoming in the 1880s, Alexander Legge found work with the McCormick Harvesting Machine Company in Omaha. In 1902, he was made manager of domestic sales in the company that had since become the International Harvester Company. By 1918, he had become senior vice president of the entire company. In 1917, he joined **Bernard Baruch** in the raw materials division of the **War Industries Board**, and he later became manager of the Allied Purchasing Commission. In 1918, Legge joined the foreign mission of the War Industries Board and was involved in formulating economic provisions in the **Versailles Peace Treaty**.

After the war, Legge returned to International Harvester and was made president in 1922. He advised **Herbert Hoover** on the reorganization of the Department of Commerce and he took part in President **Warren Harding's Unemployment Conference**. When Hoover became president, he asked Legge to become secretary of commerce, but Legge declined the offer. He became chair of the **Federal Farm Board** in 1929 and in 1932 served as a member of the National Transportation Committee. In 1933, Legge established the Farm Foundation to encourage cooperation among farmers. He had earlier established the Katherine Legge Memorial to care for working women.

LEHMAN, HERBERT HENRY (1878–1963). Herbert Lehman, New York's longest serving governor, began work in a textile company in 1899. By 1906, he had risen to become vice president and treasurer of the company. In 1908, he joined his father's investment banking company, Lehman Brothers. Lehman worked for a number of charitable organizations, particularly the Joint Distribution Committee formed during **World War I** to aid Jews in Eastern Europe. During the war, he served in the General Staff Corps in Washington, D.C., as a captain and was responsible for purchase and traffic.

After the war, Lehman entered **Democratic** politics as a friend and associate of **Alfred E. Smith** and had various roles in Smith's election campaigns in 1924 and 1928. Lehman became **Franklin D. Roosevelt**'s lieutenant governor in 1928, a position he held until 1932. In 1932, he was elected governor in his own right, and re-elected again in 1934 and 1936. In 1938, he was elected to the first four-year term in the same capacity. Under his direction New York established a "little **New Deal**" of relief and recovery programs to alleviate the impact of the **Depression**, including unemployment insurance, minimum wages, and public housing. He resigned as governor in 1942 to become head of the Office of Foreign Relief and Rehabilitation Operations in the State Department. In 1943, this became the United Nations Relief and Rehabilitation Administration (UNRRA), and Lehman was chosen as director general. He held the position until his resignation in 1946.

Unsuccessful in his bid for a seat in the United States Senate in 1946, Lehman was elected in 1950, where he fought for liberal causes and opposed Senator Joseph McCarthy. He retired from the Senate in 1956.

LEMKE, WILLIAM FREDERICK (1878–1950). William Lemke studied at the University of North Dakota, Georgetown University, and Yale University. After gaining his law degree, he set up practice in Fargo. Associated with farmers and farmers' movements, Lemke became attorney for the **Nonpartisan League** in 1916. The league captured control of the state's **Republican Party** and Lemke became party chairman. In 1920, he was elected state attorney general. However, his reputation was seriously damaged that year when he and others were accused of allowing state funds to be invested in an insolvent private institution. Although the charges were quashed, Lemke was defeated in a recall election in 1921. He retired to his law practice for the remainder of the decade.

In 1932, Lemke was elected to the United States House of Representatives where he sponsored legislation to ease bankruptcy proceedings against farmers and a proposal for the federal government to assist farmers in paying off their mortgages. When **Franklin D. Roosevelt**'s administration opposed this last measure, Lemke turned against the **New Deal** and joined Father Charles Coughlin, Dr. Francis Townsend, and Gerald K. Smith in the National Union. He was nominated the Union's presidential candidate in 1936 but secured less than 2 percent of the national vote. He failed to win election to the Senate in 1940 but remained in Congress for the rest of his life.

LENROOT, IRVINE LUTHER (1869–1949). Irvine Lenroot studied law and was admitted to the bar in Superior, Wisconsin, in 1897. A **Republican** and supporter of **Robert M. La Follette**, he was elected to the state assembly in 1900 and served as the speaker in 1903 and 1905. Unsuccessful in an attempt to gain the gubernatorial nomination in 1906, Lenroot was elected to the United States House of Representatives in 1908 where he became one of the leaders of the progressive Republicans. In 1917, his support for La Follette ended when Lenroot supported war against Germany. In 1918, Lenroot defeated La Follette's candidate for the nomination for the vacant Senate seat and then won the general election. He was re-elected in 1920.

Lenroot played a prominent role in the Senate's deliberations over the **Treaty of Versailles** and **League of Nations**. He was in favor of mild reservations to the treaty, and he wrote several of the **"Lodge amendments"** adopted by the Senate but rejected by **Woodrow Wilson**. Lenroot continued in his role as a moderate Progressive during the administrations of **Warren Harding** and **Calvin Coolidge** and chaired the Committee on Public Lands. However, some critics felt he was slow to respond to the **Teapot Dome** scandal and he failed to be renominated in the senatorial primary election in 1926.

In 1929, Coolidge nominated Lenroot to a judgeship of the United States Court of Customs Appeals, and President **Herbert Hoover** resubmitted his nomination when Congress returned from adjournment. He served on the court, renamed Court of Patent and Customs Appeals, until 1944.

LEOPOLD AND LOEB CASE. In 1924, two well-to-do Chicago students, 19-year-old Nathan Leopold, Jr., the son of a millionaire box manufacturer, and 18-year-old Richard Loeb, son of a retired Sears Roebuck vice president, were charged with the abduction and murder of Robert Franks, aged 14. The trial became a sensation because of the relationship between the two murderers and their motive for the crime. The trial involved detailed psychiatric debate and raised the issue of the death penalty to national prominence. Loeb deliberately set out to commit the perfect crime and Leopold, his lover, was apparently influenced by Friedrich Nietzsche's notion of a "superman" beyond moral codes, a role in which he saw Loeb. After murdering Franks, the boys disfigured his body with acid and hid it in a drain. They then created the impression that Franks had been kidnapped. The two were only linked to the murder when a pair of spectacles were discovered near the body that were traced back to Leopold, and both boys eventually confessed under questioning.

Clarence Darrow was hired for the defense and he changed the "not guilty" pleas to "guilty" in order not to face a jury and to avoid the death sentence. Both sides used psychiatric evidence and even Sigmund Freud was consulted. Ultimately, Darrow's impassioned argument in a 12-hour summation, that the boys were victims of their own psyche and that the death penalty would be as cruel as the murder, won the day. Judge John Caverly sentenced both boys to life imprisonment and 99 years.

Loeb died in 1936 following a razor attack in Joliet prison. Leopold studied languages, mathematics and physics, organized the prison library, and took part in experiments to combat malaria in prison. He was released in 1958 and moved to Puerto Rico, where he graduated with an M.A., taught mathematics, worked in hospitals, and produced a study, *The Birds of Puerto Rico*. He died in 1971.

LEOPOLD, NATHAN FREUDENTHAL (1904–1971). *See* LEOPOLD AND LOEB CASE.

LEVER FOOD AND FUEL ACT, 1917. The Food and Fuel Act empowered President **Woodrow Wilson** to establish and maintain government control "of foods, feeds, and fuel" in order to "prevent scarcity, monopolization, hoarding, injurious speculation, manipulation . . ." Under this measure, the president established the **United States Food Administration** and the **United States Fuel Administration** to maintain adequate supplies and prevent shortages or profiteering during **World War I**.

LEWIS, JOHN LLEWELLYN (1880–1969). John L. Lewis began work in the coal mines in Iowa in the 1890s. In 1907, he moved to Illinois and he was elected president of the United Mine Workers of

America (UMWA) local in 1910. In 1911, Lewis was appointed as field representative for the **American Federation of Labor** (AFL) and in 1917 became vice president of the UMWA. He was elected president in 1920, and Lewis held the position until his retirement in 1960.

UMWA membership declined during the 1920s as the coal industry shrank in the face of foreign competition and the increased use of oil. The deterioration in membership increased with the onset of the **Depression** in the 1930s. Lewis, however, capitalized upon the change of political climate with the advent of the **New Deal** and began to mobilize the union membership. Lewis argued for the AFL to take a more militant approach and to focus on organizing workers on an industry-wide basis rather than crafts. As differences within the AFL exploded into physical conflict in 1935, Lewis joined with **Sidney Hillman** and **David Dubinsky** to establish a Committee for Industrial Organization (CIO). The CIO became the leading force in increasing union membership during the 1930s and Lewis played an active role in these developments. In 1938 the CIO became an autonomous labor organization, the Congress of Industrial Organizations.

Lewis became increasingly critical of the administration of **Franklin D. Roosevelt** and in 1940 openly supported the **Republican** candidate, Wendell Willkie. In 1940, he also stepped down as president of the CIO. Lewis's growing opposition to Roosevelt's war administration caused differences with the CIO leadership, and in 1942 Lewis took the UMWA out of the organization. His conflict with Roosevelt heightened when Lewis led the miners in a series of strikes in 1943. He continued his confrontational methods after the war, and strikes in the face of a federal injunction in 1946 resulted in massive fines for the union. In the 1950s, Lewis collaborated more with mine owners in return for pension and health care programs for the coal miners. After his retirement, Lewis was director of the union retirement and welfare funds and some of his decisions with regard to investments were detrimental to the funds' viability. *See also* TRADE UNIONS.

LEWIS, SINCLAIR (1885–1951). Sinclair Lewis was born Harry Sinclair Lewis in Sauk Centre, Minnesota. After graduating from Yale

University, he worked as a newspaper reporter in Iowa and California, and then in publishing in New York City. Between 1912 and 1920, he wrote several novels and short stories for the *Saturday Evening Post*. However, it was with his critique of small town life in *Main Street* (1920) that Lewis achieved a national reputation. He followed this up with a portrait of a small town businessman, *Babbitt* (1922), which, like *Main Street*, was judged by some reviewers and readers to be too critical of American life and values. Lewis's next book, *Arrowsmith* (1925), dealt with the failures of the medical profession and was awarded the Pulitzer Prize. Lewis rejected the award on the grounds that the terms of the honor, requiring the presentation of the "wholesome atmosphere of American life," inhibited authors from writing freely. In *Elmer Gantry* (1927), Lewis turned his attack on the hypocrisy of religious fundamentalists, while *Dodsworth* (1929) offered a more sympathetic portrait of the businessman/inventor.

Not all critics, many of whom argued that he showed America in too negative a light, welcomed Lewis's award of the Nobel Prize for literature in 1930. In his acceptance speech, Lewis in turn criticized the American literary establishment. Although he published a number of novels in the 1930s, Lewis did not reach the heights of his previous work. Only his satirical study of American fascism, *It Can't Happen Here* (1935), was particularly successful both as a novel and then as a play. *Kingsblood Royal* (1947), which dealt with the issue of race and racial identity, also achieved some critical acclaim if only for its treatment of a vital social issue, but most of Lewis's other postwar writing was judged to have little merit.

LIBERTY LOANS. Liberty Loans were the series of five bonds issued by the Treasury between May 1917 and April 1919 to raise money to help finance the war effort (the last was known as the Victory Bond). With interest rates of between 3.5 and 4.5 percent and purchase symbolic of patriotism, the bonds were over-subscribed and raised over $21 billion dollars. Finance was also raised through the increased taxation brought about by the Revenue Acts of 1916 and 1917.

LINDBERGH, CHARLES AUGUSTUS (1902–1974). Charles Lindbergh became a national hero after making the first single-handed nonstop transatlantic flight from New York to Paris in his airplane called *The Spirit of St. Louis* on 20 May 1927. He previously had flown in the Army Air Service and as an airmail pilot between Chicago and St. Louis. As a result of his flight, he was awarded the Congressional Medal of Honor and *Time* magazine made him its first "Man of the Year." He subsequently worked to promote aviation and was employed by various airline companies. Lindbergh was in the headlines again in 1932 when his 20-month-old son was abducted and found dead two months later.

The Lindberghs left the United States in 1935 to live first in England and then France. While in Europe, Lindbergh inspected air forces in Germany, Poland, and Czechoslovakia, and became convinced that Germany had a superior airforce and that any war could destroy Western civilization. He returned to the United States in 1939 and became a leading noninterventionist and a member of the America First Committee. He was much criticized for comments that appeared anti-Semitic and pro-Nazi.

With American entry into World War II in 1941, Lindbergh tested aircraft as a civilian. Nonetheless, he flew combat missions in the Pacific in 1944. After the war, Lindbergh continued to work for the United States Air Force and Defense Department and in 1954 President Dwight D. Eisenhower promoted him to brigadier general. His autobiography, *The Spirit of St. Louis* (1953), was awarded a Pulitzer Prize in 1954.

LINDSAY, (NICHOLAS) VACHEL (1879–1931). Vachel Lindsay attended Chicago Art Institute from 1901 to 1903 and the New York School of Art from 1903 to 1904. He was unsuccessful in getting his poetry published so took to the road, selling his verse on the streets and giving lectures and spoken performances. Lindsay's poem "General William Booth Enters into Heaven" was published in *Poetry* in 1913 and won considerable recognition. **Charles Ives** set it to music in 1914. Collections of his poetry were published in 1913 and 1914. Lindsay toured extensively, gave recitals before **Woodrow Wilson**'s cabinet, and met with reformers, industrialists, and filmmakers. In 1920, he visited England and was acclaimed as "easily the most important living American poet." His career declined following the poor reception given to his prose work, *The Golden Book of Springfield*

(1920), and he suffered increasingly from financial hardship and ill health. He committed suicide in 1931.

LIPPMANN, WALTER (1889–1974). Walter Lippmann made a name as a brilliant student at Harvard. He left university in 1910 to become a journalist on the socialist *Boston Common*. Part of the radical **Greenwich Village** set, Lippmann produced a call for reform in his *Preface to Politics* in 1912. In 1914, he published *Drift and Mastery,* which captured much of the **Progressive** ethos in advocating government run scientifically by a public-minded elite. The same year Lippmann joined the staff of the *New Republic*. He supported United States entry into **World War I** and joined a team of planners to draw up plans for the postwar world. He was one of the group of American advisors at the **Versailles Peace Conference** but was disillusioned by the terms of the peace treaty and became a critic of it and the **League of Nations**. His wartime experience also made him skeptical of the democratic process and his *Liberty and the News* (1920) and *Public Opinion* (1922) suggested that government was best left to experts.

In 1922, Lippmann joined the New York *World* where he established a reputation as one of the leading journalists of his day. His book, *A Preface to Morals* (1929), also found a wide readership. Lippmann became a contributor to the conservative *New York Herald-Tribune* in 1931, and his columns were widely syndicated, nationally and internationally. In the late 1930s, he advocated United States support for Great Britain against Nazi Germany and during the war wrote a best-seller entitled *United States Foreign Policy: Shield of the Republic* (1943) advocating a continuation of the Grand Alliance with Great Britain and the USSR. When the alliance broke up after the war, Lippmann wrote a critical study of containment, *The Cold War* (1947), and was probably the originator of the phrase used to describe postwar relations with the Soviet Union.

Lippmann was awarded the Presidential Medal of Freedom in 1964 and worked on the CBS television network for a number of years. However, he became increasingly critical of Lyndon Johnson's policies in Vietnam and he retired from journalism in 1967.

LITERACY TEST. Literacy testing was proposed by **Henry Cabot Lodge** in 1891 as an addition to **immigration** legislation in order to restrict the number of immigrants. Bills introducing such a measure were vetoed by Presidents Grover Cleveland (in 1897), **William Howard Taft** (in 1913), and **Woodrow Wilson** (in 1915 and 1917). The law was passed over Wilson's veto in 1917.

LLOYD, HAROLD CLAYTON (1893–1971). The comedian Harold Lloyd began work in the theater as a child and then in 1913 worked with the Edison Film Company in San Diego. Later that year, he moved to Los Angeles and worked with Hal Roach at Universal Pictures. In 1917, he conceived his film character, Harold. Wearing his trademark horned-rimmed glasses and straw hat, Lloyd went on to make many **movies** involving remarkable stunts that he performed himself. In his best-known movie, *Safety Last* (1923), Lloyd was filmed hanging onto the clock face of a tall building. His later films included *Girl Shy* (1924), *The Freshman* (1925), *For Heaven's Sake* (1926), *The Kid Brother* (1927), and *Speedy* (1928). With the coming of sound, Lloyd's films were less successful, but with **Charlie Chaplin** and **Buster Keaton,** he was one of the greatest silent film comics.

LOCKE, ALAIN (1886–1954). The **African American** writer and critic, Alain Locke was a brilliant student and graduated from Harvard University *magna cum laude* in 1907. The first African American Rhodes Scholar, he studied in Berlin and Paris before assuming a position at Howard University in Washington, D.C. He completed his Ph.D. at Harvard in 1918 and became chair of the philosophy department at Howard, a position he held until 1953. In 1925, Locke edited a selection of articles from *Survey Graphic* showing the talent of new African American writers and published them as *The New Negro*. Locke actively encouraged and supported writers who were emerging as part of the **Harlem Renaissance**, and with T. Montgomery Gregory, he edited *Plays of Negro Life* in 1927. Locke was a regular reviewer and critic of black art and culture and a leader in the field of education.

LODGE, HENRY CABOT (1850–1924). A leading conservative **Republican** politician and historian, Lodge was one of the first people to gain a Ph.D. in history in the United States. He taught at Harvard

University and published several historical biographies before turning to politics. He served as a member of the House of Representatives for Massachusetts from 1887 to 1893 and as senator from 1893 to 1924. Although essentially conservative on domestic matters, Lodge supported most of the policies of **Theodore Roosevelt**, particularly in foreign affairs. He remained loyal to **William Howard Taft** in 1912 despite his friendship with Roosevelt. He was one of **Woodrow Wilson's** greatest critics, and as chair of the Senate Foreign Affair Committee he successfully led the opposition to the Covenant of the **League of Nations**. His reservations were expressed in the **Lodge amendments**. Lodge was a delegate to the **Washington Naval Conference** and successfully guided the agreement through the Senate in 1922.

LODGE AMENDMENTS. On 6 November 1919, Senator **Henry Cabot Lodge** tabled 15 proposed amendments to the **Versailles Peace Treaty** and **League of Nations** covenant specifically aimed at limiting American participation in the League. These amendments or reservations included allowing the United States to determine its own financial and military obligations to the League and exempting the Monroe Doctrine from external interference. When President **Woodrow Wilson** refused to accept any amendments, the opposition was such as to prevent ratification of the treaty.

LOEB, RICHARD ALLEN (1905–1936). *See* LEOPOLD AND LOEB CASE.

LOGAN, RAYFORD WHITTINGHAM (1897–1982). The **African American** historian Rayford Logan graduated from Williams College in 1917 and joined the army where he rose to lieutenant. Disillusioned by the discrimination he experienced in the army, Logan remained in France for five years after **World War I** ended. He returned to the United States in 1924 and taught at Lincoln University while completing his Ph.D. from Harvard (1936). He also taught at Atlanta University from 1933 to 1938, before moving to Howard University where he worked for the remainder of his career. Logan's *The Diplomatic Relations of the United States with Haiti* was published in 1941.

Logan campaigned for full black inclusion in the war effort in World War II and was a leader of **A. Philip Randolph**'s March on Washington Movement in 1941. In 1944, he edited *What the Negro Wants* spelling out African American opposition to segregation. After World War II, Logan was chief adviser on international affairs for the **National Association for the Advancement of Colored People** (NAACP). He was the author of *The Negro in American Life and Thought, 1877–1901* (1953).

LOMBARD, CAROLE (1908–1942). Born Jane Alice Peters, Carole Lombard had her first role in motion pictures in 1920. Fox studios employed her when she was 16. Despite facial scarring from an automobile accident, Lombard was able to sign a contract with the **Mack Sennett** company in 1927 and appeared in a number of comic roles before she left in 1928. In 1930, Lombard joined Paramount Pictures and made several minor movies before making a name for her acting in *Twentieth Century* (1934), *Hands Across the Table* (1935), *My Man Godfrey* (1936), *True Confession* (1937), and *Nothing Sacred* (1937). Her "screwball" comic roles reflected the mood of the 1930s. During World War II, Lombard campaigned across the country to help sell war bonds. She died when her flight back from one of these appearances crashed near Las Vegas.

LONDON NAVAL CONFERENCE, 1930. A follow-up to the **Washington Naval Conference**, the conference of the United States, Great Britain, France, Italy, and Japan convened in London to agree limits on smaller naval vessels not covered in the previous agreement. The French and Italians withdrew when other delegates refused to increase their ratios. Agreements were reached between United States, Great Britain, and Japan on a ratio of cruisers and destroyers of 10:10:7 and equal tonnage in submarines.

LONG, HUEY PIERCE (1893–1935). Known as the "Kingfish," Long was a largely self-taught lawyer who entered Louisiana politics as a member of the **Railroad** Commission (1918–21), which then became the Public Service Commission (1921–28). After failing to win election in 1924, he was elected Governor of Louisiana for the **Democratic Party** in 1928 and built a reputation as a populist reformer.

He raised taxes to pay for school books and embarked upon a program of bridge and road building and improving the University of Louisiana at Baton Rouge. He ran the state largely as a one-party state using patronage and intimidation to maintain control.

Long was elected to the United States Senate in 1930 but continued as governor until one of his supporters could replace him in 1932. Initially sympathetic, Long became increasingly critical of **Franklin D. Roosevelt's New Deal**. In 1934, he outlined his "Share Our Wealth" program, which promised every family a guaranteed cash income, old age pensions, and reduced working hours financed by placing a ceiling on incomes and property ownership. In 1935, he announced his candidacy for the Democratic presidential nomination and it appeared likely that he could attract as much as 10 percent of the vote. Franklin Roosevelt, who described him as one of the "two most dangerous men in America," regarded him as a serious threat and the revenue bill he submitted to Congress was in part a response to Long's challenge. However, Long died on 10 September 1935, after being gunned down on the steps of the state capitol in Baton Rouge by the son-in-law of a political opponent.

LONGVIEW, TEXAS. In July 1919, tension between the black and white populations of the rural community of Longview, Texas, erupted in violence. Following the murder of two black men, 100 national guardsmen were drafted into the town to restore order. Texas Rangers arrested 17 white men and 21 **African Americans**, but none were tried. The Longview riot was one of 25 in the **"Red Summer"** following **World War I**.

LONGWORTH, NICHOLAS (1869–1931). Born into one of Cincinnati's oldest and wealthiest families, Nicholas Longworth was educated at Harvard and Cincinnati Law School from where he graduated in 1894. A **Republican**, he was elected to the Cincinnati Board of Education in 1898, the Ohio House of Representatives in 1899, and Ohio Senate in 1901. In 1902, Longworth was elected to the United States House of Representatives. In 1912, he was defeated due to the split in the Republican Party, but he was re-elected in 1914 and served until his death. In 1923, he became Republican majority floor leader and worked with **Calvin Coolidge**'s administration to ensure tax reductions, a veterans' bonus, and the settlement of the European war debt. Longworth's ability as a conciliator helped to bring about the passage of 594 bills between 1923 and 1925 and was recognized in his appointment as speaker of the House in 1925. As a speaker, Longworth exercised considerable authority and introduced a number of reforms in the business of the House including making the *Congressional Record* more reliable and ending some of the discriminatory practices against **women**.

LOOS, (CORINNE) ANITA (1893–1981). The author Anita Loos began her career as a child actress before writing screenplays, the first of which was produced in 1912. In 1915, she moved to Hollywood and began writing for **D. W. Griffith**. Loos wrote and cowrote over 200 film scripts during her years in Hollywood. However, her greatest success was with the novel *Gentlemen Prefer Blondes* first serialized in *Harper's Bazaar* in 1925. Loos produced a successful dramatized version of the book and it eventually became a **movie** starring Marilyn Monroe in 1953. A sequel, *But Gentlemen Marry Brunettes*, was published in 1928. In 1931, Loos began work at MGM and wrote the screenplay for several successful sound films, beginning with *Red-Headed Woman* (1932). She also continued to write for the theater and produced the script for *Gigi* in 1951. Her autobiography was published in two volumes, *A Girl Like I* (1966) and *Kiss Hollywood Good-By* (1974).

LOWDEN, FRANK ORREN (1861–1943). After studying at rural schools, Frank Lowden became a teacher in Minnesota at the age of 14. In 1885, he graduated from the University of Iowa and went on to study law at the Union College of Law, Chicago. He graduated in 1887 and practiced law in Chicago where he entered politics as a **Republican**. He was first appointed to Congress in 1906 and elected to the post in 1908. He retired from Congress in 1910 but remained active in state politics. In 1916, Lowden was elected governor of Illinois and continued his reputation as a moderate reformer. In 1920, he was a contender for the Republican presidential nomination but returned to private life after **Warren Harding**'s victory. In the 1920s, he was active in a number of farming organizations and campaigned for the **McNary-Haugen** Bill. In 1929, Lowden became head of the Country Life Commission. In the 1930s, he was an isolationist and active in the America First Committee.

LUCE, HENRY ROBINSON (1898–1967). The son of a missionary, Henry Luce was born in China. He was a student at Yale and became a commissioned officer in the United States Army in 1918. He returned to college in 1919 and graduated in 1920. After a brief period of study at Oxford, England, Luce returned to the United States, where, with Briton Hadden, he established *Time* magazine in 1923. In 1930, Luce founded *Fortune*, a journal aimed at businessmen. Time, Inc., expanded and in 1935 began a documentary newsreel series, *The March of Time*. In 1936, Luce began production of *Life*, a magazine of photojournalism. *Time* and *Life* became enormously influential journals and had a huge circulation until they were undermined by the advent of television.

In an editorial entitled "The American Century" in *Life* in 1941, Luce argued that America should abandon **isolationism** and take a lead in rebuilding a peaceful world after an Allied victory. Luce supported the presidential campaign of the **Republican** Wendell Willkie in 1940. After the war, Luce was an advocate of resistance to perceived Soviet expansion. In 1949, Luce blamed Harry S. Truman's administration for the "loss" of China to the communists and supported the election of Dwight D. Eisenhower in 1952. Later Luce supported the war in Vietnam. Luce retired in 1964.

LUHAN, MABEL DODGE (1879–1962). A leading patron of the arts during the interwar years, Mabel Dodge Luhan (born Mabel Ganson) established a salon on Fifth Avenue, New York, where intellectuals, such as **Max Eastman, Emma Goldman, Walter Lippmann,** and **John Reed,** were entertained. Luhan herself contributed articles on pacifism to the radical journal *The Masses* during **World War I**. After the war, she married a Native American, Tony Luhan, and established an artist colony in Taos, New Mexico. Among her guests there were the English author D. H. Lawrence and the American artist **Georgia O'Keefe**. Mabel Luhan wrote several volumes of autobiography, including *Intimate Memories* (1933), *European Experiences* (1936), and *Edge of Taos Desert* (1937).

LUSITANIA. The British passenger liner, torpedoed and sunk by a German submarine off the coast of Ireland, 7 May 1915, en route from New York to Liverpool. One of the largest and fastest ships of its day, the *Lusitania* sank within 20 minutes of being hit by two torpedoes.

Of 651 crew and 1,255 passengers, 1,198, including 124 Americans, died. The sinking of the ship caused great outrage in the United States despite the fact that passengers boarding in New York had been warned they were at danger. It also transpired that the vessel was carrying armaments. President **Woodrow Wilson** described the sinking as an illegal and inhuman act and warned the German government that any further such action would be regarded as "deliberately unfriendly." Secretary of State **William Jennings Bryan** felt this response was too strong and resigned.

LUSK LAWS. The Lusk laws expressing the antiradical sentiment that followed World War I were produced by New York state senator Clayton R. Lusk and were intended particularly to prevent unpatriotic or subversive activities in schools by issuing licenses to teachers.

LYND, HELEN MERRELL (1896–1982). The sociologist and social philosopher Helen Lynd obtained a B.A. from Wellesley College in 1919. After two years teaching in school, she began postgraduate studies and earned an M.A. (1922) and Ph.D. (1944) from Columbia University. She was best known for her work with her husband **Robert S. Lynd** and their famous study of Muncie, Indiana, *Middletown: A Study in Contemporary American Culture* (1929) and *Middletown in Transition: A Study of Cultural Conflicts* (1937). Helen Lynd taught at Sarah Lawrence College from 1928 to 1965. Her own work covered a number of fields and she published *England in the Eighteen Eighties* (1945), *Field Work in College Education* (1945), and *Shame and the Search for Identity* (1958). During the 1950s, she was attacked for alleged communist sympathies, an accusation she denied when called before the Senate Internal Security Committee in 1953. She later wrote a defense of civil liberties included in a collection of reviews, *Toward Discovery*, published in 1965.

LYND, ROBERT STAUGHTON (1892–1970). The famous sociologist and coauthor with **Helen Lynd** of one of the key studies of American society during the 1920s, Robert Lynd graduated from Princeton University in 1914. He then worked for four years as an assistant magazine editor before serving briefly in the field artillery during **World War I**. After the war, Lynd became a Unitarian and earned his D.D. from the Union Theological Seminary in 1923. In the early 1920s, he served as a missionary preacher and wrote articles based on his experiences in the oil fields. In 1923, Lynd and his wife Helen began a study of small-town life sponsored by the Committee on Social and Religious Surveys. Their work, based on Muncie, Indiana, resulted in the book, *Middletown: A Study in Contemporary American Culture* (1929). *Middletown* became a classic study that contrasted white urban values in the age of mass consumption with the sense of community and harmony the Lynds believed had existed in the 1890s. Lynd's research earned him a Ph.D. from Columbia University, where he became professor of sociology in 1931. A further study of Muncie, *Middletown in Transition: A Study of Cultural Conflicts*, appeared in 1937 and Lynd's final book, *Knowledge for What?* appeared in 1939. The Lynds' *Middletown* ranked with the writing of **Sinclair Lewis** and **H. L. Mencken**, and like them offered a critical view of the narrow-minded conformity and materialism that was evident in parts of the United States in the 1920s.

– M –

McADOO, WILLIAM GIBBS (1863–1941). William McAdoo studied law in Tennessee and for a while was president of the Knoxville Street Railway Company. In 1892, he moved to New York City to sell **railroad** bonds and secured the funding for the Hudson River tunnels. In 1902, McAdoo became president of the Hudson & Manhattan Railroad, the company that developed the rapid-transit tunnels between New York City and New Jersey. He was vice chairman of the Democratic National Committee in 1912 and served as **Woodrow Wilson**'s secretary of treasury from 1913 to 1918. During **World War I**, McAdoo chaired the Federal Reserve Board and **War Finance Corporation** and was director general of the railways when the government took over the temporary running of the system. Married to the president's daughter, McAdoo was seen by many as the **Democratic Party**'s "heir apparent" in 1920. However, he did not campaign openly nor did he receive Wilson's endorsement. McAdoo's support for **Prohibition** might also have contributed to his failure to win the nomination. He established a home in California, from where he unsuccessfully fought for the Democratic presidential nomination against **Al Smith** in 1924. Faced with a deadlock between the two, the convention turned instead to **John W. Davis**. McAdoo was elected United States senator for California in 1932 and served until 1938 when he was defeated.

MacARTHUR, DOUGLAS (1880–1964). Douglas MacArthur graduated first in his class from West Point in 1903. He was a member of the General Staff in France during **World War I** and commanded the 42nd (Rainbow) Division. After the war MacArthur became superintendent at West Point from 1919 to 1922. He became a major general in 1928 and commander of the Philippines Department in 1928. From 1930 to 1935, MacArthur was general and chief of staff of the United States Army. In 1932, he led the troops who forcibly ejected the **Bonus Army** from Washington, D.C. He was director of organization of national defense for the Philippines from 1935 to 1937 when he retired. Recalled to active service in 1941 as a lieutenant general, MacArthur was placed in command of the United States Forces in the Far East. He was forced to flee the Philippines following the Japanese invasion in 1941 but announced "I shall return."

MacArthur was made supreme commander of Allied Forces in the Southwest Pacific in 1942. As he had promised, MacArthur led the forces that retook the Philippines in 1944. He received the Japanese surrender in Tokyo in September 1945 and became Supreme Commander for the Allied Powers in Japan until 1951. In 1950, MacArthur became commander of the United Nations forces that responded to the attack of North Korea upon the South. He was dismissed in 1951 because of his public differences with President Harry S. Truman, but returned to the United States as a public hero. He clearly had presidential ambitions, but after playing a key role at the **Republican Party** convention in 1952, he failed to get the nomination and faded from the political scene.

McCORMICK, MEDELL (1877–1925). After graduating from Yale University in 1900, McCormick began work as a police reporter on the *Chicago Tribune,* which was owned by his grandfather. By 1907, McCormick was vice president, secretary, and treasurer of the Tribune Company. In 1908, he went to Europe to be treated for depression by Carl Jung. In 1909, he left the *Tribune* and turned to politics. He joined the **Progressive Party** in 1911 and was the vice chairman of the Progressive National Committee from 1912 to 1914. In 1912, McCormick was one of the Progressives elected to the Illinois House of Representatives. He was re-elected in 1914. In 1914, McCormick also went to Mexico as a reporter for *Harper's*.

In 1915, McCormick resigned from the Progressive Party and in 1916 became chairman of the Illinois State Republican Convention. Now a **Republican**, McCormick was elected state representative at large for Illinois and as such he became a critic of **Woodrow Wilson**'s administration. In 1918, he was elected to the United States Senate where he became prominent among the group of **"Irreconcilables"** opposed to the **Versailles treaty** and United States participation in the **League of Nations**. In domestic politics, McCormick supported budget reform, proposed the **Child Labor** Amendment, called for the replacement of the Department of Interior with departments of public works and public welfare, and endorsed civil government in the United States protectorates of **Haiti** and Santo Domingo. In 1924, he committed suicide after his defeat in the Republican primary.

McCOY, FRANK ROSS (1874–1954). Frank McCoy graduated from West Point in 1897 and served in Cuba, the Philippines, Mexico in 1915, and the **American Expeditionary Force**, 1917–19. He was assistant to the governor of the Philippines, 1921 to 1925, and director of the Red Cross in Japan in 1923. In 1928, President **Calvin Coolidge** appointed McCoy to oversee the elections in Nicaragua and the following year he chaired the mediation commission between Bolivia and Paraguay. In 1932, McCoy was a member of the **League of Nations'** commission investigating the Japanese invasion of Manchuria.

McKAY, CLAUDE (1890–1948). Born Festus Claudius McKay in Jamaica, McKay had already published two volumes of poetry when he emigrated to the United States in 1912. He initially enrolled at Tuskegee Institute in Alabama, but moved to Kansas State College before finally settling in New York City in 1914, where he became editor of a Socialist journal, *The Liberator*. McKay became one of the best-known voices of the **"New Negro"** with the publication of his poem of defiance, "If We Must Die," in 1919. McKay lived in London between 1919 and 1921 then returned to the United States. His poetry collection *Harlem Shadows* was published the following year and his novel *Home to Harlem* appeared in 1928. For much of the 1920s, McKay traveled in Europe and Africa. He returned to the United States in 1934 and was employed on the Federal Writers Project. He published his autobiography, *A Long Way from Home*, in 1937, and a nonfiction work, *Harlem: Negro Metropolis*, in 1940, the year he became a United States citizen.

McLEMORE, ATKINS JEFFERSON (JEFF) (1857–1929). Jeff McLemore worked for a time as a cowboy, miner, and newspaper reporter in Texas, Colorado, and New Mexico before starting a full-time career in journalism in Texas in 1883. In 1892, he was elected as a **Democrat** to the Texas House of Representatives. He served two terms and then moved to Austin where he became a member of the board of city aldermen. In 1914, McLemore was elected the Democratic congressman at large for Texas. McLemore was an outspoken critic of the **Prohibition** Movement. He was also increasingly critical of **Woodrow Wilson** administration's position with regard to neutrality after 1914, and with Senator **Thomas Gore** of Oklahoma was responsible for the Gore-McLemore Resolution in 1916 warning United States citizens against traveling on armed belligerent vessels. McLemore was re-elected in 1916, but having voted against the declaration of war in 1917, he was defeated in 1918. He published a newspaper in Texas after 1919 and failed to gain election to the Senate in 1928.

McNARY, CHARLES LINZA (1874–1944). Charles McNary was admitted to the bar in Oregon in 1898 and was appointed dean of the law school at Willamette University in 1908. In 1913, he became an associate justice to the Oregon Supreme Court. In 1917, McNary, a progressive **Republican**, was appointed to fill the vacant Senate seat for Oregon. He supported **Woodrow Wilson**'s war policies and was elected to a full Senate term in 1918. During the 1920s, he sponsored a number of bills to protect the nation's forests and to assist the country's farmers. He was cosponsor of the **McNary-Haugen Bill**. Although associated with western **Progressives**, McNary backed

Calvin Coolidge rather than La Follette in 1924. In 1932, he became Republican Senate minority leader. He supported much of the New Deal up until Franklin D. Roosevelt's attempt to alter the composition of the Supreme Court in 1937. He was inclined toward isolationism until the attack on Pearl Harbor in 1941. In 1940, McNary ran as Wendell Willkie's running mate and after the election declined Roosevelt's offer of a cabinet position.

McNARY-HAUGEN BILL. Between 1924 and 1928, five bills were introduced in Congress known as McNary-Haugen Bills after their proposers, congressman Gilbert Haugen and Senator Charles McNary. The intention of these measures was to alleviate the economic situation of farmers by establishing an export corporation to purchase agricultural surpluses and sell them in overseas markets in order to maintain domestic prices. The last two bills passed Congress but were vetoed by President Calvin Coolidge. *See also* AGRICULTURE.

McPHERSON, AIMEE SEMPLE (1890–1944). Born in Canada and christened Aimee Elizabeth Kennedy, Aimee Semple McPherson was an evangelist who founded the International Church of the Foursquare Gospel. She had undergone a Pentecostal evangelical conversion in 1907 and married a preacher, Robert Semple, with whom she went as a missionary to Asia in 1910. When her husband died, she returned to the United States and married Harold McPherson. She conducted a revival campaign in the eastern states from her "gospel automobile" from 1916 to 1918 and started a monthly paper, the *Bridal Call*.

In 1918, McPherson moved to Los Angeles, from where she conducted widespread revival meetings. She established a permanent base for her "Foursquare Gospel" movement with the opening of a temple in 1923. Her radio station, the first full-time religious station, began broadcasting from the temple in 1924 and the International Church of the Foursquare Gospel was officially incorporated in 1927. A consummate publicist, McPherson became a national figure and the leading female evangelist. In 1926, she mysteriously disappeared while swimming and was assumed drowned. A month later, she reappeared and claimed to have been kidnapped. Her accounts to a grand jury led to a charge of perjury in 1927, but the case was dropped. Nonetheless McPherson had achieved national celebrity status. She continued her evangelical activities in the United States and overseas through the 1930s, and the church continued to grow until her death in 1944.

McREYNOLDS, JAMES CLARK (1862–1946). James McReynolds graduated from Vanderbilt University in 1882 and the University of Virginia Law School in 1884. He established a law practice in Nashville where he became a leading member of the legal, political, and social establishment. In 1903, McReynolds was hired by the Justice Department and was the chief prosecutor of the American Tobacco Trust. He resigned in 1911 but in 1913 was appointed attorney general by **Woodrow Wilson**. He was again responsible for filing several major antitrust suits. In 1914, Wilson nominated McReynolds to serve on the **Supreme Court**. McReynolds did not play a particularly significant role on the court until the 1930s when he became a persistent critic of **Franklin D. Roosevelt** and opponent of the extension of federal power under the **New Deal**. Critics regarded McReynolds as one of the worst and most conservative justices to serve on the court. In 1941, he retired in despair following Roosevelt's third election victory.

MARCH, PEYTON CONWAY (1864–1955). Peyton C. March trained at the United State Military Academy at West Point from 1884 to 1888 and became a specialist in artillery. During the Spanish-American War in 1898, he organized an artillery battery financed by John Jacob Astor and took it to the Philippines, where he fought in the battle of Manila. From 1899 to 1901, March saw action against the Philippine guerrillas in Luzon. He received five citations for gallantry.

After his return to the United States, March held a number of administrative positions before joining the General Staff in 1903. From 1911 to 1916, he served as an adjutant general with the War Department. With the United States entry into **World War I**, March was promoted to major general and went to France with the **American Expeditionary Force** (AEF) in command of artillery. In March 1918, he was recalled to the United States as a general to take over as chief of staff. March's efficient leadership and centralized direction speeded up the flow of troops to France, and he was also responsible for organizing their return from 1918 to 1919. After the war, he drew up plans for a peacetime army of 500,000, but Congress rejected the proposal. March resigned in 1921 and spent several years traveling. In 1953, President Dwight D. Eisenhower awarded him the Thanks of Congress for his efforts during World War I.

MARIN, JOHN CHERI (1870–1953). John Marin studied mechanical engineering and then became an architectural draftsman in the 1890s. From 1899 to 1905, he studied fine art in Philadelphia and New York and then spent six years in Europe, mainly in Paris. Marin produced a number of water colors and etching during his travels and exhibited in Paris and in **Alfred Stieglitz**'s 291 Gallery in the United States. Marin returned to the United States in 1912 and he demonstrated the modernist influences in his many paintings of New York City. Some of his work was shown at the **Armory Show** in 1913. During the 1920s, when he became the country's leading watercolorist, Marin produced many paintings of Maine's ocean scenes. Some of his best known work includes *Sun, Isles, and Sea* (1921), *Deer Island, Maine* (1922), *Lower Manhattan* (1922), *Rocks and Seas* (1932). The first large-scale public showing of his work, outside of Stieglitz's galleries, was in the Museum of Modern Art in 1936. Marin continued to paint through the 1940s, and in 1948 a survey of artists and art critics in *Look* magazine voted him the number one painter in the United States.

MARNE, BATTLE OF. The second battle of the Marne took place in response to the German offensive across the river Marne in July 1918. (The first battle took place in September 1914 when the German armies were halted in their advance into France.) The attack was met with a successful **Allied** counteroffensive that involved 275,000 United States troops.

MARSHALL, THOMAS RILEY (1854–1925). Twenty-eighth vice president of the United States. Thomas Marshall attended Wabash College, studied law, and was admitted to the bar in 1875 and established a law practice in Columbia City, Indiana. In 1908, he was elected **Democratic** governor of the state. Marshall sponsored a considerable amount of reform legislation, most notably proposals for a new state constitution. Although he was unsuccessful in this and a number of other measures, he did succeed in seeing through a **Child Labor** Law. Marshall was nominated as the Democratic vice presidential candidate in 1912 and served two terms under **Woodrow Wilson**. Marshall's role was largely to serve as a representative of the administration at social and official functions. He is best known for the remark made in the Senate in 1917, "What this country needs is a really good five cent cigar." Marshall was the first vice president to chair cabinet meetings while Wilson was absent at the **Versailles Peace Conference**. After leaving office, Marshall resumed his law practice and wrote his memoirs. He was a member of the Federal Coal Commission from 1922 to 1923.

MASTERS, EDGAR LEE (1869–1950). Qualified as a lawyer, Edgar Masters practiced law in Chicago but also began writing a series of poems about experiences in Illinois in 1914. These were published as the *Spoon River Anthology* in 1915. The poems took the form of dramatic graveside monologues from a representative group of individuals from a midwestern small town. Although Masters continued writing poetry, novels, and biographies for almost 30 years, it was this collection that made his reputation. His biographies included *Lincoln* (1931), *Vachel Lindsay* (1935), *Whitman* (1937), and *Mark Twain* (1938).

MAYER, LOUIS BURT (1885–1957). The legendary Hollywood **movie** producer Louis B. Mayer was born Lazar Meir (or Eliezer Mayer) in either Dumier in the Ukraine or Minsk, Russia. His family emigrated to St. John, New Brunswick, in 1887. After working in his father's scrap metal business, in 1904 Mayer moved to Boston and bought the first of a chain of movie theaters near the city in 1907. Building on his success, Mayer established his own distribution company in 1914, and in 1917 he established Louis B. Mayer Pictures. His first film was *Virtuous Wives*. Mayer moved to Los Angeles in 1918 and in 1924 formed Metro Goldwyn Mayer (MGM) with Marcus Loew and **Samuel Goldwyn**. Mayer was to be production chief from 1924 until 1951 and with **Irving Thalberg** as producer established MGM as the leading film studio by the mid-1930s.

Mayer regarded the company as a film factory with the movie stars as "assembly line workers." The studio produced massive hits, ranging from *Ben Hur* (1926) to *Grand Hotel* (1932), and produced major stars such as **Greta Garbo**, **Lon Chaney**, Joan Crawford, Clark Gable, and **John** and **Lionel Barrymore**. In 1927, Mayer helped to establish the Academy of Motion Picture Arts and Sciences. His career effectively ended in 1951 when he resigned from MGM after a difference over production styles.

MELLON, ANDREW WILLIAM (1855–1937). Andrew Mellon took over his father's banking business with his brother Richard and in 1889 established the Union Trust Company of Pittsburgh. In addition to holding interests in various industries, Mellon helped establish the Aluminum Company of America (now ALCOA) and was a multimillionaire. In 1921, he became secretary of the Treasury, a post he held until 1932 under presidents **Warren Harding**, **Calvin Coolidge**, and **Herbert Hoover**. He was associated with the conservative fiscal policy that produced the reduction of income and corporation taxes and surtaxes. He still managed to reduce the national debt from $24 billion in 1920 to $16 billion in 1930. Mellon served as ambassador to Great Britain from 1932 to 1933. He founded the Mellon Institute of Industrial Research in Pittsburgh in 1913 and in 1937 donated his own art collection to the nation and funded the building of the National Gallery of Art in Washington, D.C.

MENCKEN, HENRY LOUIS (1880–1956). After graduating from Baltimore Polytechnic, H. L. Mencken worked for two years in his father's cigar factory. In 1898, he became a reporter on the Baltimore *Herald* and by 1905 he had risen to become editor. In 1906, he became the editor of the Sunday edition of the Baltimore *Sun*. Mencken also published a volume of poetry, *Ventures into Verse* (1903), and two scholarly works, *George Bernard Shaw: His Plays* (1905) and *The Philosophy of Friedrich Nietzsche* (1908). In 1908 Mencken became literary editor of a monthly publication, the *Smart Set*, and he was later to become coeditor of the magazine with **George Jean Nathan**. He and Nathan founded the *American Mercury* in 1923, and Mencken remained as editor until 1933.

Mencken became one of the distinctive voices of the 1920s through his columns and reviews. He was often a scathing critic of American values and morality, and was particularly savage about the American South and small towns, which he claimed, were occupied by the "booboisie." Mencken was equally critical of politicians and clergymen. His accounts of the **Scopes Monkey Trial** were widely reprinted and he described **William Jennings Bryan** in his obituary as a "peasant come home to the dung-heap."

In addition to his social comment, Mencken was famous for his studies of *The American Language* (first printed in 1919), six volumes of *Prejudices* (1919–27), *Notes on Democracy* (1926), and a later series of autobiographical works. He continued to work on these and new editions of *The American Language* through World War II. He suffered a severe stroke in 1948 that left him incapacitated. His autobiography, *My Life as Author and Editor*, was not published until after his death.

MERCHANT MARINE ACT, 1920. An act passed in order to liquidate the government-owned merchant fleet built during **World War I**, and run by the **United States Shipping Board**, and yet maintain a large merchant fleet. The act provided for the disposal of ships to private companies, and those companies were also given heavy mail subsidies. Preferential tariffs were to be applied to goods carried on American-owned ships. Many of the ships were sold at a fraction of their cost, and further subsidies were granted in a second Merchant Marine Act in 1928. However, the United States merchant fleet continued to be inferior to foreign competition and many companies collapsed in the **Depression**.

MERRIAM, CHARLES EDWARD (1874–1953). The political scientist Charles Merriam took his first degree at Lenox College, Hopkinton, taught for a year, studied law at the State University of Iowa for a year, and then went to Columbia University, where he completed his M.A. in 1897 and his Ph.D. in 1900. Merriam took a teaching position at the University of Chicago in 1900 and by 1911 had risen to full professor. He was active in Chicago's reform politics and was elected as **Republican** alderman to the city council in 1909 and served until 1917. Having sat on three city council commissions,

Merriam ran for mayor in 1911 as a progressive Republican but was narrowly defeated. With **Harold Ickes** Merriam established the Illinois Progressive Party and backed first **Robert M. La Follette** and then **Theodore Roosevelt**.

Merriam worked as an examiner for the Chicago Aviation Board and later the **Committee of Public Information** during **World War I**. In 1918, he acted as American High Commissioner of Information in Rome. In the 1920s, Merriam built up the Political Science Department at Chicago into one of the leading schools of its type. In 1923, he was one of the founders of the Social Science Research Council and in 1925 he was elected president of the American Political Science Association. From 1929 to 1933, Merriam served on President **Herbert Hoover**'s Research Committee on Social Trends that issued its report in 1933. In 1933, **Franklin D. Roosevelt** appointed Merriam to the National Planning Board and he remained one of the team of planners throughout the **New Deal**. Merriam's many publications included *American Political Ideas* (1920), *The American Political System* (1922), and *New Aspects of Politics* (1925).

MEUSE-ARGONNE, BATTLE OF. The assault on a 25-mile front along the river Meuse in France from September 26 to November 11, 1918, was the last general push by the **Allied** forces during **World War I**. It was led by the United States forces under the command of General **John Pershing** and ended with the capture of Sedan and the negotiation of the general **armistice**. The United States forces captured 48,800 prisoners and 1,424 guns and suffered 117,000 dead and wounded during the offensive.

MEXICAN PUNITIVE EXPEDITION. *See* PUNITIVE EXPEDITION.

MEXICO. United States relations with Mexico deteriorated following the overthrow and execution of Francisco Madero by Victoriano Huerta in February 1913. **Woodrow Wilson** refused to recognize the new Mexican government and offered support to the opposition to Huerta led by Venustiano Carranza. Relations further deteriorated following the Tampico incident and later the seizure of **Vera Cruz** by

United States Marines in April 1914. Relations improved slightly when Carranza replace Huerta, but the raid on **Columbus, New Mexico**, by **Pancho Villa** in 1916 led to a **punitive expedition** by United States troops into Mexico. Ongoing negotiations were further threatened by the release of the **Zimmerman telegram** by the British government in 1917, but further conflict did not follow.

Relations between the two nations improved a little under the postwar **Republican** administrations. Secretary of State **Charles Hughes** attempted to arrive at a resolution of outstanding differences with Carranza's successor. When legislation by the Mexican Congress in 1925 threatened the considerable American property holdings in Mexico, President **Calvin Coolidge**'s ambassador to Mexico, **Dwight Morrow**, was able to reach some agreement on these issues. A goodwill visit by **Herbert Hoover** prior to his inaugural also helped to continue the improving relations and paved the way for **Franklin D. Roosevelt**'s "Good Neighbor" policies.

MILLAY, EDNA ST. VINCENT (1892–1950). Already publishing poetry in high school, Edna St. Vincent Millay graduated from Vassar College in 1917 and her collection of poetry *Renascence and Other Poems* was published the same year. She joined the **Greenwich Village** literary set in New York City, wrote several pieces in *Vanity Fair*, and published her second volume *A Few Figs from Thistles* in 1920. The latter, which included "My Candle Burns at Both Ends," did much to establish her reputation as a liberated "new" **woman**. *The Harper-Weaver and Other Poems* was published in 1923, and Millay wrote the libretto for **Deems Taylor**'s opera, *The King's Henchman* (1927). In 1923, Millay became the first woman poet to be awarded the Pulitzer Prize. She was elected to the National Institute of Arts and Letters in 1929 and the American Academy of Arts and Letters in 1940. Her later work included *The Buck in Snow* (1928), *Fatal Interview* (1931), *Wine from These Grapes* (1934), *Conversation at Midnight* (1937), and *Huntsman, What Quarry?* (1939).

In addition to writing poetry that captured aspects of the mood of the 1920s, Millay was one of many intellectuals who defended **Sacco and Vanzetti**. She was arrested and jailed during a protest following their execution in 1927.

MILLIKAN, ROBERT ANDREWS (1868–1953). Robert Millikan earned a master's degree in physics at Oberlin College in 1893 and then undertook postgraduate research at Columbia University. Millikan took up a teaching position at Chicago University in 1896 and wrote several introductory physics textbooks that included the widely published *A First Course in Physics*. He also taught courses on X-rays, radioactivity, and quantum and electron physics, and carried out major research in those areas. During **World War I**, Millikan chaired the General Antisubmarine Committee for the National Research Council. In 1921, he took up an appointment at the new California Institute of Technology, where he established a world-class physics department. He was awarded the Nobel Prize in 1923 for his work in electron physics. Millikan's work included articles in popular magazines and a book on *Evolution in Science and Religion* (1927). His subsequent work focused on cosmic rays and he published *Cosmic Rays* in 1939. He retired in 1945.

MILLS, OGDEN LIVINGSTON (1884–1937). Ogden Mills, a graduate of Harvard University, was admitted to the New York bar in 1908 and practiced law in the city. He became active in **Republican Party** affairs in 1911 and was treasurer of the Republican County Committee of New York until 1926. He stood unsuccessfully for Congress in 1912 but was elected to the state senate in 1914 and served until 1917 when he enlisted in the U.S. Army. He served as a captain in France and was elected to the House of Representatives from New York in 1921 and served until 1927. He was an unsuccessful candidate in the New York gubernatorial election in 1926 but was appointed undersecretary of the treasury by **Calvin Coolidge** in 1927. President **Herbert Hoover** appointed him secretary of the treasury in 1932 following the resignation of **Andrew Mellon** to become ambassador to Great Britain. Mills supported a conservative fiscal policy, a balanced budget, and the gold standard. After leaving the Treasury Department in 1933, he was highly critical of the **New Deal** and published his views in *What of Tomorrow* (1935) and *The Seventeen Million* (1937). He continued to be active in business as a director for several large corporations including, the Lackawanna Steel Company and Shredded Wheat Company.

MISSISSIPPI FLOODS, 1927. Following abnormally high rainfall from September 1926, exceptionally heavy rains in April 1927 brought some of the worst flooding of the Mississippi River in history. From Cairo, Illinois, to New Orleans, Louisiana, the Mississippi and its tributaries flooded, covering some 26,000 square miles. At some points, the Mississippi was 60 miles across. An estimated 246 people died in the floods, but hundreds more are thought to have died of exposure or illness subsequently as more than 600,000 were forced to leave their homes. Almost half of those affected were **African Americans**. Secretary of Commerce **Herbert Hoover** directed Red Cross relief operations that established 154 camps for the homeless. Hoover's popularity increased as a result, ensuring his nomination as President **Calvin Coolidge**'s successor in 1928. The Flood Control Act of 1928 increased the role of the United States Army Corps of Engineers in improving flood defenses as outlined by **Edgar Jadwin**.

MITCHELL, WESLEY CLAIR (1874–1948). After obtaining his Ph.D. at the University of Chicago in 1899, Wesley Mitchell taught at the University of California, Columbia University, and the New School for Social Research. During **World War I**, he served as head of the Price Section of the **War Industries Board**. Mitchell founded the National Bureau of Economic Research in 1920 to undertake quantitative studies of the United States business cycle. Mitchell published a number of key texts, including two works entitled *Business Cycles* (1913, 1927). In 1921, he took part in the **President's Unemployment Conference**. Mitchell succeeded **Charles Merriam** as chair of the Social Science Research Council in 1927, led the group that produced the President's *Report on Recent Economic Changes* (1929), and he chaired the **President's Research Committee on Recent Social Trends** that reported in 1933. That year, Mitchell was appointed to the National Planning Board created to serve the Public Works Administration. He resigned in 1935.

MITCHELL, WILLIAM LENDRUM (1879–1936). The **World War I** air ace "Billy" Mitchell served as a private in the infantry in the Spanish-American War of 1898. He received a commission in the Signal Corps and served in Cuba, the Philippines, and Alaska. In 1915, he was assigned to the aviation section of the Signal Corps.

During World War I, Mitchell commanded air forces in a number of important engagements and he was awarded the Distinguished Service Cross and Distinguished Service Medal in addition to the *Croix de Guerre* for his services. After the war, Mitchell became assistant chief of the Army Air Service and an advocate for the development of United States air power and unified air force. His outspoken criticism of military policy and accusations of incompetence on the part of the War and Navy Departments after the loss of the dirigible, *Shenandoah*, in 1925 led to his court-martial. Demoted and suspended in rank, Mitchell resigned in 1926. He was posthumously awarded the Congressional Medal of Honor in 1946 for his contribution to the development of an American air force.

MODEL T FORD. Known as the "tin lizzie" **Henry Ford**'s mass-produced **automobile** was intended to make car ownership a possibility for the masses by producing a simple but serviceable vehicle (the buyer could have any color as long as it was black) using standard interchangeable parts. First manufactured in 1908, by 1927 the company had produced over fifteen million Model T Fords and the price had fallen from just under $1,000 to just under $300. The new Model A Ford was introduced in 1927.

MOONEY, THOMAS JOSEPH (1882–1942). Tom Mooney was a radical labor activist involved in various socialist and labor organizations in California. In 1913, he and Warren Billings (1893–1972) were involved in a protracted and bitter electrical workers' strike in San Francisco. Billings was found carrying dynamite and he and Mooney were charged with illegal possession of explosives. After three trials, Mooney was eventually acquitted in 1914 and he resumed his labor activities. However, when a bomb went off during the Preparedness Day Parade in San Francisco on 22 July 1916, killing 10 people, Billings and Mooney were both rearrested. Billings was tried and sentenced to life imprisonment. Mooney, tried separately, was found guilty and sentenced to death despite the lack of real substantial evidence against him. A supposed eyewitness was later found to have perjured himself in his statement.

Mooney's sentence caused an outcry of protest from labor leaders and reformers both nationally and internationally and in 1918 President

Woodrow Wilson intervened to ask Governor William D. Stephens of California to delay execution. A review of the case led to the commutation of Mooney's sentence to life imprisonment. Legal efforts continued to secure a retrial for both Mooney and Billings over the next 20 years, but it was not until 1939 that Mooney was granted a pardon and released. Billings was also released and finally pardoned in 1961.

MORGENTHAU, HENRY (1856–1946). Henry Morgenthau emigrated to the United States from Germany in 1866 with his family. He graduated from Columbia Law School and established a law practice in New York City after he graduated in 1877. Morgenthau later established his own real estate businesses, but in 1913 he turned to public service. In 1907, he had helped to found the Free Synagogue that was committed to community service. In 1911, he established Bronx House, a **settlement house** and music school. Morgenthau was a generous supporter of **Woodrow Wilson** and served as chairman of the Democratic National Committee's finance committee in 1912. In 1913, Wilson appointed him as ambassador to Turkey and after the **Allied** nations broke off relations with Turkey in 1914, he also represented their citizens. He was decorated by Great Britain and France for this service and offered a cabinet post by the Turkish government. Morgenthau resigned in 1916. In 1917, he was sent to negotiate a separate peace with Turkey, but the mission was aborted.

After the war, Morgenthau campaigned on behalf of United States membership in the **League of Nations**, took part in the establishment of the International Red Cross (1919), advised on Turkish issues at the **Versailles Peace Conference**, and was vice president of the Armenian Relief Committee. He was appointed as ambassador to **Mexico** in 1920, but the appointment was not confirmed because of the unrest in Mexico. In 1923, Morgenthau successfully chaired the League of Nations' Greek Refugee Settlement Commission. In 1933, he was a technical delegate to the World Monetary and Economic Conference in London.

MORROW, DWIGHT WHITNEY (1873–1931). A graduate of Amherst College in 1895, and Columbia Law School in 1899, Dwight Morrow practiced law in New York City. In 1914 he accepted a partnership with J. P. Morgan and worked with the company until

1927. During **World War I**, Morrow played a major part in the Allied Maritime Transport Council allocating shipping resources. In 1921, he advised on the reorganization of Cuba's finances. In 1927, **Calvin Coolidge** appointed Morrow as ambassador to **Mexico** and he worked to improve relations between the two countries for three years. Morrow was a delegate to the **London Naval Conference** in 1930. Later that year, he was elected to the U.S Senate for New Jersey and became a close advisor to President **Herbert Hoover**. He was to lead the United States delegation to the World Disarmament Conference in 1931 when he died suddenly.

MORTON, "JELLY ROLL" (FERDINAND JOSEPH) (1890–1941). Born Ferdinand Lamothe, Morton acquired a new name when his mother remarried. A Creole, he grew up with the **African American jazz** musicians in New Orleans, where he learned to play the piano and began to compose his own tunes including "New Orleans Blues" (1902?) and "Jelly Roll Blues" (1905). From 1907 to 1917, Morton traveled around the United States before settling in Los Angeles in 1922. He then moved on to Chicago, where he made his first recordings with the New Orleans Rhythm Kings in 1923. Morton also made a considerable number of solo recordings in the 1920s.

In 1928, Morton moved to New York City, but increasingly his New Orleans and ragtime style were becoming outdated as swing and boogie woogie played by people like **Duke Ellington** and **Fletcher Henderson** began to dominate. Nonetheless, recordings made in the 1940s with the musicologist Alan Lomax for the Library of Congress demonstrated the breadth of his talent as a pianist and composer and his knowledge of the history of jazz. *See also* ARMSTRONG, LOUIS; BECHET, SIDNEY.

MOSKOWITZ, BELLE LINDNER ISRAELS (1877–1933). After attending the Teachers' College at Columbia University for a year, Belle Moskowitz began work as a resident **social worker** at the Educational Alliance, a Jewish **settlement house** on New York's Lower East Side, in 1900. After her marriage in 1903, Moskowitz worked part-time for the journal *Survey* and on various projects for the United Hebrew Charities and the New York State Conference on Charities and Corrections. In 1908, she was responsible for the implementation of licensing of commercial dance halls. From 1913 until 1916, Moskowitz worked with the Dress and Waist Manufacturers' Association in their grievance and arbitration service. She then established a firm of industrial consultants.

In 1918, Moskowitz supported **Alfred Smith**'s gubernatorial election campaign. Following his victory Moskowitz was appointed executive secretary to New York State's Reconstruction Commission that proposed many ideas that Smith later enacted. Moskowitz became a close adviser to Smith and she helped secure his election again in 1922. She became publicity director for the New York State Democratic Committee and acted as a speech writer and public relations consultant for the governor. She helped to mobilize support for Smith's successful bid to win the **Democratic** nomination in 1928 and she was the only woman on the executive committee of the Democratic National Committee. Moskowitz continued as Smith's press agent after his defeat. She died in 1933 following a car accident.

MOTION PICTURES. *See* MOVIES.

MOTON, ROBERT RUSSA (1867–1940). The **African American** educator received his training at Hampton Institute, Virginia, and he remained there in a number of roles after his graduation in 1890. In 1915, he succeeded the black leader Booker T. Washington as head of Tuskegee Institute in Alabama. During **World War I**, Moton was successful in leading the call for a black officer training program and the use of black troops in combat roles. He also helped to secure the appointment of **Emmett Scott** as special adviser to the secretary of war. In 1918, Moton was sent by President **Woodrow Wilson** to report on the conditions of African American servicemen and did much to challenge accusations of black military failure. However, in general, Moton continued Booker T. Washington's accommodationist policies and while in Europe he urged the black soldiers not to challenge the racial status quo on their return home. He continued to develop Tuskegee in the 1920s and was awarded the Harmon Foundation Award for his contribution to improved race relations in 1930 and the Spingarn Medal in 1932. In addition to contributions to **Alain Locke**'s *New Negro* (1925), Moton authored *Racial Good Will* (1916), *What the Negro Thinks* (1929), and his autobiography, *Finding a Way Out* (1920).

MOTT, JOHN RALEIGH (1865–1955). John Mott attended Iowa University from 1881 until 1885 when he went to Cornell University, where he obtained a Ph.D. in 1888. While at Cornell, Mott attended a Christian student conference and pledged to work in foreign missions. From 1888 until 1928, he worked with the Young Men's Christian Association (YMCA) in a variety of roles. He was general secretary of the YMCA's foreign department from 1901 to 1915, general secretary of the International Committee of the YMCA, 1915–28, and president of the YMCA's World Committee, 1926–37. In addition, Mott held positions in the Student Volunteer Movement and the World Student Christian Federation, which he helped to create in 1895. Mott personally toured many countries encouraging student Christian organizations. President **Woodrow Wilson** asked Mott to become United States ambassador to China while Mott was there in 1913, but he declined the offer. He did, however, take part in the High Commission sent to **Mexico** in 1916 to defuse tension following the **punitive expedition** in pursuit of **Pancho Villa**. In 1917, Mott went to Moscow with the United States mission following the revolution, and he also attended the **Versailles Peace Conference**.

During **World War I**, Mott became general secretary of the YMCA War Work Council established to provide social service programs for the military. After the war, he was involved in the Interchurch World Movement and the later Institute of Social and Religious Research. During the 1920s, he devoted more of his time to the International Missionary Council, which he chaired until 1941, encouraging ecumenical movements around the world. He was involved in the foundation of the World Council of Churches after World War II and was appointed its honorary president. In 1946, Mott shared the Nobel Peace Prize with **Emily Greene Balch**.

MOVIES. Moving film images emerged at the end of the 19th century from revolving discs with images in kinemascopes or kinematographs. W. K. L. Dickson's development of moving film for Thomas Edison in 1894 and then the use of film projectors led to the silent film shorts shown in five-cent theaters called "nickelodeons." The first film with a story was *The Great Train Robbery* (1903) and by 1907 there were over 5,000 theaters and the term "movie" was well established. Most of the early films were made in New York City or New Jersey, but gradually producers such as **D. W. Griffith** and

Cecil B. De Mille moved to California. There, the climate, access to space, and cheap labor led to the growth of Hollywood, outside of Los Angeles, as the center of the film industry. Griffith also led the way in making movies beyond the one-reel shorts and developing the cinematic devices of panning shots, close ups, and film editing in narrating complicated plots. These were best exemplified in his three-hour epic, *The Birth of a Nation* (1915).

It was in Hollywood that the studio system developed in the 1920s, following the breakup between 1912 and 1918 of the Edison Motion Picture Patents Company's (MPPC) monopolistic control of cameras and projectors. **Adolph Zukor** began the process of vertical integration that gave studios control of the film "product" from its making to distribution through cinema chains all owned by his Paramount company. Other companies, such as Warner Brothers, **Samuel Goldwyn** and **Louis B. Mayer**'s Metro-Goldwyn-Mayer (MGM), **William Fox**'s Fox Film (later Twentieth Century-Fox), and Radio-Keith-Orpheum (RKO), quickly joined Paramount to dominate the growing industry. Smaller companies, including Carl Laemmle's Universal Pictures, Jack and Harry Cohn's Columbia Pictures, and United Artists, formed in 1919 by the movie stars and director **Charlie Chaplin**, **Douglas Fairbanks**, **Mary Pickford**, and D. W. Griffith, also added to the growth industry. There were also a handful of independent producers like **David O. Selznick**.

By 1926, nickelodeons were being replaced by huge "picture palaces," the motion picture industry was grossing $1.5 billion a year, and cinema attendance averaged 60 million a week. Actors like Chaplin, Fairbanks, Pickford, **Clara Bow**, **Rudolph Valentino**, **Lillian Gish**, **Gloria Swanson**, and **Greta Garbo** became huge stars whose life on and off the screen became the subject of personal interest. Sound (music and special effects) was first used in 1926. The first feature-length film using talking sound (the "talkie") was Warner Brothers' *The Jazz Singer* (1927), starring **Al Jolson**. By 1930, an average of 80 million people a week were going to the movies. Movie audiences did fall in the early years of the **Great Depression**, but after 1933, attendance rose once more and the movie industry enjoyed its greatest years during the 1930s and 1940s. *See also* ARBUCKLE, ROSCOE; CHANEY, LON; FIELDS, W. C.; HAYS, WILLIAM HARRISON; KEATON, BUSTER; LLOYD,

HAROLD CLAYTON; LOMBARD, CAROLE; NEGRI, POLA; SENNETT, MACK; VIDOR, KING WALLIS.

MUMFORD, LEWIS (1895–1990). Lewis Mumford studied at City College, Columbia University, and the New School for Social Research, but did not graduate. Despite this lack of a degree, Mumford was to become an intellectual polymath, philosopher, architectural critic, urban historian and planner, and expert in American studies. He became visiting professor at Dartmouth, Stanford, Berkeley, the University of Pennsylvania, Wesleyan, and Massachusetts Institute of Technology. He was to receive honorary degrees from Edinburgh and Rome and was awarded the Presidential Medal of Freedom (1964), the National Medal for Literature (1972), and the National Medal of Arts (1986).

Mumford served in the United States Navy from 1918 to 1919 and joined the staff of *The Dial* in 1919. His first book, *The Story of Utopias* (1922), was an examination of ideal societies from Plato to the 19th century. His *Technics and Civilization* (1934) was a history of technology, and *The Culture of Cities* (1938) and *The City in History* (1961) used history to argue for smaller, planned, and balanced urban development. Mumford was one of the founders of the Regional Planning Association of America in 1923, and he advised on a number of urban developments. He was the author of a number of works on architecture, starting with *Sticks and Stones* in 1924. Mumford also wrote on American culture in *The Golden Day* (1926) and *Herman Melville* (1929).

Mumford also spoke out on political issues; he opposed appeasement in the 1930s and supported American intervention in World War II. He campaigned against atomic weapons and was one of the first to speak out against the war in Vietnam in the 1960s.

MUSTE, ABRAHAM JOHANNES (1885–1967). Clergyman, labor activist, pacifist, and exponent of nonviolent protest, Muste was born in Holland and moved to the United States with his family in 1891. Ordained to the ministry of the Dutch Reformed Church in 1918, Muste became a minister in the Society of Friends (Quakers) and later worked for the **American Civil Liberties Union**. He played a leading role in the strike of textile workers in Lawrence, Massachusetts, in

1919 and was general secretary of the Amalgamated Textile Workers of America in 1920 and 1921. He was educational director at Brookwood College, New York, from 1921 to 1933. Muste was the founder of the radical Conference for Progressive Labor Action in 1929. This organization later became the American Workers' Party and then later merged with the Trotskyite Communist League of America. He was executive director of the Fellowship of Reconciliation, an organization of reformist and pacifist clergymen, from 1940 to 1953, and author of *Non-violence in an Aggressive World* (1940). In his later years, Muste was an advisor to Martin Luther King, Jr. and an active campaigner against the war in Vietnam.

– N –

NATHAN, GEORGE JEAN (1882–1958). George Nathan began his career as writer and critic while attending Cornell University (1900–1904), where he edited the student newspaper and literary magazine. In 1905, he became a reporter with the *New York Herald* and then a writer for magazines such as *Harper's Weekly*, *Puck*, *Judge*, *Vanity Fair*, and *Esquire*. In 1908, he began writing for the *Smart Set* and in 1914 became coeditor with **H. L. Mencken**. Together, the two men turned the magazine into one of the leading publications of the early 1920s, renowned for its famous contributors, such as **F. Scott Fitzgerald**, and for its lively independent style. In 1923, Nathan and Mencken left the *Smart Set* to set up the *American Mercury*, but Nathan resigned in 1924 although he continued as drama critic. In the 1930s, Nathan, together with **Eugene O'Neill**, Ernest Boyd, and **Theodore Dreiser**, launched the *American Spectator*, a more literary journal than the *Mercury*. Nathan gave this up in 1935 and resumed work for the *Mercury* during the 1940s. He also published an annual *Theater Book of the Year* until 1951. Nathan also wrote works of literary and social criticism and in total published some 40 volumes.

NATIONAL AMERICAN WOMAN SUFFRAGE ASSOCIATION (NAWSA). Formed in 1890 with a merger of the National Woman Suffrage Association and the American Woman Suffrage Association,

NAWSA was the leading organization demanding votes for **women**. Led by **Carrie Chapman Catt** from 1900, NAWSA campaigned not on the grounds of their equality with men but on the claim that they were morally superior and would introduce higher standards to government. Fighting both at the local and national level, their campaign eventually secured the passage of the **Nineteenth Amendment** in 1920. *See also* WOMEN'S SUFFRAGE.

NATIONAL ASSOCIATION FOR THE ADVANCEMENT OF COLORED PEOPLE (NAACP). Formed in 1910 as an outgrowth of the 1909 National Negro Congress called by **Oswald Garrison Villard**, **Mary White Ovington**, and William Walling following the race riot in Springfield, Illinois, the NAACP became the leading civil rights organization in the United States until the 1950s. With its monthly journal, *The Crisis*, edited by **W. E. B. Du Bois**, the NAACP quickly grew in size and by 1919 had a membership of 90,000. Although many of the leading officers were white, the organization was increasingly influenced by its **African American** national secretary, **James Weldon Johnson**, and field secretary, **Walter White**. The NAACP organized a silent protest following the **East St. Louis Race Riot** in 1917, led the campaign against lynching in the 1920s, took part in the defense of the **Scottsboro Boys**, and in the 1930s initiated the legal challenges to segregation that culminated in the *Brown v. Topeka Board of Education* decision in 1954.

NATIONAL CONSUMERS LEAGUE (NCL). A consumer protection and social advocacy organization formed in 1899 to campaign for the protection and welfare of consumers and workers. Its aim was to ensure that goods were of reasonable quality and price and produced in "fair, safe, and healthy working conditions." It was one of a number of **Progressive** organizations that campaigned for minimum wages, limited working hours, and the protection of **women** workers. The NCL was led by **Florence Kelley** until her death in 1932 and its members included **Grace** and **Edith Abbott**, **Jane Addams**, **Emily Balch**, and **Eleanor Roosevelt**, among many others.

NATIONAL DEFENSE ACT, 1916. The National Defense Act was passed as part of the Preparedness campaign prior to United States entry into **World War I**. It authorized an increase in the size of the regular army, provided for the federalization of the National Guard, and created civilian training camps and military schools at universities. The act also empowered the secretary of war to make a census of industrial capacity with regard to potential war orders.

NATIONAL ORIGINS ACT, 1924. *See* QUOTA ACT.

NATIONAL PROHIBITION ACT, 1919. Known as the Volstead Act, the National Prohibition Act was passed in October 1919 to implement the provisions of the **Eighteenth Amendment**. The act defined intoxicating liquor as anything that contained one half of one per cent alcohol by volume, but allowed the sale of alcohol for medicinal, sacramental, or industrial purposes. The act was more easily passed than enforced, and the rise of criminal activity associated with the illegal sale of alcohol, and increased public opposition to the legislation, led to its repeal. *See also* PROHIBITION.

NATIONAL URBAN LEAGUE (NUL). The National Urban League was formed in New York City in 1911 in response to the increasing migration of **African Americans** from the South. The Urban League helped to find housing and work and carried out research into race discrimination. In 1923, the League began to publish a journal, *Opportunity*, to publicize its research and to offer opportunities for black writers.

NATIONAL WAR LABOR BOARD (NWLB). The National War Labor Board was established on 9 April 1918 to "settle by mediation and conciliation" any labor disputes threatening war production. It followed the recommendations of the War Labor Conference Board established in response to the wave of strikes in 1917. The Board recognized the right to collective bargaining and established minimum wage levels and the eight-hour day as the norm in settling disputes. The Board adjudicated in some 1,245 cases.

NATIONAL WOMAN'S PARTY (NWP). Alice Paul and others frustrated by the slow progress of the **National American Woman Suffrage Association's** state-by-state campaign to enfranchise **women**

formed the National Woman's Party as the successor to the **Congressional Union** in 1916. The NWP instead focused on the federal government and opposed whatever party was in power. In 1917, the NWP began picketing the White House and several women were jailed. When they went on a hunger strike, they were force-fed. After the passage of the **Nineteenth Amendment** the NWP began a campaign in favor of an Equal Rights Amendment. It continued to campaign into the 1960s.

NATIVE AMERICANS. From the late 19th century to the late 20th century Native Americans constituted the poorest and most overlooked minority in the United States. Native Americans numbered 250,000 in 1900, and the majority of them were located on reservations in the West and Southwest. Although the massacre at Wounded Knee in 1890 may have been the last chapter in the subjugation of the Indian tribes, it did not mark the end of their suffering. The Dawes Severalty Act of 1887 encouraged the breakup of Indian lands and allowed the disposal of land not allotted to families. By 1930, almost half of their territory, over 86 million acres, had gone to white Americans. A proposal by Senator Holm Bursum of New Mexico to dispossess the Pueblo Indians of lands led to the first Pueblo council meeting since the 17th century in 1922. White reformers and the American Indian Defense Association led by John Collier also protested, and the Bursum bill was dropped.

During **World War I**, 17,000 Native Americans registered for military service and 8,000 were inducted. Unlike **African Americans**, they were not segregated because many reformers hoped that the war would facilitate their assimilation into white society. Partially as a result of this service and also to remove inconsistencies and confusion, full citizenship was granted to Native Americans in the **American Indian Citizenship Act** in 1924. In the mid-1920s, Secretary of the Interior **Hubert Work** established a commission under Lewis Meriam to conduct a survey of conditions on the reservations. The report, *The Problem of Indian Administration* (1928), declared categorically that "an overwhelming majority of Indians are poor, even extremely poor." The commission called for changes in federal policy and more spending on health, education, and welfare provision. Further surveys were conducted under the administration of **Herbert**

Hoover and some changes took place in education. However, little else had changed and the **Great Depression**, coupled with the effects of drought in the 1930s, exacerbated the already poor conditions. It was not until the **New Deal** and the appointment of Collier as Indian Commissioner that the problems of Native Americans first began to be tackled seriously.

NEARING, SCOTT (1883–1983). A socialist and pacifist, Scott Nearing was the author of *The Solution of the Child Labor Problem* (1911) and *Women and Social Progress* (1912) whose outspoken critiques of industrial employers led to his dismissal from the University of Pennsylvania in 1915. He was subsequently offered a position at the University of Toledo in Ohio but was dismissed in 1917 for his opposition to United States entry into the war. Nearing joined the **Socialist Party** and was employed at the radical Rand School of Social Science in New York City. He was charged under the **Espionage Act** following the publication of his antiwar pamphlet, *The Great Madness* (1917), and stood trial in February 1919. Although the American Socialist Party was fined for publishing the pamphlet, Nearing was acquitted. He was an active campaigner for black civil rights and author of *Black America* (1929) and *Freeborn* (1932).

NEGRI, POLA (1899–1987). Born Barbara Apolonia Chalupiec in Poland, Pola Negri trained in ballet and appeared in a number of early Polish and then German films. In 1923 she began a contract with Paramount films in the United States and she made a series of movies as the femme fatale: *Bella Donna*, *The Cheat*, *The Spanish Dancer,* and *Hotel Imperial*. Her career was enhanced by publicity attached to her private life, particularly her affair with **Rudolph Valentino**. Her entry into sound pictures in 1932 with *A Woman Commands* was a failure and she returned to Germany. She returned to the United States in 1941 but did not make any more films of significance.

NESS, ELIOT (1903–1957). Eliot Ness found fame as the special agent leading a team of so-called "Untouchables" in the war against organized crime during the **Prohibition** Era. Ness, a graduate from the University of Chicago in 1925, found work first investigating insurance applicants for the Retail Credit Company and then in the Prohibition Bureau of the United States Treasury Department. In 1928, Ness was transferred to the Justice Department as a special agent where, with a team of agents, he targeted the **bootlegging** businesses of the mob in Chicago. Ness's team was disbanded following the conviction of **Al Capone** in 1931 and the repeal of Prohibition two years later.

In 1934, Ness moved to the Alcohol Tax Unit in Cleveland, Ohio, and a year later became director of public safety in Cleveland responsible for attacking corruption in the police force. He resigned the post in 1942 and found employment with the Federal Social Protection program in Washington, D.C. In 1944, he became the chairman of a safe and lock company in Cleveland and then treasurer and vice president of an import/export company. He was defeated in his attempt to become mayor of Cleveland in 1947. In 1957, he wrote *The Untouchables* but he did not live to see it published or the successful television series that sprang from it in 1959. An equally successful film version was made in 1987.

NEW DEAL. Addressing the **Democratic Party** convention in Chicago in June 1932 the newly nominated presidential candidate **Franklin D. Roosevelt** pledged "a new deal for the American people." The term *New Deal* was then applied to his program of relief, recovery, and reform to tackle the problems of the **Depression**. The New Deal was to become one of the greatest periods of political change in United States history.

NEW FREEDOM. The New Freedom was the title given to **Woodrow Wilson**'s political program in 1912. It reflected the influence of the Progressive lawyer **Louis D. Brandeis** and proposed that federal power be used positively to correct monopoly abuses of competition and restore a more open economic order with social justice and opportunity for all. Rather than the "regulated monopoly" proposed in **Theodore Roosevelt**'s "New Nationalism," Wilson wanted "regulated competition." This would be achieved through the use of antitrust legislation and the reduction of protectionist tariffs. Wilson felt he had achieved these aims with the introduction of the **Underwood-Simmons Tariff Act**, the **Federal Reserve Act**, the **Clayton Antitrust Act**, and the creation of the **Federal Trade Commission**.

"NEW NEGRO." Following the outbreaks of violence directed against **African Americans** in the **Red Summer** of 1919, a new mood of anger and assertiveness emerged among the black population evident in their willingness to fight back against white oppression. This was apparent both in the armed resistance to white violence in the riots in Washington, D.C., and Chicago, in rising black membership of the National Association for the Advancement of Colored People (NAACP), and in the statements of leaders such as **W. E. B. Du Bois**. This new mood found voice, too, in the work of writers such as **Claude McKay** and in the **Harlem Renaissance.**

NINETEENTH AMENDMENT. The Nineteenth Amendment to the Constitution, first introduced in 1878, ratified on 18 August 1920, recognized **women**'s right to vote. It had been passed by Congress in 1919 and achieved the two-thirds majority needed for ratification when it was approved by Tennessee. It came into operation with the elections in 1920. (*See* appendix II.)

NONPARTISAN LEAGUE. The Nonpartisan League was established by the former Socialist, **Charles A. Townley**, in North Dakota in 1915 and it quickly spread into neighboring states. The League represented mainly farmers and others disgruntled by monopoly control in the wheat trade. It echoed many of the demands of the Populist movement in calling for public ownership of marketing facilities, grain elevators, flour mills, railroads, and banks. The program was adopted by the North Dakota legislature in 1919 and the movement had some electoral success in other midwestern states. However, its membership declined following the war although elements of it were evident in the **"Farm Bloc"** and in the **Progressive Party** of 1924.

NORBECK, PETER (1870–1936). Peter Norbeck established an artesian well-drilling company in South Dakota in the 1890s, and was elected to the state senate where he served from 1909 to 1915. He was one of the leaders of the **Progressive Republicans** who supported first **Robert M. La Follette** and then **Theodore Roosevelt** in 1912. Norbeck was elected lieutenant governor in 1914 and became governor of South Dakota in 1916 and 1918. As governor, Norbeck led a program of reform that included rural credits for farmers, highway building schemes, workmen's compensation, and reform in state government. In 1920, Norbeck was elected to the United States Senate where he served until his death. In Congress, he supported farm relief programs such as the **McNary-Haugen** Bills and the later Agricultural Adjustment Act (1933). Norbeck supported most **New Deal** measures.

NORRIS, GEORGE WILLIAM (1861–1944). George Norris qualified in law in Indiana in 1883. He moved to Nebraska in 1885 and established a law practice. A **Republican**, Norris won election as a county prosecuting attorney in 1892, judge in 1895, and congressman to the United States House of Representatives in 1902. He held that position until 1912, when he was elected to the United States Senate, a seat he held almost until his death. An independently minded Progressive, Norris opposed United States intervention in the affairs of Latin American nations and he supported neutrality in the war in Europe. Norris was one of the six senators (**Robert M. La Follette, James K. Vardaman, William Stone**, Asle J. Gronna [Republican, N. Dakota], and Harry Lane [Democrat, Oregon] being the others) who voted against the declaration of war in 1917. He voted against the **Versailles Peace Treaty** and entry into the **League of Nations** in 1919.

Throughout the 1920s, Norris increasingly sided with Republican insurgents in favor of policies to aid the farmers and he supported the **McNary-Haugen** Bills. He was particularly conspicuous in calling for public ownership and development of the Muscle Shoals facilities in Alabama. Norris was cosponsor of the **Norris-La Guardia Anti-Injunction Act of 1932** that extended some protection to organized labor in the event of strikes. He also sponsored the **Twentieth Amendment** to the Constitution, ending the "lame duck" congresses that had sat from December to March following elections.

Although a Republican, Norris supported **Franklin D. Roosevelt** and the **New Deal** during the 1930s and led the fight in favor of the Tennessee Valley Authority (TVA) in 1933. He also increasingly supported Roosevelt in foreign affairs, moving away from his earlier **isolationist** stance. In 1936, Norris was re-elected as an Independent Progressive but was defeated in 1942 and retired from public life.

NORRIS-LA GUARDIA ANTI-INJUNCTION ACT, 1932. Co-sponsored by **George Norris** and **Fiorello La Guardia** this act declared "Yellow Dog Contracts" that prohibited a worker from joining a union unenforceable in federal courts. It also prevented federal courts from issuing injunctions against striking workers, those encouraging others to strike, or those picketing, speaking, or writing in support of strikes. Similar measures were passed at the state level in the following years. *See also* TRADE UNIONS.

– O –

OGBURN, WILLIAM FIELDING (1886–1959). William Ogburn got a Ph.D. in sociology from Columbia University in 1912 and then taught in Portland, Oregon, and at the University of Washington. He returned to Columbia in 1919 and taught there until 1927. He established his reputation with the publication of *Social Change with Respect to Cultural and Original Nature* (1922) in which he outlined his theory of "cultural lag," arguing that changes in material culture occur before changes in cultural life occur in response. He also later argued that because scientific discoveries were made by more than one person, inventions were inevitable. Ogburn's use of statistical analysis was also evident in his work on "How Women Vote" published in *Political Science Quarterly* [34] in 1919.

Ogburn was managing editor of the *Journal of the American Statistical Association* from 1920 to 1926 and became president of the American Sociological Society in 1929. In 1931, he was president of the American Statistical Association, and from 1937 to 1939 chair of the Social Science Research Council. In 1927, he became professor of sociology at the University of Chicago and in 1933 was appointed Sewell L. Avery Distinguished Service Professor. He remained at Chicago until his retirement in 1951. In 1929, Ogburn was one of several social scientists increasingly employed by the federal government when **Herbert Hoover** appointed him director of the **President's Research Committee on Recent Social Trends**, which reported in 1933. From 1933 to 1935, he was director of the Consumer's Advisory Board of the National Recovery Administration and from 1935 to 1943 a research consultant to the Science Committee of the National Resource Committee. Ogburn's *Sociol-*

ogy (1940), written with Meyer Nimkoff, became a standard text for many years.

O'HARE, KATE RICHARDS (1876–1948). Born Carrie Kathleen Richards, Kate O'Hare worked as a machinist and was one of the first **women** to join the International Association of Machinists. After working in social welfare in Kansas City in the late 1890s, O'Hare became a Socialist, married Patrick O'Hare, and trained as a party organizer. She wrote for the *Appeal to Reason* and in 1910 assumed leadership of the Kansas **Socialist Party**. O'Hare became a major figure on the socialist speaking circuit and held several leading positions in the party. She was a candidate for the party's vice presidential nomination in 1916 and she was the first ever woman to run for the U.S. Senate, albeit unsuccessfully. She consistently spoke out against United States involvement in **World War I** and was jailed under the **Espionage Act** following an antiwar speech in 1917. Woodrow Wilson commuted her sentence in 1920. O'Hare then campaigned for prison reform and an amnesty for all political prisoners. In the 1930s O'Hare supported **Upton Sinclair**'s End Poverty in California campaign and then worked as assistant to the state director of the California Department of Penology.

O'KEEFE, GEORGIA (1887–1986). Georgia O'Keefe studied art at the Art Institute of Chicago and Art Student's League in New York. In 1909, she began work as an illustrator in Chicago, briefly taught in Amarillo, Texas, and at the University of Virginia, and in 1915 at Columbia College in South Carolina. O'Keefe returned to New York in 1916, where her work was shown by **Alfred Stieglitz** in his "291" exhibition. Stieglitz showed her work again in 1918, 1923, and 1924. Having married O'Keefe that year, Stieglitz was to show O'Keefe's work regularly thereafter and to include her and her work in his own photographs. O'Keefe's painting included Texan landscapes, close-ups of flowers and seashells, and studies of bones, skulls, and antlers in the New Mexico desert and incorporated rich vivid colors in powerful images. By the 1930s, her work was widely viewed and her reputation as one of America's leading artists was established. In 1946, the New York Museum of Modern Art showed her work in their first one-woman exhibition. O'Keefe continued painting through to the 1960s until her eyesight failed.

O'NEILL, EUGENE (1888–1953). Born Eugene Gladstone O'Neill, the future great dramatist had an erratic school education and spent two semesters at Princeton University, 1906–07. From 1909 to 1912, O'Neill wandered various parts of the world (Honduras and Argentina) and worked his passage to England on a number of occasions. He was confined to a sanatorium due to ill health in 1912, but began writing one-act plays shortly thereafter. In 1914, O'Neill went to Harvard University where he spent a year studying playwriting. After spending some time in **Greenwich Village** O'Neill moved to Provincetown, Massachusetts where, with a group of writers and artists, he formed "The Provincetown Players" who put on plays in New York City. Several of O'Neill's one-act plays were staged and some were published in *Seven Arts* and *The Smart Set*. His first professional success came with *Beyond the Horizon*, awarded the Pulitzer Prize in 1920. O'Neill produced a number of plays in 1919 and 1920, most significantly *The Emperor Jones* (1920). He received his second Pulitzer for *Anna Christie* (1921), and in 1923 he was awarded a gold medal by the National Institute of Arts and Letters. That same year *All God's Chillun Got Wings*, dealing with miscegenation, appeared, followed the next year by *Desire under the Elms*, which dealt with incest.

O'Neill won his third Pulitzer for *Strange Interlude*, which appeared in 1928 and ran for over 400 performances in New York City before it toured the United States and then Europe. Further success came with *Mourning Becomes Electra* in 1929. In 1936, O'Neill was awarded the Nobel Prize for literature. In 1939, he completed one of his greatest works, *The Iceman Cometh*, and this was followed by *Long Day's Journey into Night* (1939–41), which won a posthumous Pulitzer, and *A Moon for the Misbegotten* (1943). O'Neill was regarded as one of the greatest 20th-century playwrights. He defied convention in terms of content, subject, and style.

OPEN SHOP MOVEMENT. *See* AMERICAN PLAN.

ORGANIC ACT OF PUERTO RICO, 1917. Also known as the Jones Act, the Organic Act of Puerto Rico was an amendment to the original legislation, the Foraker Act (1900), that had established a government of Puerto Rico following its acquisition from Spain in 1898.

The legislation passed in 1917 conferred United States citizenship upon Puerto Ricans and established an elected upper house. The power to veto legislation and appoint the governor and senior officials still remained with the United States president. Greater autonomy was granted in a further act of 1947, and Puerto Rico adopted its own constitution in 1952.

OVERMAN ACT, 1918. A measure introduced by Senator Lee Overman of South Carolina in 1918. The Overman Act extended President **Woodrow Wilson**'s wartime powers to enable him to redistribute personnel, functions, and powers of federal agencies as necessary and without congressional approval.

OVINGTON, MARY WHITE (1865–1951). After attending Packer Collegiate Institute and Radcliffe College, in 1893 Mary White Ovington opened a **settlement house** in New York City known as the Greenpoint Settlement of the Pratt Institute Neighborhood Association. Following her resignation due to illness in 1903, Ovington began to study the problems of **African Americans**. She became involved with the Niagara Movement, a protest organization formed by black leaders including **W. E. B. Du Bois**, and with the Lincoln settlement for African Americans. Her study, *Half Man: The Status of the Negro in New York*, was published in 1911. Ovington was instrumental in calling the meeting that led to the National Conference on the Negro following the race riot in Springfield, Illinois, in 1908. The outcome of the conference was the formation of the **National Association for the Advancement of Colored People** (NAACP) in 1910. Ovington held a number of positions in the NAACP and was chair of the board from 1919 until 1932 when she became treasurer. She retired from the NAACP in 1947.

OWEN, CHANDLER (1889–1967). A graduate of Virginia Union University in Richmond, Chandler Owen moved to New York City, where he received one of the **National Urban League**'s first social work fellowships to study at Columbia University and the New York School of Philanthropy. Together with **A. Philip Randolph**, whom he met in 1915, Owen joined the **Socialist Party**. The two young **African Americans** established and edited *The Messenger*, a left-wing monthly journal, from 1917 to 1928. They were critical of American entry into **World War I**, which they opposed as a class war and a "white man's war." Owen and Randolph were charged under the **Sedition Act** with impeding the war effort, but a judge who could not accept that the antiwar publications were their own work dismissed the charges. Owen was inducted into the army in 1918 and served until the war ended.

During the **Red Scare**, *The Messenger* was classed by the Justice Department as "the most dangerous Negro magazine" but the two editors escaped further prosecution. For a while, Owen still supported the Socialist Party and he ran for election to the New York state assembly in 1920, but failed. He and Randolph were extremely critical of **Marcus Garvey** and in 1923 Owen was one of a number of African Americans who wrote to the attorney general urging speedy prosecution of the West Indian. In 1923, Owen moved to Chicago and edited the *Chicago Bee* and later became a regular columnist for the *Chicago Daily News*. He later joined the **Republican Party** and ran unsuccessfully for election to the House of Representatives in 1928. After 1941, both Owen and Randolph were supporters of United States involvement in World War II and Owen wrote a widely circulated government pamphlet *Negroes and the War* in 1942. He also wrote speeches for the Republican presidential candidates Wendell Willkie and Thomas Dewey and later campaigned on behalf of Dwight D. Eisenhower. Owen's influence was, however, largely limited to the 1920s and 1930s.

OWEN, RUTH BRYAN (1885–1954). Ruth Owen, daughter of **William Jennings Bryan**, was educated at the University of Nebraska. Owen married a British man and after spending several years in Jamaica, West Indies, she moved to London, England, in 1912. Owen worked with the American Women's War Relief Fund during the war and served as a nurse in the Voluntary Aid Detachment during the Egypt-Palestine campaign, 1915–18. After the war, Owen settled in Miami, where she was a Lyceum and Chautauqua lecturer, vice president of the University of Miami board of regents, and a member of the faculty, 1926–28.

Owen was the first woman elected to Congress from Florida when she became the **Democratic Party** representative in 1928. Her election was challenged on the grounds that she had not been a citizen for the required period (having taken her husband's citizenship on marriage). Owen won her case (her husband had died and she had "renaturalized") and she was re-elected in 1930. She failed to regain the nomination in 1932 but became the first American woman diplomat when **Franklin D. Roosevelt** appointed her minister to Denmark in 1933. Owen held the position until 1936 when she resigned, having married a Dane. Owen was a member of the Advisory Board of the Federal Reformatory for Women, 1938–54, and in 1945 acted as a special assistant at the San Francisco Conference. She continued to lecture and to write on various subjects.

– P –

PACIFICISM. *See* PEACE MOVEMENTS.

PACT OF PARIS. *See* KELLOGG-BRIAN PACT.

PALMER, A. (ALEXANDER) MITCHELL (1872–1936). The **Democratic Party** politician and attorney general, A. Mitchell Palmer, was educated at Swarthmore College and worked as an attorney in Pennsylvania. He served in the House of Representatives from 1909 to 1915. As a member of the Democratic Party National Committee, he helped secure the nomination for **Woodrow Wilson** in 1912. Palmer was defeated in his bid to become a United States senator in 1914 by the conservative Republican Boies Penrose. In 1916, Wilson appointed him **Alien Property Custodian** responsible for enemy-owned property in the United States during **World War I**. He became attorney general in 1918. Palmer used wartime powers to obtain injunctions against striking miners and railroad workers in 1919.

In response to pressures from Congress, the wave of postwar strikes, and several bomb attacks in 1919, including one on his own home, which encouraged the belief that an attempted revolution was imminent (a fear known as the as **Red Scare**), he instigated the **Palmer Raids** of January 1920. It was believed that Palmer hoped to win the Democratic presidential nomination by capitalizing on anti-radical feelings, but his biographer points out that Palmer, who had a

Quaker and reform background, had been criticized for delay in dealing with the imagined revolutionary threat. The criticism provoked by his actions, particularly against labor, ensured his defeat in the campaign for the presidential nomination and he returned to his private law practice. Palmer's last significant political act was to draft the Democratic platform in 1932. He was working on the platform for 1936 when he died.

PALMER RAIDS, 1919–1920. Following a wave of industrial strikes and a postal bombing campaign in April and June 1919, Attorney General **A. Mitchell Palmer** determined to crack down on radical activities. Using the powers provided in the 1918 Immigration Act, on 7 November 1919, the Justice Department arrested some 600 people in raids in 11 different cities across the country. A further 3,000 people were detained in a second series of raids in January 1920. Over 800 were deported as undesirable aliens, among them the long-time residents in the United States, anarchists **Emma Goldman** and Alexander Berkman, but the vast majority of the arrests were dismissed by the acting secretary of labor, Louis B. Post. When the Bolshevik rising predicted by Palmer (advised by **J. Edgar Hoover**) for May 1 failed to occur, there was increasing criticism of Palmer's actions and the threat to civil liberties involved.

PARIS PEACE CONFERENCE. *See* VERSAILLES PEACE CONFERENCE.

PARKER, DOROTHY (1893–1967). Dorothy Parker had her first poem published in *Vanity Fair* in 1915 and she was hired as a caption writer, first for *Vogue* then for *Vanity Fair*. In 1918, she succeeded P. G. Wodehouse as the drama critic at *Vanity Fair*. Parker also published some of her more acerbic and satirical pieces in *Ainslee's* and *Life* and she wrote fiction and essays for the *Saturday Evening Post* and *Ladies' Home Journal*. Parker was soon well known for her wit, puns, and epigrams. Parker's first book of poems, *Enough Rope*, was published in 1926, and her second, *Sunset Gun*, in 1928. As well as a humorist and a poet, Parker expressed social concerns about racial and gender discrimination. In 1927, she was arrested in Boston for protesting against the execution of **Sacco and Vanzetti**.

In 1927, Parker joined the staff of the *New Yorker* as a book reviewer and later as drama critic. Two volumes of her short stories, *Laments for the Living* and *After Such Pleasures*, were published in 1930 and 1933, and her third volume of poetry, *Death and Taxes*, appeared in 1931. During the 1930s, Parker turned to writing Hollywood screenplays. She also helped to organize the Anti-Nazi League and she reported on the Spanish Civil War. As a consequence of her activities in the 1930s, the House Un-American Affairs Committee questioned Parker in 1952. During the 1950s, she wrote very little. She was inducted into the American Academy of Arts and Letters in 1959 and taught briefly at California State College, Los Angeles, in the 1960s. She lived most of her last years in solitude in New York City, where she died.

PAUL, ALICE (1885–1977). A Quaker, Alice Paul was educated at Swarthmore College and the University of Pennsylvania, from where she gained her Ph.D. in 1912. She later gained a law degree from Washington College and a Ph.D. in law from American University in 1928. Paul studied at Woodbridge Quaker College in England and the London School of Economics from 1907 to 1910. Paul was active in the British suffragette movement, and after returning to the United States in 1910 she organized demonstrations for the **National American Woman's Suffrage Association**.

In 1916, Paul and Lucy Burns established the more militant **National Woman's Party**. She mobilized pickets outside the White House in 1917 demanding that "America be made safe for democracy" and was jailed. When she went on a hunger strike, Paul was force-fed. Once the vote had been gained, Paul led the campaign for equal rights in support of the Equal Rights Amendment first introduced in 1923. In the 1930s, Paul traveled to Europe, where she established a World Woman's Party. She continued to campaign for the Equal Rights Amendment and in the 1960s was involved in protests against the war in Vietnam. *See also* WOMEN'S SUFFRAGE.

PEACE MOVEMENTS. Peace movements had a long history in the United States stretching back to the late-18th to early-19th centuries and Quaker and other religious groups. The "largest and oldest" group still in existence in 1900 was the American Peace Society

(APS), formed in 1828. The peace movement experienced a surge of interest following the Spanish-American War (1898) and in response to international imperialism. **Progressivism** too, with its emphasis on rational solutions to man-made problems encouraged action to outlaw war as a means of settling disputes. Many Americans attended the first Hague Peace Conference in 1899, and between 1901 and 1914 some 45 new peace organizations came into existence in the United States. Chief among these were **Jane Addams**'s International Welfare Organization (1904), **Elihu Root**'s American Society of International Law (1906), and the World Peace Foundation and Carnegie Endowment for Peace, both formed in 1910.

The American peace activists continued their campaigns after the outbreak of **World War I** in 1914, and called for a negotiated peace. A Woman's Peace Parade in New York City in August 1914 led to the formation of the **Woman's Peace Party** (WPP) in 1915 involving **Carrie Chapman Catt** and **Rosika Schwimmer**. The WPP lost some support following its backing of **Henry Ford**'s failed "Peace Ship" mission in 1915, and it lost more supporters after the United States entered the war in 1917. **Women's** involvement in the international peace movement found fruition in the Women's International League for Peace and Freedom (WILPF) formed in The Hague in April 1915 with Jane Addams as its first president.

After 1917, the American peace movement was thrown into disarray as most organizations patriotically supported the war. Opposition to the war came chiefly from the **Socialist Party** and radical peace activists who formed the **American Union Against Militarism**. The terms of the **Treaty of Versailles** also divided American peace activists as some felt the terms were too harsh and other were prepared to accept it in order to ensure participation in the **League of Nations**. The postwar reactions to the horrors of World War I did, however, lead to support for disarmament and backing for the **Washington** and **London Naval Conferences** and the **Kellogg-Briand Pact**. New organizations like the Women's Committee for World Disarmament and National Council for Prevention of War joined the older groups in the 1920s.

PEEK, GEORGE NELSON (1873–1943). George Peek studied briefly at Northwestern University, Illinois, in 1891. He then worked first as an office assistant and subsequently found employment with Deere and Webber, a branch of the John Deere Plow Company. In 1901, Peek became general manager of the Deere Company in Omaha and in 1914 vice president in charge of sales in Deere's main offices in Moline, Illinois. During **World War I**, he was an industrial representative on the **War Industries Board** and in 1918 became commissioner of finished products. In 1919, Secretary of Commerce William C. Redfield appointed Peek to chair the Industrial Board of the **Department of Commerce**, but Peek resigned after a few months due to conflict with the railroad director, **Walker D. Hines**, over price issues.

From 1919 to 1923, Peek was president and general manager of the Moline Plow Company. He resigned over differences with the company's vice president **Hugh S. Johnson**. As president of the American Council of Agriculture, Peek supported government farm support initiatives as proposed in the **McNary-Haugen** Bills between 1924 and 1928. He was an active supporter of **Franklin D. Roosevelt** in 1932 and was appointed to head the Agricultural Adjustment Administration (AAA) in 1933. However, Peek did not accept that there was a farm surplus and opposed the program to reduce production at the heart of the AAA, and Roosevelt was forced to ask for his resignation after a few months. He was appointed instead as adviser on foreign trade and president of the Export-Import Bank but again differences over policy led to his resignation in 1935. Peek increasingly became a critic of **New Deal** farm policies and of Roosevelt's interventionist policies. Peek was a member of the national committee of the America First Committee established in 1940 to keep the United States out of the European war.

PERKINS, FRANCES (1882–1965). Born Fannie Coralie Perkins, Frances Perkins was a graduate of Mount Holyoke College and Columbia University. She became executive secretary of the New York Consumer's League from 1910 to 1912 and worked as an authority on industrial safety with the New York Committee of Safety (1912–17). Perkins served on the Industrial Commission of New York State in 1921 and was appointed chair of the New York State Industrial Board in 1926. She held the position until 1929 when she became New York secretary of labor under Governor **Franklin D. Roosevelt.** Following his election to the presidency, Roosevelt made Perkins the first woman cabinet officer when he appointed her secretary of labor in 1933. Perkins was a member of the United States Civil Service Commission in 1946. She held a number of teaching positions after World War II, and in the late 1950s held a visiting professorship at Cornell.

PERMANENT COURT OF INTERNATIONAL JUSTICE. Often referred to as the World Court, the Permanent Court of International Justice was established under Article XIV of the covenant of the **League of Nations**. It was intended that the court would act as arbiter in international disputes and offer advice on disputes to the Council of the League. Although the United States did not become a member, **Charles Evans Hughes** and **Frank B. Kellogg** were among four Americans who served as judges.

PERSHING, JOHN JOSEPH (1860–1948). Pershing was a career soldier who graduated from West Point in 1886 and served in the Indian wars and Spanish American War (1898). In 1916, he led the **punitive expedition** into **Mexico** in pursuit of **Francisco ("Pancho") Villa** following the attack on **Columbus**, New Mexico. Although unsuccessful, Pershing carried out his orders to the letter and without upsetting the Mexican government. As a result, he became commander in chief of the **American Expeditionary Force (AEF)** in 1917. He successfully maintained the unity of the American army rather than have it divided among other **Allied** forces, and he supported the strategy of concentrating on the western front over other theaters in the war. In 1921, Pershing was appointed chief of staff of the United States Army, a position he held until he retired in 1924.

PICKFORD, MARY (1892–1979). Mary Pickford, who was to become one of the great stars of the silent **movies**, was born Gladys Louise Smith in Toronto, Canada. When her father died in 1897, the family turned to the stage to make a living. After some success on Broadway, Pickford turned to movies in 1909 when she found work at the Biograph studio with director **D. W. Griffith** with whom she made over 20 films. After a brief return to Broadway, Pickford joined **Adolph Zukor**, head of the Famous Players company that eventually became Paramount Studios. In the five years at Famous Players, Pickford achieved enormous financial success, having negotiated a share of net profits from her movies. Her many roles, in films such as *A Poor Little Rich Girl* (1917) and *Rebecca of Sunnybrook Farm* (1917), generally depicted a very young, almost child-like figure with the distinctive girlish curls, by which she became known.

In 1917, Pickford met **Douglas Fairbanks** and together, with **Charlie Chaplin** and D. W. Griffith, they established the United Artists Company. She and Fairbanks married in 1920. During their honeymoon in Europe, crowds of ecstatic fans mobbed them. Her first films with United Artists *Pollyanna* (1920) and *Little Lord Fauntleroy* (1920) (in which she played both the boy of the title and his mother), were major successes. Attempts to play more adult roles were less successful and she returned to her normal type in the box-office smash *Little Annie Rooney* in 1925. However, it was becoming increasingly difficult for Pickford to play the young parts. In 1928, she was given an Academy Award for best actress in her first talkie, *Coquette*. In 1929, she costarred for the first and only time with Fairbanks in *The Taming of the Shrew*. She effectively retired from acting in 1933, and she and Fairbanks were divorced in 1935. In 1934, Pickford's book *Why Not Try God?* was a best-seller and she wrote a novel, *The Demi-Widow*, in 1935 and her autobiography, *Sunshine and Shadow*, in 1955. She became more and more a recluse in later years and sent a taped message of thanks to the Motion Picture Academy in 1976 in response to the award of an honorary Oscar.

PINCHOT, AMOS RICHARDS ENO (1873–1944). Not as well-known as his famous older brother **Gifford Pinchot**, Amos Pinchot studied at Yale University and dropped out of Columbia Law School to serve in the Spanish-American War, 1898. He subsequently qualified in law, served briefly as deputy district attorney in New York City (1900–01), and became active in politics following Gifford Pinchot's dismissal in 1910. Amos Pinchot became committed to exposing what he saw as the threat to government of organized wealth, and he wrote several articles on the subject. Together with Gifford, he established the National Progressive Republican League in 1911 to secure the election of Progressive candidates and supported the creation of the **Progressive Party**.

Pinchot opposed America's entry into the **World War I** and supported conscientious objectors. In 1920, he headed the **Committee of Forty-Eight** in an attempt to resurrect the defunct Progressive Party. His *History of the Progressive Party* was published posthumously in 1958. Pinchot was opposed to **Franklin D. Roosevelt's New Deal** and was an early member of the **isolationist** America First Committee.

PINCHOT, GIFFORD (1865–1946). The first head of the forestry division in the Department of Agriculture in 1898 and then the United States Forest Service in 1905, Pinchot graduated from Yale University in 1889 and studied conservation in France and Germany. In 1896, he was appointed to the National Forest Commission and became head of the Division of Forestry in the Department of Agriculture in 1898. Pinchot became a leader in the conservation movement in the administration of **Theodore Roosevelt**. Pinchot favored controlled commercial use of the national forest reserves, rather than their preservation simply as wilderness areas. His conflict with President **William Howard Taft**'s secretary of the interior, Richard A. Ballinger, over conservation practices in Alaska, led to Pinchot's dismissal in 1910 and resulted in division in the **Republican Party**. Pinchot and his brother **Amos** were involved in founding the National Progressive Republican League in 1911 and aiding the return of Roosevelt to the political arena. After campaigning on Roosevelt's behalf Pinchot established and taught at the forestry school at Yale and was then elected governor of Pennsylvania in 1923 until 1927 and again from 1931 to 1935. He modernized the Pennsylvania administration and increased regulation of state utilities. He also introduced a "mini-**New Deal**" in the state during the **Depression**.

PLUMB PLAN. Proposed in 1919 by Glenn E. Plumb, counsel for **railroad** unions, the plan called for a degree of federal-public ownership of the railroads to replace the wartime Railroad Administration. The government would purchase the railroads at approved values and a corporation representing government, employees, and operators would run the system. Congress did not accept the measure, but the railroads experienced greater government regulation after 1920.

POMERENE, ATLEE (1863–1937). Atlee Pomerene qualified in law and was admitted to the bar in Cincinnati in 1886. He served on the city board of education and in 1896 was elected county prosecuting attorney. As a **Democrat**, he was a supporter of the reformer Tom L. Johnson. In 1910, Pomerene was elected as Ohio's lieutenant governor, but the state legislature immediately chose him as United States senator. Pomerene was re-elected in 1916 and won a reputation as an independent-minded Progressive. He opposed both the **Eighteenth** and **Nineteenth Amendments** and failed to retain his seat in the 1922 election. In 1924 President **Calvin Coolidge** named Pomerene as one of the two special counsels to prosecute those involved in the **Teapot Dome** scandals. He successfully secured the cancellation of the leases and the conviction of **Albert Fall** for taking bribes. In 1927, he was appointed as special assistant to the attorney general to assist in further related prosecutions. Pomerene failed to gain re-election to the Senate in 1926 and failed to gain the Democratic nomination for the presidency in 1928. President **Herbert Hoover** named Pomerene to chair the **Reconstruction Finance Corporation** in 1932, but his nomination was never confirmed. Pomerene was an outspoken critic of the **New Deal**, particularly its banking and farm policies.

PORTER, COLE (1891–1964). The prolific songwriter Cole Porter was educated at Worcester Academy, Yale, and Harvard's law and music schools. Having already written several musical comedies and hundreds of songs at Yale, in 1916 he and T. Lawrason Riggs wrote a musical comedy, *See America First*, produced on Broadway in 1916. Porter went to France in 1917. A number of his songs were included in English musical shows from 1918 to 1922. Porter's music was included in *Within the Quota* performed in Paris and New York in 1923, the *Greenwich Village Follies* in 1924, *Paris* in 1928, *La Revue des Ambassadeurs* (Paris, 1928), and *Wake Up and Dream* (London 1929). Porter rose to even greater prominence in the 1930s with songs for shows and **movies**, the most famous being "Night and Day" from *The Gay Divorcee* (1932), "I Get a Kick Out of You" from *Anything Goes* (1934), "Begin the Beguine" from *Jubilee* (1935), "I've Got You under My Skin" from the movie *Born to Dance* (1936), and "In the Still of the Night" in the film *Rosalie* (1937). He continued to write through the 1940s and 1950s, most notably for *Kiss Me, Kate* (1948), *Can-Can* (1953), and the film *High Society* (1956) for which Porter's song "True Love" won an Academy Award. However, Porter's sophisticated, languid, and often sensual music seemed to belong more appropriately in the interwar period.

POUND, EZRA (WESTON) LOOMIS (1885–1972). Ezra Pound studied at the University of Pennsylvania and Hamilton College in Clinton, New York, and graduated with an M.A. from Pennsylvania in 1906. After being dismissed from a teaching position in 1907 for "bohemian" behavior, Pound traveled in Europe before settling in London where he became part of the literary avant-garde from 1908 until 1920. He remained an expatriate for the rest of his life. Pound's first volume of poetry, *A Lume Spento*, was published in 1908. This was followed by *Personae* (1909), *Canzoni* (1911), and *Ripostes* (1912). During this period, Pound established the Imagist movement and later joined the Vorticists with whom he published two volumes of *BLAST: A Review of the Great English Vortex* between 1914 and 1915. After the World War I, Pound published *Hugh Selwyn Mauberley* (1920) and worked with **T. S. Eliot** on Eliot's manuscript of the *Waste Land.* In 1921, Pound joined the expatriate set including **Gertrude Stein** and **Ernest Hemingway** in Paris, but in 1924 moved to Rapallo, Italy, where he remained until the end of World War II.

During the interwar period, Pound produced his *Cantos* series of poems, published from 1925 to 1940. He increasingly identified with Italy and Mussolini and between 1941 and 1943 made several broadcasts for Radio Rome attacking United States policies. Accused of treason, Pound was arrested in 1945, and after an imprisonment in Pisa was transferred to Washington, D.C., where he was found unfit to stand trial. From 1945 until 1958, Pound was held in an insane asylum. His work the *Pisan Cantos* appeared in 1948 and was awarded the Bollingen Poetry Prize in 1949. Pound was awarded the Pulitzer Prize for poetry in 1950. Those who felt that Pound had been a traitor during the war criticized both awards. Pound published several other works before his death, but none reached the levels of his earlier poetry.

PRESIDENT'S EMERGENCY COMMITTEE FOR EMPLOYMENT, 1930–31. Established by President **Herbert Hoover** in 1930 the Committee for Employment consisted of the secretaries of agriculture, commerce, interior, labor, and the treasury and was intended to encourage local and state relief activity in response to the **Depres-**

sion. Provided with only a limited budget, the committee could do very little and it was replaced by the **President's Organization on Unemployment Relief**.

PRESIDENT'S ORGANIZATION ON UNEMPLOYMENT RE- LIEF, 1931–1932. **Herbert Hoover** established the President's Organization on Unemployment Relief in 1931 to encourage, coordinate, and gather information about local and state provision of relief for the increasing number of people left unemployed. Chaired by **Walter Gifford**, the organization relied on traditional voluntary and charitable relief agencies to tackle the problems of the **Depression** and it soon proved ineffectual.

PRESIDENT'S RESEARCH COMMITTEE ON RECENT SO- CIAL TRENDS. Established by President **Hoover Hoover** in 1929, the Committee on Recent Social Trends was instructed to carry out a survey of the nation's social development to provide a basis for future government policy. The committee of leading social scientists and other academics was chaired jointly by **Charles Merriam** and **Wesley Mitchell** and funded by the Laura Spelman Rockefeller Memorial. Its detailed report, published as *Recent Social Trends in the United States* in 1933, provided a useful source of information for future historians but was little use at the time as the country was hit by the **Depression**.

PRESIDENT'S UNEMPLOYMENT CONFERENCE, 1921. Suggested and chaired by Secretary of Commerce **Herbert Hoover**, President **Warren Harding** called a conference of social scientists and trade officials in response to the recession following World War I. The committee called for local voluntary relief programs and for detailed study of economic trends. Such a study was undertaken under the leadership of **Wesley Clair Mitchell** between 1927 and 1929 and resulted in a two-volume study, *Recent Economic Changes in the United States* (1929). Much of the report was made redundant by the impact of the **Depression**.

PROGRESSIVE PARTY, 1912. The Progressive Party, or "Bull Moose" Party, sprang from **Republicans** disaffected with **William**

Howard Taft's presidency. Originally supporting **Robert M. La Follette**, the dissidents threw their backing behind **Theodore Roosevelt** and his "New Nationalism" in February 1912. When the Republican Party managers ensured that Taft was renominated despite overwhelming victories for Roosevelt in the primaries, Roosevelt and his followers broke away to establish the Progressive Party in August 1912 with Roosevelt as presidential candidate and **Hiram Johnson** as his running mate. The party platform included political reform, **women's suffrage**, further antitrust legislation, **tariff** reform, prohibition of **child labor** and regulation of female labor, and legislation to protect workers. In the election, Roosevelt was ahead of Taft with over 4 million votes, but the split in the Republican Party gave victory to the Democrats and **Woodrow Wilson**.

PROGRESSIVE PARTY, 1924. Republicans disillusioned with the return to conservatism in the postwar era joined forces with elements of the "**Farm Bloc**," members of the **American Federation of Labor** and Socialists to endorse the third party candidature of **Robert M. La Follette**. The party platform called for further legislation against monopolies, greater farm relief, and the public ownership of utilities and the **railroads**. La Follette won almost 5 million votes and carried his own state of Wisconsin but trailed in third behind **Calvin Coolidge** and **John W. Davis**.

PROGRESSIVISM. The "Progressive Era" was the period from about 1890 to World War I in which Americans from different backgrounds and parties responded to the problems produced by the rapid industrialization and urbanization of the United States. Progressivism was a diverse movement that almost defies definition. On the one hand, reformers wanted to regulate industry to allow for fairer competition, protect workers and consumers, and on the other hand they wished to democratize the political processes and make government more accountable. They also attempted to tackle urban problems such as poor housing, sanitation, and public transport, and many reformers worked in the **settlement houses**. Some reformers were more concerned with moral issues such as **prohibition** or prostitution, while others emphasized "Americanization" and issues related to **immigration**.

The origins of the Progressive movement lay in the earlier agrarian Populist movement and abolitionism. It also reflected a religious revival with the rise of the "Social Gospel" and development of the Young Men's Christian Association (YMCA) (1851) and the Salvation Army (1880). The increase in the number of college educated professional workers influenced by the new social sciences and also by "human interest" stories written in the new journals such as *Harper's* and *McClure's* by journalists (described by **Theodore Roosevelt** as "Muckrakers") was also an important factor. Significant, too, was the rise in the number of college educated **women**, many of whom found an outlet for their skills in the settlement houses. Increased employment of women brought calls for regulation and reform, and many women contributed to the growing call for **women's suffrage**. A wave of social unrest with violent strikes in the 1890s, and the rise of new movements like the **Socialist Party of America** and **Industrial Workers of the World**, motivated many among the middle classes to demand reform.

As the Progressive movement spread from the city to state to national level, it influenced both major parties and spawned new ones such as the **Progressive Party** and Prohibition Party. In 1912, the presidential election was contested by **Woodrow Wilson** (Democrat), **William Howard Taft** (Republican), Roosevelt (Progressive), and **Eugene V. Debs** (Socialist Party), all of whom could claim to be Progressive.

Among the Progressive movement's many accomplishments were: reform in city and state government, improvements in housing and the provision of public utilities, regulation of industry to improve safety and to protect workers, regulation of monopolies to make for fairer competition, **tariff** regulation, protection for consumers, and a more democratic political system with the use of referenda, initiatives, recall, the direct election of senators (**Seventeenth Amendment**), and votes for women (**Nineteenth Amendment**). Some Progressives also supported **Prohibition** and immigration control.

PROHIBITION. The Prohibition movement had its origins in the temperance movement that began in colonial America and grew with the religious and reform movements of the 1830s. The Prohibition Party originated in 1869 and in 1892 the party gained over 270,000 votes in the presidential election. **Women**'s groups were particularly associated with the movement and in 1874 the Women's Christian Temperance Union (WCTU) was founded in Cleveland, Ohio. Led by Frances Willard from 1879 to 1898, the WCTU was a powerful force. It was aided by the Anti-Saloon League created in 1893, and together the organizations mobilized a campaign to achieve the legal prohibition of alcohol. By 1914, 14 states had passed prohibition legislation.

During **World War I**, the need to conserve grain and anti-German feelings directed against brewers strengthened the call for national prohibition. In December 1917, Congress passed the **Eighteenth Amendment**. It was ratified on 16 January 1919. The legal ban on the manufacture, sale, or transportation of alcohol in the United States came into force following the passage of the amendment and **National Prohibition Act** (known as the Volstead Act) from midnight on 16 January 1920 until its repeal in 1933. Prohibition gave the 1920s a colorful reputation for violence and lawlessness associated with the rise of criminal organizations producing and distributing **"bootleg"** alcohol to "speakeasies" (illegal saloons) as it appeared that broad sections of the public were prepared to break the law. However, annual per capita consumption of alcohol fell from 2.6 gallons before the war to 0.97 gallons in 1934. Opposition was mobilized by the Association Against the Prohibition Amendment that secured the passage of the **Twenty-First Amendment** in December 1933. After repeal, liquor control once more became a matter of state, rather than federal government.

PUERTO RICO. *See* ORGANIC ACT OF PUERTO RICO.

PUNITIVE EXPEDITION, 1916–1917. Following the murder of 16 American citizens taken from a train near Chihuahua City, **Mexico**, and of 19 more in an attack on **Columbus**, New Mexico, by **Pancho Villa**, a force of 15,000 American troops led by Brigadier General **John Pershing** crossed into Mexico on 15 March 1916 in pursuit of Villa and his men. Initially, the Mexican government agreed to this punitive raid, but as United States troops penetrated several hundred miles into Mexico, there were armed clashes with Mexican troops with casualties sustained on both sides. As relations deteriorated, war between the United States and Mexico seemed a real possibility. Protracted negotiations took place from September to January 1917 and finally **Woodrow Wilson**'s administration recalled the expedition in February although Villa had not been captured.

– Q –

QUOTA ACT, 1921. Also known as the Emergency Quota Act, this legislation signed on 19 May 1921, was one of the first of President **Warren Harding**'s administration. The act limited the number of **immigrants** from any nationality to 3 percent of the number of that nationality resident in the United States as determined by the census of 1910. The measure, which was renewed in 1922 for a further two years, was intended to favor immigrants from northern and western Europe over those of southern and eastern Europe. When it failed to achieve this objective, it was replaced by the **Quota Act of 1924**.

QUOTA ACT, 1924. Also known as the Johnson-Reed Act or Immigration Act, the Quota Act of 1924 replaced the Emergency Quota Act. It reduced the proportion of **immigrants** of any national group to 2 percent of that nationality resident in the United States in 1890 and was intended to reduce the number of "new" immigrants arriving from southern and eastern European countries. While it exempted countries in the western hemisphere, it abrogated previous agreements with Japan and prohibited all further immigration from that country. Under the legislation, a new quota based on the proportion of people from any nationality group to the American population as a whole resident in the United States in 1920 was to come into effect in 1927 with a maximum total immigration of 150,000.

– R –

RADIO. Before **World War I**, radio, only developed in the 1890s by Guglielmo Marconi, was still in its infancy and used as a means of communication between individuals. New developments, particularly during the war, enabled the transmission of sound and a shift in emphasis to broadcasting to a wide audience. The Radio Corporation of America (RCA) was chartered in 1919 and the first announced broadcast was made when the Westinghouse company's KDKA station in Pittsburgh broadcast the presidential election returns on 2 November 1920. The new medium spread rapidly; by 1922, 3 million homes had radios and by the mid-1920s there were 530 local stations with an estimated audience of 50 million. The RCA network was joined by the National Broadcasting Company (NBC) in 1926 and the Columbia Broadcasting System (CBS) in 1927. Federal regulation was initiated with the **Federal Radio Commission** in 1927. The spread of commercial radio encouraged the consumer boom through advertising and with the **movies** helped to further "nationalize" American culture.

RAILROAD LABOR ACT, 1926. Following the bitter **Railroad strike of 1922**, the Railroad Labor Act (known as the Watson-Parker Act) abolished the **Railroad Labor Board** and replaced it with a National Board of Mediation. The Board of Mediation was to hear all disputes not settled by bipartisan boards of adjustment created by **railroads** to represent management and labor. Where settlements were not reached the Board could refer disputes to courts of arbitration. The intention of the act was to allow collective bargaining and voluntary agreements to settle disputes in the railroad industry. However, the railroads failed to establish boards of adjustment and continued to maintain company unions, and the Board had no power to impose penalties on the employers. Nonetheless, the Act marked a step toward union recognition in the railroads. In providing a mechanism for mediating public disputes and introducing a cooling-off period in which no changes could be made to existing conditions, it also brought some peace to the troubled industry. *See also* TRADE UNIONS.

RAILROAD LABOR BOARD. Created under the **Railroad Transportation Act** of 1920, the Railroad Labor Board was a nine-man tribunal with three members each representing public, labor, and management respectively, and it was empowered to settle labor disputes and make awards relating to hours and wages. In any event, the Board proved unable to enforce its decisions and was abolished in 1926 by the **Railroad Labor Act**. *See also* RAILROADS.

RAILROAD STRIKE, 1922. When the **Railroad Labor Board** withdrew wage increases granted in 1920 and at the same time failed to enforce agreements to abandon company unions, the **railroad** shop and nonoperative unions went on strike. The employers also demanded an end to union seniority rights in the industry and employed strikebreakers to keep the lines running. In 1923, Attorney General **Harry Daugherty** obtained a sweeping injunction prohibiting picketing and even communication between the strikers and their supporters, and the strikers were forced to return to work. *See also* TRADE UNIONS.

RAILROAD TRANSPORTATION ACT, 1920. Known as the Esch-Cummins Act, the Railroad Transportation Act was passed to ease the transition from wartime government control back to private ownership after the war. It increased the size of the Interstate Commerce Commission from 7 to 11 members and gave the commission power to fix rates to yield a return of 6 percent of the estimated value of **railroads**. An appropriation of $200 million was made to help railroads re-establish their prewar status and a $300 million "revolving fund" was created to provide loans to financially weak companies. The commission was also authorized to draw up plans for the consolidation of the railroads into between 20 and 35 systems. The Act also prohibited multiple directorships after December 1921.

RAILROADS. The railroad industry, which began in the early 19th century and grew with increasing rapidity from the 1830s on, was central to American economic growth. By 1860, there were more than 30,000 miles of rail track in the United States, two-thirds of it in northern states. The greatest wave of railroad construction came after the Civil War in conjunction with westward expansion and settlement and massive industrialization in the east. The first transcontinental railroad was completed in 1869 and by the start of the 20th century over 200,000 miles of track had been laid.

The railroad industry also witnessed the development of huge corporations headed by entrepreneurs often described as "robber barons." Despite the beginning of regulation with the creation of the

Interstate Commerce Commission in 1886, the ruthless profiteering and shady business practices of such men led to calls for reform and was a key element in both the Populist and **Progressive** movements. Legislation aimed at curbing railroad monopolies and the control of the rates charged by companies was passed under both **Theodore Roosevelt** and **Woodrow Wilson**. During **World War I**, the government took over running the railroads and although there were calls for this to continue, they were returned to private ownership under the **Railroad Transportation Act** of 1920. Postwar readjustments led to labor conflict in the industry and a major **railroad strike** in 1922. The development of the **automobile** and of air transportation, and the earlier overexpansion of uneconomic lines, placed the industry in an increasingly unfavorable position from the 1920s on. Railroad mileage, which had peaked at 254,000 miles in 1916, had fallen to 249,619 by 1930.

RANDOLPH, ASA PHILIP (1889–1979). A. Philip Randolph was born in Florida and attended the Cookman Institute. In 1911, he moved to New York City and took courses at City College. Together with **Chandler Owen**, Randolph opened an employment office in Harlem to try to unionize fellow **African American** migrants and enlist black recruits for the **Socialist Party**. In 1917, Randolph and Owen began to produce *The Messenger*, a left-wing journal aimed at black audiences. Their opposition to African American participation in the war effort during **World War I** led to them being charged under the **Sedition Act**, but the charge was dismissed because the judge believed they were the dupes of white radicals. During the **Red Scare** *The Messenger* was described as the "most able and most dangerous" of all black publications.

After World War I, Randolph voiced opposition to **Marcus Garvey**'s call for racial separatism and from 1925 on was involved in trying to organize the Pullman Car porters into a union. He established the Brotherhood of Sleeping Car Porters (BSCP) with *The Messenger* as its official publication. The BSCP was finally given a charter by the **American Federation of Labor** in 1935 and was recognized by the Pullman Company in 1937. Randolph was the BSCP president until his retirement in 1968. Randolph was appointed to the New York City Commission on Race in 1935 and also became president of

RANKIN, JEANETTE (1880–1973) • 233

the National Negro Congress concerned with the economic situation of African Americans. Faced with continued discrimination in the developing defense industries, in 1940 Randolph called for a March on Washington to protest in July 1941. Threatened by a potentially embarrassing demonstration, President **Franklin D. Roosevelt** issued an executive order outlawing discrimination and establishing a Fair Employment Practices Committee to investigate complaints, and the march was called off. Randolph unsuccessfully campaigned for the establishment of a permanent fair employment practices act. With the reintroduction of Selective Service after World War II, Randolph mobilized black opinion to protest against segregation in the armed forces and in 1948 President Harry S. Truman issued an executive order initiating the integration of the military.

During the 1950s, Randolph organized a Prayer Pilgrimage in Washington, D.C., in 1957 and supported Youth Marches for Integrated Schools in 1958 and 1959. In 1955 Randolph was appointed one of the vice presidents of the newly merged AFL-CIO. It was Randolph who in 1963 suggested a March on Washington for Jobs and Freedom for African Americans. The March was one of the highpoints of the civil rights demonstrations of the 1960s. However, Randolph subsequently agreed to a moratorium on demonstrations in order to support Lyndon Johnson in the presidential election. The same year, Randolph established the Randolph Institute to encourage links between labor organizations and the civil rights movement. Although such actions separated him from the increasingly militant and separatist Black Power groups, Randolph remained an influential figure in civil rights until his death. *See also* TRADE UNIONS.

RANKIN, JEANETTE (1880–1973). Jeanette Rankin was a graduate of the University of Montana (1902) and the New York School of Philanthropy (1909). She was a **social worker** in Seattle in 1909 and then became involved in the **women's suffrage** campaign. Following Montana's acceptance of female suffrage in 1914, Rankin was the first woman to serve in the United States Congress when she was elected on a progressive **Republican** platform in 1916. She voted against America's entry into **World War I**. Having failed to be elected to the Senate in 1918, Rankin returned to social work and became active in a number of **women**'s causes and was particularly active in peace organizations. She returned to the House of Representatives in 1940 and once again voted against war in 1941. Rankin did not seek re-election in 1942, but turned instead to lecturing and work for the **National Consumers League** and Women's International League for Peace and Freedom. She later campaigned against the war in Vietnam.

RANSOM, JOHN CROWE (1888–1974). The southern poet John Ransom graduated from Vanderbilt University, Nashville, in 1909, studied at Oxford as a Rhodes Scholar from 1910 to 1913, and then took a teaching position at Vanderbilt, where he remained until 1937. Ransom served in the artillery in France during **World War I** and shortly after his first book, *Poems about God*, was published. His second volume, *Chills and Fever* appeared in 1924 and the third, *Two Gentlemen in Bonds* in 1927. Ransom wrote little new poetry after this, but was still highly regarded. His book, *Selected Poems* (1963), was awarded the National Book Award in 1964.

Ransom was one of a group of 16 poets including **Donald Davidson, Allen Tate**, and Robert Penn Warren known as the Fugitives. They met in Nashville from 1915 to 1928 to read and criticize one another's work and to produce a magazine, *The Fugitive* (1922–25), in which they explored the southern heritage but offered an alternative to the old cliches of the South. They responded to the criticism of southern ways in coverage of the **Scopes Monkey Trial**, and in *I'll Take My Stand* (1930) Ransom and others defended agrarian culture. Ransom offered a defense of religion in his *God without Thunder: An Unorthodox Defense of Orthodoxy* (1930).

Ransom moved to Kenyon College, Ohio, in 1937. There he edited the *Kenyon Review* from 1939 to 1959 and together with the publication of *The New Criticism* (1941), with its emphasis on close, systematic textual analysis, this made him one of America's most respected literary figures.

RECONSTRUCTION FINANCE CORPORATION (RFC). The Reconstruction Finance Corporation was established by Congress on the recommendation of **Herbert Hoover** in 1932 "to provide emergency financing facilities for financial institutions," and "to aid in financing agriculture, commerce, and industry" in order to counter the effects of the **Depression**. Its primary concern was to halt the run on **banks** and to restore faith in the financial system in order to encourage a revival of industry. It was headed initially by **Charles Dawes** and was described by some as a "rich man's dole." Before the end of the Hoover administration, the RFC had lent $1.5 billion to banks, mortgage loan companies, **railroads**, insurance companies, and agricultural credit organizations. Although it was not particularly successful, the RFC's life was extended and it was grouped with other agencies as the Federal Loan Agency in 1939. It survived in various forms and was involved in financing a number of war-related activities. Its capital stock, originally $500 million, was reduced in 1948 to $100 million. Revelations of various financial irregularities and misuse of funds in the 1950s led to its abolition in 1954.

RED SCARE, 1919. Following the end of World War I, the United States was gripped by a wave of antiradical hysteria that was directed against real or imagined Bolsheviks (supporters of the 1917 Russian communist revolution). Strikes, such as those in **Seattle** and the **Boston police strike**, were characterized as the work of "reds," and fears of impending revolution were fanned by a wave of bombing outrages in April and June. Radical groups and **trade unionists** celebrating May Day were attacked. Attorney General **A. Mitchell Palmer** and a Justice Department official **J. Edgar Hoover** announced that a revolution was planned and launched the **Palmer Raids** in December 1919. When no revolution materialized, many observers began to protest against the attack on civil liberties and gradually the violence declined. However, xenophobia continued to be evident in the legislation to limit **immigration**, in the rise of the **Ku Klux Klan**, and in the trial and execution of **Sacco and Vanzetti**.

The Red Scare can be seen in part as a reaction to the dislocations of war and uncertainty about the postwar settlement. It was also a continuation of the anti-German hysteria and "100 percent Americanism" of the war years and of the anti-immigrant sentiment evident in the prewar years.

RED SUMMER, 1919. As well as a wave of anti-radicalism in the **Red Scare**, 1919 witnessed an upsurge of violence directed against **African Americans**. Lynching, which had been increasing during

World War I, reached an even higher level when more than 80 African Americans were brutally murdered by mobs in 1919. In addition, 25 race riots, varying in scale and intensity, broke out across the country in towns and cities as far apart as Charleston, South Carolina; **Longview**, Texas; Omaha, Nebraska; **Elaine**, Arkansas; and in Washington, D.C., itself. The worst incidents took place in **Chicago**, where at least 23 African Americans and 15 white Americans died. However, out of the mood of disillusionment emerged a **"New Negro,"** more assertive and less prepared to turn the other cheek.

REED, JOHN SILAS (1887–1920). The writer and revolutionary, John Reed went to Harvard University from 1906 to 1910. Shortly after his graduation, Reed joined the **Greenwich Village** bohemian community and began writing for the *American Magazine*, *Collier's*, and other publications. In 1912, he became an editor of *The Masses*, a radical journal dedicated to free expression. In 1913, Reed went to Paterson, New Jersey, to report on the strike of silk workers. He and his friends then staged a pageant in Madison Square Garden in support of the strike. He subsequently went to **Mexico** to cover the revolution for the *New York World* and his reports helped to popularize **Pancho Villa** in the United States. When war in Europe broke out in 1914, Reed attempted to get to the western front but failed. Instead he went to Russia and published *The War in Eastern Europe* in 1916. After a brief sojourn in the United States, where he and his partner Louise Bryant established the Provincetown Players with **Eugene O'Neill**, Reed returned to Russia to cover the outbreak of the revolution. When he arrived back in the United States in 1918, Reed was put on trial under the **Espionage Act** for his antiwar writing in the *The Masses*. He was acquitted, arrested and tried a second time, and once more acquitted with his fellow editors. In 1919, he published *Ten Days That Shook the World*, his account of the Russian Revolution. Reed helped to found the Communist Labor Party in America and began editing its journal in 1919. He returned to Russia in 1919, was detained in Finland trying to return to the United States, and was forced to return to Russia. Suffering from typhus, Reed died in Moscow and was buried in the Kremlin. In the 1920s and 1930s, groups who shared his left-wing sympathies established several John Reed clubs in the United States.

REPUBLICAN PARTY. For much of the latter half of the 19th and early years of the 20th centuries, the party of Abraham Lincoln dominated politics, controlling both the White House and Congress. However, from the turn of the century on, the conservative element in the party was increasingly challenged by **Progressive** insurgents demanding reform. For a while, both factions united uneasily behind **Theodore Roosevelt**, but the divisions reappeared during the presidency of **William Howard Taft** and culminated in the defection of many reformers to Roosevelt and the **Progressive Party** in 1912. As a result of this split, **Woodrow Wilson** won the presidential election and the **Democrats** gained control of both the House and the Senate. The demise of the reform impulse and the reaction to the **Versailles peace settlement** and **League of Nations** at the end of **World War I** restored some unity to the Republican Party. In control of the White House under presidents **Warren Harding, Calvin Coolidge**, and **Herbert Hoover**, they had majorities in the House and Senate from 1919 until the **Depression** brought a Democratic landslide in the election of 1932. However, the continued presence of a reformist element, united with the midwestern **Farm Bloc**, ensured that none of the presidents in the interwar years could completely rely on partisan support for their policies.

RICKENBACKER, EDWARD VERNON (1890–1973). Edward Rickenbacker worked in automobile manufacturing and sales before **World War I**. In 1909, he took up motorcar racing and became a full-time driver in 1912. With the outbreak of war in 1917 Rickenbacker joined the army and became a driver, but then learned to fly and was commissioned in the Army Air Service. By the time the war ended, Rickenbacker had become America's top air ace, having fought in 134 aerial contests and downed 26 German airplanes and balloons. He was awarded the French Croix de Guerre, the American Distinguished Service Cross with oak leaf clusters, and the Congressional Medal of Honor.

After the war, Rickenbacker created an automobile manufacturing company but took to speedway management when his business failed. In 1934, he became manager of Eastern Airlines and then became president and general manager in 1938. Although originally opposed to American involvement in the World War II, once the country had entered the conflict, Rickenbacker toured the United States, the Pacific, China, and the Soviet Union on morale-boosting and diplomatic missions. He survived three weeks at sea on a raft after his airplane had crashed in the Pacific in 1942. In 1953, Rickenbacker became chairman of the Eastern Airlines board of directors.

ROARING TWENTIES. The decade of the 1920s was described variously as "the **Jazz** Age," "the age of prosperity," and the "roaring twenties." The latter suggested a rapid period of change—the adjective had been applied first to the 1840s as "the roaring forties." A **movie** titled *The Roaring 20s* about bootlegging and starring James Cagney appeared in 1939.

ROBERTS, OWEN JOSEPHUS (1875–1955). The **Supreme Court** justice Owen Roberts was educated at the University of Pennsylvania and the University of Pennsylvania Law School, where he graduated in 1898. He practiced law in Philadelphia and for 22 years also taught at the University of Pennsylvania Law School. In 1918, Roberts became a special deputy United States attorney and was involved in prosecutions under the **Espionage Act**. In 1924, President **Calvin Coolidge** appointed Roberts, together with **Atlee Pomerene**, to prosecute those involved in the **Teapot Dome** scandal.

In 1930, President **Herbert Hoover** nominated Roberts to fill the seat on the Supreme Court vacated following the death of **Edward Sanford**. With the new chief justice **Charles Evans Hughes**, Roberts held the balance between the conservatives and liberals in the court. Increasingly the court became more liberal on issues of freedom of speech and, in the case of the **Scottsboro Boys**, on the right of defendants to have counsel appointed for their defense. However, Roberts tended to side with the conservatives in cases concerning the extension of government authority under the **New Deal**. But following **Franklin D. Roosevelt**'s attempt to alter the composition of the court Roberts made "a switch in time that saved nine," and sided with the liberal group to uphold minimum wage laws, the National Labor Relations Act (1935), and the Social Security Act (1935). Roberts tended to be more conservative on civil rights and civil liberties and supported white primaries in 1935, and compulsory flag salutes and the pledge of allegiance in public schools in 1940. However, he dissented against the decision to uphold the evacuation of Japanese Americans during World War II.

Following his retirement in 1945, Roberts was dean of the University of Pennsylvania Law School from 1948 to 1951. He was also chair of the security board of the Atomic Energy commission (AEC). His Holmes lectures at Harvard Law School in 1951 were published as *The Court and the Constitution.*

ROBERTSON, ALICE MARY (1854–1931). Largely self-educated, Alice Robertson became a clerk in the Indian Office in Washington, D.C., in 1873. In 1879, she returned to Oklahoma Indian Territory to teach. Robertson was appointed government supervisor of Creek Indian Schools from 1900 to 1905 and was postmaster of Muskogee, Oklahoma, 1905 to 1913. In 1920, she was elected as a Republican to the United States Congress, but failed to win re-election in 1922. President **Warren Harding** appointed her as a welfare worker at the Veterans' Hospital in Muskogee in 1923. *See also* NATIVE AMERICANS.

ROBESON, PAUL LEROY BUSTILL (1898–1976). The great American singer, actor, athlete, and civil rights activist Paul Robeson attended Rutgers University (then a college). An outstanding scholar and athlete, he became the first **African American** all-American in football. After his graduation in 1919, Robeson went to Columbia University Law School where he obtained his degree in 1923 and began work in a New York City law firm. Following a racial slight, Robeson gave up law and joined **Eugene O'Neill**'s Provincetown Players and starred in *All God's Chillun Got Wings* and *The Emperor Jones* in 1924. Robeson began his solo singing career with a performance of gospel songs at Carnegie Hall in 1925 and became celebrated for singing and acting in various musicals, most famously for his rendition of "Ol' Man River" in *Showboat* (1928). In 1930, he achieved critical acclaim for his portrayal of *Othello* in London. Robeson went on to appear in 11 **movies** including *Song of Freedom* (1936), *King Solomon's Mines* (1937), and *Proud Valley* (1940), in addition to film versions of his stage successes and was the best-known black entertainer of his day.

Embittered by race prejudice in the United States, Robeson increasingly spent time performing in Europe after 1928. In the 1930s, he visited the Soviet Union and became an advocate of communism. He returned to the United States with the outbreak of World War II and achieved a great success when he became the first African American to play the lead in *Othello* in America. After the war Robeson's communist sympathies led to his investigation by congressional committees and his blacklisting as an entertainer. His passport was revoked from 1950 to 1958, effectively destroying his career. Robeson left the United States in 1958 and did not return until 1963. He lived out his remaining in years in virtual seclusion, but was remembered in several awards for his contributions to the arts and to civil rights.

ROBINS, MARGARET DREIER (1868–1945). Margaret Robins (née Dreier, sister of **Mary Dreier**) committed herself to voluntary work while still a teenager. In 1902, she joined the New York Charities Aid Association and the Women's Municipal League, and in 1904 she joined the Women's Trade Union League (WTUL). Robins was to devote most of her career and her personal wealth to the WTUL. Originally treasurer, in 1907 Dreier became president of the WTUL, a position she held until 1922. She also edited the WTUL journal, *Life and Labor*, for several years. Dreier campaigned for municipal reform and for **women's suffrage**, worked on behalf of the **Progressive Party** in 1912, and supported **Republican Charles Evans Hughes** in 1916.

During **World War I**, Robins was involved in the Illinois Women's Council of National Defense. After the war, she convened the first International Congress of Working Women and organized the International Federation of Working Women in 1922. During the 1920s, Robins was active in the national Republican Party, but later supported the **New Deal**.

ROBINSON, EDWIN ARLINGTON (1869–1935). Regarded as the first major American poet of the 20th century, Edwin Arlington studied at Harvard University from 1891 to 1893 but was forced to leave due to family difficulties. His first poetry was published as *The Torrent and the Night Before* in 1897 and *The Children of the Night* in

1897. With the support of President **Theodore Roosevelt**, he found a job at the New York Customs House from 1905 to 1909 that enabled him to continue writing. He published *The Town down the River* in 1909. A series of Arthurian poems, *Merlin, Lancelot,* and *Tristram* were published in 1917, 1920, and 1927 respectively. Robinson's volume of *Collected Poems* was awarded the first Pulitzer Prize for poetry in 1921 and he won a second Pulitzer for *The Man Who Died Twice* (1924) and a third for *Tristram*. His other writings included *Avon's Harvest* (1921), *Roman Bartholow* (1925), *The Glory of the Nightingales* (1930), and *Nicodemus* (1932). Robinson was awarded honorary degrees from Yale and Bowdoin.

ROBINSON, JAMES HARVEY (1863–1936). The historian James Robinson completed his undergraduate and master's degrees at Harvard University in 1888 and traveled to Europe where he studied for his Ph.D. A year after his graduation in 1890, Robinson began teaching European history at the University of Pennsylvania. His emphasis on the use of primary sources led to the publication of five volumes of Translations and Reprints in 1894. In 1895, Robinson was appointed professor in European history at Columbia University, where he remained until 1919. At Columbia, Robinson became one of America's leading historians, inspiring a generation of scholars, including **Charles A. Beard**, Carl Becker, and Arthur Schlesinger, Sr., who would later become famous in their own right. In his many publications, Robinson stressed the "new history," incorporating social, economic, and cultural aspects rather than merely concentrating on the political and military. He also argued that history was relevant to contemporary issues. His books included *An Introduction to the History of Western Europe* (1902, 1903), *Readings in European History* (1904, 1906), *The Development of Modern Europe* (1907–08) [with Charles A. Beard], and *Outlines of European History* (1912) [also with Beard]. In *The New History* (1912) Robinson argued that history must draw upon the social sciences to better understand the past.

Robinson became increasingly disillusioned during **World War I** and, after Columbia dismissed two professors for their opposition to American entry into the war, he resigned to establish the New School for Social Research in 1919. The new institution had no entry requirements and offered no degrees. Robinson left in 1921 to concentrate on his own writing. He produced *The Mind in the Making* (1921), *The Humanizing of Knowledge* (1922), and *The Ordeal of Civilization* (1926). Robinson was elected president of the American Historical Association in 1929.

ROCKEFELLER, ABBY ALDRICH (1874–1948). Abby Greene Aldrich, the daughter of Nelson Aldrich, senator for Rhode Island, grew up in Providence, Rhode Island, and was educated by private tutor and in a girls' school. She traveled in the United States and Europe. In 1901, she married **John D. Rockefeller, Jr.**, one of the world's richest men. She had six children between 1903 and 1915. In addition to raising a family, Abby Rockefeller was involved on her own and with her husband in many philanthropic activities. The Rockefellers supported the restoration of Colonial Williamsburg and Abby donated to the Rockefeller Folk Art Collection there. Abby was also instrumental in the creation of the New York Museum of Modern Art in 1929 and was an active supporter throughout her life. She served on the board of trustees and donated several works by Matisse, Picasso, Rivera, and others, and with her son Nelson, she established a purchase fund for the museum.

ROCKEFELLER, JOHN DAVISON, JR. (1874–1960). John D. Rockefeller was the only son of the head of Standard Oil, millionaire industrialist John D. Rockefeller, Sr. Rockefeller, Jr. graduated from Brown University in 1897 and began work as an associate in Standard Oil. Ill health led to his retirement from the business and he began instead to manage the various Rockefeller philanthropic organizations. In 1913, he became president of the newly created Rockefeller Foundation.

Rockefeller supported a wide range of concerns including religious groups such as the Interchurch World Movement, conservation projects including the establishment of the Grand Teton National Park in Wyoming and Arcadia National Park in Maine, and the development of Colonial Williamsburg in Virginia. The foundation also financed an International Education Board to support academic research activities abroad and "International Houses" to provide residences for foreign students at United States universities. From 1918 to 1929, Rockefeller was president of the Laura Spelman Rockefeller

Memorial that provided philanthropic support for concerns related to women and children. Rockefeller also supported preservation and building projects in New York City, including work on the Cloisters Museum and the Palisades Park. In 1928, building began on the Rockefeller Center in New York City, originally as a home for the Metropolitan Opera. When the Opera withdrew, RCA became the tenant of "Radio City."

ROCKNE, KNUTE (1888–1931). Born Knute Kenneth Rokne (sic) in Voss, Norway, Rockne arrived in the United States with his family in 1893 and settled in Chicago. After working at a variety of jobs, Rockne entered Notre Dame University in 1910 and took part successfully in a number of sports. He shone particularly at football as captain of the team. After graduating in chemistry and pharmacology in 1914, Rockne took a coaching post at a high school, but later that year he was appointed as a chemistry instructor and assistant football coach at Notre Dame, where he became head coach in 1918. The team dominated the game from 1919 to 1924 and Rockne became a national celebrity. His team was famous for its backfield, known as the "Four Horsemen of Notre Dame": Harry Stuhldreher, Donald Miller, James Crowley, and Elmer Layden. In 1928, Rockne's Notre Dame team achieved near mythical status when his halftime appeal to the memory of a former halfback, George Gipp, resulted in an emotional 12-6 upset victory over the Army team. The team won the national championships again in 1929 and 1930. In 1931, Rockne died in an airplane crash en route to help make a film, *The Spirit of Notre Dame*. A film of his life, *Knute Rockne, All-American*, was made in 1940.

ROGERS, WILL (WILLIAM PENN ADAIR) (1879–1935). A Cherokee born in the Indian Territory of Oklahoma, Will Rogers began his career as a cowboy in Texas in 1898. In 1902, he traveled to Argentina as a cowhand, and then onto South Africa. It was in South Africa that Rogers found work in a Wild West Show riding and roping. He toured New Zealand and Australia before returning to the United States. During performances with the Ziegfeld *Follies* in 1916, Rogers developed his style of humorous social commentary. In 1920, he began to write columns for the press and particularly for the *Saturday Evening Post*. In 1918, Rogers also began appearing in motion pictures and he made

48 silent comedies before turning to sound film in 1929. A series of **movies** in which he played different western persona appeared in the 1930s: *State Fair* (1933), *David Harum* (1934), and *Steamboat 'Round the Bend* (1935). Rogers became a well-known radio personality during the 1930s and his folksy wit and humorous observations on political and other matters seemed to capture a popular mood for nostalgia. When he died in an airplane crash in Alaska in 1935, Rogers was much mourned.

ROOSEVELT, (ANNA) ELEANOR (1884–1962). Eleanor Roosevelt was born in New York City into America's social elite. Her uncle was President **Theodore Roosevelt**, and Eleanor benefited from the best education available, despite the death of her parents at an early age. When she returned from her schooling in London Eleanor joined the **National Consumers League** and worked with immigrant children. In 1905, she married **Franklin Delano Roosevelt**, a sixth cousin once removed. She bore him six children between 1906 and 1916, one of whom died as an infant. She was for a long time dominated by her husband's mother, but during **World War I** Eleanor began to develop an independent public role when she worked for the Red Cross and Navy League. She came to an accommodation with Franklin after discovering his affair with her own social secretary, Lucy Mercer, and became more involved in activities with **women's suffrage** groups and **trade unions**, particularly the **League of Women Voters**, the Women's Trade Union League, and the Women's Division of the Democratic Committee. Her independence developed further in 1921 following Franklin's affliction with poliomyelitis, a crippling viral infection that left him permanently disabled. Eleanor helped him to overcome the disability and to continue his political career.

By 1928, Eleanor headed the Women's Division of the **Democratic Party** and when Franklin became governor of New York, she often carried out inspections of state facilities on his behalf. Once Franklin Roosevelt became president, Eleanor took on the role as an active first lady, transforming the position much as her husband did the presidency. She was often attacked for her actions on behalf of women and **African Americans** and for her views expressed in speeches, radio broadcasts, and her daily newspaper column, "My Day," that began in 1935. In 1939, Eleanor Roosevelt publicly announced her resignation from the Daughters of the American Republic (DAR) after the organization had refused to allow the black opera singer Marian Anderson to perform in Constitution Hall. Roosevelt helped to arrange an alternative performance at the Lincoln Memorial. She continued to campaign on behalf of African Americans during World War II.

During the war, Mrs. Roosevelt was briefly assistant director of the Office of Civil Defense, but this ended following congressional criticism. She worked energetically throughout the war on morale-raising activities, visiting many parts of the United States, the Caribbean, the Pacific, and Great Britain. Following Franklin Roosevelt's death in 1945, Eleanor was appointed U.S representative to the United Nations, a position she held until 1953. She chaired the Human Rights Commission from 1946 to 1951 and was instrumental in the adoption of the Universal Declaration of Human Rights in 1948. Eleanor twice visited the USSR in the 1950s. She also campaigned on behalf of birth control and continued to have some influence in the Democratic Party. John F. Kennedy appointed her as representative to the UN once more in 1961 and as chair of the National Commission on the Status of Women.

ROOSEVELT, FRANKLIN DELANO (1882–1945). Thirty-second President of the United States. Born in Hyde Park, New York, into a wealthy family, Franklin Roosevelt was educated at Groton, Harvard, and Columbia Law School. He briefly practiced law in New York City before entering the state senate as a **Democrat** in 1910. In 1913, he was appointed assistant secretary of the navy, a post previously held by his uncle **Theodore Roosevelt**. His role in the Navy Department enhanced his reputation and after the war he was nominated as the Democratic Party's vice-presidential candidate to run with **James M. Cox** in the unsuccessful campaign of 1920. In 1921, he developed polio, which left him severely paralyzed and threatened to destroy his political career. However, aided by his wife **Eleanor Roosevelt**, he fought to overcome the handicap and in 1928 succeeded **Al Smith** as governor of New York. As the effects of the **Depression** began to tell, Roosevelt introduced measures to develop public electric power, reduce utility rates, and provide relief for the unemployed. He defeated Smith and **John Nance Garner** to win the Democratic presidential nomination in 1932 and he broke with tradition and flew to Chicago to accept the nomination. In his speech on 2 July, he promised "a new deal for the American people" and this quickly became the label applied to his program. His election campaign was impressively vague in specifics, but he projected a positive air and promised an "enlightened administration." He was critical of **Herbert Hoover** for failing to balance the budget and for increasing government bureaucracy.

Roosevelt won a convincing victory with 57 percent of the popular vote to Hoover's 40 percent and 472 electoral college votes to 59. He did little between his victory and his inauguration, but did survive **Guiseppe Zangara**'s assassination attempt in February 1933. However, declaring there was "nothing to fear but fear itself," in his inaugural address in March he promised a wide-ranging program of measures to combat the deepening Depression. He followed this up with a remarkable wave of action in what became known as the "First Hundred Days" establishing the **New Deal** as a reforming administration of unprecedented proportions. The New Deal was to form the basis of the modern welfare state and the framework of American politics for the next half century. Roosevelt served an unprecedented four terms having been re-elected in 1936, 1940, and 1944. He successfully led the nation through World War II and in the process assumed the leading role in international diplomacy through his meetings with Prime Minister Winston Churchill of Great Britain and Premier Josef Stalin of the USSR.

ROOSEVELT, THEODORE (1858–1919). Twenty-sixth president of the United States. Theodore Roosevelt was born in New York City into a wealthy family. Sickly as a child, he improved his health and physique through exercise and subsequently remained a life-long advocate of the strenuous life. He was educated privately and then at Harvard University and Columbia Law School. His first book, *The Naval War of 1812*, was published in 1882. Roosevelt visited the West in 1883, acquired a ranch, became a cowboy, and developed a lasting affinity with that region. He wrote an account of *Hunting Trips of a Ranchman* (1885) and a four-volume history, *Winning the West* (1889–96).

In 1881, Roosevelt was elected to the New York State Assembly and served from 1882–84. He was a member of the United States

Civil Service Commission, 1889–95 and president of New York City Board of Police Commissioners, 1895–97. He was appointed assistant secretary of the navy by President William McKinley in 1897, but resigned in 1898 to organize a volunteer cavalry unit, the "Rough Riders," to serve in the Spanish-American War. Roosevelt rose to national prominence when he led the "Rough Riders" in the battle at San Juan Hill, Cuba, in 1898. He enhanced his reputation as a reformer while governor of New York, 1899–1900, and was chosen by the **Republican Party** as William McKinley's vice-presidential running mate largely in order to keep him in control. However, Roosevelt became president after an anarchist assassinated McKinley in 1901. He was elected in his own right in 1904.

Flamboyant and assertive, Roosevelt reinvigorated the presidency. Beginning with the antitrust proceedings against J. P. Morgan's Northern Securities Company, Roosevelt made a reputation as "trust-buster" in restricting industrial monopolies in 43 separate actions under the Sherman Antitrust Law (1890). In 1903, Roosevelt created the Department of Commerce and Labor and supported the regulation of the **railroads**. He initiated policies of land conservation and approved the Pure Food and Drug and Meat Inspection Acts in 1906. Roosevelt backed an aggressive **foreign policy** in the Caribbean, using the phrase to "talk softly and carry a big stick" and asserting "dollar diplomacy" to further United States interests, particularly in Panama. Under Roosevelt, United States troops occupied Santa Domingo (1904) and Cuba (1907). He supported the expansion of United States naval strength and was active in bringing about a number of international arbitration treaties. His role as mediator in the Russo-Japanese War (1905) won him the Nobel Peace Prize.

Having promised in 1904 not to seek re-election, Roosevelt was responsible for the nomination of **William Howard Taft** as his successor in 1908. When Taft failed to continue his policies, particularly on conservation, Roosevelt attempted to regain the Republican Party nomination in 1912. When he was unsuccessful, he assumed the leadership of the National **Progressive Party**, but was defeated by the **Democratic** candidate, **Woodrow Wilson**. He was critical of many of Wilson's policies and after the outbreak of war in Europe in 1914 called for the strengthening of the United States military. Once America entered **World War I**, he proposed raising another volunteer regiment and unsuccessfully sought a military appointment. Roosevelt called for total loyalty and spoke out against "hyphenated Americans." He gave only qualified support for the **League of Nations** and was insistent that America remained an independent military power.

ROOT, ELIHU (1845–1937). Elihu Root graduated from New York University Law School in 1867 and started his own law firm in 1869. From 1883 to 1885, Root served as United States attorney in the southern district of New York and it was there he developed his relationship with **Theodore Roosevelt**. In 1899, President McKinley appointed Root secretary of war. He was largely responsible for developing policies with regard to the territories acquired from Spain in 1898 (Puerto Rico and the Philippines) and for establishing the basis for Cuban independence. He resigned from the post in 1904 but returned to office as secretary of state in 1905. Root began the process of professionalizing the foreign service, and he established better relations with Latin America and cosponsored the Central American Peace Conference in 1907. Root also resolved disagreements with Canada over North Atlantic coastal fishing rights. Through the Root-Takahira agreement with Japan in 1908, Root secured Japanese agreement to maintain the status quo in the Pacific and accept the independence and integrity of China. In 1912 he was awarded the Nobel Peace Prize for his work.

Root resigned as secretary of state in 1909. He was elected senator for New York in 1908 and served until 1915. He supported **William Howard Taft** in 1912. In April 1917, **Woodrow Wilson** appointed Root to head a mission to Russia following the overthrow of the Tsar. The appointment was not a success and as a result Root was not included in the **Versailles Peace Conference**. Root favored ratification of the **League of Nations** with reservations, a proposal rejected by the **"Irreconcilables"** to United States membership. Root was a delegate to the **Washington Naval Conference** and was a member of the commission of international law experts appointed by the League of Nations to draft the constitution of the **Permanent Court of International Justice**. He declined an invitation to become one of the court's judges, but remained an advocate of American membership. Root was also president of the Carnegie Endowment for International Peace.

ROSENWALD, JULIUS (1862–1932). The business executive and philanthropist Julius Rosenwald entered the clothing business in 1879. He established his own clothing manufacturing company in Chicago in the 1880s. In 1896, Rosenwald joined the Sears & Roebuck mail-order company. He was vice president of the company from 1895 to 1910, president from 1910 to 1925, and chairman of the board, 1923 to 1932. In addition to expanding the business and establishing retail outlets, Rosenwald established health-care provision and profit-sharing schemes for employees. Rosenwald's investments in the company made him a multimillionaire. By 1925, he was worth an estimated $125 million. Rosenwald aimed to use one-third of his wealth for charity and became a leading philanthropist. The Julius Rosenwald Fund was established in 1917, through which over $4 million was given toward the construction of 5,357 public schools, shops, and teachers' homes in **African American** communities in the South. He also made donations to the University of Chicago, Chicago's Museum of Science and Industry, the Young Men's Christian Association (YMCA) and Young Women's Christian Association (YWCA), and a number of Jewish causes.

ROSEWOOD MASSACRE, 1923. Following unconfirmed reports that an **African American** male had assaulted a white woman near the black township of Rosewood, Florida, on 1 January 1923, a white mob gathered, set fire to the buildings in Rosewood, and murdered eight people. The rest of the 120 black inhabitants fled the town and did not return. No one was ever indicted for the incident.

ROSS, EDWARD ALSWORTH (1866–1951). Edward Ross was educated at Coe College, Iowa, then studied in Berlin, France, and England before taking his Ph.D. at Johns Hopkins in 1891. Following his graduation, Ross held a succession of teaching posts in Indiana, Cornell, and Stanford Universities. His contract at Stanford was terminated because of his outspoken progressive views and the furor that followed led to the campaign to secure tenured protection for academics. Ross was employed as professor of sociology at the University of Nebraska from 1901 to 1906 when he was appointed professor in sociology at the University of Wisconsin, a position he held until 1937. In 1914 and 1915, Ross was elected president of the American Sociological Society. Ross wrote many academic works, chiefly *Social Control* (1901), *Foundations of Sociology* (1905), *Sin and Society* (1907), and *Social Psychology* (1908). Widely traveled, he also wrote *The Changing Chinese* (1911), *Russia in Upheaval* (1918), *The Social Revolution in Mexico* (1923), and *The Russian Soviet Republic* (1923). From 1940 to 1950, Ross was chair of the **American Civil Liberties Union**.

ROSS, NELLIE TAYLOE (1876–1977). In 1924, Nellie Tayloe Ross became the first female state governor when she completed the term of office of her deceased husband, William Bradford Ross, in Wyoming. She served out the two remaining years in office and saw a number of measures such as a new **banking** code and a **Child Labor Law** passed. Although selected to run again by the Wyoming **Democrats**, Ross failed to win re-election in 1926 in her solidly **Republican** state. She continued to be active within the Democratic Party and was vice chair of the party's national convention in 1928. She moved to Washington, D.C., that year and was active in mobilizing Democratic **women**. Her support for **Franklin D. Roosevelt** was rewarded with her appointment as head of the U.S. Mint in 1933, a position she held for 20 years.

ROTHSTEIN, ARNOLD (1883–1928). A professional gambler from an early age, Arnold Rothstein ran gambling houses in New York City, Saratoga Springs, and Long Beach, operated a racing stable, a real estate business, and a bail bond firm. Rothstein was alleged to have been behind the fixing of the 1919 **World Series** when the Chicago White Sox lost to the Cincinnati Reds. Rothstein was shot and killed in a New York hotel while playing cards.

RURAL CREDITS ACT, 1916. Passed as part of the "preparedness" campaign prior to United States entry into **World War I**, the Rural Credits Act established 12 Federal Farm Banks similar to those in the **Federal Reserve**. The Farm Banks were to provide long term mortgages to farmers at low interest rates to reduce farm debt and encourage greater production. *See also* FARMING.

RUSSIAN CIVIL WAR, INTERVENTION IN, 1918–1920. While the Bolshevik (Communist) Revolution of October 1917 was greeted with some misgivings by **Woodrow Wilson**'s administration, it was not until the new Soviet government had signed the Treaty of Brest-Litovsk with Germany and withdrawn from **World War I** in March 1918 that the United States government became openly antagonistic. In August 1918, three regiments of United States troops were sent as part of an allied force to Murmansk, Archangel, and Vladivostok, ostensibly to protect United States personnel and property but in practice aiding the anti-Bolshevik forces. Some 8,000 troops were in Russia until their eventual withdrawal in April 1920 and 275 died in various confrontations with the Soviet forces.

RUTH, GEORGE HERMAN "BABE" (1895–1948). The great baseball player, Babe Ruth, was committed to an industrial school for boys in Baltimore as a delinquent child in 1902. It was there that Ruth developed his early prowess as a baseball player. In 1914, he was signed by the Baltimore Orioles where he acquired his nickname, "Babe." Later that year, Ruth was sold to the American League side, the Boston Red Sox. Initially an outstanding pitcher, he switched to the outfield in 1919 and rapidly made his mark as a batter, establishing a league record by hitting 29 home runs. In 1920, Ruth was sold to the New York Yankees for a then-record $125,000.

In New York, Ruth became a national figure and the best-known sportsman of his day as the "Sultan of Swat." His presence helped bring about the Yankees' domination of major league baseball and in 1923 they moved to a newly built Yankee Stadium, popularly known as "the House that Ruth Built." Ruth was a legend not just for his baseball but also for his legendary appetite for food, beer, and women. By 1925, he was overweight, playing badly, and often in conflict with Yankees' manager, Miller Huggins. However, he regained his home run title in 1926 and kept it for six seasons. In 1927, he hit 60 home runs, a record not beaten until 1961. Ruth played his last game for the Yankees in 1934, joined the Boston Braves as assistant manager, but retired after only 28 games in 1935. Ruth's big-hitting style of play helped to transform baseball and his presence on and off the field made him the most widely acclaimed sportsman and best-known figure of his day. His total of 714 home runs survived until the 1970s. He was among the first five players admitted to the National Baseball Hall of Fame when it opened in Cooperstown, New

York, in 1939. When he died of cancer in 1948, 200,000 fans passed his body as it lay in state at Yankee Stadium and 100,000 watched the funeral procession. For many observers, Ruth remains the greatest baseball player ever.

– S –

SACCO, NICOLA (1891–1927). The Italian **immigrant** famously convicted with **Bartolomeo Vanzetti** in the **Sacco and Vanzetti case** was born in Torremaggiore, Italy. He emigrated to the United States in 1908 and found work in shoe factories in Massachusetts. Between 1912 and 1917, Sacco and Vanzetti were active as fundraisers and in strike activities for the anarchist movement. In 1917, both men fled to Mexico to avoid the draft. They returned to the United States and resumed their association with the anarchist movement and were arrested in May 1920 with other Italians in connection with those activities. However, Sacco and Vanzetti were subsequently charged with robbing two shoe factories and killing a guard and paymaster at the factory in South Braintree, Massachusetts. Found guilty in 1921, they were electrocuted at Charlestown State Prison on 23 August 1927.

SACCO AND VANZETTI CASE. The arrest, trial, conviction, and ultimate execution of the two Italian anarchists, **Nicola Sacco** and **Bartolomeo Vanzetti**, became an international *cause célèbre* between 1921 and 1927. Arrested initially for their political activities, the two men were subsequently charged with the robbery of two shoe factories in 1920 involving the killing in one at South Braintree, Massachusetts, of a guard and the paymaster. The trial in Dedham, Massachusetts, took place against a background of hysteria during the **Red Scare** and the **Palmer Raids**, and the trial was conducted in a prejudicial manner in focusing on their **immigrant** backgrounds, avoidance of the draft, and anarchist involvement. Their conviction on 14 July 1921, despite obvious weaknesses in the prosecution case and evidence of bias on the part of the judge, led to national and international protests. After eight motions for retrial were denied and the Massachusetts Supreme Court upheld their convictions, Sacco and

Vanzetti were sentenced to death in April 1927. A commission appointed by the state governor also found that "on the whole" the trial and appeals process had been fair. The two men were electrocuted on 23 August 1927. Arguments about their guilt or innocence are still the subject of much historical debate.

SANDBURG, CARL (1878–1967). After a time as an itinerant worker and serving in the Spanish-American War, the poet and writer Carl Sandburg became a reporter in Milwaukee and then for the Chicago *Daily News*. His poetry celebrating the city and working people, *Chicago Poems* (1915), *Cornhuskers* (1918), and *Smoke and Steel* (1920), won him prizes and national and international recognition as a "poet of the people." He was awarded a Pulitzer Prize in 1940 for his four-volume biography of Abraham Lincoln, *The War Years*, (1939) and for his *Complete Poems* in 1951. He was awarded the gold medal of the American Academy of Arts and Letters in 1952 for his work in history and biography. He published *Harvest Poems* in 1960 and *Honey and Salt* in 1963.

SANFORD, EDWARD TERRY (1865–1923). The **Supreme Court** justice, Edward Sanford, studied at the University of Tennessee, Harvard University, and Harvard Law School, where he obtained his LL.B. in 1889. He practiced law in Knoxville, Tennessee, until 1907 when he became assistant attorney general. Sanford also taught law at the University of Tennessee between 1897 and 1916. From 1908 until 1923, he sat as federal trial judge in Tennessee, earning a reputation for patience and impartiality. In 1923, President **Warren G. Harding** appointed Sanford to the Supreme Court on the recommendation of **William Howard Taft**. Sanford was often among the more liberal minority in court decisions about federal and economic regulation and voted to invalidate all-white primaries in *Nixon v. Herndon* (1927). However, he wrote the decision upholding racially restrictive covenants. His most important contribution was in cases relating to the First Amendment in which he argued that speeches advocating the violent overthrow of government had a "bad tendency" that placed them outside of the protection of free speech. In the course of his argument, Sanford extended the Bill of Rights to apply to the states through the Fourteenth Amendment's "due process" clause, a position that was to have considerable significance in the 1950s. Co-incidentally, Sanford died on the same day as Taft.

SANGER, MARGARET HIGGINS (1883–1966). Margaret Sanger trained as a nurse and studied under Havelock Ellis, the sexual psychologist, and Dr. Marie Stopes, the pioneer birth control advocate. In 1914, she became editor of *Woman Rebel*, which encouraged the use of contraception. When the publication was declared indecent, Sanger was arrested but fled to England. In 1916, she opened the first birth control clinic in the United States and was charged with maintaining a public nuisance and jailed for 30 days. In 1921, she founded the American Birth Control League, which she headed until 1929 when she established the National Committee on Federal Legislation for Birth Control. The Planned Parenthood Federation of America emerged from this in 1942.

ST. MIHIEL SALIENT. German position held in the **Argonne** for four years during **World War I**. The salient was attacked by the American 1st Army on 12 September 1918 and taken by 16 September. The victory may have inflated the self-esteem of the United States forces, leading them to underestimate the task that faced them in the subsequent Argonne offensive, but it did provide an important boost to **Allied** morale and vindicated **Pershing's** policy of maintaining the United States Army as an independent force.

***SCHENCK V. UNITED STATES*, 1919.** One of several cases brought to the **Supreme Court** to test the validity of the wartime **Espionage** and **Sedition Acts**. Justice **Oliver Wendell Holmes** used not only the consequences of the actions in question, but also the circumstances of "clear and present danger" to uphold the conviction of the socialist Charles T. Schenck for distributing literature encouraging resistance to the draft. The decision of the court was unanimous.

SCHURMAN, JACOB GOULD (1854–1942). Born in Canada, Jacob Schurman attended university in London and Edinburgh, followed by a further period of study in Europe. He began teaching in Canada in 1880 and published *Kantian Ethics and the Ethics of Evolution* in 1881. In 1886, he was appointed professor of philosophy at Cornell, where he remained for 28 years becoming president of the university in 1892. Schurman published several works, including *The Ethical Import of Darwinism* (1888), and was the founding editor of the *Philosophical Review* from 1892 to 1905.

Schurman became a naturalized United States citizen in 1892 and was involved in political affairs. He opposed the annexation of the Philippines in 1898, but in 1899 was appointed president of the first United States commission to the islands. From 1912 to 1913, Schurman was the United States minister to Greece and Montenegro and published a study of *The Balkan Wars, 1912–1913* (1914). Following his retirement from Cornell in 1920, Schurman was appointed United States minister to China and ambassador to Germany in 1925. He held that position until 1930.

SCHWAB, CHARLES MICHAEL (1862–1939). Charles Schwab began his career in the steel industry aged 17 and in 1889 became superintendent of the Carnegie Homestead Works in Pennsylvania. In 1897, Andrew Carnegie made Schwab president of the Carnegie Steel Company. When the company was sold to John Pierpoint Morgan in 1901, Schwab became president of the newly created United States Steel Company. In 1903, he resigned and assumed control of the Bethlehem Steel Corporation, which he built up to become the largest independent steel company. During **World War I**, **Woodrow Wilson** appointed Schwab head of the Emergency Fleet Corporation. After the war, he lived in semiretirement but from 1927 to 1932 was president of the Iron and Steel Institute.

SCHWIMMER, ROSIKA (1877–1948). Born in Budapest, Hungary, Rosika Schwimmer organized the National Association of Women Office Workers in 1897 and the Hungarian Association of Working Women in 1903. Inspired by the American suffragist **Carrie Chapman Catt**, Schwimmer organized the Hungarian Feminist Association in 1904. In 1914, she drew up a proposal for a conference of neutral nations to end **World War I** and she traveled to the United States to appeal to **Woodrow Wilson** and **William Jennings Bryan** for support. In 1915, she joined with **Jane Addams** to create the **Women's Peace Party**. Schwimmer was the international secretary. In 1915, Schwimmer persuaded **Henry Ford** to sponsor a peace conference in Sweden and she sailed on the peace ship, *Oscar II*, to convene the conference in February 1916. The conference ended in failure and Schwimmer remained in Europe. In 1918, the Hungarian government appointed her minister to Switzerland.

Following a counterrevolution in Hungary, Schwimmer fled first to Austria and then in 1921 to the United States. In America she was labeled a radical and pacifist and in 1928 her application for citizenship was denied. Her case was argued before the **Supreme Court** in *Schwimmer v. United States* but was denied on the grounds that she was "an uncompromising pacifist with no sense of national loyalty." Justices **Oliver Wendell Holmes** and **Louis D. Brandeis** dissented from the majority decision. Schwimmer remained in the United States as a resident alien and continued to work for world government. She was nominated for the Nobel Peace Prize by several international representatives in 1948 but died before an award was made.

SCOPES, JOHN T. (1900–1970). John Scopes was a high school biology teacher in Dayton, Tennessee, charged with breaking the Butler Act, a state law passed in 1925 that prohibited the teaching of the theory of evolution. His trial, known as the **Scopes Monkey Trial** became famous nationally and internationally.

SCOPES MONKEY TRIAL. The trial in Dayton, Tennessee, of **John Scopes**, the biology teacher accused of breaking the Tennessee law prohibiting the teaching of the theory of evolution. The trial lasted from 10 July to 25 July 1925, and was known as the "Monkey Trial" because it was argued that evolutionists believed men were descended from apes. The defense, funded by the **American Civil Liberties Union** and argued by the famous labor lawyer, **Clarence Darrow**, challenged the constitutionality of the law given the scientific validity of evolution. The prosecution was led by **William Jennings Bryan** who supported the literal interpretation of the Bible. The climax of the trial came when Darrow put Bryan on the stand to defend his fundamentalist views and exposed him to public ridicule. Although Scopes was found guilty of breaking the law, he was given the minimum penalty of a 100-dollar fine. The Butler Act, the law forbidding the teaching of evolution, remained on the statutes until 1967.

SCOTT, EMMETT JAY (1873–1957). The **African American** educator and publicist Emmett Scott attended Wiley College in Texas briefly before leaving to become a journalist in 1890. After becoming a reporter at the Houston *Post*, Scott became an editor of the black newspaper, the *Texas Freeman* in 1894. In 1897, he was hired as private secretary to the African American spokesman and principal of Tuskegee Institute, Booker T. Washington. Scott helped Washington to influence and control elements of the black press and other black leaders. He was involved in the creation of the Negro Business League and was its secretary from 1900 to 1922. In 1909, President **William Howard Taft** appointed Scott as one of the members of the American Commission to Liberia in Africa.

During **World War I**, Scott was appointed assistant to the secretary of war, **Newton D. Baker**, to advise on race relations and he was to write *Scott's Official History of the American Negro in the World War* (1919) and *Negro Migration during the War* (1920). From 1919 to 1932, Scott was secretary-treasurer and business manager at Howard University in Washington, D.C. A supporter of the **Republican Party**, he was a specialist adviser on race to the Republican National Convention in 1924 and assistant publicity director for the National Republican Committee from 1939 to 1942. During World War II, Scott established an African American shipyard at the Sun Shipbuilding Company in Chester, Pennsylvania. He retired when the war ended.

SCOTTSBORO BOYS. In March 1931, nine **African American** teenagers riding a freight train from Chattanooga to Memphis, Tennessee, were seized in Alabama and accused of raping two young white women riding the same train. Tried in Scottsboro, the case of the boys became an international *cause célèbre* because of the doubts about the evidence and the racial nature of the trials. Eight of the boys were convicted by an all-white jury and sentenced to death. One conviction was reversed on the grounds that the accused was a juvenile when the crime was committed. (The nine boys were Roy and Andy Wright, Eugene Williams, Heywood Patterson, Ozie Powell, Clarence Norris, Olen Montgomery, Charlie Weems, and Willie Roberson. Roy Wright's trial was declared a mistrial.)

Clarence Darrow was originally involved in the boys' defense following their first conviction. However, he withdrew because of the role of the **Communist Party** in the defense committee. In November 1932, the **Supreme Court** reversed the convictions on the other eight boys because Alabama had failed to provide adequate assistance of counsel. In subsequent retrials, despite doubts about the evidence of the two supposed victims, the boys were once against found guilty and sentenced to death, but in 1935 the Supreme Court overturned the convictions because African Americans were excluded from juries in Alabama. The boys were subsequently retried once more and four were convicted, two of whom were sentenced to death. Charges were dropped against the remaining four. The death sentences were commuted and by 1950 all of the Scottsboro boys were free by parole, appeal, or escape.

SEABURY, SAMUEL (1873–1958). Samuel Seabury qualified and practiced law in New York City. From 1907 to 1914, he served as a justice on the Supreme Court of New York and from 1914 to 1916 was associate judge to the New York Court of Appeals. Seabury rose to national prominence as chairman of the committee investigating crime in New York City politics, 1930–31. The results of the investigation led to the resignation of Mayor **James J. Walker** in 1932 and subsequent election of **Fiorello La Guardia** on a reform Fusion ticket. Seabury was the author of *The New Federalist* (1950).

SEATTLE GENERAL STRIKE, 1919. On 21 January 1919, shipyard workers in Seattle went on strike over a wage claim. Support from other unions turned this into a general strike on 6 February as 60,000 workers withdrew their labor. The strike was characterized by Mayor **Ole Hanson** as the work of Bolsheviks and the first step toward revolution in the United States. Hanson mobilized the police and military against the strikers, and faced with growing public disapproval, the strikers ended their action on 10 February. The strike was one of several major labor disputes that year contributing to the mood of unrest that provoked the **Red Scare**. *See also* TRADE UNIONS.

SECOND CHILD LABOR LAW, 1919. Passed after the **Supreme Court** had invalidated the **Keating-Owen Act**, 1916, the second Child Labor Law imposed a tax of 10 percent on the profits of any factory employing children younger than 14 or mines and quarries employing children under the age 16. The law was declared unconstitutional by the Supreme Court in *Bailey v. Drexel Furniture Company*, 1922.

SEDITION ACT, 1918. In May 1918, the **Espionage Act** was amended to prohibit any incitement of disloyalty or refusal of duty, or "the uttering, printing, writing, or publishing" of "any disloyal, profane, scurrilous, or abusive language about the form of government of the United States, or the Constitution of the United States, or the military or naval forces . . . , or the flag . . . , or the uniform." Convictions were punishable by a fine of up to $20,000 and up to 20 years' imprisonment. Under this and the previous legislation some 450 conscientious objectors were sentenced to military prison, a total of 2,168 cases of sedition were brought of which by 1921, 1,055 had been convicted. Among those convicted were the Socialists **Victor Berger** and **Eugene Debs** and the **Industrial Workers of the World** leader "Big Bill" **(William) Haywood**. The Espionage and Sedition legislation was upheld by the **Supreme Court** in *Schenck v. United States*. The Sedition Act was repealed in 1921.

SELECTIVE SERVICE ACT, 1917. Passed in May 1917, the Selective Service Act was effectively the first full military draft law passed in United States history and was passed despite some opposition both inside and outside Congress. The act required all men between the ages of 21 and 30 to register for military service on 5 June. Draft boards were established in 4,648 districts and they administered the four calls for service issued during **World War I**. A total of 26 million men out of a male population of 54 million were registered, and 4 million were drafted.

SELZNICK, DAVID O. (1902–1965). David Selznick took over his father's film-making business in 1923 and after some success moved to Metro-Goldwyn-Mayer (MGM) and became a producer. He moved to Paramount in 1928 and produced a number of successful **movies**. He established his own production unit in 1931 and then worked for RKO for whom he made *King Kong* in 1933. Selznick returned to MGM in 1933 and produced some famous films, particularly versions of literary works such as *David Copperfield* (1935) and

Anna Karenina (1935). His later productions included *Little Lord Fauntleroy* (1936), *The Prisoner of Zenda* (1937), and *Gone with the Wind* (1939). Selznick later made a number of major movies with the director Alfred Hitchcock, including *Rebecca* (1940) and *Spellbound* (1945). Following the success of *Gone with the Wind* Selznick was awarded the Irving G. Thalberg Memorial Award by the Academy of Arts for his outstanding contribution to the movie industry. He continued to produced films into the 1950s, despite declining success and failing health.

SENNETT, MACK (1880–1960). The future pioneer of silent **movie** comedies, Mack Sennett was born Michael Sinnott in Canada. His family moved to the United States in 1897 and he found work in burlesque theater before getting a job with the Biograph Film Company in 1908. Sennett successfully developed a number of slapstick comic films while at Biograph. In 1912, he became production head of the Keystone Film Company where he made several successful films, particularly those featuring the crazy antics of the Keystone Kops. Sennett's success faded in the later 1920s and by 1929 he worked for a minor company, Educational Pictures. He was declared bankrupt during the 1930s. In 1937, Sennett received a special Academy Award for his contribution to screen comedy.

SETTLEMENT HOUSES. The Settlement House movement that sprang up in the late-19th and early-20th century across the United States was a major part of the **Progressive movement**. Inspired by the example of Toynbee Hall in London, the settlement house was a residential community center established in poor, working class, or **immigrant** urban areas to provide social welfare, educational and leisure facilities. Stanton Coit and Charles B. Stover established the first settlement in the United States at the University Settlement in New York City in 1886. It was followed in 1889 by the Hull Street Settlement in Chicago established by **Jane Addams** and the Henry Street Settlement in New York City in 1893 led by **Lillian Wald**. By 1916, there were some 400 settlements in different towns and cities. Some 70 percent of the workers in them were female and the settlement houses were closely linked with the **women's suffrage** campaign as well as the calls for wider social and political reform. *See also* SOCIAL WORK.

SEVENTEENTH AMENDMENT, 1913. The Seventeenth Amendment, passed by Congress in May 1912 and ratified 31 May 1913, established the direct popular election of United States senators rather than by state legislatures. (*See* appendix II.)

SHARKEY, JACK (1902–1994). Born Josef Paul Zukauskas, Jack Sharkey changed his name shortly before he left the navy and became a professional boxer in 1924. After a rapid rise through the ranks of heavyweight boxers, Sharkey fought **Jack Dempsey** in 1927, but was knocked out in the seventh round. After beating a number of other contenders, Sharkey fought Max Schmeling of Germany for the heavyweight championship in 1930, but he lost by disqualification for a low blow. In 1932, Sharkey won the rematch and became the world heavyweight champion. He lost the title in 1933 to the Italian Primo Carnera. After a comeback in 1935, Sharkey fought the **African American** Joe Louis in 1935, but he was knocked out in the third round and retired from boxing.

SHEELER, CHARLES RETTEW (1883–1965). Charles Sheeler studied art in Philadelphia at the Pennsylvania Academy of Fine Arts. He traveled widely in Europe and was influenced by the Impressionist painters in his paintings of still life and architecture. In 1910, he began work as a commercial photographer while also continuing to paint. Several of his paintings were included in the **Armory Show** in 1913 and the 1916 Forum Exhibition of leading modern American artists. In 1919, Sheeler moved to New York City and established a reputation for his photographs and paintings of the city. He also produced photographs for *Vogue*, *Vanity Fair*, and advertising agencies. In 1927, he completed a widely published series of photographic studies of **Henry Ford**'s River Rouge factory in Michigan. In addition to photographs, Sheeler also painted many industrial landscapes, and his career, which continued through to the 1950s, included commissions from Kodak, United States Steel, and **General Motors**. In 1962, Sheeler was awarded the American Academy of Arts and Letters' Merit Medal and he was elected to the National Institute of Arts and Letters in 1963.

SHEPPARD, MORRIS (1875–1941). Morris Sheppard graduated in law from the University of Texas in 1897 and obtained a master of law degree from Yale in 1898. After practicing law in Texas, he was elected to Congress as a progressive **Democrat** in 1902 and served until 1913 when he was elected to the United States Senate on a pro-hibition platform. Sheppard introduced a constitutional amendment providing for **Prohibition** in 1913; it was passed in 1917 and ratified as the **Eighteenth Amendment** in 1919. Sheppard coauthored the **Sheppard-Towner Act** and was also one of the founders of the con-gressional **"Farm Bloc"** formed in 1921 to lobby on behalf of agri-cultural interests. He supported **Franklin D. Roosevelt** and the **New Deal**, but was chair of the Senate Investigating Committee on Cam-paign Expenditures that criticized the political role played by mem-bers of the Works Progress Administration. As chair of the Military Affairs Committee, Sheppard supported the administration's prepara-tions for war including the introduction of Selective Service in 1940.

SHEPPARD-TOWNER ACT. Passed in 1921, the Sheppard-Towner Act or Maternity and Infancy Care Act, provided federal-state fund-ing for child and maternal health centers, some three thousand of which were established between 1921 and 1929 when its funding was ended by Congress. *See also* SHEPPARD, MORRIS.

SIMMONS, WILLIAM JOSEPH (1880–1945). The founder of the second **Ku Klux Klan,** William Simmons went into the church min-istry at an early age. After service in the Spanish-American War (1898), Simmons was licensed to preach for the Methodist Church and he preached in Florida and Alabama until 1912. After breaking with the church, Simmons worked with fraternal organizations and became district manager of the Woodmen of the World in Atlanta. In-spired by **D. W. Griffith**'s film *The Birth of a Nation*, Simmons launched the Ku Klux Klan in 1915.

In 1920, Simmons hired Edward Y. Clarke and Elizabeth Tyler of the Southern Publicity Association to expand Klan membership. Cap-italizing on the conservative postwar mood, Clarke and Tyler in-creased membership from a few thousand to two million and the Klan spread beyond the South into Indiana and Illinois and into urban ar-eas. Clarke and then Hiram W. Evans replaced Simmons as "imperial wizard" in 1922. Simmons attempted to regain control in 1923 and eventually agreed to sell his interests back to the Klan for $90,000 in

1924. Simmons established another organization, the Knights of the Flaming Sword, but like the Klan it faded away, and with it, so did Simmons.

SINCLAIR, HARRY FORD (1876–1956). Harry Sinclair first qualified as a pharmacist and ran his father's drugstore in Wheeling, West Virginia. Having lost the business in 1901, he began work in the oil industry buying and selling oil leases. He was successful enough to buy his own well in 1905 and, following a series of successful investments, Sinclair established the Sinclair Oil and Refining Corporation in 1916. He served as a member of the oil subcommittee of an advisory committee to the **Council of National Defense**. After the war, he continued to build up his business empire and in 1923 it was revealed in a Senate investigation that he had leased naval oil reserves in **Teapot Dome**, Wyoming, from the Department of Interior without competitive bidding. Sinclair refused to testify before the Senate committee and was held in contempt. In 1927, he was tried with Secretary of the Interior **Albert Fall** on a charge of criminal conspiracy, but the case ended in a mistrial. He was tried again in 1928 after Fall had been convicted separately on other charges. Sinclair refused to testify and was found in contempt for shadowing jurors. He was jailed for nine months in 1929 on the two contempt charges, but was never convicted for other charges relating to Teapot Dome.

Sinclair's oil business continued to grow even through the **Depression**. During World War II, he served on the Petroleum Industry War Council. By 1950, the Sinclair Oil Company was the seventh largest integrated petroleum company in the United States.

SINCLAIR, UPTON BEALL (1878–1968). Educated at the City College of New York and Columbia University, the author Upton Sinclair began publishing with his *Springtime Harvest* in 1901. This was followed by several other books, but his first major success came with *The Jungle* in 1906, an exposé of the life and working experience of **immigrants** in Chicago. Sinclair's writing reflected his socialism and among his other more successful books were *Cry for Justice*, an anthology of social protest published in 1915, and the novels *King Coal* (1917) and *Oil* (1927). His *Boston* (1928) dealt with the **Sacco and Vanzetti case**.

Sinclair moved to California after World War I and stood, unsuccessfully, as the **Socialist** candidate for the United States House of Representatives in 1920 and for governor of California in 1926 and 1930. In 1934, he ran for governor on the **Democratic** ticket and a platform to End Poverty in California (EPIC). He was unsuccessful. Sinclair later wrote a number of political novels dealing with Hitler and the rise of Fascism and his "Lanny Budd" novels, *World's End* (1940), *Between Two Worlds* (1941), and *Wide Is the Gate* (1943), for which he was awarded the Pulitzer Prize. Altogether, Sinclair wrote more than 90 books.

SISSLE, NOBLE (1889–1975). The **African American** songwriter and bandleader, Noble Sissle, began singing professionally in 1908 and formed his first orchestra in 1915 and also performed as a singer. During **World War I**, Sissle was a drum major in the 369th United States Infantry band under James Reese Europe. After the war, Sissle toured with his partner in song-writing, pianist Eubie Blake. Together, they wrote the music for *Shuffle Along*, which opened on Broadway in May 1921. *Shuffle Along* included famous songs such as "Love Will Find a Way" and "I'm Just Wild about Harry." The production helped popularize jazz dancing, and is regarded by some critics as the opening of the **Harlem Renaissance**. Other musicals followed: *Elsie* (1923), *Chocolate Dandies* (1924), and *Keep Shufflin'* (1928). In 1926, Sissle and Blake toured in Europe and Sissle continued to perform in Paris and London, with visits back to the United States, through to 1930. Through the 1930s, Sissle and Blake were reunited, and their band included at various times such performers as **Sidney Bechet**, **Duke Ellington**, and Lena Horne. Sissle performed in various tours for troops during World War II, and continued playing through to the 1960s. He was one of the founders of the Negro Actors' Guild and was its first president.

SIXTEENTH AMENDMENT, 1913. Passed by Congress in 1909, the Sixteenth Amendment was ratified on 30 March 1913. It provided Congress with the power to tax incomes. (*See* appendix II.)

SLEMP, CAMPBELL BASCOM (1870–1943). A graduate of Virginia Military Institute and the University of Virginia Law School,

Campbell Slemp practiced law in Virginia until 1907, when he was elected as a **Republican** to fill his dead father's seat in the United States House of Representatives. Slemp was a staunch supporter of **William Howard Taft** and then of **Warren Harding** and he helped secure the Republican victories in southern states in 1920. In 1923, he became secretary to President **Calvin Coolidge** and in 1924 was Coolidge's campaign manager. Slemp resigned his position as secretary in 1925 and resumed his law practice in Washington, D.C. Slemp published a positive account of Coolidge's presidency in *The Mind of the President* in 1926. He continued to be active in the Republican National Committee and supported **Herbert Hoover** in 1928. He was appointed American commissioner general at the French Colonial Exposition in 1931.

SMITH, ALFRED EMANUEL (1873–1944). "Al" Smith as he came to be known was born and brought up in New York City, where he worked in a variety of jobs including the fish market. He was involved in local politics at an early age and was elected to the New York State legislature in 1903, and served until to 1915, becoming **Democratic Party** leader in 1911 and speaker in 1913. Smith took part in the state factory commission established after the Triangle Shirtwaist factory fire that killed 146 people in 1911, and he sponsored a number of bills to protect the health and safety of workers, particularly **women** and children. Smith was sheriff of New York County from 1915 to 1917 and president of the New York Board of Aldermen in 1917. In 1918, he was elected governor of New York and he served for four terms 1919–20, 1923–28. Following his failure to win re-election in 1920, Smith served on the National Board of Indian Commissioners and Port of New York Authority. He also acted as chairman of the United States Trucking Corporation.

Smith's period as governor was associated with the continuation of a reform program: limiting the working hours of women and children, improving **railroad** safety, expanding public education, and reforming state government. Smith also supported measures to repeal **Prohibition**. In 1924, Smith failed to win the Democratic Party's presidential nomination for the presidency. He won the nomination in 1928, but lost the election in part because of his Catholic, Irish background and his opposition to Prohibition. However, given the apparent prosperity at the time, **Herbert Hoover**'s election victory for the **Republicans** was probably fairly inevitable. Hoover gained more than 58 percent of the popular vote and won 444 Electoral College votes to Smith's 87.

Following his defeat, Smith became manager of the company that managed the Empire State Building in New York City. He supported **Franklin D. Roosevelt**'s nomination in 1932 but increasingly became critical of the **New Deal** for creating what he saw as class conflict. In 1936, he campaigned against Roosevelt and in favor of the Republican Alfred M. Landon. In 1940, Smith supported Wendell Willkie.

SMITH, BESSIE (1894–1937). The great blues singer, Bessie Smith, began performing on the streets of Chattanooga, Tennessee, at the age of nine. She joined other **African American** performers in a touring show in 1912 and spent several years in minstrel and vaudeville shows. By 1920, Smith was established as a star among the black community and in 1921 she produced her first record, but she was not signed by Columbia Records until 1923. Her first single sold 780,000 copies in six months and the "Empress of the Blues," as Smith was billed, became probably the most successful African American performer of the 1920s. She made over 180 recordings, performed in a number of revues, and appeared in one film, *St. Louis Blues*, made in 1929. Smith's career began to wane in the 1930s, but she continued to tour theaters in the South and to perform occasionally in **Harlem**, New York. In 1937, she was seriously injured in a car crash in Mississippi, but denied treatment at the nearest white hospitals, she died having been taken 200 miles to an African American hospital. *See also* JAZZ.

SMITH-HUGHES ACT, 1917. The Smith-Hughes Act established a Federal Board for Vocational Education to encourage training in agriculture, home economics, vocational subjects, commerce, trade, and industry by providing federal funds to states on a matching basis.

SMITH-LEVER ACT, 1914. The Smith-Lever Act provided an appropriation of $500,000 with additional appropriations of the same amount annually until 1923 to be distributed equally to the states to support adult education in agriculture.

SMOOT, REED (1862–1941). A graduate of Brigham Young University, Reed Smoot was a banker and official in the Mormon Church prior to becoming the first Mormon elected to the United States Senate by the state legislature in 1902. He held his seat until 1933. Smoot was a conservative **Republican** and he opposed the **League of Nations**. In 1930, he cosponsored the **Hawley-Smoot Tariff Act**. He was defeated in the election of 1932 and returned to Salt Lake City. *See also* TARIFFS.

SNYDER, RUTH (1895–1928). Ruth Snyder became the center of public attention in 1927 after she and her lover, Judd Gray, were arrested for the murder of her husband, the editor of *Motor Boating*, Albert Snyder. The trial was the subject of a great deal of lurid news coverage in which Ruth Snyder was painted as the "femme fatale." Found guilty on 9 May 1927, Snyder became only the second **woman** to be electrocuted when she was executed in Sing Sing prison, New York, on 12 January 1928. Thomas Howard photographed the moment of her death using a concealed camera and the shocking picture appeared on the front page of the *New York Daily News*. Judd was executed shortly after Snyder. The murder formed the basis of the film *Double Indemnity* made in 1944.

SOCIAL WORK. The social work profession emerged in the period between the late 19th century and the late 1930s out of the philanthropic, charitable, and community welfare programs. As industrialization, **immigration**, and urbanization developed from the 1870s on, mounting concern about urban poverty, crime, and ill-health brought a variety of responses. The Charity Organization Societies (COS) sought to better organize the traditional voluntary charitable responses to poverty, unemployment, and hardship through investigators who would assess need and allocate resources. Other educated middle-class workers, many of them **women** like **Jane Addams**, turned to **settlement houses** to provide assistance, education, and a meeting point for the immigrant working classes and American middle classes. Many of the people concerned about social problems joined the **Progressive movement** to call for political reform to improve conditions at work and in the cities and to make politics more responsive to social need.

The study of social problems and provision of different forms of social welfare led to the emergence of professional social workers. The National Conference of Charities and Corrections (NCCC), formed in 1874, became the National Conference of Social Work in 1917. People like **Edith Abbott** and **Sophonisba Breckinridge** established new educational programs and schools, and an American Association of Social Workers (AASW) was created in 1921. Increasingly in the 1920s, the focus was less on the social aspect and more on case studies and the individual and psychological causes of social problems. With the coming of the **Great Depression**, however, social welfare once more became a national issue. Under the reform programs of the **New Deal** social work moved from the private into the public sector and completed the professionalization of social work in a modern, often federally funded, welfare system.

SOCIALIST PARTY OF AMERICA. In 1897, **Eugene V. Debs** established a Social Democratic Party and in 1901 this joined with reformist elements of the Socialist Labor Party led by **Morris Hillquit** to establish the Socialist Party of America. The Socialist Party was committed to state ownership of the means of production and the equitable distribution of wealth among the working classes. It sought to achieve these ends through evolutionary rather than revolutionary means, and it supported social and economic reform through the political process. Support for the Socialist Party was particularly strong in working-class **immigrant** communities, but it began to attract middle-class intellectuals like **Upton Sinclair**, **Walter Lippmann**, and **John Reed** in the years before 1914. However, when the party opposed America's entry into **World War I**, many people deserted it, and the majority of its leaders were jailed under the **Espionage** and **Sedition Acts**. Debs ran as the party's presidential candidate in every election except 1916 up to and including that of 1920, when he received almost a million votes despite being in prison. In 1912, he secured 6 percent of the popular vote with over 900,000 votes. At the end of the war, the party divided between those who wished to follow a revolutionary path along Russian lines and those who continued to espouse a reformist path. The **"Red Scare"** further discredited and weakened them and its membership fell from 24,661 in 1921 to a mere 8,477 by 1926. In the 1930s and 1940s, the leader of the party was **Norman Thomas**, but even at the height of the **Depression**, he could attract only less than 900,000 votes, about 2 percent of the vote (the total number of voters having increased considerably since 1912 with the enfranchisement of **women**). *See also* TRADE UNIONS.

SPEAKEASY. Speakeasies were illegal, unlicensed drinking establishments. Although they had existed before the passage of the **National Prohibition Act** in 1919, speakeasies reached a height of popularity during the mid-1920s. Speakeasies varied from restaurants, clubs, or basic bars to which admittance was gained by payment of a fee or private membership. *See also* BOOTLEGGING; PROHIBITION.

SPINGARN, JOEL ELIAS (1875–1939). After obtaining a Ph.D. from Columbia in 1899, Joel Spingarn took up a teaching position in literature at the university. He became a professor in 1909 but was dismissed in 1911 for his criticism of university policy. Although he published several collections of poetry, Spingarn established a reputation as a literary critic, publishing several works including *The New Criticism* (1911). In 1919, he became one of the founders of the Harcourt, Brace and Company publishers and edited its European library series.

Spingarn was active in Progressive politics and attended the **Progressive Party** conventions in 1912 and 1916. In 1910, he became a member of the executive of the **National Association for the Advancement of Colored People** (NAACP) and succeeded **Oswald Garrison Villard** as chairman in 1914. In 1913, he established the Spingarn Medal, an annual award to **African Americans** of achievement. In 1917, Spingarn, who served as an army intelligence officer, used his influence to win the establishment of a segregated officer training school for black soldiers. Spingarn was president of the NAACP from 1930 to 1939.

STARR, ELLEN GATES (1859–1940). Ellen Starr, who with **Jane Addams** founded **Hull House**, studied briefly at Rockford Female Seminary before taking up teaching in 1878. She and Addams traveled to Europe in 1888 and opened Hull House in Chicago the following year. Starr was particularly interested in art and education and in 1894 she formed the Chicago Public School Art Society to place art in school classrooms. In 1897, Starr went to London, England, to study bookbinding and returned in 1898 to open a bookbindery at Hull House. Starr was actively involved in a number of industrial disputes between 1895 and 1915, and she campaigned against low wages, long hours, and the exploitation of **women** workers. She helped to found the Chicago branch of the Women's Trade Union League in 1904. Starr joined the **Socialist Party** and stood unsuccessfully as a candidate in local elections. She converted to Catholicism in 1920 and, suffering from ill health, she entered a convent in 1930. *See also* SETTLEMENT HOUSES; TRADE UNIONS.

STEEL STRIKE, 1919. Encouraged by gains in membership and strength during **World War I**, the **American Federation of Labor** hoped to organize the steel industry in the aftermath of the conflict. Organized labor had failed to make inroads in the steel industry since major defeats in the 1890s and in 1902. The labor force often worked a 12-hour day, seven days a week. A National Committee for Organizing Iron and Steel Workers was established under the leadership of **William Z. Foster** and the strike began on 22 September 1919 when 250,000 workers came out. The employers, led by **Elbert Gary** of United States Steel, characterized the strikers and Foster as "Bolsheviks" and refused to take part in any collective bargaining. They used strikebreakers, police, and federal troops to overcome the strike that was effectively over by December, and was officially called off on 8 January 1920. The 12-hour day remained in force until the mid-1920s. *See also* TRADE UNIONS.

STEIMER, MOLLIE (1897–1980). Born in Russia, Mollie Steimer emigrated to the United States with her family in 1913. Steimer found work in the garment industry in New York City and became active in the **trade union** movement. She became an anarchist and was part of a group that opposed United States entry into **World War I**. Steimer and five others were arrested under the **Espionage Act** in 1918. Steimer was sentenced to 15 years in jail and a $500 fine. Her conviction was upheld despite protests from people such as **Roger Baldwin** and **Margaret Sanger**. While in prison, it was decided that Steimer should be deported with other radicals, including **Emma Goldman**, held in the **Palmer Raids**, and she was sent to Russia. In

1922, she was arrested for political activities and sent to Siberia. In 1923, Steimer was deported to Germany and settled in Berlin. She fled Germany following Hitler's rise to power and eventually settled in Mexico, where she died, still true to her anarchist beliefs.

STEIN, GERTRUDE (1874–1951). A graduate of Radcliffe College, Gertrude Stein lived in Paris from 1902, where the salon she established was the center of the group of American literary exiles, including **Sherwood Anderson, F. Scott Fitzgerald**, and **Ernest Hemingway**, during the interwar period. It was Stein who characterized Hemingway and others as a "lost generation." She was the author of several books and essays, many marked by an avant-garde style. Among the best-known are *Three Lives* (1908), *Making of Americans* (1925), *The Autobiography of Alice B. Toklas* (1933), *Four Saints in Three Acts* (1934), and *Picasso* (1938). Her style was very much that of the avant-garde stream of consciousness.

STIEGLITZ, ALFRED (1864–1946). Educated first in New York, Alfred Stieglitz moved with his family to Europe and continued his education in Berlin, Germany, in the 1880s. It was while in Germany that Stieglitz began to study photography and he began to exhibit and publish his photographs. He returned to New York in 1890 and set up the Photochrome Engraving Company. Stieglitz was not committed to business and in 1893 he became the editor of *American Amateur Photographer*. In 1896 he was involved in the foundation of the Camera Club of New York and he established the official publication, *Camera Notes*, the following year. By the turn of the century he had established himself through publications and exhibitions as the best-known photographer in the United States. He helped to establish the Photo-Secession group with Edward Steichen and edited *Camera Work* from 1903 to 1917. The studio he and Steichen established, known simply as "291," was famous for showing the work of young American artists and leading European artists such as Picasso, Matisse, and Rodin. Stieglitz later established other galleries in New York City where he continued to show the work of new photographers and artists. He married **Georgia O'Keefe** and encouraged her artistic development in the 1920s. Stieglitz gave his last one-man exhibition in 1934.

STIMSON, HENRY LEWIS (1867–1950). One of America's longest serving statesmen, Henry Stimson graduated from Yale University in 1888, attended Harvard Law School qualified in law and practiced in New York City. Stimson was United States attorney for southern New York State and in 1910 ran unsuccessfully as the **Republican** candidate for governor. In 1911, President **William Howard Taft** appointed him secretary of war. During **World War I,** Stimson served as a colonel with the artillery in France. In 1927, President **Calvin Coolidge** appointed Stimson to mediate between warring factions in Nicaragua. From 1927 to 1929, he served as governor general of the Philippines and resisted early moves toward independence.

In 1928, President **Herbert Hoover** appointed Stimson as Secretary of State and in that capacity he chaired the United States delegation to the **London Naval Conference**, 1930–31. In 1931, Stimson issued a statement that became known as the "Stimson Doctrine" expressing United States opposition to the Japanese conquest of Manchuria and refusing to accept any change in territorial possession as a consequence of the invasion. Stimson tried to mobilize European opposition to Japanese aggression and would have preferred to take stronger action, but bowed to Hoover's wishes to maintain a purely limited diplomatic response. In 1940, Stimson was one of two Republicans appointed to the cabinet when President **Franklin D. Roosevelt** made him secretary of war. Stimson was also the president's senior adviser on atomic weapons. During World War II, he recommended offering the Japanese terms for surrender that would allow them to keep the emperor. He also supported the dropping of the atomic bombs in 1945 and was responsible for the choice of targets.

STOCK MARKET CRASH. *See* WALL STREET CRASH.

STOKES, ROSE PASTOR (1879–1933). Stokes was born Rose Wieslander in Poland, but moved first to London, England, and then to Cleveland, Ohio, as a child. In 1900, she became a journalist for the Cleveland *Yidisher Tageblatt* then moved to New York City where she met and, in 1905, married James Graham Phelps Stokes, a leader in the **settlement house** movement. Stokes became an active campaigner for reform and socialist causes. She supported United States entry into **World War I** and initially broke with the **Socialist Party**

of America. However, she returned to the party following the Bolshevik Revolution in Russia and in 1918 was charged under the **Espionage Act** for criticizing the involvement in the war. Her conviction was overturned on appeal. She joined the **Communist Party** after the war and was one of the few **women** elected to the executive committee.

STONE, HARLAN FISKE (1872–1946). Harlan Fiske Stone graduated from Amherst College in 1894 and Columbia Law School in 1898. He practiced law in New York City and in 1902 became first professor then in 1910, dean in the Columbia Law School. Stone held that post until he was appointed attorney general by President **Calvin Coolidge** to succeed **Harry S. Daugherty** in 1924. In 1925, Coolidge appointed Stone to the **Supreme Court**, where, with **Oliver Wendell Holmes** and **Louis Brandeis**, he became one of the liberal dissenting voices. He defended legislation to protect the rights of **women**, children, and workers and in 1940 became chief justice.

STONE, WILLIAM JOEL (1848–1918). A graduate of the University of Missouri and a qualified lawyer, William Stone was elected **Democratic** congressman to the United States House of Representatives for three terms from 1884 to 1890 and then governor of Missouri from 1893 to 1897. As governor, he supported the employers' liability law but was defeated by opposition from the **railroad** companies. Stone was also conspicuous for his support of "free silver," the use of silver coinage to expand currency supply in the mid-1890s. In 1903, he was elected to the United States Senate and served until his death. As a senator, Stone supported **Woodrow Wilson** and helped to secure the passage of the **Underwood-Simmons Tariff** in 1913.

As chair of the Senate Foreign Relations Committee from 1914, Stone increasingly disagreed with Wilson's policies with regard to Germany and in 1917 was one of the "little group of willful men" who opposed giving the president the power to arm merchant ships. Once America had entered **World War I**, Stone offered his full support and although coming from a state with a large German-American population, said there could be "no divided patriotism." Stone supported the notion of a "peace without victory," but died before the war had ended.

STRATTON-PORTER, GENE (1863–1924). Gene Stratton-Porter's career initially began as a photographer and naturalist. Her photographs of birds and moths were published in the magazines *Recreation* and *Outing* and she acted as photographic consultant for *National Geographic*. She combined her interest in nature with romance in works of fiction and her first novel *Song of the Cardinal* was published in 1903. The following year Stratton-Porter achieved popular success with *Freckles*, a novel that idealized the values of hard work and bravery and a love of nature. Similar themes featured in *A Girl of the Limberlost* (1909), *The Harvester* (1911), and *Laddie* (1913). Her other work included *Michael O'Halloran* (1915), *A Daughter of the Land* (1918), *Her Father's Daughter* (1921), and the posthumous *The Magic Garden* (1927). In addition, Stratton-Porter wrote editorials advancing **women**'s equality in *McCall's* and in 1922 she established her own film company. At the time of her death in an automobile accident, Stratton-Porter was one of the country's most popular writers.

STRONG, BENJAMIN (1872–1928). After a successful career in **banking** in 1914, Benjamin Strong became governor of the newly established **Federal Reserve** Bank of New York in 1914. Strong provided effective leadership during **World War I** when the "Fed" operated as the fiscal agent for the Treasury. After the war, Strong worked to ensure the "Fed's" independence. He was also active in trying to bring stability to the currencies of Germany, Belgium, Italy, and Poland during the 1920s.

SULLIVAN, MARK (1874–1952). Mark Sullivan began his career in journalism while he was still at high school writing for a small-town paper that he also co-owned. He attended Harvard University and Harvard Law School and graduated in 1903. Sullivan found work first with *McClure's* in 1905 and then with *Collier's* in 1906. He edited *Collier's* from 1914 to 1917. Sullivan supported **Theodore Roosevelt** and the **Progressives**. After **World War I**, he reported on the **Versailles peace settlement** for *Collier's* and then wrote first for the *New York Evening Post* and then the *New York Tribune* (later the *Herald-Tribune*). He became one of the United States' best-known journalists.

Sullivan was a friend and supporter of **Herbert Hoover**. He opposed **Franklin D. Roosevelt**'s election in 1932, but initially seemed open-minded about the **New Deal**. Gradually, he became more critical of the Roosevelt administration. In addition to his success as a journalist, Sullivan also published an informative six-volume history *Our Times: The United States 1900–1925* between 1926 and 1935. He retired from journalism in 1945.

SUNDAY, BILLY (1862–1935). Born William Ashley Sunday, Billy Sunday achieved early success as a baseball player in Nevada, Iowa, and then Marshalltown. In 1883, he joined the Chicago White Stockings and then the Pittsburgh Alleghenies in 1888, before moving on to the Philadelphia Phillies in 1890. In 1891, at the height of his success, Sunday quit sport to become an evangelist with the Chicago Young Men's Christian Association (YMCA). After a few years, Sunday became a traveling evangelist and achieved a national reputation that survived into the 1920s. In 1920, he unsuccessfully sought the **Republican** presidential nomination and then agreed to run on a Prohibitionist Party ticket, but the party failed to organize. Nonetheless, Sunday was credited with aiding the passage of the **Eighteenth Amendment**. Although his following gradually declined as the 1920s progressed, thousands of mourners gathered to view his coffin after he died in Chicago.

SUPREME COURT. The highest federal court in the land consisting of nine justices, each appointed by the president for life, had in the late 19th century increasingly upheld the principles of laissez faire and notions of freedom of contract to empower business corporations often to the detriment of **trade unions**. There was a slight shift in the court's attitudes during the **Progressive** period, particularly with the appointment of **Oliver Wendell Holmes**, **John H. Clarke**, and **Louis Brandeis**, who recognized the law should respond to social change. Prior to **World War I**, the court upheld limitations on working hours where the health and safety of workers, men and **women**, were affected, but not where it violated workers' rights to accept whatever working conditions they chose. Regulation of trusts was upheld, but increasingly narrowed to apply only to "unreasonable" restraint of trade. Shortly after the war, the court upheld the limitations imposed on civil liberties in the **Espionage** and **Sedition Acts** in *Schenck v. United States* and *Abrams v. United States* although Holmes and Brandeis dissented.

In the 1920s, the court once more tended to protect business and private property. **Warren Harding**'s appointment of **William Howard Taft** as chief justice, with three other conservative justices (**Pierce Butler, Edward Sanford**, and **George Sutherland**), resulted in decisions against **child labor laws** (*Bailey v. Drexel Furniture*) and a minimum wage law for women (*Adkins v. Children's Hospital*), but upheld restrictions on trade unions. Faced with a predominantly conservative body that threatened to undermine the **New Deal** in the 1930s, President **Franklin D. Roosevelt** attempted to alter the court's composition. Although his "court packing" failed, the court increasingly adopted a more liberal position and approved the later reform measures. *See also* CARDOZO, BENJAMIN; FRANKFURTER, FELIX; McREYNOLDS, JAMES; ROBERTS, OWEN; VAN DEVANTER, WILLIS.

SUSSEX. The *Sussex* was a French liner torpedoed by a German submarine on 24 March 1916. Not only was this an apparent breach of the pledge made after the sinking of the *Arabic*, but also among those injured were four Americans. On 19 April, President **Woodrow Wilson** announced that if such attacks were not suspended, his administration would sever diplomatic links with the German government. On 4 May, the German government pledged that all vessels would be visited for inspection prior to any future submarine attack. *See also LUSITANIA*.

SUTHERLAND, (ALEXANDER) GEORGE (1862–1942). Born in England, George Sutherland moved to Utah with his family in 1864. Sutherland graduated from the Brigham Young Academy in 1881 and later enrolled in the University of Michigan Law School. Having qualified in law Sutherland established a practice in Salt Lake City. He was elected state senator in Utah's first state legislature in 1896 as a **Republican** and in 1900 became Utah's congressman in the United States House of Representatives. In 1905, the legislature elected him to the United States Senate. In 1915, Sutherland introduced a constitutional amendment to grant **women** the vote. Like the amendment, Sutherland was defeated in his bid for re-election in 1916 and established a law practice in Washington, D.C.

Sutherland supported the election of **Warren Harding** in 1920 and in 1922 was appointed to the **Supreme Court**. Generally a conservative in outlook, Sutherland wrote the majority opinion in *Adkins v. Children's Hospital* (1923) against the law allowing the federal government to fix minimum wages for women in Washington, D.C. However, in *Powell v. Alabama* in 1932, he wrote the opinion setting aside the conviction of one of the **Scottsboro Boys** because he had been denied adequate counsel. Sutherland retired in 1938 after **Franklin D. Roosevelt**'s attempt to alter the composition of the Supreme Court had failed but also after *Adkins* had been overturned in *West Coast Hotel v. Parrish*. *See also* BRANDEIS, LOUIS; BUTLER, PIERCE; McREYNOLDS, JAMES; ROBERTS, OWEN J.; STONE, HARLAN F.; VAN DEVANTER, WILLIS.

SWANSON, GLORIA (1899–1983). The **movie** actress Gloria Swanson was born Gloria May Josephine Svensson. She began her acting career as an extra in Chicago and moved to California in 1915, where she adopted her stage name. Swanson worked for **Mack Sennett** at the Keystone Film Company. She later moved to the Triangle Picture Company, but became a star after joining Paramount in 1919 and working with **Cecil B. De Mille**. Swanson starred in *For Better, for Worse* (1919), *Male and Female* (1919), *Why Change Your Wife?* (1920), *The Great Moment* (1921), *Her Gilded Cage* (1922), *Prodigal Daughters* (1923), *Bluebeard's Eighth Wife* (1923), *Zaza* (1923), and *The Humming Bird, A Society Scandal, Manhandled, Her Love Story*, and *Wages of Virtue* all in 1924.

By the mid-1920s, Swanson was the best-known silent screen actress famous for her looks and her often-extravagant costumes. In 1926, she left Paramount to form her own company, which released films through United Artists. She made *The Love of Sunya* in 1927 and *Sadie Thompson*, a movie version of Somerset Maugham's novel *Rain*, in 1928, and *The Trespasser* in 1929. Her various films in the 1930s were generally less than successful and she went into retirement. Swanson's comeback after World War II was not successful either, but she did gain an Academy Award for her role in

Sunset Boulevard in 1950. Her last appearance in the movies was as herself in *Airport* (1975).

SWOPE, GERARD (1872–1957). Swope was an engineer with the Western Electric Company in Chicago who served as an assistant to **George W. Goethals** during **World War I**. In 1919, he joined General Electric as president of its international operations and became chairman of General Electric itself in 1922. With **Owen Young** as chairman, Swope took control of day-to-day running of the company and with great attention to detail helped to increase sales and production through increased efficiency and a reduced workforce. Swope, who had lived and worked at **Hull House settlement** in the 1890s, was instrumental in the introduction of policies of **"welfare capitalism,"** but was unsuccessful in gaining employee approval for an unemployment insurance plan.

In response to the **Wall Street Crash**, Swope proposed the "Swope Plan" in 1931 that called upon companies to organize by industry and agree codes of fair competition with agreed working hours and conditions. Elements of the plan were discernable in the **New Deal's** National Recovery Administration (NRA). Swope chaired the **Department of Commerce**'s Business Advisory and Planning Council formed to advice the NRA in 1933. He later worked toward the implementation of social security and labor relations legislation and was a member of the National Labor relations Board. He accepted union recognition within General Electric between 1936 and 1939 and after his retirement in 1939 he served as chair of the New York City Housing Authority. He briefly returned to General Electric during World War II. After the war he chaired the Institute of Pacific Relations looking at United States **foreign policy** in the Far East.

– T –

TAFT, WILLIAM HOWARD (1957–1930). Twenty-seventh president of the United States. Born in Cincinnati, Ohio, William Howard Taft graduated from Yale University in 1878 and Cincinnati Law School in 1880. He was admitted to the bar and practiced law in

Cincinnati. Taft served as a judge in the Ohio Superior Court, 1887–90, United States Solicitor General, 1890–92, United States Circuit Court judge, 1892–1900, and as first governor of the Philippines, 1901–04. He was appointed secretary of war by **Theodore Roosevelt** in 1904, and in 1908, largely at Roosevelt's suggestion, was nominated as the **Republican Party**'s presidential candidate. He defeated the **Democratic** candidate **William Jennings Bryan** by 7.6 million votes to 6.4 million and by 321 Electoral College votes to 162. As president, Taft created a separate **Department of Labor** in 1913 and established the **Children's Bureau.** He also supported the Mann-Elkins Act (1910) regulating **railroads** and supported United States business investments overseas as part of "dollar diplomacy."

Taft vigorously continued Roosevelt's antitrust policies but lost his mentor's support over tariff issues and the dismissal of the chief forester, **Gifford Pinchot.** He lost the presidency to **Woodrow Wilson** in 1912, when many Republicans supported Roosevelt and the **Progressive Party.** Taft became professor of constitutional law at Yale from 1913 to 1921 and during the war he cochaired the War Labor Conference Board with **William Wilson** and served on the **War Labor Board.** He was appointed chief justice of the **Supreme Court** by **Warren Harding** in 1921 and served until 1930. He generally took a conservative position, writing the majority opinion in *Bailey v. Drexel Furniture Co.* (1922), but he dissented from the decision that invalidated minimum wages for **women** in the capital in *Adkins v. Children's Hospital* (1923). Taft was the only person in history to hold the office of president and chief justice.

TARBELL, IDA MINERVA (1857–1944). Ida Tarbell was educated at Allegheny College and then at the Sorbonne, in Paris, from 1891 to 1894. She became the most famous female journalist of her day through her work with *McClure's*, particularly the series of exposés of the practices of the Standard Oil Company that she wrote between 1902 and 1904 and published as the *History of the Standard Oil Company* in two volumes in 1904. From 1906 to 1915, Tarbell contributed to the *American Magazine*. Tarbell also authored *The Business of Being a Woman* (1912) and *The Ways of a Woman* (1915), both of which revealed something of her conservatism with regard to female equality. She was not a supporter of **women's suffrage** and expressed fairly traditional views on women's "true nature." After **World War I**, Tarbell served on President **Woodrow Wilson**'s **Industrial Conference** in 1919 and on President **Warren Harding**'s **Unemployment Conference** in 1921. Tarbell also authored a number of books on history and economics, including a *Life of Abraham Lincoln* (1900).

TARIFFS. The system of duties or taxes levied on imports to raise revenue and to protect United States manufacturers began with the policies of Alexander Hamilton and the tariff of 1789 and continued through various forms and amendments thereafter. Attempts to reform the tariff system in order to lower prices became a part of the **Democratic Party**'s platform in the late-19th century, particularly after the McKinley tariff of 1890 had raised duties to new levels. Tariff reform was a central part of **Woodrow Wilson**'s **New Freedom** program to bring about fairer competition. He succeeded with the passage of the **Underwood-Simmons Act** of 1913.

President Wilson vetoed an Emergency Agricultural Tariff Bill in 1920, but **Warren Harding** passed it in 1921. The attempt to protect United States farm prices and the expansion of industry into the South and West helped to erode tariff opposition and enabled the passage of the **Fordney-McCumber Act** in 1922 raising tariffs to a new high. The **Hawley-Smoot Tariff Act** (1930) raised tariffs yet further in an attempt to stave off the deepening economic **Depression** after the **Wall Street Crash**. It turned out to be counterproductive as other nations were unable to earn dollars to purchase United States commodities and they also responded with their own protective measures.

TARKINGTON, BOOTH (1869–1946). The novelist and playwright Booth Tarkington first achieved literary success with the publication of *The Gentleman from Indiana* in 1899. He wrote a series of bestsellers examining life in Indiana, including *The Two Vanrevels* (1902), *The Conquest of Canaan* (1905), *The Flirt* (1913), *The Turmoil* (1915), and a play that was a box-office success, *The Man from Home* (1908). His collections of boys' stories, beginning with *Penrod* in 1914, were also very popular with all ages. His best-known work, later a famous film, was *The Magnificent Ambersons* (1918), which won Tarkington a Pulitzer Prize. *Alice Adams* (1921) won him a second Pulitzer. During the early 1920s, Tarkington wrote several successful plays. In addition to his studies of Indiana and Indianapolis, Tarkington wrote novels about Maine and more children's stories through to the 1940s.

TATE, (JOHN ORLEY) ALLEN (1899–1979). The critic and poet Allen Tate studied at Vanderbilt University, Nashville, between 1918 and 1923. While there, he joined a group of poets and writers known as the Fugitives, including **John Crowe Ransom, Donald Davidson,** and **Robert Penn Warren,** who were part of the southern literary renascence. In 1924, Tate moved to New York City where he contributed reviews and articles to journals such as the *New Republic* and the *Nation.* In 1928, Tate published a collection of poems, *Mr. Pope and Other Poems* (which included "Ode to the Confederate Dead"), and a biography, *Stonewall Jackson,* followed in 1929 by *Jefferson Davis.* In 1930, Tate, with other Fugitives, was a contributor to the defense of southern agrarianism in *I'll Take My Stand.* In addition to further collections of poetry, Tate published a Civil War novel, *The Fathers,* in 1938. He then became poet in residence at Princeton University until 1942. In 1943, he was appointed consultant in poetry at the Library of Congress and in 1944 he began to edit the *Sewanee Review.* In 1948, two further collections of poetry and essays were published and Tate accepted a three-year appointment at New York University. In 1951, he went to the University of Minnesota where he remained until 1968. Tate continued to publish essays and poetry through the 1950s and in 1956 he was awarded the Bollingen Prize.

TAYLOR, (JOSEPH) DEEMS (1885–1966). After graduating from New York University in 1906, Deems Taylor worked for a number of encyclopedias including *Encyclopedia Britannica.* However, Taylor's career lay in music and he began writing musical works while still a student. He composed *The Siren Song* in 1912, *Through the Looking Glass* (1918), and *Jurgen* (1925). He achieved some popular success with his operas, *The King's Henchman* (1927) based on a libretto by **Edna St. Vincent Millay,** and again with *Peter Ibbetson* in 1931. Taylor supported himself by journalism and was music critic for the *New York World* from 1921 to 1925, editor of *Musical America* 1927–29, and music critic for the *New York American.* In the 1930s and 1940s, he worked as a radio commentator on music programs.

From 1933 until 1966, Taylor was a director of the American Society of Composers, Authors, and Publishers (ASCAP) and its president from 1942 to 1948.

TEAPOT DOME. Near Salt Creek, Wyoming, Teapot Dome was the location of United States navy oil reserves, which, together with those in Elk Hills, California, were transferred to the authority of the Department of the Interior in 1921. In 1922, the secretary of the interior, **Albert B. Fall** leased the reserves to oil companies owned by **Harry F. Sinclair** and **Edward L. Doheny** without any competitive bidding in return for bribes totaling $400,000. This arrangement became public in 1924 following the Senate investigations initiated by **Robert M. LaFollette** and led by **Thomas J. Walsh**. Civil and criminal suits eventually resulted in Fall's conviction for corruption and Sinclair's for criminal contempt. Teapot Dome subsequently became synonymous with the corruption surrounding the administration of **Warren G. Harding**.

THALBERG, IRVING GRANT (1899–1936). Irving Thalberg went into business straight from high school and in 1918 entered the **movie** industry where he was employed as a private secretary by the head of Universal Studios, Carl Laemmle. By 1920, Thalberg was general manager in charge of production at Universal City in California. He successfully managed the production of two box office hits, *Foolish Wives* (1921) and *The Hunchback of Notre Dame* (1923). That same year, Thalberg joined **Louis B. Mayer** and was involved in the formation of Metro-Goldwyn-Mayer. The studio soon became the richest and most important in Hollywood.

Thalberg developed a reputation for detailed planning and organization of movie production. He also opposed **trade unions** and fought to keep them out of the industry. In his long career, Thalberg was associated with the production of such classics as *The Big Parade* (1925), *The Barretts of Wimpole Street* (1934), *Mutiny on the Bounty* (1935), and *Romeo and Juliet* (1936). *See also* GOLDWYN, SAMUEL.

THOMAS, NORMAN MATTOON (1884–1968). Socialist leader Norman Thomas studied politics under **Woodrow Wilson** at Princeton University and then turned to theology. He was a Presbyterian pastor and worked in the New York **settlement houses** until 1918. A pacifist, Thomas opposed entry into **World War I** and was one of the founders of the Fellowship of Reconciliation, a group of pacifist clergymen. He was also one of the founders of the **American Civil Liberties Union**. He was an associate editor of *The Nation* (1921–22) and codirector of the League of Industrial Democracy from 1922–37. Thomas ran unsuccessfully as the Socialist candidate in the New York gubernatorial campaign in 1924 and as the party's presidential candidate in 1928, 1932, and 1936 offering a moderate, non-Marxist brand of socialism critical of Soviet-style communism. He supported United States entry into World War II, but opposed certain government policies, such as the internment of Japanese Americans. He became the Socialist presidential candidate again in 1940, 1944, and 1948, but later suggested that the party should abandon such campaigns and support progressive **Democrats**. Thomas resigned his official positions in the party in 1955 but continued as its leading spokesman. In his later years, he spoke out against United States military involvement in Vietnam.

THOMPSON, WILLIAM BOYCE (1869–1930). The mining entrepreneur and financier William Thompson attended Phillips Exeter Academy, New Hampshire, and Columbia University School of Mines. In 1897, Thompson established a mining investment company in Butte, Montana, and in 1899 created the Colorado Mining Company, which successfully developed profitable mines in Arizona and in Nevada. His mining interests quickly spread to other states, and by 1914 he also had investments in mines in Peru and Brazil. Thompson joined with **Bernard Baruch** to develop other mines in Asia and he also worked with J. P. Morgan. During **World War I**, Thompson helped to raise funds for **Herbert Hoover**'s Belgian Relief Fund, for the **Liberty Loans**, and for the Red Cross. He also visited Russia and tried to aid the Kerensky regime following the first Russian Revolution. After the war Thompson called for the recognition of the Soviet Union. In 1918 and 1919, Thompson provided financial support for the Republican Party and supported **Theodore Roosevelt**'s bid for the presidential nomination. When Roosevelt died, Thompson led the call for a national memorial. During the 1920s, Thompson was involved in oil investments and was linked with **Henry Sinclair**.

THOMPSON, WILLIAM HALE (1867–1944). After working for a number of years as a cowboy, William Thompson assumed the management of his family's real estate business in Chicago in 1891. He became known nationally as an outstanding football player for the Chicago Athletic Club. In 1900, Thompson entered politics as a **Republican** alderman on the Chicago city council. He then served as Cook County commissioner from 1902 to 1904. After a period out of political office, Thompson was elected mayor of Chicago with a huge majority in 1915. Opposed to American entry into **World War I**, Thompson ran for the United States Senate in 1918 on an **isolationist** platform. He was unsuccessful, but in 1919 regained the mayor's position by a narrow margin. Thompson's victory was due in large measure to the support of **African American** voters and during the **1919 race riots** he delayed in calling in the National Guard for three days.

Thompson's second term as mayor was notable for a major program of public works, but it was also marked by a wave of gangsterism and crime in part due to Thompson's failure to enforce **Prohibition**. Thompson did not seek re-election in 1923. He regained the position in 1927 and promised to recognize individual civil liberties, i.e., not uphold Prohibition. He received financial aid from **Al Capone**. Thompson also made a national reputation for his outspoken anti-British views and he suspended the Chicago superintendent for allowing the use of pro-British history texts in school. Despite his undoubted success in appealing to black, German, and Irish voters, Thompson was defeated in the election of 1931. He was defeated in the gubernatorial election in 1936 and failed to gain the Republican nomination for governor in 1939. He ran as an independent but was defeated.

TILDEN, WILLIAM ("BILL") TATUM (1893–1953). Bill Tilden dominated tennis in America throughout the 1920s. He began playing tennis as a child. In 1913 and 1914, he won the United States mixed doubles title with Mary Kendall Browne. Tilden enlisted in the army during **World War I** and played exhibition games around the country. In 1918, while still in the service, he won the national clay court championship and the United States doubles championship with Vinnie Richards. After winning the Wimbledon championship in

London in 1920, Tilden went on to win his first United States singles title the same year. He held on to the first ranking in the United States for six years, winning six United States singles titles, a second Wimbledon title, the World Hard Court title in 1921, and 15 Davis Cup singles contests. In addition, Tilden held various clay court doubles and mixed doubles titles. He won the U.S title again in 1929 and his last Wimbledon championship in 1930, the year he retired from the amateur game.

In 1930, Tilden became a tennis professional, playing exhibition matches and coaching. He won the professional championship singles titles in 1931 and 1935 and doubles titles in 1931 and 1932 with Frank Hunter and Bruce Barnes respectively. Tilden continued to play exhibition fund-raisers during World War II. In 1945, Tilden was one of the organizers of the Professional Tennis Players Association. His reputation was, however, shattered in 1946, following his arrest and conviction for committing a homosexual act with a minor. He served a one-year prison sentence, but was convicted of a similar offense in 1949. Despite this, he was regarded for a long time as the greatest tennis player during the first 50 years of the 20th century. In addition to playing tennis, Tilden wrote several books about the game and authored a number of stage plays.

TOKLAS, ALICE BABETTE (1877–1967). Born in San Francisco Alice B. Toklas moved to Paris, France, in 1907. There, she became **Gertrude Stein**'s partner in the famous salon that became a center for members of the "lost generation" of American writers, such as **Ernest Hemingway**, who became voluntary exiles in Europe during the 1920s. Toklas published Stein's work and after her friend's death wrote two cookbooks and her own memoirs, *What Is Remembered* (1963).

TOOMER, (NATHAN) JEAN (1894–1967). Jean Toomer attended a number of colleges and universities without graduating before finding employment in 1921 in a small college in Sparta, Georgia. While there, Toomer began writing short stories that were published in various journals. In 1923, his book, *Cane*, was published to critical acclaim and was seen as part of the **Harlem Renaissance**. Toomer subsequently became a disciple of the Russian mystic, Georgi Gurdjieff, and he dedicated his life to teaching Gurdjieff's lessons, first in Harlem, then Chicago, and later Taos, New Mexico. He published little other than a few short stories after *Cane*.

TOWNER, HORACE MANN (1855–1937). The **Republican** congressman from Iowa, Horace Towner, was educated at the University of Chicago and Union College of Law and admitted to the bar in 1877. He served as county superintendent of schools in Adams County, Iowa, from 1880 to 1884 and was elected judge of the third judicial district in 1890 and served until 1911. Towner also lectured on constitutional law at the University of Iowa. He was elected to the United States House of Representatives in 1910 and served until 1923 when he was appointed governor of **Puerto Rico**. Towner held that position until 1929, when he returned to his private law practice. As a legislator Towner was best known for cosponsoring the **Sheppard-Towner Act** (1921).

TOWNLEY, CHARLES ARTHUR (1880–1959). After failing as a farmer in North Dakota in 1912, Charles Townley became involved with the **Socialist Party**. In 1915 Townley formed an organization to focus simply on the needs of farmers known as the **Nonpartisan League** (NPL). Under Townley's effective leadership, the NPL endorsed a number of successful candidates in 1916, including Governor Lynn J. Frazier. However, Townley opposed United States entry into **World War I** and he was twice tried under the **Espionage** and **Sedition Acts** and served a brief jail sentence. Unsuccessful in his attempt to win election to congress from North Dakota in 1920, Townley's influence declined and he resigned from the position of leader in 1922.

During the 1930s, Townley was involved in organizing the Farm Holiday Association and he edited a farmers' newspaper. During the 1950s, he supported Joseph McCarthy and accused some of his former colleagues of being communist sympathizers. Townley died in a car accident.

TRADE UNIONS. The organization of working people in a particular craft or industry began in the early 19th century in response to industrialization and the rise of the factory system. The growing power of industrial corporations after the Civil War (1861–65) and the decline of the independent craftsman led to different attempts to organize. Following the failure of the reformist all-inclusive Knights of Labor in the 1880s, the **American Federation of Labor** (AFL) headed by **Samuel Gompers** emerged as an organization of skilled workers using collective bargaining to achieve better wages and conditions in the workplace. While the AFL concentrated on skilled workers, the unskilled **immigrant** and **African American** workers were largely ignored.

The failure of unions to organize the steel industry in 1892 and the **railroad** workers in 1894 saw the rise of more radical bodies. The **Socialist Party**, led by **Eugene Debs**, sought political solutions and the **Industrial Workers of the World** (IWW) attempted to mobilize all workers, particularly the unskilled, in one big union, in order ultimately to bring about a revolutionary change in society. These radical challenges did much to prompt **progressive** reformers into action but in the long run had only a limited appeal to American workers.

During **World War I**, unions gained in strength and recognition as a consequence of labor shortages and their participation in the mobilization of manpower. While the AFL hoped to capitalize upon these gains at the end of the war, employers were equally determined to return to the prewar position. This conflict led to a series of strikes in 1919, one of the most significant being the **steel strike**. Most of these disputes ended in failure for the unions, and the 1920s witnessed a decline in membership from a high of five million to less than three million as prosperity and the employers use of **welfare capitalism** to some extent undermined their appeal. The conservative attitude of the **Republican** administrations and the antipathy of the **Supreme Court** also contributed to this weakened position.

Faced with even greater losses during the **Great Depression**, some union leaders, particularly **John L. Lewis**, called for a revitalized effort to organize workers on an industrial basis, including the unskilled. This caused a rift with the AFL and was to lead to the emergence of the Congress of Industrial Organizations (CIO) in 1935. Granted recognition under the Labor Relations Act of the **New Deal**, unions were to go through one of their greatest periods of growth during the 1930s. These gains were consolidated during World War II as trade unions finally became an established part of American life. The

AFL and CIO merged in the 1950s. *See also* DUBINSKY, DAVID; GREEN, WILLIAM; HAYWOOD, WILLIAM DUDLEY; HILLMAN, SIDNEY.

TRADING WITH THE ENEMY ACT, 1917. Passed in October 1917, the Trading with the Enemy Act prohibited trade with the **Central Powers** and established a blacklist of all companies suspected of having commercial links with enemy countries. The act also established the office of the **Alien Property Custodian**. *See also* WORLD WAR I.

TROTTER, WILLIAM MONROE (1872–1934). The **African American** leader William Monroe Trotter grew up in Boston and was educated at Harvard University where he earned both a bachelor's and master's degree. In 1901, Trotter established a crusading weekly newspaper, *The Boston Guardian*, which he edited until his death. Trotter was among the first African Americans to criticize Booker T. Washington's "accommodationist" leadership and in 1903 was involved in disrupting a public meeting in Boston addressed by Washington. Trotter was briefly jailed for his part in the so-called Boston Riot. In 1905, Totter joined with **W. E. B. Du Bois** to establish the Niagara Movement, a civil rights organization that helped pave the way for the **National Association for the Advancement of Colored People** (NAACP). Trotter wanted the latter organization to be exclusively black and disagreed with Du Bois on this and other issues.

In 1914, Trotter was among a delegation of African Americans who met **Woodrow Wilson** at the White House. When Trotter insistently chided the president for his failure to combat lynching, Wilson terminated the meeting. Trotter also encouraged African Americans to protest against **D. W. Griffith**'s film *The Birth of a Nation* for its glorification of the **Ku Klux Klan**. In 1919, Trotter managed to attend the **Versailles Peace Conference**, despite being denied a passport by the United States government, and in doing so helped to publicize race issues. His stormy temperament, however, ensured that Trotter was always a rather marginal figure. He lost his newspaper in 1934 in the **Depression** and committed suicide shortly after.

TULSA RACE RIOT, 1921. Tulsa, Oklahoma, was the scene of the three-day race riot in which at least 50 white and 200 black people were killed in the confrontation that began on 31 May 1921. The riot began after members of the **African American** community, who had gathered to ensure the safety of a black man in police custody, exchanged shots with gathering white men. Most of Greenwood, the area inhabited by Tulsa's 8,000 African Americans (sometimes known as the "Black Wall Street"), was destroyed by the white mob. Governor J. B. A. Robertson declared martial law and mobilized units of the National Guard to restore order. A commission established in 1997 held the police largely responsible for not preventing the conflict.

TUMULTY, JOSEPH PATRICK (1879–1954). Qualified as a lawyer in New Jersey, Joseph Tumulty established a practice in Jersey City in 1902 and became involved in **Democratic Party** politics. He served on the New Jersey Assembly from 1907 to 1910 when he became Governor **Woodrow Wilson**'s personal secretary. He continued in that position when Wilson entered the White House in 1912. Tumulty was an influential figure until after Wilson's second marriage in 1916. His relationship with the president finally ended in 1922 and he returned to the private practice of law.

TUNNEY, (JAMES JOSEPH) GENE (1897–1978). Gene Tunney began his career as a professional boxer in 1916. In 1918, he enlisted in the Marine Corps and was sent to France, where he became the camp boxing champion, and lightweight champion of the **American Expeditionary Force**. Back in civilian life, Tunney won the United States light heavyweight title in 1922. From then until 1925, Tunney won all but one contest as a light heavyweight, losing and regaining his title to Harry Greb (1922, 1923) and famously defeating Georges Carpentier in 1924.

In 1926, Tunney defeated the heavy weight champion **Jack Dempsey** in front of a record audience of 120,000. Another 100,000 watched the rematch in 1927. The fight became one of the most famous in boxing history. Having led for six rounds, Tunney was knocked down in the seventh, but benefited from a famous "long count" because Dempsey did not retire to a neutral corner. Tunney recovered and won the fight. In 1928, Tunney retired as undefeated heavyweight champion. He went on to write articles on health and fitness and two autobiographies (*A Man Must Fight* [1933], *Arms for a Living* [1941]) and after 1928 became a business executive. During World War II, Tunney directed the United States Navy's physical fitness program.

TWENTIETH AMENDMENT. Passed on 3 March 1932, and ratified on 23 January 1933, the Twentieth Amendment reduced the gap between the election of a new president and Congress in November to January rather than March. It also ended "lame duck" Congresses that had met from December to March and had included congressmen defeated in the November elections. (*See* appendix II.)

TWENTY-FIRST AMENDMENT. Passed in February 1933 and ratified on 5 December 1933, the Twenty-First Amendment repealed the **Eighteenth** and so ended **Prohibition** in the United States. The amendment was ratified directly by state conventions, the first time such a device had been used since the approval of the Constitution itself. The vote for delegates in favor of repeal was approximately 73 percent of votes cast. Control of alcohol after 1933 became a state rather than a federal issue. (*See* appendix II.)

– U –

UNDERWOOD, OSCAR WILDER (1862–1929). After studying at the University of Virginia, Oscar Underwood established a successful law practice in Birmingham, Alabama, in 1884. In 1895, he was elected as a **Democrat** to the United States House of Representatives, lost the seat in 1896, but was returned in 1897. He remained in the House until 1915, when he was elected to the Senate on an anti-**Prohibition** platform. As a congressman, Underwood became chair of the House Ways and Means Committee and, following the election of **Woodrow Wilson**, led the Democrats to secure passage of the president's **New Freedom** program including **tariff** reform. The latter was achieved with the **Underwood-Simmons Tariff Act**. Underwood supported Wilson's war program and also the **Treaty of Versailles**. In 1920, Underwood became Senate minority leader. He was a delegate to the **Washington Naval Conference** in 1921 and helped to secure ratification of the treaties. Underwood resigned as minority leader in 1923 and planned a campaign to secure the Democratic presidential nomination in 1924. His opposition to the **Ku Klux Klan** cost him the support of the South, and his bid was unsuccessful. He did not seek re-election in 1926.

UNDERWOOD-SIMMONS TARIFF. Passed in 1913, the Underwood-Simmons Act was a key measure in **Woodrow Wilson's New Freedom** program. It was the first significant reform of the **tariff** since the Civil War and it reduced tariffs on 958 goods or items. However, rates were left unchanged on over 300 items maintaining the protectionist element.

UNEMPLOYMENT CONFERENCE, 1921. *See* PRESIDENT'S UNEMPLOYMENT CONFERENCE.

UNITED STATES EMERGENCY FLEET CORPORATION (USEFC). The Emergency Fleet Corporation, headed by **Charles Schwab**, replaced the **United States Shipping Board** in following America's entry into **World War I** in April 1917. It embarked on a huge shipbuilding program, spending more than $1 billion. During the war, the number of shipyards increased from 61 to 341, with an increase in the workforce from 45,000 to 380,000. By 1921, the tonnage of U.S. vessels involved in foreign trade had risen from about 3 million to 11 million. After the war, government-built ships were sold to private operators.

UNITED STATES FOOD ADMINISTRATION. Established under the **Lever Food and Fuel Act** in 1917 the Food Administration was responsible for ensuring the adequate production and for controlling the price and supply of food and feeds during the war. As head of the Administration, **Herbert Hoover** set the prices of certain commodities such as wheat, sugar, and hogs but refused to introduce rationing. The Food Administration relied on voluntary cooperation mobilized by a massive program of exhortation and propaganda urging the population to conserve food supplies and observe "wheatless, meatless and porkless" days.

UNITED STATES FUEL ADMINISTRATION. The Fuel Administration was established with the United States **Food Administration** in 1917 under the **Lever Food and Fuel Act** in order to ensure the adequate provision of fuel for the war effort. **Harry Garfield**, president of Williams College and son of former President James Garfield, headed the Administration. He took action to stabilize coal prices but, faced with continuing shortages and a transportation deadlock, he ordered all factories east of the Mississippi to close for a week in January 1918. Although this helped to resolve the situation, it led to considerable criticism of **Woodrow Wilson**'s administration.

UNITED STATES HOUSING CORPORATION (USHC). Faced with considerable housing shortages in many war industry centers in 1918, President **Woodrow Wilson** approved the creation of the United States Housing Corporation to build homes for war workers. Although short-lived the Corporation built some 6,000 homes in 80 cities across the country. After the war, completed projects were sold off, but the USHC established an important precedent for later federal housing programs.

UNITED STATES RAILROAD ADMINISTRATION (USRA). Following America's entry into **World War I** in 1917, the various **railroad** companies attempted to coordinate their services voluntarily through a Railroads War Board. However, this proved inadequate and by December of that year the system had virtually come to a standstill. Using his wartime executive authority, President **Woodrow Wilson** established the United States Railroad Administration to take over the temporary running of the system. Headed by Secretary of the Treasury **William Gibbs McAdoo**, the new agency successfully coordinated timetables, pooled rolling stock, unified the use of terminals, and built additional rail cars. The railroad companies were guaranteed annual compensation and the federal government paid all railroad costs for the duration of the war.

UNITED STATES SHIPPING BOARD (USSB). The five-man U.S. Shipping Board was created under the Merchant Marine Act on 7 September 1916 to build, purchase, lease, and operate merchant ships during **World War I** and for a five-year period after. In April 1917 it became the **United States Emergency Fleet Corporation**. The Shipping Board assumed a largely regulatory role under the **Merchant Marine Act** of 1920.

– V –

VALENTINO, RUDOLPH (1895–1926). Born Rodolfo Alfonzo Raffaele Pierre Philibert Guglielmi in Italy, Rudolph Valentino entered the United States in 1913, where he became one of the greatest silent **movie** idols in the role as the Latin lover. He began work as an extra in the movies after working variously as a gardener, waiter, and café dancer. His big breakthrough came with *The Four Horsemen of the Apocalypse* (1921). Valentino then starred in a series of movies as a male seducer who was tamed by his would-be victim, beginning with *The Sheik* (1921). His other films in a similar role included *Blood and Sand* (1922), *Monsieur Beaucaire* (1924), and *The Son of the Sheik* (1926). Valentino's funeral after his sudden death of peritonitis in New York attracted huge crowds of hysterical women and he remained the personification of the male screen heart-throb for generations.

VAN DEVANTER, WILLIS (1859–1941). Willis Van Devanter graduated from Cincinnati Law School in 1881 and practiced law in Indiana for three years before establishing a practice in Wyoming. Van Devanter was actively involved in Wyoming politics as a **Republican** and was a Cheyenne City attorney from 1887 to 1888 and then representative to the state legislature. In 1889, Van Devanter was appointed chief justice of the territorial supreme court and then became first chief justice of Wyoming's Supreme Court after it achieved statehood in 1890. He abandoned the position for private practice.

In 1897, Van Devanter was appointed assistant United States attorney general in the Department of Interior, and in 1903 became judge of the Eighth Circuit Court of Appeals. In 1910, President **William Howard Taft** appointed him to the United States **Supreme Court**. Van Devanter was a staunch conservative. He was a strong supporter of property rights and business interests and opposed demands for labor reform. Van Devanter was one of the authors of the

Judiciary Act of 1925 that gave the Supreme Court power to regulate and control its own business and so determine which cases it would examine. He wrote the opinion upholding the **Eighteenth Amendment** and **Prohibition** and was steadfast in his opposition to the **New Deal** in the 1930s. Van Devanter was the first justice to retire with full pay under the terms of the Supreme Court Retirement Act (1937).

VAN DOREN, CARL (CLINTON) (1885–1950). Carl Van Doren studied at Illinois University and Columbia University where he gained his Ph.D. in 1911. He was an assistant professor in the English Department at Columbia from 1911 to 1934, during which time he edited the *Cambridge History of American Literature* (1917–21), was literary editor of *The Nation* (1919–22) and *Century Magazine* (1922–25), and editor for the Literary Guild (1926–34). Van Doren was particularly important in encouraging black writers in the **Harlem Renaissance**.

VAN RENSSELAER, MARTHA (1864–1932). Martha Van Rensselaer was for a while a schoolteacher before she became school commissioner for Cattaraugus County, New York, from 1893 to 1899. In 1911, she joined Cornell University to organize an extension program of home economic courses for agriculture communities, and in 1911 Van Rensselaer became professor of home economics. She was a leading writer on home economics and contributed regularly to the *Ladies Home Journal*. From 1914 to 1916, Van Rensselaer was president of the Home Economic Association. During **World War I**, she was a member of the **United States Food Administration**. In 1923, she was voted one of the most outstanding **women** in the United States.

VAN VECHTEN, CARL (1880–1964). Following his graduation from the University of Chicago in 1899, Carl Van Vechten began work as a society reporter and photographer for the *Chicago American*. In 1906, Van Vechten moved to New York City where he became the assistant music critic of the *New York Times*. He was the paper's Paris correspondent from 1908 to 1909 and then continued as art and music critic until 1913. Van Vechten was a close acquaintance of **Mabel Dodge Luhan**, **Gertrude Stein**, and the literary and artistic inhabitants of **Greenwich Village**. Van Vechten wrote several novels dealing with this social milieu—*Peter Whiffle* (1922), *The Blind Bowboy* (1923), *The Tatooed-Countess* (1924)—and also several works of music criticism—*Music after the Great War* (1915), *The Music of Spain* (1918), and *Red: Papers on Musical Subjects* (1925).

Perhaps Van Vechten's greatest significance, however, was in his role as a popularizer of **African American** arts and entertainment and as a supporter of the **Harlem Renaissance**. Van Vechten captured something of the excitement of New York's black community in his novel *Nigger Heaven* (1926), although some African Americans disliked the book's title and subject matter. During the 1930s, Van Vechten became a keen portrait photographer and captured many of the images of famous black and white personalities for posterity.

VANZETTI, BARTOLOMEO (1888–1927). Born in Villafalletto, Italy, Bartolomeo Vanzetti emigrated to the United States in 1908. He worked in a number of menial jobs and became a fish peddler. With **Nicola Sacco**, he was involved in anarchist activities, which led to his arrest in 1920. He and Sacco were, however, subsequently charged with robbery and murder. Following their trial, conviction, and death sentence, the **Sacco and Vanzetti case** became an international *cause célèbre*. Despite protests from around the world, both men were electrocuted at Charlestown State Prison on 23 August 1927.

VARDAMAN, JAMES KIMBLE (1861–1930). After studying law at Carrollton University, Mississippi, James Vardaman was admitted to the bar in 1881 and began a law practice in Winona, where he also became editor of the Winona *Advance*. He continued to practice law and publish newspapers after his move to Greenwood, Mississippi. A **Democrat**, Vardaman served in the state house of representatives, 1890–96, and was speaker in 1894. He was an unsuccessful candidate for governor of Mississippi in 1895 and 1899 and served in Cuba during the Spanish-American War. In 1904, Vardaman was elected governor following his virulent criticism of **African Americans**. He served one term before winning election to the United States Senate on his third attempt in 1912. Vardaman was one of the six senators who opposed American entry into **World War I** in 1917, and because of this he failed to be re-elected in 1918 and again in 1922. His other notable contribution as a senator was to oppose **selective service** and particularly the recruiting of African Americans into the services. Vardaman retired to Birmingham, Alabama, in 1922.

VERA CRUZ. In 1913, Victoriano Huerta seized power in **Mexico**. The American president, **Woodrow Wilson**, refused to recognize the new regime. Following an incident in which United States seamen were arrested in Tampico, Mexico, in 1914, Admiral Henry Mayo demanded a salute for the United States flag in addition to the release of the servicemen, which had already occurred. When this was refused, Wilson approved the bombardment and seizure of Vera Cruz. On 21 April, his instructions were carried out with the loss of 200 Mexican and 19 American lives. The United States forces were withdrawn in June after a mediated settlement negotiated by Argentina, Brazil, and Chile, but relations with Mexico continued to be fragile for several years. *See also* ABC MEDIATION.

VERSAILLES, TREATY OF, 1919. The treaty that emerged from the **Versailles Peace Conference** ending **World War I** was signed by 32 nations in June 1919 and presented to the German representatives for signature. It consisted of 440 articles, many of a punitive character. These included: a war guilt clause; acceptance of the demilitarization of the Rhineland; the cession of Alsace and Lorraine and the Saar to France, Sudentenland to the newly created Czechoslovakia, and other territory to Belgium and to Poland, and the loss of all colonies; the scrapping of the German navy and air force; and the imposition of reparations, which were to be agreed at a future date. The last clause provided for the establishment of a **League of Nations**. President **Woodrow Wilson** accepted the treaty as politically expedient on the expectation that it could be modified subsequently by the League of Nations. However, many Progressives, both in- and outside of the **Democratic Party**, were dismayed by the harsh terms of the treaty. Conservatives in both major parties were not prepared to accept the commitments involved in the League of Nations and as a consequence the treaty failed to get the two-thirds support needed for ratification in the United States Senate. The United States ended formal hostilities with Germany by a two-nation agreement in 1921.

VERSAILLES PEACE CONFERENCE. Following the **armistice** in November 1918, the victorious **Allies** met from 18 January to 28 June 1919 in Versailles to agree on the terms of the peace settlement. Although attended by representatives from 32 countries initially working through various committees, the conference was dominated by the "Big Five," President **Woodrow Wilson**, Georges Clemenceau of France, Prime Minister David Lloyd George of Britain, Vittorio Orlando of Italy, and Saionji of Japan. Ignoring the principle of "open convenants openly arrived at," as proposed in Wilson's **Fourteen Points**, the meetings were held behind closed doors.

VIDOR, KING WALLIS (1894–1982). The motion picture producer and director began work in the film industry in Texas producing films of real events, such as the Galveston hurricane and the Houston sugar refining industry. In 1915, Vidor moved to California and began work with the Vitagraph studio. After working for a number of companies, Vidor established his own in 1920 and produced several **movies** starring his wife, Florence Vidor. From 1924 until 1933, he worked as a director for Metro-Goldwyn-Mayer. He produced the sound musical *The Big Parade* in 1925. Vidor's first big success came with *La Bohème* starring **Lillian Gish** in 1926. His film *The Crowd* won an Academy Award nomination the same year. Several more successful films followed. Vidor worked as an independent producer-director for several years after 1933, but returned to MGM in 1938. *The Citadel*, his first film that year, won four Academy Award nominations; *Northwest Passage* (1940) was a huge box-office success.

During World War II, Vidor served in the photographic unit of the armed forces and, after the war, he worked on several films with producer **David O. Selznick**. Vidor's last film was *Solomon and Sheba* (1959). Vidor received many awards in recognition of his contribution to filmmaking and in 1979 the Academy gave him its Lifetime Achievement Award.

VILLA, FRANCISCO ("PANCHO") (1877–1923). Born Doroteo Arango, Pancho Villa was a Mexican revolutionary and bandit who fought against the government first of Victoriano Huerta (1911–15) and then of Venustiano Carranza (1914–15). Initially supported by the United States government and admired in the press that dubbed him "the Robin Hood of Mexico," **Woodrow Wilson**'s administration ceased supplying Villa arms once Carranza assumed power. In January 1916, Villa seized a train and killed 16 American passengers in an attempt to discredit Carranza and provoke United States intervention. When that failed, Villa crossed the border into Texas and New Mexico, where he burned the town of **Columbus** and killed 19 inhabitants on 9 March 1916. Villa was then pursued unsuccessfully by a **punitive expedition** led by General **John Pershing** deep into **Mexico**. In 1919, Villa agreed to retire to his ranch, but he was assassinated in 1923.

VILLARD, OSWALD GARRISON (1872–1949). Born in Germany, Villard was the grandson of the abolitionist and pacifist William Lloyd Garrison. After graduating from Harvard University, he began work as an editorial writer on his father's newspaper, the New York *Evening Post*. When his father died in 1900, Villard became owner/editor of the *Post* and its weekly edition, the *Nation*. He turned the latter into a leading liberal journal and was an advocate of **women's suffrage**, recognition of **trade unions**, and civil rights. He was one of the founders of the **National Association for the Advancement of Colored People** (NAACP) in 1909. As a pacifist, Villard opposed United States entry into **World War I** and as a result was forced to sell the *Post* in 1918. He bought the *Nautical Gazette* the same year and owned it until 1935. In 1918, Villard wrote critical accounts of the **Versailles conference** and **peace settlement** for *The Nation*, and during the 1920s he campaigned on behalf of imprisoned conscientious objectors, in support of antilynching legislation, and against **Prohibition**. During the 1920s and 1930s, he published material on newspapers and journalism, several studies of German history and development, a critique of the United States defense establishment, and his own autobiography, *Fighting Years: Memoirs of a Liberal Editor*, in 1939.

VINSON, FREDERICK MOORE (1890–1953). Frederick Vinson graduated from Kentucky Normal College in 1908 and gained his law degree from Center College, Danville, in 1911. He established a law practice in Louisa, Kentucky, and served as city attorney from 1913 to 1914. Vinson was elected commonwealth attorney for the 32nd judicial district of Kentucky in 1921, a position he held until his election as a **Democrat** to the United States House of Representatives in 1924. He was defeated in 1928 and resumed his law practice in Ashland, Kentucky. Vinson returned to the House of Representatives in 1931 and held his seat until 1938.

A supporter of the **New Deal**, Vinson was appointed associate justice to the United States Circuit Court of Appeals in the District of Columbia and he served in that position from 1938 until 1943. From 1943 until 1945, he was director of the Office of Economic Stabilization, a wartime agency. In 1945, he was appointed first as Federal Loan Administrator and then director of War Mobilization and Reconstruction. President Harry S. Truman appointed Vinson as secretary of the treasury in 1945 and he was involved in drawing up the Bretton Woods Agreement in 1944 and in establishing the International Monetary Fund. Following the death of Chief Justice **Harlan F. Stone** in 1946, Truman appointed Vinson as replacement and he served until his death. Not especially outstanding, Vinson approved the decision in 1951 to uphold the conviction of 11 members of the **Communist Party** charged under the Smith Act (1940).

VOLSTEAD, ANDREW JOHN (1860–1947). Andrew Volstead was admitted to the Minnesota bar in 1884 and in 1886 was elected **Republican** prosecuting attorney for Yellow Medicine County. He was elected to the United States House of Representatives in 1902 and served until 1923. He consistently opposed **Woodrow Wilson**'s **New Freedom** legislation. As chair of the Judiciary Committee Volstead gave his name to the legislation to enforce **Prohibition**. Volstead was defeated in the election of 1922 and became legal adviser to Minnesota's Northwest Prohibition Enforcement District until 1931, when he returned to his law practice.

VOLSTEAD ACT. The Volstead Act was the popular name for the **National Prohibition Act** that was introduced in Congress by Congressman Andrew Volstead of Minnesota in 1919 to enforce the **Eighteenth Amendment**. Initially vetoed by **Woodrow Wilson**, Congress overrode the president and the act went into force on 1 January 1920.

– W –

WAGNER, ROBERT FERDINAND (1877–1953). Robert Wagner was born in Germany and emigrated to the United States with his family in 1885. They settled in New York City, where Wagner went on to qualify and practice in law. He was elected as a **Democrat** to the New York state assembly in 1905 and then to the state senate. He was chairman of the State Factory Investigating Committee from 1911 to 1915 and justice of the supreme court of New York, 1919 to 1926. Together with **Al Smith**, Wagner promoted several pieces of reform legislation to improve labor conditions in New York. He was elected to the United States Senate in 1926, where he served until his resignation due to ill health in 1949.

Wagner chaired several committees and sponsored several pieces of social reform legislation, such as the National Industrial Recovery Act and the Social Security Act. He was best known as the author of the National Labor Relations Act (Wagner Act) of 1935 that established the National Labor Relations Board and recognized workers' rights of free collective bargaining. He was a delegate to the United Nations Monetary and Financial Conference at Bretton Woods in 1944.

WALD, LILLIAN (1867–1940). Lillian Wald was a nurse, **social worker**, and public health official active in the Progressive reform movement as a social worker and **women**'s activist. Wald trained as a nurse in the New York Hospital training school and graduated in 1891. Having become aware of the plight of **immigrant** workers in the Lower East Side, Wald abandoned her training to become a doctor and with Mary Brewster established the Henry Street Settlement in New York City in 1893. Wald pioneered public health nursing when she developed the Visiting Nurse Society to provide health care among the immigrant population. She also persuaded Columbia University to establish a department of nursing and health. In 1912, Wald became the first president of the National Organization for Public Health Nursing.

Wald was influential in securing the establishment of the Federal **Children's Bureau** and the Red Cross rural nursing service, both in 1912. Wald was also a supporter of **women's suffrage** and of the peace movement. When American entered **World War I**, she chaired the Committee on Community Nursing of the American Red Cross and led the campaign to combat the outbreak of **influenza** in 1918. In 1919, she represented the United States at the international Red Cross conference in France. She attended the International Conference on Women for Peace in Zurich that led to the foundation of the Women's International League for Peace and Freedom. Wald was a supporter of the **League of Nations**. Wald's prewar pacifism and her friendship with people like **Emma Goldman** led her to be listed as a radical during the **Red Scare**. Nonetheless, in 1922 the *New York Times* named Wald one of the 12 greatest living American women. Paradoxically, Wald lobbied in support of **Prohibition** and also supported **Al Smith**'s candidacy for president in 1928. Wald wrote two autobiographical accounts: *The House on Henry Street* (1915) and *Windows on Henry Street* (1934). She retired from Henry Street in 1933 due to ill health.

WALKER, JAMES JOHN (1881–1946). Although he completed a law degree in 1904, "Jimmy" Walker first worked as a songwriter. However, in 1909 Walker began his political career when he was elected to the state assembly and in 1914 he entered the New York state senate. He served until 1925, supporting a series of progressive social welfare measures. In 1925, Walker successfully campaigned to become mayor of New York City and he was re-elected in 1929, defeating Republican **Fiorello La Guardia**.

Although his administrations witnessed the expansion of the transit system, improved public hospitals, and a new sanitation department, Walker left the details of government to others, particularly the machine politicians of Tammany Hall. Walker enjoyed the good life and a colorful private life. His extravagant lifestyle and casual approach to the business of government lost its appeal with the onset of the **Depression** and investigations headed by **Samuel Seabury** in 1931 revealed widespread corruption in the Walker administration. Walker resigned in September 1932. Despite all this, Walker remained popular in New York. In 1937, he was appointed assistant counsel of the New York State Transit Commission and in 1940 La Guardia appointed him as "impartial chairman" of the Women's Cloak Industry.

WALL STREET CRASH, 1929. The greatest financial crash in the history of the United States occurred in October 1929. Following several months in which security prices fell, on "Black Thursday," 24 October, over 13 million shares were traded on the stock exchange. On 29 October, "Black Tuesday," "the most devastating day in the history of the New York stock market," more than 16 million shares were sold and share prices fell by $40 billion. By July 1933, the decline in value was $74 billion and the great boom in stocks, the "bull-market" of the 1920s, was over.

The speculation boom of the 1920s was fueled by the expansion of manufacturing and the growth of consumerism based on new products, such as the **automobile, radio,** and other electrical appliances. The mood of optimism was reflected in rising share prices, and shares themselves then became seen as a way of making money quickly, rather than as investments in the country's industrial future. The market, however, was largely unregulated and suffered serious flaws. Investors could buy shares on "margin," that is paying a fraction (sometimes as little as 10 percent) of the value of the shares and borrowing the rest from brokers. As prices rose, shares could be sold, the balance paid off, and a profit made; when prices fell, panic set in as investors realized the yield would not meet outstanding balance. Holding companies and investment trusts sprang up offering shares that often bore little relation to industrial assets or profits and sometimes were simply exercises in speculation. Brokers' loans rose from $3.5 million in June 1927 to $8 million in September 1929 and about 4 million Americans owned stock, 1.5 million of them using brokers. When share prices began to fall, panic quickly set in—especially among those who had bought on margin.

The Crash wiped out the savings of individuals and the investments of **banks** and insurance companies. The loss of confidence in financial institutions, because of failure and tales of fraud and embezzlement, added to this downward spiral. The rush of savers to withdraw money from banks compounded the crisis that led to a general collapse in financial institutions. By 1932, almost 4,000 **banks** had failed. This in turn contributed to the onset of the **Great Depression** as investment in industry fell and loans to companies, farms, homeowners, and international banks were called in.

WALLACE, HENRY CANTWELL (1866–1924). Henry Cantwell Wallace studied briefly at Iowa State Agricultural College before taking over one of his father's farms in 1887. In 1892, he was appointed professor of dairying at Iowa State College. In 1895, he joined his father in taking over what became *Wallaces' Farmer* and he helped turn it into an influential agricultural journal. He was active in the wartime mobilization of farming during **World War I** but opposed **Herbert Hoover**'s policies as Food Administrator. In 1921, **Warren Harding** appointed Wallace secretary of agriculture. Wallace expanded the role of the Department of Agriculture and he supported the proposed **McNary-Haugen** plan to maintain farm prices. However, the plan had little support from the Harding administration and was opposed by President **Calvin Coolidge** under whom Wallace served briefly before he succumbed to illness. Wallace's son, Henry Agard Wallace, also became secretary of agriculture and later secretary of commerce in **Franklin D. Roosevelt**'s administration.

WALSH, THOMAS JAMES (1859–1933). The lawyer and **Democratic Party** politician, Thomas Walsh gained a degree in law at the University of Wisconsin, settled briefly in Dakota Territory, and in 1890 established a law practice in Montana. He was unsuccessful in his bid to win election to the United States House of Representatives in 1906 but was elected to the Senate in 1912 and held the position until his death. Walsh managed **Woodrow Wilson**'s western campaign in 1916 and supported Wilson's program in peace and war. It was Walsh whose investigations while chair of the Public Land Committee after the war opened up the **Teapot Dome** Scandal and won him a reputation for probity. In 1932, Walsh supported the nomination of **Franklin D. Roosevelt** and he was offered the appointment of attorney general in the new administration. He died while en route to the inaugural ceremonies.

WAR FINANCE CORPORATION (WFC). The War Finance Corporation was created in 1918 to provide credit facilities for war industries by making loans to banks. After **World War I** it provided loans to **railroad** companies. The powers of the WFC were augmented in

1919 to aid exporters. In 1921 the WFC provided funds to help agricultural exporters and by 1924, when it was abolished, had lent $700 million.

WAR INDUSTRIES BOARD (WIB). The War Industries Board was established in 1917 to coordinate United States industrial mobilization, fix prices, allocate raw material, and determine production levels during **World War I**. In 1918, the WIB's powers were further increased and **Bernard Baruch** was appointed chairman. Although the WIB relied on voluntary methods and utilized an enormous number of committees staffed primarily with "dollar-a-year men" from business who could afford to work for a nominal salary, it did have enforcement powers. Such was its power that some commentators viewed the Board as a form of "war socialism." The WIB was abolished in January 1919.

WAR LABOR BOARD (WLB). The War Labor Board was established in April 1918 to mediate in labor-management disputes in defense industries and lessen the potential disruption of the war effort by strikes. The WLB recognized the right to collective bargaining and the need for a minimum living wage and a basic eight-hour day. It adjudicated in over 1,200 cases during the war.

WASHINGTON NAVAL CONFERENCE, 1921–1922. A conference held in Washington, D.C., to consider the limiting of naval armaments involving the United States, Great Britain, France, Italy, the Netherlands, Belgium, Portugal, Japan, and China. The conference resulted in several treaties: the **Washington Naval Treaty**, **Four Power Treaty**, Nine Power Treaty, and a "naval holiday." Significantly, it left Japan as the strongest naval power in the Far East.

WASHINGTON NAVAL TREATY. The Washington Naval Treaty, or Five Power Treaty, was signed by the United States, Great Britain, Japan, France, and Italy at the **Washington Naval Conference**. It provided for the scrapping of a number of battleships and a "naval holiday" to establish a ratio in terms of ships' tonnage to 5:5:3 for the United States, Britain, and Japan, and 1.75 each for France and Italy.

WATERS, ETHEL (1896–1977). The **African American** singer and actress Ethel Waters began performing in vaudeville in 1917. She began recording for Black Swan Records in 1921 and performed in a number of musical plays and reviews, including *African* (1927), *Blackbirds of 1930* (1930), *As Thousands Cheer* (1933), in **DuBose Heyward**'s *Mamba's Daughters* (1938), and in *Cabin in the Sky* (1940). Waters also appeared in films, most notably the **movie** version of *Cabin in the Sky* with **Louis Armstrong** and other leading African American performers in 1943. She was nominated for the best supporting actress Academy Award for her role in *Pinky* in 1949. Waters also appeared on radio shows and later as "Beuhla" on television.

WEBB-POMERENE ACT. Passed in April 1918, the Webb-Pomerene Act, or Webb Export Act, exempted export trade associations from the provisions of antitrust legislation provided that they did not attempt to restrain competition or prices within the domestic market. The act was intended to stimulate foreign trade.

WEEKS, JOHN WINGATE (1860–1926). John Weeks graduated from Annapolis Naval Academy in 1881 and served in the navy for two years. After working as a surveyor in Florida, he moved to Boston where he successfully established a banking and brokerage company. Weeks served briefly in local politics before being elected to Congress as a **Republican** representative for Massachusetts in 1904. He served until 1913. He played a part in drawing up the Currency Act in 1908 and the Postal Savings Bank in 1910. He was elected to the United States Senate by the Massachusetts legislature in 1913 and played an important part in securing the passage of the **Federal Reserve Act** in 1913. Weeks lost his seat to his Democratic opponent in 1918. However, he continued to be active in Republican Party politics. As a member of the National Committee in 1920 Weeks supported **Warren G. Harding**'s nomination. He was rewarded with the appointment as secretary of war in 1921. Untainted by the scandals in the Harding administration, he kept his position under **Calvin Coolidge** until ill health forced him to retire in 1925.

WEISSMULLER, JOHNNY (1904–1984). Born Janos Weissmuller in Rumania, the future swimming champion was brought to the United States as an infant. He changed his name in 1924. Weissmuller began entering swimming competitions in 1921 and using the new crawl stroke he had set 67 world records at different distances by 1922. Weissmuller won three gold medals at the 1924 Paris Olympics and five in the 1928 games at Amsterdam. Having turned professional in 1929 Weissmuller became an international **movie** star in the 1930s as Tarzan, the hero of the novels by **Edgar Rice Burroughs**. Weissmuller established the formulaic characteristics of the primitive hero (his limited speech, his famous jungle yodel, and his athleticism) in a series of movies from *Tarzan the Ape Man* (1932) through to *Tarzan and the Mermaids* (1948) and in similar movies through to the 1950s. Weissmuller retired in the late-1950s. He was elected a charter member to the U.S. Olympic Hall of Fame in 1983.

WELFARE CAPITALISM. A term applied to programs introduced by large corporations during the 1920s to improve labor relations, stabilize the workforce, and limit the appeal of **trade unions**. They included offering profit sharing and stock subscription schemes to workers, pension and insurance plans, paid vacations, social and welfare clubs and activities, and improved facilities on the shop floor. These plans were more paternalistic forms of the **American Plan** that had emerged in defense of the open shop and in response to union gains during **World War I**. Company unions were often allowed, but without bargaining rights or the right to strike, and benefits were generally determined by the length of service. By 1926, 50 percent of the top 1,500 companies had comprehensive plans in operation and more than 400 companies had pension plans available to their four million workers. Such schemes rarely reached the smaller businesses, nor did they do much to avert the impact of the **Depression**.

WESTON, EDWARD HENRY (1886–1958). The photographer Edward Weston took courses in photography at the Illinois College of Photography and began work as a commercial photographer in 1911. The Photographers' Association of America recognized Weston as a leading pictorialist photographer in 1916 and he was a frequent prizewinner. Weston's work was, however, becoming increasingly more artistic and he gradually abandoned his commercial career. He moved to Mexico in 1923 and began to produce photographs of ordinary objects shot from unusual perspectives. In 1928, he opened a studio in San Francisco before settling the following year in Carmel. Studies of landscapes, rock formations, and sand dunes now followed his photographs of stones, shells, and other objects. Weston continued to produce prints of his work until his death. With **Alfred Stieglitz,** Weston helped to establish modern American photography.

WHARTON, EDITH NEWBOLD (1862–1937). The writer Edith Wharton was born of wealthy parents in New York City. She began writing early in life and had already published several poems by the age of 16. After her marriage in 1885, she traveled frequently to Europe and wrote a number of books on European architecture. Several of her short stories were published in collections as *The Greater Inclination* (1899), *Crucial Instances* (1901), and *The Descent of Man* (1904). Wharton's first novel *The Valley of Decision* was published in 1902, but her critical and popular success as an author began with her critique of New York high society in *The House of Mirth* in 1905. *Ethan Frome* (1911), reflecting her own personal experience, was concerned with a love triangle.

Wharton's support of France during **World War I** and her activities on behalf of Belgian refugee's won her the award of the Legion of Honor and Order of Leopold. In 1920 her novel, *The Age of Innocence*, mourning the loss of tradition in the war, won the Pulitzer Prize. Her subsequent writing, written in France, was less successful.

WHEELER, BURTON KENDALL (1882–1975). After gaining a law degree from the University of Michigan in 1905, Burton Wheeler established a law practice in Butte, Montana. He served a term as a **Democrat** in the Montana House of Representatives from 1910 to 1912 and then became United States district attorney for Montana from 1913 to 1918. He was unsuccessful in his attempt to become governor of Montana in 1918 but was elected senator in 1920 and served until he lost the Democratic primary in 1946. As a western progressive, Wheeler fought against the power of the Anaconda Copper Mining Company in Montana and the popular hysteria during **World War I.**

Wheeler led the hearings in 1924 into Attorney General **Harry Daugherty**'s failure to investigate the **Teapot Dome** scandal and was the vice presidential running mate with **Robert M. La Follette** and the **Progressive Party** the same year. In 1930, Wheeler was one of the first Democrats to support the nomination of **Franklin D. Roosevelt** for the presidency, and he supported most of Roosevelt's **New Deal** measures. However, Wheeler opposed Roosevelt's attempt to alter the composition of the **Supreme Court** in 1937. He also was a supporter of neutrality and opposed Roosevelt's increasing support for Great Britain and France and spoke at America First rallies across the country in 1941. He supported the war effort after Pearl Harbor, and voted for American membership of the United Nations in 1945. After leaving the Senate, he practiced law in Washington, D.C.

WHITE, EDWARD DOUGLASS (1845–1921). Edward White left Georgetown College (now a University) in 1861 to fight for the Confederacy in the Civil War. After the war, White studied law and was admitted to the Louisiana bar in 1868. In 1874, he was elected to the Louisiana Senate and in 1879 was appointed to the Louisiana Supreme Court. Because of a new age requirement, he gave up his seat in 1880 and practiced law. In 1888, White was elected to the United States Senate as a **Democrat**.

In 1894, President Grover Cleveland appointed White to the United States **Supreme Court** and in 1910 President **William Howard Taft** raised him to chief justice, the first time a sitting justice had assumed the position. White held the position until his death and provided stability in the court during a period of rapid change in personnel. His position was generally conservative, supportive of business rather than labor interests or social reform measures, and upheld racial segregation. White argued for a narrow reading of the Sherman Antitrust Act and opposed a number of decisions against monopolies. In 1908, he wrote the opinion in the *Employers' Liability Cases* against federal laws making **railroads** liable for injuries to their workers and was in the majority in *Adair v. United States* upholding "yellow dog contracts" prohibiting union membership. White was also in the majority decision against the prohibition of **child labor** in *Hammer v. Dagenhart* (1918). He did, however, dissent when the Court ruled against a law limiting working hours in

Lochner v. New York (1905) and he joined the unanimous decision in *Muller v. Oregon* (1908) that upheld the law limiting the hours women could work. In both cases, White believed the states had policing powers in the workplace.

White supported the federal government's broad taxation rights in a series of cases and also the federal power to suppress civil liberties. He voted to uphold all of the federal prosecutions during **World War I** under the **Espionage** and **Sedition Acts**. White also voted to uphold racial segregation in decisions from *Plessy v. Ferguson* on. However, he did agree with decisions against "grandfather clauses" that undermined the right to vote. White's major contribution to constitutional law was in developing the "insular doctrine" that stated that constitutional rights and guarantees did not "follow the flag" without express congressional approval, but otherwise his role in the Supreme Court was largely unmemorable.

WHITE, WALTER FRANCIS (1893–1955). The **African American** civil rights leader graduated from Atlanta University in 1916 and worked for two years in insurance. In 1918, he was appointed assistant executive secretary to the **National Association for the Advancement of Colored People** (NAACP). He held the position until 1929 and then became executive secretary of the organization. White took advantage of his light color to investigate and report on lynching in the South during the 1920s, and his reports were used in support of the **Dyer Antilynch Bills** in 1922, 1937, and 1940. His book on the subject, *Rope and Faggott: A Biography of Judge Lynch*, was published in 1929. White also wrote two novels, *The Fire in the Flint* (1924) and *Flight* (1926), and actively supported other members of the **Harlem Renaissance**. He later wrote of the situation of black soldiers during World War II in *A Rising Wind* (1945) and his autobiography, *A Man Called White* (1948).

White and the NAACP successfully opposed the nomination of John J. Parker to the **Supreme Court** in 1930 because of racist comments he had made during his career. White was also instrumental in initiating the NAACP's legal challenges to discrimination and through his friendship with **Eleanor Roosevelt** gained some influence in the White House. His marriage to a white woman in 1949 alienated some white and African American supporters of the

NAACP, and White increasingly had differences with fellow activists in the organization before his death.

WHITE, WILLIAM ALLEN (1868–1944). William Allen White was a leading **Progressive** newspaper editor, journalist, and writer. He was educated at Emporia College and the University of Kansas. In 1891, he began work with the *Kansas City Journal* but soon moved to the *Kansas City Star*. White established his own paper, the *Emporia Gazette*, in 1895 and turned it into a commercial success. White wrote for magazines and published several collections of short stories and novels. After meeting and becoming friendly with **Theodore Roosevelt**, White became a leading voice among progressive Republicans. He joined a number of like-minded writers at *The American Magazine* and published a series of his articles there as *The Old Order Changeth* (1910). White supported the **Progressive Party** in 1912, but returned to the **Republicans** in 1916. White supported **Woodrow Wilson**'s wartime domestic programs and the **League of Nations**. In 1923, White's editorial in defense of free speech won him a Pulitzer Prize. He stood unsuccessfully as an independent candidate for governor of Kansas in 1924 in order to challenge the influence of the **Ku Klux Klan**, but was outspoken in his attacks on **Al Smith** in 1928. In 1930, he became a member of the committee appointed by President **Herbert Hoover** to study conditions in **Haiti**. White was lukewarm in his support for **Franklin D. Roosevelt** and the **New Deal** due to the increased power of the federal government. In 1940, he led the Committee to Defend America by Aiding the Allies and helped secure support for the Lend-Lease Act in 1941. White's *Autobiography of William Allen White* was published posthumously in 1946 and awarded the Pulitzer Prize.

WHITEMAN, PAUL SAMUEL (1890–1967). Paul Whiteman grew up in a musical family and played viola with the Denver Symphony Orchestra at the age of 16. He moved to San Francisco in 1912 and worked with the San Francisco Symphony Orchestra until 1916 when he turned to **jazz**. In 1917, Whiteman joined the United States Navy and served as a bandleader. After **World War I**, Whiteman formed his own band and in 1920 moved to New York to perform on Broadway and make recordings. He had major hits in 1920 with "Whispering" and "Japanese Sandman," and even greater success with "Three O'Clock in the Morning" in 1926. In 1924, the Whiteman orchestra performed the first jazz symphony in New York with **George Gershwin** playing "Rhapsody in Blue." Whiteman was one of the leading musical influences in the 1920s. His band toured Great Britain several times and did much to make jazz widely known. Whiteman also wrote popular books on jazz. His first film in 1930 was *The King of Jazz* and he appeared in several more films subsequently. After a break due to illness, Whiteman returned to radio in 1942 and later made television appearances. He was vice president of the ABC network from 1947 to 1955. Whiteman, although white, was often known as the "King of Jazz" because he gave many white jazz performers, such as Bix Beiderbecke, Tommy Dorsey, Hoagy Carmichael, and singer Bing Crosby, their start in show business.

WICKERSHAM, GEORGE WOODWARD (1858–1936). George Wickersham qualified as a lawyer at University of Pennsylvania and practiced law in New York City from 1883 until his death. In 1909, **William Howard Taft** appointed him attorney general. Wickersham brought more than 80 prosecutions under the Sherman Antitrust Act against companies, including Standard Oil and American Tobacco. He returned to his law practice after 1912 but remained active in **Republican Party** politics. Wickersham was a strong internationalist and supported United States involvement in the **League of Nations**. He served on the League's committee to codify international law and was president of the International Arbitral Tribunal from 1932 to 1936. In 1929, President **Herbert Hoover** appointed Wickersham to chair the National Commission on Law Observance that reported on **Prohibition** in 1931. The Commission concluded that the enforcement of Prohibition was a failure that had undermined law enforcement generally and led to widespread corruption. However, the report did not categorically reject the principle of prohibition itself.

WILDER, THORNTON NIVEN (1897–1975). Thornton Wilder was educated at Oberlin College and Yale University and was awarded an M.A. in French Literature from Princeton in 1926. Wilder served in the coastguard during **World War I**. He taught French and English at Lawrenceville School and at the University of Chicago from 1930 to

1937. As a writer, Wilder used myth and allegory to explore the meaning of life and the themes of love and tolerance. His best-known book, *The Bridge of San Luis Rey* (1927), won a Pulitzer Prize, as did *Heaven's My Destination* (1935) and the plays *Our Town* (1938) and *The Skin of Our Teeth* (1942). Wilder enlisted during World War II, served in the air force, and was awarded the Legion of Merit and the Bronze Star. In the 1950s, he held a chair in poetry at Harvard University and was awarded the National Medal for Literature in 1962. His comedy, *The Matchmaker* (1954), was successfully turned into the film musical *Hello, Dolly!* in 1969. Wilder continued to write until his death. His last book, *Theophilus North*, was published in 1973.

WILSON, EDITH BOLLING GALT (1872–1961). The second wife of **Woodrow Wilson**, Edith Wilson was previously married to Norman Galt, a jeweler. When Galt died in 1908, Edith took over the operation of the jewelry store for a number of years before selling the business. In 1915, she met and married President Wilson. Mrs. Wilson accompanied the president whenever he traveled and advised him on many political matters. She accompanied him to the **Versailles Peace Conference** in 1919 and on his tour of the United States to support the **Versailles settlement** and United States entry into the **League of Nations**. When the president suffered a stroke, Mrs. Wilson played a key, even controversial, role in vetting his visitors and the business he handled. Edith Wilson cared for her husband until his death in 1924 and after helped in the publication of his authorized biography. Her own book, *My Memoir* (1938), was critical of many politicians for failing her husband. She continued to attend political functions until her death.

WILSON, ELLEN AXSON (1860–1914). The first wife of President **Woodrow Wilson**, Ellen Wilson was a graduate of Rome Female College in Georgia. She married Wilson in 1885 and bore him three daughters. While supporting her husband in his professional and political career, Ellen Wilson developed her own work in art from the 1890s on. Some of her work won prizes and she held several exhibitions. As first lady, Mrs. Wilson organized the running of the White House and participated in official functions. Although not a prominent public figure, she also supported a number of social issues relating to conditions for federal employees and housing conditions in the capital.

WILSON, WILLIAM BAUCHOP (1862–1934). Wilson was the first secretary of labor in the United States following the creation of the **Department of Labor** in 1912. A former miner and a member of the Mine Workers' union, he served in congress as a **Democratic** representative from Pennsylvania 1907–1913. During **World War I**, he cochaired the War Labor Conference Board with **William Howard Taft** and served on the **War Labor Board**. After the war Wilson was president of the International Labour Conference in 1919 and he chaired the Federal Board for Vocational Training from 1920 to 1921 and also the second **Industrial Conference**. In 1926, Wilson made an unsuccessful attempt to win the Democratic Party nomination to become senator for Pennsylvania.

WILSON, (THOMAS) WOODROW (1856–1924). Twenty-eighth President of the United States. Born in Staunton, Virginia, and educated at Princeton and the University of Virginia, Woodrow Wilson was admitted to the bar in 1882 and practiced law in Atlanta, Georgia. In 1886 he obtained his Ph.D. in history from Johns Hopkins University. His thesis was published as *Congressional Government* in 1885. He was to write a number of other studies in politics and history, including a five-volume *History of the American People* (1902). Wilson taught political science and history at Bryn Mawr, Weslyan, and Princeton where he became president from 1902 to 1910. He introduced a number of reforms to the university system, including challenging the exclusive eating clubs. Faced with opposition to these measures he resigned in 1910.

In 1910, Wilson became **Democratic** governor of New Jersey and served from 1911 to 1913. He disassociated himself from the old state party machine and supported a corrupt practices act, workmen's compensation legislation, the direct primary, and regulation of public utilities. He was nominated as the Democratic Party's presidential candidate in 1912 with the support of **William Jennings Bryan**. Wilson won the 1912 presidential election in a three-corned contest against the **Progressive** candidate, **Theodore Roosevelt**, and **Republican William Howard Taft**. Wilson gained 6,296,547 votes,

Roosevelt 4,118,571, and Taft 3,486,720 but won 435 Electoral College votes to Roosevelt's 88 and Taft's 8. Wilson was the first southerner to become president since the Civil War.

Wilson's **"New Freedom"** program was essentially a classical liberal program of using government power to restore free market competition. Like Theodore Roosevelt, Wilson saw the presidency as central to an activist federal government. He met with Democratic Party leaders to formulate policy and broke with tradition in going directly to address Congress in person. He continued the antitrust policies of his Republican predecessors and established the **Federal Trade Commission**, supported the **Clayton Antitrust Act**, federal workmen's compensation, and a federal **Child Labor Law**. He reduced **tariffs** in 1913, and introduced income tax to recoup the lost revenues, and provided for **bank** regulation with the passage of the **Federal Reserve Act**. On other issues such as race relations and votes for **women**, Wilson was a conservative. Racial segregation in the federal government increased under his administration, and it was only after 1915 that he began to support **women's suffrage**. Wilson was re-elected again in 1916, narrowly defeating **Charles Evans Hughes** by 9,127, 695 votes to 8,533,507 and 277 Electoral College votes to 254.

When the war in Europe broke out in 1914, Wilson called upon Americans to remain impartial "in thought as well as action" and he initiated a policy of neutrality. However, Americans were not forbidden from traveling on ships of belligerent nations nor from traveling to Europe. Nor were they were forbidden from trading with European powers. Instead the Wilson administration insisted that American citizens had the right to free passage on the high seas. Such policies brought the government into conflict with both Great Britain and Germany but particularly the latter when they announced a policy of unrestricted submarine warfare in 1915. Although the president protested following the sinking of the *Lusitania*, he also said that there was such a thing as being "too proud to fight." Support for his policy was indicated when, in the course of Wilson's nomination at the Democratic Party convention, the slogan "he kept us out of war" emerged as a campaign slogan. President Wilson also attempted to bring an end to the conflict through mediation in 1915 and again in 1916. In 1917, he called for "peace without victory," but this was rejected when the German government announced the resumption of unrestricted submarine warfare. The subsequent sinking of several American vessels made war inevitable. The decision was made easier by the publication of the **Zimmerman telegram**, indicating that Germany might form an alliance with **Mexico** in the event of war with the United States. In his address to Congress on 2 April 1917, Wilson said the war was to make the world "safe for democracy." America entered the war on April 6.

During **World War I**, the Wilson administration took steps to mobilize the population through the **Committee on Public Information** and to suppress opposition via **Espionage** and **Sedition** legislation. Control over food and fuel was achieved through the **Food** and **Fuel** administrations, and industrial mobilization was led by the **Committee for National Defense** and the **War Industries Board**. A National **War Labor Board** was created to mediate in labor disputes in defense industry. In total, during the war, government powers were extended to unprecedented levels.

President Wilson spelled out his program for the postwar settlement and a liberal new order in his **Fourteen Points** speech to Congress on 8 January 1918 promising a liberal world order based on national self-determination. It was on this basis that Germany sued for peace in October 1918 and the **armistice** was agreed in November. Wilson went to Paris to take part personally in the peace conference at **Versailles**. Although forced to compromise with the British leader Lloyd George and the French premier Georges Clemenceau on a number of issues, he won acceptance for the **League of Nations** central to his promise of a world without war. The Germans were forced to accept the treaty, including a war guilt clause and demand for reparations, in June 1919.

On his return to the United States, President Wilson met considerable opposition from **Republicans** and some Democrats to the commitments implied in the League of Nations. Wilson, however, refused any compromise and would accept no amendments. Faced with congressional opposition led by **Henry Cabot Lodge**, Wilson went to the country to appeal to the people directly. On 2 October 1919, he suffered a massive stroke and was severely incapacitated. The treaty was rejected in November 1919. With the defeat of the Democrats in the 1920 election, Wilson retired to his home in Washington, D.C.

WOLFE, THOMAS (1900–1938). The author Thomas Wolfe was a graduate of Chapel Hill, North Carolina, and Harvard Universities. From 1924 until 1930, he worked in the English department of Washington Square College in New York City. In 1929, his study of small-town southern life based on his own family was published to critical acclaim as the novel *Look Homeward, Angel*. The sequel, *Of Time and the River*, was published in 1935. A collection of short stories was also published in 1935 as *From Death to Morning*. A memoir, *The Story of a Novel*, appeared in 1936 and *The Web and the Rock* (1939) and *You Can't Go Home Again* (1940) were both produced from manuscripts after his death.

WOMAN'S PEACE PARTY (WPP). Founded following a meeting of peace campaigners led by **Jane Addams** in 1915. By 1917, the WPP had a membership of between 25,000 and 40,000. The party was somewhat discredited when it was linked with **Henry Ford's** failed peace campaign in 1916 and declined in support after the United States entered **World War I** in 1917. It was renamed the Women's International League for Peace and Freedom in 1921. *See also* PEACE MOVEMENTS.

WOMEN. The situation of women in the United States went through considerable change from the late-19th century up to the 1930s. Following the Civil War (1861–65), there was a considerable increase in opportunities for women in higher education, and the number of women students more than doubled between 1880 and 1900. At the same time, there was also an increase in female employment. In 1870, less than 15 percent of women (four million) were in paid work; by 1910 this was 24 percent (eight million). The great majority of these (85 percent) were single and under the age of 25 and the biggest single area of employment was domestic service. Most working women were **immigrants** or **African Americans**. However, new job opportunities, other than the traditional ones of teaching and nursing, were growing for native-born American women with the development of the typewriter, telephone, and cash register. Many college-educated women, like **Jane Addams** and **Edith** and **Grace Abbott**, also found a vocation in the **settlement house** movement, 70 percent of whose workers were female.

The changing status of women was reflected in the **Progressive movement's** calls for regulation of women's work and in the demand for the vote. The **women's suffrage** movement grew in support in the late-19th and early-20th centuries and was reinvigorated under the new leadership of people like **Carrie Chapman Catt** and **Alice Paul** and also by the inspiration of the suffragettes in Great Britain. **World War I** brought further gains through the increased use of women in war work and in the stress placed on the "war for democracy." While the importance of women's work was now recognized in the creation of a **Women's Bureau**, the passage of the **Nineteenth Amendment** in June 1919 finally brought women into politics and they were able to vote nationally for the first time in 1920.

For many observers, such as **Frederick Lewis Allen**, the acquisition of the vote signaled the birth of a "new woman" in the 1920s. The number of women in paid employment rose from 8.6 million to 10.7 million during the decade, and the proportion of women in clerical and sales occupations continued to rise. The proportion of female workers who were married doubled between 1900 and 1930. However, the percentage of women in paid work remained constant at around 25 percent, and equally the percentage of the labor force that was female remained at about the same figure, and 60 percent of all employed women were black or foreign.

Nonetheless, the **"flapper"** symbolized both the greater economic opportunities enjoyed by many women and a greater social and sexual liberation reflected and shaped by advertising and the **movies**. For women still tied to the home chores, work may have become lighter with the greater use of electric refrigerators, cleaners, and irons, but their roles as mothers and wives were essentially the same. These differences might account in part for the divisions within the women's movement after 1920. Although some were satisfied with the vote, there were those who campaigned for an Equal Rights Amendment, while others argued for legislation to protect women at work. The limits to the progress toward gender equality became apparent in the 1930s when, faced with impact of the **Great Depression**, many Americans felt men should be given priority over women in the workplace and a number of states tried to legislate against the employment of married women.

WOMEN'S BUREAU. Developed from the Women in Industry Service established during **World War I** in response to the increased employment of **women**, the Women's Bureau was created as an office in the **Department of Labor** in 1920 to investigate and report upon issues relating to female employment. It provided guidelines to employers on women's employment through the 1920s and 1930s and reported on conditions of female employment in specific industries.

WOMEN'S CHRISTIAN TEMPERANCE UNION (WCTU). The WCTU was created in 1874 to campaign in favor of the legal prohibition of alcohol. It quickly grew into the largest single organization of **women** in the United States and was often linked to the **women's suffrage** movement. The WCTU campaign encouraged a number of states to enact **Prohibition** prior to the introduction of the **Eighteenth Amendment** in 1920.

WOMEN'S SUFFRAGE MOVEMENT. The campaign for women's suffrage had its origins in the 1830s and was particularly associated with the Abolitionist movement. The Seneca Falls declaration (1848) was a call for equal rights. However, the movement was swallowed up in the conflict over slavery and divided after the Civil War when the Fourteenth Amendment specifically acknowledged the rights of men. In 1869, a New York-based group led by Elizabeth Cady Stanton and Susan B. Anthony, the National Woman Suffrage Association (NWSA), was formed to promote an amendment to enfranchise women. An alternative and less radical group, the American Woman Suffrage Association (AWSA), led by Lucy Stone, concentrated on local activities and state-by-state campaigns for the franchise. In 1890 the two organizations came together to form the **National American Woman Suffrage Association** (NAWSA), and this was led by Anthony from 1892 until 1900. Three western states, Wyoming, Colorado, and Utah granted women the vote in the 1890s.

There was powerful opposition to women's suffrage from the South (fearful of changes that would affect the racial status quo), the brewing industry (aware of women's support for **Prohibition**), industrialists (alarmed at the thought of regulation of female and **child labor**), and machine politicians (worried about the possibility of reform). However, under the new leadership of **Carrie Chapman Catt** (1900–04), NAWSA began to grow by appealing to middle class society and club women and the newly college educated. They also adopted the tactics used by the British suffragists. Many women in the **settlement house** and **Progressive movements** became supporters of suffrage. Catt's return to the leadership and **Alice Paul's** advocacy of militant tacts gave the movement a new vigor. Between 1910 and 1914, another 10 states granted women the vote. The final impetus to reform came during **World War I** as women harnessed their campaign to the "war for democracy," and as war work broke down some of the barriers in the workplace. The **Nineteenth Amendment** was approved by Congress in 1919 and finally ratified on 26 August 1920. Women voted for the first time nationally that November.

WOOD, GRANT (1892–1942). Grant Wood, regarded as "one of the most American of America's artists," learned his trade at the Minneapolis School of Design and in night classes at the University of Iowa and Art Institute of Chicago. He taught in Cedar Rapids, Iowa, but after military service during **World War I** was one of the many artists and writers who spent time in Paris, France. In 1927, he received a commission for a stained glass window commemorating war veterans in Cedar City. His design, using German glass, caused some controversy, a fact that influenced his satirical painting *Daughters of Revolution* (1932). A number of Wood's paintings shared this ironic view, most famously his austere depiction of a farmer and his wife in *American Gothic* (1930). Other work showing the influence of American folk art and the sense of irony included the *Midnight Ride of Paul Revere* (1931) and *Parson Weems' Fable* (1939).

In the 1930s, Wood became a leading figure in the Regionalist school of artists celebrating the richness of the land and offering a vision of hope during the **Great Depression** in work ranging from *Fall Plowing* and *Birthplace of **Herbert Hoover*** (both 1931) through to *Iowa Cornfield* (1941). During the 1930s, Wood was head of the Iowa Works Progress Administration (WPA) Art Project, and taught at Iowa University. In 1935, he was elected to the National Academy of Design and much of his work in the mid-1930s was printmaking and illustration.

WOOD, LEONARD (1860–1927). Leonard Wood qualified as a doctor at Harvard Medical School in 1884. Having been dismissed from Boston City Hospital for infringing on rules with regard to surgery, Wood entered the United States Army as a surgeon in 1885. In 1898, together with **Theodore Roosevelt,** he formed and then led the "Rough Riders," a volunteer military unit in the Spanish-American War. He subsequently became military governor of Cuba (1899–1902) and then commander of the United States forces in the Philippines (1903–08). In this latter position, he was responsible for the bloody suppression of the Moro people. Wood was appointed army chief of staff from 1910 to 1914 and became an advocate of the policy of "preparedness." He was a candidate for the Republican presidential nomination in 1916 and 1920, losing to **William Howard Taft** and **Warren Harding** respectively. As governor-general of the Philippines from 1921 until 1927, he resisted demands for self-government in the island, a policy for which he was subsequently criticized.

WOODS, ROBERT ARCHEY (1865–1925). Robert Woods was educated at Amherst College and Andover Theological Seminary. In 1892, he took over control of Andover House, the first **settlement house** in Boston. In 1895, Woods renamed it South End House and he was to develop it into one of the leading settlement houses in the country. Woods particularly stressed the need for empirical evidence in social reform and popularized the use of the social survey. His own study, *The City Wilderness: A Study of the South End*, was published in 1898 and he conducted further studies of Boston published as *Americans in Progress* in 1902.

In 1911, Woods organized the National Federation of Settlements (later the National Association of Social Workers) and he acted as president and secretary until his death. He published many articles and monographs on the nature and ethos of the settlement house movement.

WORK, HUBERT (1860–1942). Hubert Work studied at the University of Michigan and then University of Pennsylvania, where he obtained his medical qualification in 1885. Work established a practice in Colorado and founded the Woodcroft Hospital for mental illness at

Pueblo in 1896. He was director until 1917. Work was a leading activist in the Colorado medical profession and was president of the State Board of Health. In 1917, he joined the Army Medical Reserve.

Work was a leading **Republican** and a member of the National Committee from 1913 to 1919. He supported **Warren Harding** and was appointed assistant postmaster general in 1921 and postmaster general in 1922. When **Albert Fall** resigned as secretary of the interior in 1923, Harding named Work as his successor and he endeavored to overcome the taint of corruption left by his predecessor. Work called for the preservation of grazing lands and he also helped to establish the Federal Oil Conservation Board in 1924 following the **Teapot Dome** scandal. Work commissioned a study of the role of the Indian Bureau that called for widespread changes in policy when it was published in 1928. Work had, however, resigned to campaign on behalf of **Herbert Hoover**. After the victory, he retired to practice medicine in Denver, Colorado.

WORLD DISARMANENT CONFERENCE, 1932–1934. In February 1932, the **League of Nations** convened a conference of 57 nations at Geneva, Switzerland, to discuss general disarmament. The United States was one of the non-League members to be represented. Attempts to produce disarmament agreements foundered on disagreements over exact terms and the withdrawal of Germany in October 1933.

WORLD SERIES, 1919. In 1919, eight players from the Chicago White Sox were accused of throwing the World Series against the Cincinnati Reds. Few people could accept the possibility that the national sport could be corrupt, despite evidence to the contrary. Although acquitted in the trial that lasted from 1920 to 1921, the players were banned from professional baseball for life. They were known as the Chicago Black Sox. A baseball commission under **Kenesaw Mountain Landis** was subsequently established to clean up the game.

WORLD WAR I, 1914–1918. The first of two world wars in the 20th century, often known as the "Great War," World War I was caused by an explosion of a complex series of big power rivalries over colonies, naval strengths, and territorial disputes, particularly in the Balkans. The outbreak began following the assassination of Archduke Franz Ferdinand of Austria in Sarajevo, Serbia, on 28 June 1914. Two opposing alliance systems, the **Allies** and **Central Powers**, built up since the 1890s, were then drawn into the conflict as Austria, backed by Germany, issued an ultimatum to Serbia, in turn backed by Russia. When Austria mobilized and declared war on Serbia, Russia ordered general mobilization on 30 July. Fearful that Russia's ally, France, might enter any ensuing conflict, and following pre-established military plans, the German government declared war on France and on 4 August invaded Belgium, which had refused passage of German troops. The German invasion prompted a British declaration of war in honor of treaty obligations with Belgium. The war spread as Turkey was drawn in against Russia and Italy against Austria and the Japanese against Germany.

The reaction of Americans to the outbreak of war in Europe was shock and horror. Many **Progressives** were associated with **peace movements** and regarded the war as a descent into barbarity; others believed that it confirmed the validity of the policy of **isolation**. With a large **immigrant** population, particularly of German-American and Irish-American origin, and traditional links with Great Britain and France, sympathies were divided. British propaganda made much of the German invasion of Belgium and "war atrocities." It was not surprising, then, that President **Woodrow Wilson** called upon the American people to be "impartial in thought as well as in action."

Despite this intention, no restriction was imposed upon trade with belligerents nor on travel across the Atlantic. American industry was quick to supply munitions and as a consequence of British control of the seas, trade quickly began to favor the Allies. By 1916, the value of trade with Great Britain and France was $3.5 billion compared with only $1 million to the Central Powers. Germany responded by using submarines (U-boats) to attack merchant and passenger ships. President Wilson described the sinking of the *Lusitania* in 1915 as "illegal and inhuman" but later declared that there was such a thing "as a nation too proud to fight." Increasingly, however, the United States could not sit idly on the sidelines, and the Wilson administration made several unsuccessful attempts to arrive at a mediated settlement in 1915 and 1916. This culminated in his call for "peace without victory" in January 1917. Having committed so much and suffered such huge losses, neither side was prepared to accept this position.

When Germany, faced with stalemate and desperate to break the blockade, resumed the campaign of unrestricted submarine warfare in 1917, war was inevitable. Diplomatic relations with Germany were severed in February and the publication of the **Zimmerman telegram** increased the growing anti-German mood. The Russian Revolution in March ended tsarist autocracy and enabled Wilson to argue that the Allies were fighting for the cause of democracy. After several American vessels had been torpedoed, on 2 April the president went before Congress to ask for a declaration of war in order to "make the world safe for democracy." The declaration was approved in the Senate by 82 votes to 6 on 4 April and by the House of Representative, 373 votes to 50 on 6 April.

Although only directly involved for 18 months, the war had a considerable impact on American society. The mobilization of manpower for the armed forces with the introduction of **Selective Service** and the expansion of industry and **farming** to feed, clothe and arm the United States and continue to supply her allies, affected different social groups and government itself. Faced with continued opposition to the war from **Socialists**, peace groups, and some Midwestern farmers, the Wilson administration immediately established a **Committee on Public Information** (CPI) to rally public opinion. The **Espionage Act**, passed in 1917, introduced to stifle dissent and deal with enemy sympathizers, was further strengthened by the **Sedition Act** in 1918. Both were used against Socialists and the leaders of the **Industrial Workers of the World** (IWW) but also fostered a mood of "100 percent Americanism" that brought hysterical attacks on individuals of German origin and in some cases, foreigners from whatever country.

The economic mobilization was first led by the **Council of National Defense** (CND) and its **Advisory Commission** and then by the **War Industries Board** (WIB). The **Lever Food and Fuel Act** established federal agencies to maximize food production and control prices and to facilitate the best use of fuel. **Railroads** came under the control of the **United States Railroad Administration** (USRA). A **War Labor Board** (WLB) was created to settle disputes in war industries. One consequence of this was increased recognition of **trade unions** and certain minimum standards in pay and conditions. As a million additional **women** workers joined the labor force they too gained recognition in the Women in Industry Service in the **Department of Labor**. The majority of women peace activists abandoned their prewar position. The **women's suffrage** campaign, however, continued, and the participation of women in defense industries strengthened their case and contributed to the final passage of the **Nineteenth Amendment**. **African Americans** were less fortunate. Segregated and discriminated against in the military, their armed service was belittled. Employment opportunities in northern industries encouraged a **Great Migration** from the South that resulted in better jobs and greater freedom, but was met by race violence in **East St. Louis** in 1917 and in several towns and cities in the North and South during the **"Red Summer"** of 1919.

By the time the United States entered the war, the conflict had long reached a stalemate in the trench warfare on the western front. Resisting Allied calls to incorporate American forces in their own armies, the United States commander, General **John J. Pershing** insisted on the independence of an **American Expeditionary Force** (AEF). Nonetheless, in the face of a renewed German offensive in March 1918, the first United States' troops fought under French and British command and played a crucial role in the second battle of the **Marne** at **Chateau-Thierry** and **Belleau Wood**. The presence of the American troops was enormously important psychologically. In September, half a million members of the AEF fought in the battle at **St. Mihiel,** and then more took part in the **Meuse-Argonne** offensive that eventually saw success in November. By the time the war ended, four million men had joined the armed forces and the AEF had suffered 255,970 casualties, including 50,280 dead.

After four years of trench warfare in the West, a second revolution in Russia, and a total of almost 10 million war dead, the war had ended with an Allied victory. Four empires, the German, Austro-Hungarian, Russian, and Turkish, collapsed. The **Treaty of Versailles** drawn up in 1919 also established a **League of Nations** that was hoped would prevent further wars. The United States Senate's failure to approve the treaty and/or American involvement in the League, despite President Woodrow Wilson's wishes, did much to undermine the settlement.

The legacies of the war and the failures of the peace settlement in many ways paved the way for the rise of Hitler in 1933 and the outbreak of World War II in 1939.

WRIGHT, HAROLD BELL (1872–1944). The novelist Harold Bell Wright trained for the ministry at Hiram College, Ohio, 1892–94, and although he did not complete the course, he served as a minister in a number of states between 1897 and 1908. His first book, *That Printer of Udell's*, based on his readings to his congregation, was published in 1903 and sold almost 500,000 copies. His second, *The Shepherd of the Hills* (1907), was also an enormous success and Wright became a fulltime writer. In 1909, he produced another best-seller, *The Calling of Dan Matthews*, and yet another, *The Winning of Barbara Worth*, in 1911. These successes were followed by *The Eyes of the World* (1914) and *When a Man's a Man* (1916). Wright's books stressed manly virtues, hard work, patriotism and self-reliance, the benefits of outdoor life, and the power of Christian faith.

Although he continued to write through the 1920s and 1930s, Wright's later novels did not match his earlier works' success. However, film versions of *The Winning of Barbara Worth* starring Gary Cooper in 1926 and *The Shepherd of the Hills* starring John Wayne in 1941 were successful.

– Y –

YEZIERSKA, ANZIA (1880–1970). Anzia Yezierska, who also wrote under the name Hattie Mayer, was born on the Russian-Polish border. Her family emigrated to New York in about 1890. Yezierska won a scholarship to Columbia University and graduated as a domestic science teacher in 1904. She taught from 1908 to 1915 but turned increasingly to writing. Her collection of short stories, *Hungry Hearts*, was published in 1920. It was followed by her novels, *Salome of the Tenements* (1923), *Bread Givers* (1925), *Arrogant Beggar* (1927), and *All I Could Never Be* (1932). The main theme of Yezierska's writing was the struggle of **immigrant** women to escape poverty and achieve the "American Dream." Yezierska worked for the WPA during the 1930s and also wrote about the Puerto Rican community.

YORK, ALVIN CULLUM (1887–1964). York was a soldier who had originally claimed conscientious objector status on religious grounds when America entered **World War I** but was persuaded that he would be fighting for God in a righteous conflict. Having joined the Army, on 8 October 1918, York became a national hero when during the **Argonne offensive** he single-handedly killed or captured nearly 150 Germans in a single day, armed only with a rifle and colt .45. He was awarded the Medal of Honor and returned home to a hero's welcome. *Sergeant York*, a film of his life starring Gary Cooper, was made in 1941.

YOUNG, OWEN D. (1874–1962). A graduate of Boston Law School and corporation lawyer, Owen Young joined General Electric (GE) as general counsel and vice president in 1913. He settled strikes in several GE plants during **World War I** and in 1919 he served on the **Second Industrial Conference**. In 1921, he chaired the subcommittee on Business Cycles and Unemployment of President **Warren Harding's Unemployment Conference**. He also lead the American delegation to the International Chamber of Commerce's Court of Arbitration. From 1925 to 1928, Young chaired the International Chamber of Commerce itself.

In 1919, **Woodrow Wilson** asked Young to join GE with Westinghouse, AT&T, and Western Electric to form a company to prevent the British Marconi Company from monopolizing long distance radio communication. The result was the Radio Corporation of America (RCA) which, with Young as chairman until 1929, pooled American radio technology and equipment. Young entered into agreements with foreign companies dividing the world into radio zones in order to facilitate communication. Under his leadership, RCA became the largest radio company in the world. In 1926, Young also helped to establish the National Broadcasting Company (NBC) and in 1928 the movie chain, Radio-Keith-Orpheum (RKO).

In 1922, Young became chair of the board of GE with **Gerard Swope** as president. The two men were associated with the introduction of programs of **"welfare capitalism,"** which did much to influence labor relations during the 1920s.

Young was a representative to the Reparations Conference in 1924 and was instrumental in securing the acceptance of the **Dawes**

Plan. In 1929, he chaired the meetings, which agreed to the **Young Plan**. President **Herbert Hoover** appointed Young to the **President's Research Committee on Recent Economic Changes** in 1929 and as chair of the Committee on Mobilization of Relief Resources of the **President's Organization on Unemployment Relief Commission** in 1931. He chaired the American Youth Commission, 1936–42 and was a member of the New York regional committee of the War Manpower Commission in 1942. Having retired from GE in 1939, Young returned as acting chair to supervise the manufacture of war orders in 1942. He finally retired in 1944 but after the war served on President Harry S. Truman's Advisory Committee on Foreign Aid (1947) and chaired the New York Commission on the Need for a State University (1946).

YOUNG PLAN, 1929. The Young Plan was drawn up by a committee headed by **Owen D. Young** and replaced the **Dawes Plan** in setting a revised schedule of annual payments of war reparations by Germany. The Young Plan reduced the total amount of reparations to $27 billion spread over 59 years and to be paid through a Bank for International Settlement in Basel, Switzerland. As Germany was unable to make any payments in 1931–32 because of the onset of the Depression, and Hitler refused to make payments after 1933, the Young Plan was ineffective.

– Z –

ZANGARA, GUISEPPE (1900–1933). Born in Italy, Guiseppe Zangara emigrated to the United States in 1923. He worked for a while in New Jersey and California before settling in Miami, Florida. Depressed because of lack of employment, he blamed first President **Herbert Hoover** and then President-elect **Franklin Roosevelt**. When Roosevelt visited Florida in February 1933, Zangara fired several shots at him in an attempted assassination. He missed Roosevelt but wounded several bystanders and the Mayor of Chicago, **Anton Cermak**, who was meeting Roosevelt. Sentenced initially to 84 years in prison, when Cermak died from his wounds Zanagara was sentenced to death. He was executed on 20 March 1933.

ZANUCK, DARRYL FRANCIS (1902–1979). The Hollywood **movie** tycoon, Darryl Zanuck served in the United States Army from 1916 to 1918 before moving to California to establish a career as a writer. He became a screenwriter with Warner Brothers Studio in 1923 and in 1925 became head of production. Following a dispute with Jack Warner, Zanuck left the company in 1933 and began work with Twentieth Century Films, later Twentieth Century-Fox. In 1935, Zanuck became vice president and he held the position until 1956. Zanuck was responsible for the production of many significant films including *The Grapes of Wrath* (1940), *Gentlemen's Agreement* (1947), and *The Robe* (1953). During World War II, he served with the Signal Corps and made films about the war effort. After breaking with Twentieth Century-Fox in 1956, Zanuck returned to take over the company in 1962. The success of his *The Longest Day* (1962) helped get the studio back on its feet, and this was followed with *The Sound of Music* (1965) and *Planet of the Apes* (1968). Internal disputes forced Zanuck to resign in 1971.

ZIMMERMAN TELEGRAM. A telegram from the German foreign secretary Arthur Zimmerman to the German minister in **Mexico** was intercepted by the British government in January 1917. On 24 February, the note was given to the United States ambassador in London. It indicated that Germany would resume unrestricted submarine warfare and proposed a Mexican-German alliance in the event of United States entry into **World War I**. If victorious, Mexico would recover Texas, New Mexico, and Arizona. When the telegram was published on 1 March, it caused considerable public anger and added support to **Woodrow Wilson**'s call for a declaration of war on 2 April 1917.

ZUKOR, ADOLPH (1873–1976). Born in Ricse, Hungary, Adolph Zukor emigrated to the United States in 1889 and established a fur company in Chicago in 1893. In 1903, Zukor opened a penny arcade with kinetoscopes (peep-show viewers) that he eventually turned into a "nickelodeon" **movie** theater. Zukor studied filmmaking and, using the technique of employing stars from the theater, established the Famous Players Film Company in 1912. By 1918, he employed a number of the big names in the new industry, including **Mary Pickford** and **Douglas Fairbanks**. By 1916, he had added distribution to showing and producing films and had taken over the Paramount company. In 1919, Zukor began to build a chain of larger "picture places" to show first-run movies, a practice **Samuel Goldwyn** and **William Fox** were also to follow. Paramount was forced into bankruptcy in 1933 as a consequence of the **Great Depression**, but Zukor remained as chairman and later president of the reorganized company. In creating a vertically integrated company that controlled film making from production to exhibition Zukor had helped to establish the studio system that dominated the industry until 1948, when the **Supreme Court** ruled that the studio constituted a monopoly in breach of antitrust laws. His "contribution to the industry" was recognized with a special Academy Award in 1949.

APPENDIX I

Presidents and Their Administrations, 1913–1933

Woodrow Wilson 1913–1921

Presidential Election Results:

Year		Popular Votes	Electoral Votes
1912	**Woodrow Wilson**	**6,296,547**	**435**
	Theodore Roosevelt	4,118,571	88
	William H. Taft	3,486,720	8
1916	**Woodrow Wilson**	**9,127,695**	**277**
	Charles Evans Hughes	8,533,507	254

Vice President: Thomas R. Marshall (1913–21)

Cabinet:
Secretary of State
   William J. Bryan (1913–15)
   Robert Lansing (1915–20)
   Bainbridge Colby (1920–21)
Secretary of the Treasury
   William G. McAdoo (1913–18)
   Carter Glass (1918–20)
   David F. Houston (1920–21)
Secretary of War
   Lindley M. Garrison (1913–16)
   Newton D. Baker (1916–21)
Attorney General
   James C. McReynolds (1913–14)
   Thomas W. Gregory (1914–19)
   Alexander M. Palmer (1919–21)
Postmaster General
   Albert S. Burleson (1913–21)

Secretary of the Navy
Josephus Daniels (1913–21)
Secretary of the Interior
Franklin K. Lane (1913–20)
John B. Payne (1920–21)
Secretary of Agriculture
David F. Houston (1913–20)
Edwin T. Meredith (1920–21)
Secretary of Commerce
William C. Redfield (1913–19)
Joshua W. Alexander (1919–21)
Secretary of Labor
William B. Wilson (1913–21)

Warren Harding 1921–1923

Presidential Election Results:

Year		Popular Votes	Electoral Votes
1920	**Warren G. Harding**	**16,143,407**	**404**
	James M. Cox	9,130,328	127

Vice President: Calvin Coolidge (1921–23)

Cabinet:
Secretary of State
Charles Evans Hughes (1921–23)
Secretary of the Treasury
Andrew W. Mellon (1921–23)
Secretary of War
John W. Weeks (1921–23)
Attorney General
Harry M. Daugherty (1921–23)
Postmaster General
William H. Hays (1921–22)
Hubert Work (1922–23)
Harry S. New (1923)
Secretary of the Navy
Edwin Denby (1921–23)

Secretary of the Interior
   Albert B. Fall (1921–23)
   Hubert Work (1923)
Secretary of Agriculture
   Henry C. Wallace (1921–23)
Secretary of Commerce
   Herbert C. Hoover (1921–23)
Secretary of Labor
   James J. Davis (1921–23)

Calvin Coolidge 1923–1929

Presidential Election Results:

Year		Popular Votes	Electoral Votes
1924	**Calvin Coolidge**	**15,718,211**	**382**
	John W. Davis	8,385,283	136
	Robert M. La Follette	4,831,289	13

Vice President: Charles G. Dawes (1925–29)

Cabinet:
Secretary of State
   Charles Evans Hughes (1923–25)
   Frank B. Kellogg (1925–29)
Secretary of the Treasury
   Andrew W. Mellon (1923–29)
Secretary of War
   John W. Weeks (1923–25)
   Dwight F. Davis (1925–29)
Attorney General
   Harry M. Daugherty (1923–24)
   Harlan F. Stone (1924–25)
   John G. Sargent (1925–29)
Postmaster General
   Harry S. New (1923–29)
Secretary of the Navy
   Edwin Denby (1923–24)
   Curtis D. Wilbur (1924–29)

Secretary of the Interior
Hubert Work (1923–28)
Roy O. West (1929)
Secretary of Agriculture
Henry C. Wallace (1923–24)
Howard M. Gore (1924–25)
William M. Jardine (1925–29)
Secretary of Commerce
Herbert C. Hoover (1923–28)
William F. Whiting (1928–29)
Secretary of Labor
James J. Davis (1923–29)

Herbert Hoover 1929–1933

Presidential Election Results:

Year		Popular Votes	Electoral Votes
1928	**Herbert C. Hoover**	**21,391,993**	**444**
	Alfred E. Smith	15,016,169	87
1932	**Franklin D. Roosevelt**	**22,809,638**	**472**
	Herbert C. Hoover	15,758,901	59

Vice President: Charles Curtis (1929–33)

Cabinet:
Secretary of State
Henry L. Stimson (1929–33)
Secretary of the Treasury
Andrew W. Mellon (1929–32)
Ogden L. Mills (1932–33)
Secretary of War
James W. Good (1929)
Patrick J. Hurley (1929–33)
Attorney General
William DeWitt Mitchell (1929–33)
Postmaster General
Walter F. Brown (1929–33)
Secretary of the Navy
Charles F. Adams (1929–33)

Secretary of the Interior
Ray L. Wilbur (1929–33)
Secretary of Agriculture
Arthur M. Hyde (1929–33)
Secretary of Commerce
Robert P. Lamont (1929–32)
Roy D. Chapin (1932–33)
Secretary of Labor
James J. Davis (1929–30)
William N. Doak (1930–33)

APPENDIX II
Constitutional Amendments

SEVENTEENTH AMENDMENT

Passed by Congress 16 May 1912. Ratified 31 May 1913.

The Senate of the United States shall be composed of two Senators from each state, elected by the people thereof, for six years; and each Senator shall have one vote. The electors in each state shall have the qualifications requisite for electors of the most numerous branch of the state legislatures.

When vacancies happen in the representation of any state in the Senate, the executive authority of such state shall issue writs of election to fill such vacancies: Provided, that the legislature of any state may empower the executive thereof to make temporary appointments until the people fill the vacancies by election as the legislature may direct.

This amendment shall not be so construed as to affect the election or term of any Senator chosen before it becomes valid as part of the Constitution.

EIGHTEENTH AMENDMENT

Passed by Congress 17 December 1917. Ratified 29 January 1919.

Section 1. After one year from the ratification of this article the manufacture, sale, or transportation of intoxicating liquors within, the importation thereof into, or the exportation thereof from the United States and all territory subject to the jurisdiction thereof for beverage purposes is hereby prohibited.

Section 2. The Congress and the several states shall have concurrent power to enforce this article by appropriate legislation.

Section 3. This article shall be inoperative unless it shall have been ratified as an amendment to the Constitution by the legislatures of the several states, as provided in the Constitution, within seven years from the date of the submission hereof to the states by the Congress.

NINETEENTH AMENDMENT

Passed by Congress 5 June 1919. Ratified 26 August 1920.

The right of citizens of the United States to vote shall not be denied or abridged by the United States or by any state on account of sex.

Congress shall have power to enforce this article by appropriate legislation.

TWENTIETH AMENDMENT

Passed by Congress 3 March 1932. Ratified 23 January 1933.

Section 1. The terms of the President and Vice President shall end at noon on the 20th day of January, and the terms of Senators and Representatives at noon on the 3rd day of January, of the years in which such terms would have ended if this article had not been ratified; and the terms of their successors shall then begin.

Section 2. The Congress shall assemble at least once in every year, and such meeting shall begin at noon on the 3rd day of January, unless they shall by law appoint a different day.

Section 3. If, at the time fixed for the beginning of the term of the President, the President elect shall have died, the Vice President elect shall become President. If a President shall not have been chosen before the time fixed for the beginning of his term, or if the President elect shall have failed to qualify, then the Vice President elect shall act as President until a President shall have qualified; and the Congress may by law provide for the case wherein neither a President elect nor a Vice President elect shall have qualified, declaring who shall then act as President, or the manner in which one who is to act shall be selected, and such person shall act accordingly until a President or Vice President shall have qualified.

Section 4. The Congress may by law provide for the case of the death of any of the persons from whom the House of Representatives may choose a President whenever the right of choice shall have devolved upon them, and for the case of the death of any of the persons from whom the Senate may choose a Vice President whenever the right of choice shall have devolved upon them.

Section 5. Sections 1 and 2 shall take effect on the 15th day of October following the ratification of this article.

Section 6. This article shall be inoperative unless it shall have been ratified as an amendment to the Constitution by the legislatures of three-fourths of the several states within seven years from the date of its submission.

TWENTY-FIRST AMENDMENT

Passed by Congress 20 February 1933. Ratified 5 December 1933.

Section 1. The eighteenth article of amendment to the Constitution of the United States is hereby repealed.

Section 2. The transportation or importation into any state, territory, or possession of the United States for delivery or use therein of intoxicating liquors, in violation of the laws thereof, is hereby prohibited.

Section 3. This article shall be inoperative unless it shall have been ratified as an amendment to the Constitution by conventions in the several states, as provided in the Constitution, within seven years from the date of the submission hereof to the states by the Congress.

SELECTED BIBLIOGRAPHY

Contents

INTRODUCTORY NOTE

There is a huge amount of literature covering the period 1913 to 1933. Normally, the Progressive Era, World War I, and the 1920s would be dealt with separately and each area would merit its own extensive bibliography. A few general works do take a broader view: some older works such as Preston William Slosson's *The Great Crusade and After 1914–1928* and Mark Sullivan's multivolume *Our Times 1900–1925*, for example, often provide useful detail and insight. More recent works are stronger on analytic content. One of the best of these in terms of detailed basic coverage is still Arthur S. Link with William B. Catton, *American Epoch: A History of the United States since the 1890s* (2 vols. covering 1897–1920, 1921–41). Longer surveys such as Walter La Feber, *The American Century: A History of the United States since the 1890s*, and James T. Patterson, *America in the Twentieth Century: A History*, are particularly good. Also useful is Page Smith, *America Enters the World: A People's History of the Progressive Era and World War*.

The authority on Woodrow Wilson is Arthur S. Link. Link's edited *Papers of Woodrow Wilson*, Princeton, Princeton University Press, was published in 69 volumes between 1965 and 1994 and is an essential source. His definitive biography *Wilson* was also published in several volumes: *The Road to the White House* (1947), *The New Freedom* (1956), *The Struggle for Neutrality, 1914–1915* (1960), *Confusions and Crises, 1915–1916*, and *Campaigns for Progressivism and Peace, 1916–1917* (1965), all by Princeton University Press. Link's short survey *Woodrow Wilson and the Progressive Era, 1910–1917* is also extremely good on the major political developments but has little to say on social and economic matters. A stimulating comparison that reveals a great deal about the Progressive period is John M. Cooper's *The Warrior and the Priest: Woodrow Wilson and Theodore Roosevelt*. Kendrick A. Clements provides a very good overview in *The Presidency of Woodrow Wilson*.

An established authority on the entry of the United States into the war is Ernest R. May, *The World War and American Isolation, 1914–1917*. More up-to-date is John Milton Cooper, *The Vanity of Power: American Isolationism and the First World War*, and Thomas J. Knock's prize-winning study, *To End All Wars: Woodrow Wilson and the Quest for a New World Order*. Older surveys such as Frederic L. Paxson's three volume *American Democracy and the World War* are still useful although very political in emphasis.

One of the best single accounts of the American military experience during World War I is Laurence Stallings's *The Doughboys: The Story of the AEF, 1917–1918.* Two contrasting views are presented by particpants in General John Pershing's *My Experience in the Great War* and Peyton C. March's *The Nation at War.* David Trask's *The AEF and Coalition Warmaking, 1917–1918* is a critical study of Pershing's leadership, while individual campaigns are thoroughly examined in Paul F. Braim's *The Test of Battle* and James Hallas's *Squandered Victory.*

Historical works dealing with the United States home front during World War I fall essentially into two groups: the semiofficial studies written shortly after the war, often by participants, and the newer more critical studies in the later 20th century. In addition to Paxson's *American Democracy and the World War*, Grosvenor B. Clarkson's *Industrial America in the World War*, Benedict Crowell and Robert F. Wilson's six-volume *How America Went to War*, W. D. Hines's *The War History of American Railroads*, and Gordon S. Watkins's *Labor Problems and Labor Administration in the United States during World War I*, all provide detailed factual accounts. Some later work was more critical in tone: John Maurice Clark, *The Costs of the World War to the American People*, and James R. Mock and Cedric Larson, *Words That Won the War: The Story of the Committee of Public Information 1917–1919*, are two excellent examples. A more balanced view is available in the later analytical studies. Ground-breaking in offering a new analysis that combines the military experience with the domestic is David M. Kennedy's *Over Here: The First World War and American Society.*

Domestic issues are dealt with in more detail by Neil A. Wynn, *From Progressivism to Prosperity: World War I and American Society*, while a comprehensive synthesis is provided by Robert H. Zeiger, *America's Great War: World War I and the American Experience.* John Milton Cooper, Jr., in *Pivotal Decades: The United States, 1900–1920* looks at the Progressive Era and war together, while Ellis Hawley's illuminating study, *The Great War and the Search for Modern Order: A History of the American People and Their Institutions, 1917–1933*, locates the war in the context of later developments. Steven Vaughn established the links between progressivism and the propaganda activities of the Committee on Public Information in his *Holding Fast the Inner Lines: Democracy, Nationalism, and the Committee on Public Information*, while Valerie Jean Conner links prewar and postwar labor relations with the war in her excellent study *The National War Labor Board: Stability, Social Justice, and the Voluntary State in World War I.*

The impact of the war on underprivileged groups has also been increasingly a subject of study. The story of the women's campaign for the vote previously stopped in 1915 and concluded in 1920. Barbara J. Steinson's *American Women's Activism in World War I* is a useful corrective. Maurine Weiner Greenwald's examination of the economic effects, *Women, War, and Work*, is the most detailed study of this important area and helps to fill many gaps. While Arthur E. Barbeau and Florettte Henri's slim study of *The Unknown Soldiers: Black American Troops in World War I* remains the best work on the military experience of African Americans, Mark Ellis's *Race, War, and Surveillance: African Americans and the United States Government during World War I* offers the most detailed study of black attitudes and the government's response to them.

Excellent surveys of all of these subjects and a useful bibliography can be found in the Organization of American Historians' *Magazine of History*, 17,1, October 2002.

Views of the "Jazz Age" were for a long time colored by Frederick Lewis Allen's journalistic study *Only Yesterday* and the short stories and novels of F. Scott Fitzgerald, both of which tended to emphasize the "revolution in manners and morals" and apparently care-free spirit of the decade. More critical appraisals appeared after World War II with George Soule's economic reassessment in *Prosperity Decade* and William E. Leuchtenburg's broader *The Perils of Prosperity*. Although more balanced, these studies still had elements of the traditional views evident in their discussion of broad cultural developments and politics judged against the coming of the Great Depression. Leuchtenburg's sympathetic analysis of the New Deal, shared by other writers like Arthur M. Schlesinger, Jr., also colored their perspective of the 1920s. Later writers focused more on social and cultural diversity and the survival particularly of ethnic and racial divisions. Lynn Dumenil, *The Modern Temper*, Ann Douglas, *Terrible Honesty: Mongrel Manhattan in the 1920s*, and David J. Goldberg's shorter *Discontented America* are among the best of more recent work on the 1920s. However, they tend to present social history without the politics, and they should be read in conjunction with political studies. Robert and Helen Merrell Lynd's famous study of Muncie, Indiana, *Middletown: A Study in Modern American Culture* provides fascinating contemporary insights on small-town life and values, and the report by the President's Research Committee on Recent Social Trends, *Recent Social Trends in the United States*, contains much detailed information.

Just as views of the 1920s as a whole have changed, so the appreciation of presidents Harding, Coolidge, and Hoover has undergone some revision. Warren G. Harding's presidency was for a long time regarded as one of the worst in American history, associated with political scandal and failure to adapt to the changing economic and cultural forces of modern society. Revelations of corruption that emerged after his death in the investigations of Teapot Dome and other affairs involving his administration, coupled with accusations of marital infidelity and the suggestion he had fathered an illegitimate child, ensured that Harding would be dealt with harshly by historians. From the 1920s on, with works such as William Allen White's *Masks in a Pageant* through to Mark Sullivan's volume of *Our Times: The Twenties*, Harding became more of a caricature than a real figure. Revision of these portrayals began with the opening of the Harding papers in 1964, but the most substantial reconsideration did not appear until Robert K. Murray's study of *The Harding Era: Warren G. Harding and His Administration* in 1969. Robert K. Ferrell's *The Strange Deaths of President Harding* provides a stimulating survey of some of the debates surrounding the Harding administration.

President Calvin Coolidge has been placed only marginally higher than Harding in the historical rankings. While his honesty and sobriety was always emphasized, his inactivity and willingness to allow business a free hand was judged harshly by post-Depression critics. The Coolidge administration was given little consideration in Frederick Lewis Allen's *Only Yesterday* and, as the title suggests, William Allen White's biography, *A Puritan in Babylon*, only confirmed what had become the established view of the 1920s. Even almost 30 years later, Donald R. McCoy's study *Calvin Coolidge: The Quiet President* did little to alter the image of "Silent Cal" that survived until Hendrik Booraem's *The Provincial: Calvin Coolidge and His World, 1885–1895* another 25 years later. The best reassessment of the Coolidge administration can be found in John Earl Haynes's edited collection *Calvin Coolidge and the Coolidge Era: Essays on the History of the 1920s*. The bibliographic essays by John Braeman and Lynn Dumenil are especially useful and cover the decade as a whole.

Much of the rewriting of the political history of the 1920s focused on governmental structures and the rise of the "managerial" or "associational" state. Work by Ellis W. Hawley in a number of journal articles and in *The Great War and the Search for Modern Order* demonstrated that the Republican administrations were far from the *laissez faire* governments they were once portrayed as. Central to this new perspective was Herbert Hoover, both as secretary of commerce and as president. Hoover's reputation was left in tatters as a consequence of the Wall Street Crash and the catastrophic Depression that followed. Even his defenders represented him as a conservative, upholding traditional values in contrast to the later "radical" departures of the New Deal. However, as historians after World War II began to revise their views of both Progressivism and the New Deal, so Hoover's role was subject to re-examination and that process speeded up with the opening of the Hoover Library in 1966. The biographies by Joan Hoff Wilson and David Burner, *Herbert Hoover: Forgotten Progressive* and *Herbert Hoover: A Public Life*, established continuities between the reform ethos, war years, and 1920s. Increasingly, too, the Hoover administration was seen as paving the way for the New Deal, rather than standing in contrast to it. These views were expressed in different ways by Harris G. Warren in *Herbert Hoover and the Great Depression*, Albert U. Romasco in *The Poverty of Abundance: Hoover, the Nation, the Depression*, and Ellis W. Hawley, et al., *Herbert Hoover and the Crisis of American Capitalism*. This changing historiography is outlined fully in the edited collections by Martin L. Fausold and George T. Mazuzan, *The Hoover Presidency: A Reappraisal*, and Mark M. Dodge, *Herbert Hoover and the Historians*. Useful coverage of all presidential elections can be found in Arthur M. Schlesinger, Jr.'s multivolume *History of American Presidential Elections*.

The various social, cultural, and economic trends of the 1920s are clearly outlined in the books by Dumenil, Goldberg, and Leuchtenburg cited above. Paula Fass's *The Damned and the Beautiful: American Youth in the 1920s* is also very useful in examining key aspects of the decade. African American life during this period is the subject of a growing scholarship, much of it concentrating on the Great Migration and settlement in particular northern centers. Several chapters in Joe William Tuttle, Jr.'s *The African American Experience* provide a good general survey and detailed bibliography. Similarly William H. Chafe's *The American Woman: Her Changing Economic and Political Roles, 1920–1970* offers a good introduction and overview to another area of expanding literature. The prewar period in labor history is well dealt with in Melvyn Dubofsky's *Industrialism and the American Worker* while the classic study of labor in the 1920s remains Irving Bernstein's *The Lean Years*.

The Wall Street Crash and causes and consequences of the Great Depression are well handled in Robert McElvaine's *The Great Depression* and also in David M. Kennedy's Pulitzer Prize winning *Freedom from Fear*. Kennedy also provides a good synopsis of the material relating to Franklin D. Roosevelt and the New Deal and Anthony J. Badger's *The New Deal* is one of the best more recent studies of the subject.

Several archive collections are particularly useful for this period. The Library of Congress has the private papers of many of the leading figures during this period. Presidential papers, some of which are more useful than others can be found in the Library of Congress and presidential libraries. The Wilson papers in the Library of Congress and at Princeton University, New Jersey, and the Hoover papers at the Hoover Library in West Branch, Iowa, are exceptionally full collections. The records of federal agencies held in the National Archives in Washington, D.C., also provide rich sources. Some of this material can be accessed via Web sites. Information on presidents and their administrations can be found via www.whitehouse.gov/history/presidents. Material on Coolidge and the decade as a whole is included in www.calvin-coolidge.org. The Library of Congress provides a great deal of material online and particularly useful is the American Memory site, "Prosperity and Thrift: The Coolidge Era and the Consumer Economy" at http://memory.loc.gov/ammem/coolhtml/coolhome.html. Among other very useful Web sites are http://historymatters.gmu.edu and www.galeuk.com.

BIBLIOGRAPHIES AND ENCYCLOPEDIAS

Carnes, Mark C., ed. *American History*. New York: Simon & Schuster/Macmillan, 1996.

Ciment, James, ed. *Encyclopedia of the Great Depression and New Deal*. Armonk, N.Y.: M.E. Sharpe, 2000.

Garraty, John A., and Mark Carnes, eds. *The American Dictionary of National Biography*. (24 vols.) New York: American Council of Learned Societies and Oxford University Press, 1999. Also available at www.anb.org.

Hogg, Ian V. *Historical Dictionary of World War I*. Lanham, Md.: Scarecrow Press, 1998.

Howlett, Charles F. *The American Peace Movement: References and Resources*. Boston: G. K. Hall, 1997.

Kellner, Bruce. *The Harlem Renaissance: A Historical Dictionary for the Era*. New York: Methuen, 1987.

Martin, Michael, and Leonard Gelber, eds. *Dictionary of American History*. Totowa, N.J.: Littlefield, Adams, 1965.

Olson, James S. *Historical Dictionary of the 1920s: From World War I to the New Deal, 1919–1933*. Westport, Conn.: Greenwood Press, 1988.

Renshaw, Patrick. *America in the Era of the Two World Wars, 1910–1945*. New York: Addison Wesley Longman, 1996.

Schaffer, Ronald, ed. *The United States in World War I: A Selected Bibliography*. Santa Barbara, Calif.: ABC-Clio, 1978.

U.S. Bureau of the Census. *Historical Statistics of the United States, Colonial Times to 1970*. Washington, D.C.: Government Printing Office, 1976.

Venson, Anne Cipriano, ed. *The United States in the First World War: An Encyclopedia*. Hamden, Conn.: Garland, 1996.

Woodward, David R., and Robert Franklin Maddox, eds. *America and World War I: A Selected Annotated Bibliography of English Language Sources*. New York: Garland, 1985.

GENERAL SURVEYS

Graham, Otis L. *The Great Campaigns: Reform and War in America, 1900–1928*. Englewood Cliffs, N.J.: Prentice Hall, 1971.

Karl, Barry D. *The Uneasy State: The United States from 1915 to 1945*. Chicago: University of Chicago Press, 1983.

La Feber, Walter. *The American Century: A History of the United States since the 1890s* (5th edition). New York: McGraw-Hill, 1998.

Link, Arthur S., with William B. Catton. *American Epoch: A History of the United States since the 1890s*, (2 vols. 1897–1920, 1921–41). New York: Alfred Knopf, 1963.

Patterson, James T. *America in the Twentieth Century: A History*, (5th edition). Fort Worth: Harcourt, 2000.

Schlesinger, Arthur M., Jr. *History of American Presidential Elections*. New York: McGraw Hill, 1971.

Slosson, Preston William. *The Great Crusade and After 1914–1928*. New York: Macmillan, 1930.

Smith, Page. *America Enters the World: A People's History of the Progressive Era and World War II*. New York: McGraw-Hill, 1985.

Sullivan, Mark. *Our Times 1900–1925*. New York: Charles Scribner's Sons, 1925–1935.

PREWAR PROGRESSIVISM, 1913–1917

Addams, Jane. *Twenty Years at Hull House*, New York: Macmillan, 1910.

Ashby, Le Roy. *William Jennings Bryan: Champion of Democracy*. New York: Macmillan, 1987.

Chambers, Clarke A. *Paul U. Kellogg and the "Survey": Voices for Social Reform and Social Justice*. Minneapolis: University of Minnesota Press, 1971.

———. *Seedtime of Reform: American Social Service and Social Action, 1918–1933*. Ann Arbor, Mich.: University of Michigan, 1967.

Chambers, John W., III. *The Tyranny of Change: Americans in the Progressive Era, 1890–1920*. New York: St. Martin's Press, 1992.

Chatfield, Charles. *For Peace and Justice: Pacifism in America, 1914–1941*. Knoxville: University of Tennessee Press, 1971.

Cooper, John Milton, Jr. *Pivotal Decades: The United States, 1900–1920*. New York: W. W. Norton, 1990.

———. *The Warrior and the Priest: Woodrow Wilson and Theodore Roosevelt*. Cambridge, Mass.: Harvard University Press, 1983.

Davis, Allen F. *American Heroine: The Life and Legend of Jane Addams*. New York: Oxford University Press, 1973.

———. *Spearheads for Reform*. New York: Oxford University Press, 1967.

DeBenedetti, Charles. *The Peace Reform in American History*. Bloomington: Indiana University Press, 1984.

Diner, Steven J. *A Very Different Age: Americans of the Progressive Era*. New York: Hill & Wang, 1998.

Dubofsky, Melvyn. *We Shall Be All: A History of the Industrial Workers of the World*. Chicago: Quadrangle, 1969.

Forcey, Charles. *The Crossroads of Liberalism: Croly, Weyl, Lippmann and the Progressive Era, 1900–1925*. New York: Oxford University Press, 1961.

Goldman, Eric. *Rendezvous with Destiny: A History of Modern American Reform*. New York: Vintage, 1956.

Higham, John. *Strangers in the Land: Patterns of American Nativism, 1860–1925*. New York: Atheneum, 1963.

Hofstadter, Richard. *The Age of Reform*. New York: Knopf, 1955.

La Follette, Belle Case, and Fola La Follette. *Robert M. La Follette*. (2 vols). New York: Macmillan, 1953.

Lears, T. J. Jackson. *No Place of Grace: Antimodernism and the Transformation of American Culture, 1880–1920*. New York: Pantheon, 1981.

Leiby, J. *A History of Social Welfare and Social Work in the United States*. New York: Columbia University Press, 1979.

Link, Arthur. *Woodrow Wilson and the Progressive Era, 1910–1917*. New York: Harper & Row, 1954.

Link, Arthur, and Richard L. McCormick. *Progressivism*. Arlington Heights, Ill.: Harlan Davidson, 1983.

Lubove, R. *The Professional Altruist: The Emergence of Social Work as a Career 1880–1930*. Boston: Harvard University Press, 1965.

Marchand, C. Roland. *The American Peace Movement and Social Reform*. Princeton, N.J.: Princeton University Press, 1973.

May, Henry F. *The End of American Innocence: A Study of the First Years of Our Own Time, 1912–1917*. Chicago: Quadrangle, 1964.

Parrish, Michael E. *Felix Frankfurter and His Time*. New York: Free Press, 1982.

Stansell, Christine. *American Moderns: Bohemian New York and the Creation of a New Century*. New York: Metropolitan, 2000.

Steel, Ronald. *Walter Lippmann and the American Century*. Boston: Little, Brown and Company, 1980.

Urofsky, Melvin I. *Big Steel and the Wilson Administration: A Study in Business-Government Relations*. Columbus, Ohio: Ohio State University Press, 1969.

Weinstein, James. *The Corporate Ideal in the Liberal State: 1900–1918*. Boston: Beacon Press, 1968.

——. *The Decline of Socialism in America, 1912–1925*. New York: Vintage, 1969.

Wiebe, Robert. *The Search of Order, 1877–1920*. New York: Hill and Wang, 1967.

Zunz, Olivier. *The Changing Face of Inequality: Urbanization, Industrial Development, and Immigrants in Detroit, 1880–1920*. Chicago: University of Chicago Press, 1982.

WOODROW WILSON

Baker, Ray Stannard. *Woodrow Wilson: Life and Letters*. (8 vols.) New York: Doubleday, 1927–1939.

Clements, Kendrick A. *The Presidency of Woodrow Wilson*. Lawrence: University Press of Kansas, 1992.

Heckscher, August. *Woodrow Wilson*. New York: Macmillan/Collier, 1991.

Link, Arthur S. *Campaigns for Progressivism and Peace*. Princeton, N.J.: Princeton University Press, 1965.

———. *Confusions and Crises, 1915–1916*. Princeton, N.J.: Princeton University Press, 1964.

———. *The New Freedom*. Princeton, N.J.: Princeton University Press, 1956.

———. *The Road to the White House*. Princeton, N.J.: Princeton University Press, 1947.

———. *The Struggle for Neutrality, 1914–1915*. Princeton, N.J.: Princeton University Press, 1960.

———. *Woodrow Wilson and the Progressive Era, 1910–1917*. New York: Harper & Row, 1954

Mulder, John M., et al., eds. *Woodrow Wilson: A Bibliography*. Westport, Conn.: Greenwood Press, 1997.

Thorsen, Niels Aaga. *The Political Thought of Woodrow Wilson, 1875–1910*. Princeton, N.J.: Princeton University Press, 1988.

Walworth, Arthur C. *Woodrow Wilson*. (2 vols.) New York: W. W. Norton, 1958.

Weinstein, Edwin A. *Woodrow Wilson: An Medical and Psychological Biography*. Princeton, N.J.: Princeton University Press, 1981.

FOREIGN RELATIONS

Bacino, Leo J. *Reconstructing Russia: U.S. Policy in Revolutionary Russia, 1917–1922*. Kent, Ohio: Kent State University Press, 1999.

Calhoun, Frederick S. *Power and Principle: Armed Intervention in Wilsonian Foreign Policy*. Kent, Ohio: Kent State University Press, 1986.

———. *Uses of Force and Wilsonian Foreign Policy*. Kent, Ohio: Kent State University Press, 1993.

Clements, Kendrick A. *Woodrow Wilson: World Statesman*. Boston: Twayne, 1987.

Fogelsong, David S. *America's Secret War against Bolshevism: U.S. Intervention in the Russian Civil War, 1917–1920*. Chapel Hill: University of North Carolina Press, 1995.

Katz, F. *The Secret War in Mexico: Europe, the United States and the Mexican Revolution*, Chicago: University of Chicago Press, 1981.

Kindall, S. G. *American Soldiers in Siberia*. New York: R. Smith, 1945.

Levin, N. Gordon. *Woodrow Wilson and World Politics: America's Response to War and Revolution*. New York: Oxford University Press, 1968.

Link, Arthur S. *The Higher Realism of Woodrow Wilson*. Nashville, Tenn.: Vanderbilt University Press, 1971.

———, ed. *Woodrow Wilson and a Revolutionary World, 1913–1920*. Chapel Hill: University of North Carolina Press, 1982.

McFadden, D. W. *Alternative Paths: Soviets and Americans, 1917–1920*. New York: Oxford University Press, 1993.

Ninkovich, Frank. *The Wilsonian Century: U.S. Foreign Policy since 1900*. Chicago: University of Chicago Press, 1999.

Quirk, R. E. *Affair of Honor: Woodrow Wilson and the Occupation of Veracruz*. New York: W. W. Norton, 1967.

Rhodes, B. D. *The Anglo-American Winter War with Russia, 1918–1919*. Westport, Conn.: Greenwood Press, 1988.

Saul, Norman E. *War and Revolution: The United States and Russia, 1914–1921*. Lawrence: University Press of Kansas, 2001.

Silverlight, John. *The Victor's Dilemma: Allied Intervention in the Russian Civil War*. London: Barrie & Jenkins, 1970.

Tulchin, Joseph S. *The Aftermath of War: World War I and U.S. Policy Toward Latin America*. New York: New York University Press, 1971.

THE WILSON ADMINISTRATION, WORLD WAR I, AND THE VERSAILLES TREATY

Ambrosius, Lloyd E. *Wilsonian Statecraft*. Wilmington, Del.: Scholarly Resource Books, 1991.

Bailey, Thomas A. *Woodrow Wilson and Lost Peace*. London: Macmillan, 1944.

Boemeke, Manfred F., et al., eds. *The Treaty of Versailles: A Reassessment after 75 Years*. Washington, D.C.: German Historical Institute, 1998.

Cooper, John Milton. *The Vanity of Power: American Isolationism and the First World War*. Westport, Conn.: Greenwood Press, 1969.

Devlin, Patrick. *Too Proud to Fight: Woodrow Wilson's Neutrality*. New York: Oxford University Press, 1975.

Ferrell, Robert H. *Woodrow Wilson and World War I, 1917–1921*. New York: Harper & Row, 1985.

Finnegan, John Patrick. *Against the Specter of a Dragon: The Campaign for American Military Preparedness, 1914–1917*. Westport, Conn.: Greenwood Press, 1974.

Keene, Jennifer D. *The United States and the First World War*. Harlow, England: Pearson Education, 2000.

Kendrick, A. Clements. *The Presidency of Woodrow Wilson*. Lawrence: University of Kansas, 1992.

Knock, Thomas J. *To End All Wars: Woodrow Wilson and the Quest for a New World Order*. New York: Oxford University Press, 1992.

Levin, N. Gordon. *Woodrow Wilson and World Politics: America's Response to War and Revolution*. London: Oxford University Press, 1968.

May, Ernest R. *The World War and American Isolation, 1914–1917*. Cambridge, Mass.: Harvard University Press, 1959.

Mayer, Arno J. *The Political Origins of the New Diplomacy, 1917–1918*. New Haven, Conn.: Yale University Press, 1959.

———. *The Politics and Diplomacy of Peacemaking*. London: Weidenfeld & Nicholson, 1968.

Mee, Charles L. *The End of Order: Versailles, 1919*. New York: Dutton, 1980.

Nelson, Keith L. *Victors Divided: America and the Allies in Germany, 1918–1923*. Berkeley: University of California Press, 1975.

Paxson, Frederic L. *American Democracy and the World War*. (3 vols.) Boston: Houghton Mifflin, 1936–1948.

Peterson, H. C. *Propaganda for War: The Campaign against American Neutrality, 1914–1917*. Port Washington, N.Y.: Kennikat Press, 1968.

Seymour, C. *American Diplomacy during the War*. Baltimore, Md.: Johns Hopkins University Press, 1934.

Sharp, Alan. *The Versailles Settlement: Peacemaking in Paris, 1919*. New York: St. Martin's, 1991.

Smith, Daniel M. *The Great Departure: The United States and World War I*. New York: John Wiley, 1965.

———. *Robert Lansing and American Neutrality, 1914–1917*. Berkeley: University of California Press, 1958.

Walworth, Arthur S. *America's Moment: 1918: American Diplomacy at the End of the War*. New York: Norton, 1977.

———. *Wilson and His Peacemakers: American Diplomacy at the Paris Peace Conference, 1919*. New York: Norton, 1986.

THE AMERICAN EXPEDITIONARY FORCE

Ayres, L. P. *The War with Germany: A Statistical Summary*. Washington, D.C.: U.S. War Department, 1919.

Beaver, Daniel R. *Newton D. Baker and the American War Effort, 1917–1919*. Lincoln: University of Nebraska, 1966.

Braim, Paul F. *The Test of Battle: The American Expeditionary Forces in the Meuse-Argonne Campaign*. Newark: University of Delaware Press, 1987.

Chambers, John Whitelly, II. *To Raise an Army: The Draft Comes to Modern America*. New York: Free Press, 1987.

Coffman, Edward M. *The Hilt of the Sword: The Career of Peyton C. March*. Madison: University of Wisconsin Press, 1966.

———. *The War to End All Wars: The American Military Experience in World War*. Oxford: Oxford University Press, 1968.

Freidel, Frank. *Over There: The Story of America's First Great Overseas Crusade*. New York: McGraw-Hill, 1990.

Hallas, James H. *Squandered Victory: The American First Army at St. Mihiel*. Westport, Conn.: Praeger, 1995.

Harbord, James G. *The American Army in France, 1917–1919*. Boston, Mass.: Houghton Mifflin, 1936.

Johnson, Herbert A. *Wingless Eagle: U.S. Army Aviation through World War I*. Chapel Hill: University of North Carolina Press, 2001.

Lee, David D. *Sergeant York: An American Hero*. Lexington: University Press of Kentucky, 1985.

Liggett, Hunter. *Commanding an American Army: Recollections of the Great War*. Boston, Mass.: Houghton Mifflin, 1925.

March, Peyton C. *The Nation at War*. New York: Doubleday, 1932.

Mitchell, William. *Memoirs of World War I*. New York: Random House, 1960.

Palmer, F. *Our Greatest Battle: The Meuse Argonne*. New York: Dodd, 1919.

Pencak, William. *For God and Country: The American Legion, 191–1941*. Boston: Northeastern University Press, 1989.

Pershing, John J. *My Experience in the Great War*. New York: Frederick Stokes, 1931.

Smythe, Donald. *Pershing, General of the Armies*. Bloomington: Indiana University Press, 1986.

Stallings, Laurence. *The Doughboys: The Story of the AEF, 1917–1918*. New York: Harper, 1963.

Trask, David F. *The AEF and Coalition Warmaking, 1917–1918*. Lawrence: University Press of Kansas, 1993.

——. *The United States in the Supreme War Council*. Middletown, Conn.: Wesleyan University Press, 1961.

U.S. War Department. *United States Army in the World War, 1917–1919*. (17 vols.) Washington, D.C.: U.S. Government Printing Office.

Vandiver, Frank E. *Black Jack: The Life and Times of John J. Pershing*. College Station, Tex.: A&M University, 1977.

WORLD WAR I AT HOME

Baruch, Bernard. *American Industry in the War*. New York: Prentice-Hall, 1941.

Beaver, Daniel R. *Newton D. Baker and the American War Effort, 1917–1919*. Lincoln: University of Nebraska Press, 1966.

Blakey, George T. *Historians on the Homefront: American Propagandists for the Great War*. Lexington: University Press of Kentucky, 1970.

Breen, William J. *Labor Market Politics and the Great War: The Department of Labor, the States, and the First U.S. Employment Service, 1907–1933*. Kent, Ohio: Kent State University Press, 1997.

———. *Uncle Sam at Home: Civilian Mobilization, Wartime Federalism, and the Council of National Defense, 1917–1919*. Westport, Conn.: Greenwood Press, 1984.

Bristow, Nancy K. *Making Men Moral: Social Engineering during the Great War*. New York: New York University Press, 1996.

Britten, Thomas, A. *American Indians in World War I: At Home and at War*. Albuquerque: University of New Mexico Press, 1997.

Chafee, Zechariah, Jr. *Free Speech in the United States*. Cambridge, Mass.: Harvard University Press, 1941.

Clark, John Maurice. *The Costs of the World War to the American People*. New Haven, Conn.: Yale University Press, 1931.

Clarkson, Grosvenor B. *Industrial America in the World War: The Strategy Behind the Lines*. Boston, Mass.: Houghton Mifflin, 1923.

Clayton, James D., and Anne Sharp Wells. *America and the Great War, 1914–1920*. Wheeling, Ill.: Harlan Davidson, 1998.

Conner, Valerie Jean. *The National War Labor Board: Stability, Social Justice, and the Voluntary State in World War I*. Chapel Hill: University of North Carolina Press, 1983.

Cornebise, Alfred E. *War as Advertised: The Four Minute Men and America's Crusade, 1918–1918*. Philadelphia: American Philosophical Society, 1984.

Creel, George. *How We Advertised America*. New York: Harper & Brothers, 1920.

Crowell, Benedict. *America's Munitions 1917–1918*. Washington, D.C.: U.S. Government Printing Office, 1919.

Crowell, Benedict, and Robert F. Wilson. *Demobilization: Our Industrial and Military Demobilization after the Armistice, 1918–1920*. New Haven, Conn.: Yale University Press, 1921.

———. *How America Went to War*. (6 vols.) New Haven, Conn.: Yale University Press 1921.

Cuff, Robert D. *The War Industries Board: Business-Government Relations during World War II*. Baltimore: Johns Hopkins University Press, 1973.

Davis, Allen F. "Welfare, Reform, and World War I." *American Quarterly* 19, Fall 1967, 516–33.

DeBauches, Leslie Midkiff. *Reel Patriotism: The Movies and World War I*. Madison: University of Wisconsin Press, 1997.

Ellis, Edward Robb. *Echoes of Distant Thunder: Life in the United States, 1914–1918*. New York: Coward, McCann & Geoghegan, 1975.

Gilbert, Charles. *American Financing of World War I*. Westport, Conn.: Greenwood, 1970.

Grubbs, Frank L. *Samuel Gompers and the Great War: Protecting Labor's Standards*. Wake Forest, N.C.: Meridional Publications, 1982.

——. *The Struggle for Labor Loyalty: Gompers, the A. F. of L. and the Pacifists, 1917–1920*. Durham, N.C.: Duke University Press, 1968.

Gruber, Carol S. *Mars and Minerva: World War I and the Uses of the Higher Learning in America*. Baton Rouge: Louisiana State University Press, 1975.

Harries, Meirion, and Susan Harries. *The Last Days of Innocence: America at War, 1917–1918*. New York: Random House, 1997.

Haydu, Jeffrey. *Making American Industry Safe for Democracy: Comparative Perspectives on the State and Employee Representation in the Era of World War I*. Urbana: University of Illinois Press, 1997.

Hines, Walter D. *The War History of American Railroads*. New Haven, Conn.: Yale University Press, 1928.

Jantzen, Steven. *Hooray for Peace, Hooray for War: The United States during World War I*. New York: Knopf, 1972.

Jensen, Joan. *The Price of Vigilance*, Chicago: Rand McNally, 1968.

Johnson, Donald. *The Challenge to American Freedoms: World War I and the Rise of the American Civil Liberties Union*. Lexington: University of Kentucky Press, 1963.

Kennedy, David M. *Over Here: The First World War and American Society*. New York: Oxford University Press, 1980.

Kerr, K. Austin. *American Railroad Politics, 1914–1920: Rates, Wages, and Efficiency*. Pittsburgh: University of Pittsburgh Press, 1969.

Kohn, Stephen M. *American Political Prisoners: Prosecutions under the Espionage and Sedition Acts*. Westport, Conn.: Praeger, 1994.

Koistinen, Paul A. C. *Mobilizing for Modern War: The Political Economy of American Warfare, 1865–1919*. Lawrence: University of Kansas Press, 1997.

Link, Arthur S., ed. *The Impact of World War I*. New York: Harper & Row, 1969.

Livermore, Seward W. *Woodrow Wilson and the War Congress, 1916–1918*. Seattle: University of Washington Press, 1966.

Luebke, Frederick C. *Bonds of Loyalty: German-Americans and World War I*. DeKalb, Ill.: Northern Illinois University Press, 1974.

McCartin, Joseph A. *Labor's Great War: The Struggle for Industrial Democracy and the Origins of Modern Labor Relations, 1912–1921*. Chapel Hill: University of North Carolina Press, 1997.

Mock, James R., and Cedric Larson. *Words That Won the War: The Story of the Committee on Public Information, 1917–1919*. Princeton, N.J.: Princeton University Press, 1939.

Mullendore, William Clinton. *History of the United States Food Administration, 1917–1919*. Stanford, Calif.: Stanford University Press, 1941.

Murphy, Paul L. *World War I and the Origin of Civil Liberties in the United States*. New York: Norton, 1979.

Offer, Avner. *The First World War: An Agrarian Interpretation*. Oxford: Clarendon Press, 1989.

Paxson, Frederic L. *American Democracy and the World War*. (3 vols.) Boston: Houghton Mifflin, 1936–48.

Peterson, H. C., and Gilbert C. Fite. *Opponents of War, 1917–1918*. Seattle: University of Washington Press, 1968.

Polenberg, Richard. *Fighting Faiths: The Abrams Case, the Supreme Court, and Free Speech*. New York: Viking, 1987.

Preston, William, Jr. *Aliens and Dissenters: Federal Suppression of Radicals, 1903–1933*. New York: Harper & Row, 1966.

Rochester, Stuart I. *American Liberal Disillusionment in the Wake of World War I*. University Park: Pennsylvania State University Press, 1977.

Schaffer, Ronald. *America in the Great War: The Rise of the War Welfare State*. New York: Oxford University Press, 1991.

Scheiber, Harry N. *The Wilson Administration and Civil Liberties, 1917–1921*. Ithaca, N.Y.: Cornell University Press, 1960.

Thompson, John A. *Reformers and War: American Progressive Publicists and the First World War*. Cambridge, England: Cambridge University Press, 1987.

Trask, David F., ed. *World War I at Home: Readings on American Life, 1914–1920*. New York: Wiley, 1970.

Vaughn, Stephen. *Holding Fast the Inner Lines: Democracy, Nationalism, and the Committee on Public Information*. Chapel Hill: University of North Carolina Press, 1980.

Ward, Larry Wayne. *The Motion Picture Goes to War: The U.S. Government Film Effort during World War I*. Ann Arbor: University of Michigan Research Press, 1985.

Watkins, Gordon S. *Labor Problems and Labor Administration in the United States during World War I*. Urbana: University of Illinois, 1919.

Wittke, Carl. *German-Americans and the World War*. Columbus: Ohio State Archaeological and Historical Society, 1936.

Wynn, Neil A. *From Progressivism to Prosperity: World War I and American Society*. New York: Holmes and Meier, 1986.

Zeiger, Robert H. *America's Great War: World War I and the American Experience*. Lanham: Rowman & Littlefield, 2000.

POSTWAR

Bagby, Wesley M. *The Road to Normalcy*. Baltimore: Johns Hopkins University Press, 1962.

Coben, Stanley. *A. Mitchell Palmer: Politician.* New York: Columbia University Press, 1963.

——. "A Study in Nativism: The American Red Scare of 1919–1920." *Political Science Quarterly* 79, March 1964, 52–75.

Crosby, Alfred W. *America's Forgotten Pandemic: The Influenza of 1918.* Westport, Conn.: Greenwood, 1976.

Murray, Robert K. *The Red Scare: A Study in National Hysteria.* Minneapolis: University of Minnesota Press, 1955.

Noggle, Burl. *Into the 1920s: America from Armistice to Normalcy.* Urbana: University of Illinois Press, 1974.

Rochester, Stuart I. *American Liberal Disillusionment in the Wake of World War I.* University Park: Pennsylvania State University Press, 1977.

Russell, Francis. *A City in Terror, 1919: The Boston Police Strike.* New York: Viking, 1975.

THE TWENTIES: GENERAL

Alchon, Guy. *The Invisible Hand of Planning: Capitalism, Social Science, and the State in the 1920s.* Princeton, N.J.: Princeton University Press, 1985.

Allen, Frederick Lewis. *Only Yesterday: An Informal History of the Nineteen-Twenties.* New York: Harper & Brothers, 1931.

——. *Since Yesterday: The Nineteen Thirties in America, September 3, 1929–September, 3 1939.* New York: Harper & Row, 1940.

Ashby, Leroy. *The Spearless Leader: Senator Borah and the Progressive Movement in the 1920s.* Urbana: University of Illinois Press, 1972.

Berger, Michael. *The Devil Wagon in God's Country: The Automobile and Social Change in Rural America, 1892–1929.* Hamden, Conn.: Archon Books, 1979.

Braeman, John, Robert Bremner, and David Brophy, eds. *Change and Continuity in Twentieth Century America: The 1920s.* Columbus: Ohio State University Press, 1968.

Burner, David. *The Politics of Provincialism: The Democratic Party in Transition, 1919–1932.* New York: Alfred Knopf, 1968.

Carter, Paul A. *Another Part of the Twenties.* New York: Columbia University Press, 1977.

——. *The Twenties in America.* New York: Columbia University Press, 1977.

Cohen, Lizabeth. *Making a New Deal*. New York: Cambridge University Press, 1990.

Cowley, Malcolm. *Exile's Return: A Literary Odyssey of the 1920s*. New York: W.W. Norton, 1934.

Douglas, Ann. *Terrible Honesty: Mongrel Manhattan in the 1920s*. New York: Farrar, Straus, and Giroux, 1995.

Dumenil, Lynn. *The Modern Temper: American Culture and Society in the 1920s*. New York: Hill & Wang, 1995.

Fass, Paula, *The Damned and the Beautiful: American Youth in the 1920s*. New York: Oxford University Press, 1977.

Fitzgerald, F. Scott. "Echoes of the Jazz Age," (1931) in *The Crack-Up with Other Pieces and Stories*. Harmondsworth, England: Penguin, 1965.

———. *The Great Gatsby*. (1926). New York: Collier, 1992.

———. "May Day," (1920) in *The Diamond as Big as the Ritz and Other Stories*. Harmondsworth, England: Penguin, 1962.

Flink, James J. *The Automobile Age*. Cambridge, Mass.: MIT Press, 1988.

Gordon, Colin, ed. *Major Problems in American History 1920–1945*, Boston: Houghton Mifflin, 1999.

Green, Harvey. *The Uncertainty of Everyday Life*. New York: HarperCollins, 1992.

Hawley, Ellis W. *The Great War and the Search for a Modern Order: A History of the American People and Their Institutions, 1917–1933*. New York: St. Martin's Press, 1992.

Hicks, John D. *Republican Ascendancy, 1921–1933*. New York: Harper & Row, 1960.

Hoffman, Frederick J. *The Twenties: American Writing in the Postwar Decade*. New York: Free Press, 1965.

Jardim, Anne. *The First Henry Ford: A Study in Personality and Business Leadership*. Cambridge, Mass.: MIT Press, 1970.

Lacey, Robert. *Ford: The Men and the Machine*. London: Heinemann, 1986.

Leach, William. *Land of Desire: Merchants, Power, and the Rise of a New American Culture*. New York: Pantheon Books, 1993.

Leighton, Isabel, ed. *The Aspirin Age 1919–1941*, New York: Simon & Schuster, 1949.

Leuchtenburg, William E. *The Perils of Prosperity, 1914–1932*. Chicago: University of Chicago Press, 1958.

Levine, Lawrence. *Defender of the Faith: William Jennings Bryan: The Last Decade, 1915–1925*. Boston: Harvard University Press, 1987.

Link, Arthur S. "What Happened to the Progressive Movement in the 1920s?" *American Historical Review*, 64, 1959, 833–51.

Lynd, Robert S., and Helen M. Lynd. *Middletown: A Study in Modern American Culture*. New York: Harcourt Brace, 1929.

Marchand, Roland. *Advertising the American Dream: Making Way for Modernity, 1920–1940*. Berkeley: University of California Press, 1985.

Mowry, George Edwin. *The Twenties: Fords, Flappers, & Fanatics*. Englewood Cliffs, N.J.: Prentice-Hall, 1963.

Nash, Roderick. *The Nervous Generation: American Thought, 1917–1930*. Chicago: Rand McNally, 1970.

Nevins, Allan, and Frank E. Hill. *Ford: Expansion and Challenge, 1915–1933*. New York: Scribner, 1957.

Parrish, Michael E. *Anxious Decades: America in Prosperity and Depression, 1920–1941*. New York: W. W. Norton, 1992.

President's Committee on Recent Economic Changes. *Recent Economic Changes in the United States; Report of the Committee on Recent Economic Changes, of the President's Conference on Unemployment, Herbert Hoover, Chairman, Including the Reports of a Special Staff of the National Bureau of Economic Research*. (2 vols.) New York: McGraw-Hill, 1929.

President's Research Committee on Social Trends. *Recent Social Trends in the United States; Report of the President's Research Committee on Social Trends, with a Foreword by Herbert Hoover*. (2 vols.) New York: McGraw-Hill, 1933.

Rhodes, Chip. *Structures of the Jazz Age: Mass Culture, Progressive Education, and Racial Disclosures in American Modernism*. London: Verso, 1998.

Saloutos, Theodore, and John D. Hicks. *Agricultural Discontent in the Middle West, 1900–1939*. Madison: University of Wisconsin Press, 1951.

Schlesinger, Arthur M., Jr. *The Age of Roosevelt: The Crisis of the Old Order, 1919–1933*. Boston: Houghton Mifflin, 1957.

Shannon, David. *Between the Wars: America, 1919–1941*. Boston: Houghton Mifflin, 1979.

Sitton, Tom, and William Deverell. *Metropolis in the Making: Los Angeles in the 1920s*. Berkeley: University of California Press, 2001.

Sklar, Robert, ed. *The Plastic Age, 1917–1930*. New York: George Braziller, 1970.

Snowman, Daniel. *America Since 1920*. London: Heinemann Educational, 1978.

Soule, George. *Prosperity Decade: From War to Depression, 1917–1929*. New York: Rinehart, 1947.

Tindall, George B. *The Emergence of the New South, 1913–1945*. Baton Rouge: Louisiana State University Press, 1967.

Tobin, Eugene M. *Organize or Perish: America's Independent Progressives, 1913–1933*. Westport, Conn.: Greenwood Press, 1986.

WARREN HARDING AND HIS ADMINISTRATION

Britton, Nan. *The President's Daughter*. New York: Elizabeth Ann Guild, 1927.

Ferrell, Robert K. *The Strange Deaths of President Harding*. Columbia: University of Missouri Press, 1996.

Giglio, James N. *H. M. Daugherty and the Politics of Expediency*. Kent, Ohio: Kent State University Press, 1978.

Mee, Charles L. *The Ohio Gang: The World of Warren G. Harding*. New York: Evans, 1981.

Moran, P., ed. *Warren G. Harding, 1865–1923: Chronology, Documents, Bibliographic Aids*. New York: Oceana Publications, 1970.

Murray, Robert K. *The Harding Era: Warren G. Harding and His Administration*. Minneapolis: University of Minneapolis Press, 1969.

———. *The Politics of Normalcy: Governmental Theory and Practice in the Harding-Coolidge Era*. New York: Norton, 1973.

Noggle, Burl. *Teapot Dome: Oil and Politics in the 1920s*. Baton Rouge: Louisiana State University Press, 1962.

Russell, Francis. *The Shadow of Blooming Grove: Warren G. Harding in His Times*. New York: McGraw Hill, 1968.

Sinclair, Andrew. *The Available Man: The Life Behind the Masks of Warren Gamaliel Harding*. New York: Macmillan, 1965.

Stratton, David H. *Tempest over Teapot Dome: The Story of Albert B. Fall*. Norman: University of Oklahoma Press, 1998.

Trani, Eugene P., and David L. Wilson. *The Presidency of Warren G. Harding*. Lawrence: Regents Press of Kansas, 1977.

White, William Allen. *Masks in a Pageant*. New York: Macmillan, 1928.

Wilson, David L. *The Presidency of Warren G. Harding*. Lawrence: Regents Press of Kansas, 1977.

CALVIN COOLIDGE AND HIS ADMINISTRATION

Booraem, Hendrik V. *The Provincial: Calvin Coolidge and His World, 1885–1895*. Lewisburg, Pa.: Bucknell University Press, 1994.

Coolidge, Calvin. *The Autobiography of Calvin Coolidge*. New York: Cosmopolitan Book Corporation, 1929.

———. *Foundations of the Republic: Speeches and Addresses*. New York: Scribner's Sons, 1926.

———. *The Price of Freedom: Speeches and Addresses*. New York: Scribner's Sons, 1924.

Coolidge, Grace. *Grace Coolidge: An Autobiography.* (Edited by Lawrence F. Wikander and Robert H. Ferrell.) Worland, Wyo.: High Plains Publishing, 1992.

Ferrell, Robert H. *The Presidency of Calvin Coolidge.* Lawrence, Kans.: University Press of Kansas, 1998.

Fuess, Claude Moore. *Calvin Coolidge: The Man from Vermont.* Boston: Little, Brown and Company, 1940.

Haynes, John Earl, ed. *Calvin Coolidge and the Coolidge Era: Essays on the History of the 1920s.* Washington, D.C.: Library of Congress, 1998.

MacKay, Kenneth. *The Progressive Movement of 1924.* New York: Columbia University Press, 1947.

McCoy, Donald R. *Calvin Coolidge: The Quiet President.* Lawrence: University Press of Kansas, 1988.

Murray, Robert K. *The Politics of Normalcy: Governmental Theory and Practice in the Harding-Coolidge Era.* New York: Norton, 1973.

Ross, Ishbel. *Grace Coolidge and Her Era: The Story of a President's Wife.* New York: Dodd Mead, 1962.

Silver, Thomas B. *Coolidge and the Historians.* Durham, N.C.: Academic Press for the Claremont Institute, 1982.

Slemp, C. Bascom. *The Mind of the President.* Garden City, N.Y.: Doubleday, Page, 1926.

Quint, Howard H., and Robert H. Ferrell, eds. *The Talkative President: The Off-the-Record Press Conferences of Calvin Coolidge.* Amherst: University of Massachusetts Press, 1964.

White, William Allen. *A Puritan in Babylon: The Story of Calvin Coolidge.* New York: Macmillan, 1938.

HERBERT HOOVER

Barber, William J. *From New Era to New Deal: Herbert Hoover, the Economists, and American Economic Policy, 1921–1933.* Cambridge: Cambridge University Press, 1985.

Best, Gary Dean. *Herbert Hoover: The Postpresidential Years, 1933–1964.* Stanford, Calif.: Hoover Institution Press, 1983.

———. *The Politics of American Individualism: Herbert Hoover in Transition, 1918–1929.* Westport, Conn.: Greenwood, 1975.

Burner, David. *Herbert Hoover: The Public Life.* New York: Alfred A. Knopf, 1978.

Burns, Richard Dean. *Herbert Hoover: A Bibliography of His Times and Presidency.* Wilmington, Del.: Scholarly Resources, 1991.

Calder, James D. *The Origins and Development of Federal Crime Control Policy: Herbert Hoover's Initiatives*. Westport, Conn.: Praeger, 1993.

Dodge, Mark M., ed. *Herbert Hoover and the Historians*. West Branch, Iowa: Herbert Hoover Presidential Library Association, 1989.

Fausold, Martin L. *The Presidency of Herbert C. Hoover*. Lawrence: University Press of Kansas, 1985.

Fausold, Martin L., and George Mazuzan, eds. *The Hoover Presidency: A Reappraisal*. Albany: State University of New York Press, 1974.

Gelfand, Lawrence E., ed. *Herbert Hoover: The Great War and Its Aftermath, 1914–1923*. Iowa City: University of Iowa Press, 1979.

Hawley, Ellis W., ed. *Herbert Hoover as Secretary of Commerce: Studies in New Era Thought and Practice*. Iowa City: University of Iowa Press, 1981.

Hawley, Ellis W., et al. *Herbert Hoover and the Crisis of American Capitalism*. Cambridge, Mass.: Schenkman, 1973.

Hoover, Herbert C. *The Memoirs of Herbert Hoover*. (3 vols.) New York: Macmillan, 1951–1952.

Lichtman, Allan J. *Prejudice and the Old Politics: The Presidential Election of 1928*. Chapel Hill: University of North Carolina Press, 1979.

Lisio, Donald J. *Hoover, Blacks, and Lily-Whites: A Study of Southern Strategies*. Chapel Hill: University of North Carolina Press, 1985.

———. *The President and Protest: Hoover, MacArthur, and the Bonus Riot*. Columbia: University of Missouri Press, 1974.

Lloyd, Craig. *Aggressive Introvert: A Study of Herbert Hoover and Public Relations Managment, 1912–1932*. Columbus: Ohio State University Press, 1973.

Nash, George H. *Herbert Hoover and Stanford University*. Stanford, Calif: Hoover Institution Press, 1988.

———. *The Life of Herbert Hoover*. (3 vols.) New York: W. W. Norton, 1983–1996.

Nash, Lee, ed. *Understanding Herbert Hoover: Ten Perspectives*. Stanford, Calif.: Hoover Institution Press, 1987.

Norton, Richard. *An Uncommon Man: The Triumph of Herbert Hoover*. New York: Simon & Schuster, 1989.

O'Brien, Patrick G. *Herbert Hoover: A Bibliography*. Westport, Conn.: Greenwood, 1993.

Olson, James S. *Herbert Hoover and the Reconstruction Finance Corporation, 1931–1933*. Ames: Iowa State University Press, 1977.

———. *Saving Capitalism: The Reconstruction Finance Corporation and the New Deal, 1933–1940*. Princeton, N.J.: Princeton University Press, 1988.

Romasco, Albert U. *The Poverty of Abundance: Hoover, the Nation, the Depression*. New York: Oxford University Press, 1965.

Rosen, Elliott A. *Hoover, Roosevelt, and the Brains Trust: From Depression to New Deal*. New York: Columbia University Press, 1977.

Schwarz, Jordan A. *The Interregnum of Despair: Hoover, the Nation, and the Depression*. Urbana: University of Illinois Press, 1970.

Smith, Gene *The Shattered Dream: Herbert Hoover and the Great Depression*. New York: William Morrow, 1970.

Smith, Richard Norton. *An Uncommon Man: The Triumph of Herbert Hoover*. New York: Simon & Schuster 1984.

Wilson, Joan Hoff. *Herbert Hoover: Forgotten Progressive*. Boston: Little Brown, 1975.

FOREIGN AFFAIRS

Adler, Selig. *The Uncertain Giant, 1921–1941: American Foreign Policy between the Wars*. New York: Macmillan, 1965.

Aldcroft, Derek. *From Versailles to Wall Street, 1919–1929*. Berkeley: University of California Press, 1977.

Buckley, Thomas H. *The United States and the Washington Conference, 1921–1922*. Knoxville: University of Tennessee Press, 1970.

Costigliano, Frank. *Awkward Dominion: American Political, Economic and Cultural Relations with Europe, 1919–1933*. Ithaca, N.Y.: Cornell University Press, 1984.

Curry, Earl R. *Hoover's Dominican Diplomacy and the Origins of the Good Neighbor Policy*. New York: Garland, 1979.

DeBenedetti, Charles. *Origins of the Modern American Peace Movement, 1915–1929*. New York: Kraus International, 1978.

DeConde, Alexander. *Herbert Hoover's Latin American Policy*. Stanford, Calif.: Stanford University Press, 1951.

Ellis, L. Ethan. *Republican Foreign Policy, 1921–1933*. New Brunswick, N.J.: Rutgers University Press, 1968.

Feis, Herbert. *The Diplomacy of the Dollar, 1919–1932*. New York: Norton, 1966.

Ferrell, Robert H. *American Diplomacy in the Great Depression: Hoover-Stimson Foreign Policy, 1929–1933*. New Haven, Conn.: Yale University Press, 1957.

———. *Peace in Their Time: The Origins of the Kellogg–Briand Pact*. New Haven, Conn.: Yale University Press, 1952.

Glad, Betty. *Charles Evans Hughes and the Illusions of Innocence*. Urbana: University of Illinois Press, 1966.

Grieb, Kenneth J. *The Latin American Policy of Warren G. Harding*. Fort Worth: Texas Christian University Press, 1976.

Kamman, William. *A Search for Stability: United States Diplomacy toward Nicaragua, 1925–1933*. Notre Dame, Ind.: University of Notre Dame Press, 1968.

Kuehl, Warren, and Lynne Dunn. *Keeping the Covenant: American Internationalists and the League of Nations, 1920–1939*. Kent, Ohio: Kent State University Press, 1997.

Leffler, Melvyn P. *The Elusive Quest: America's Pursuit of European Stability and French Security, 1919–1933*. Chapel Hill: University of North Carolina Press, 1979.

Marks, Sally. *The Illusion of Peace: International Relations, 1918–1933*. New York: Palgrave Macmillan, 2003.

Myers, William Starr. *The Foreign Policies of Herbert Hoover, 1929–1933*. New York: Scribners, 1940.

O'Connor, Raymond G. *Perilous Equilibrium: The United States and the London Disarmament Conference of 1930*. Lawrence: University of Kansas Press, 1962.

Randall, Stephen J. *United States Foreign Oil Policy, 1919–1948*. Kingston, Ontario: McGill-Queens University Press, 1986.

Tulchin, Joseph S. *The Aftermath of War: World War I and U.S. Foreign Policy toward Latin America*. New York: New York University Press, 1971.

Wilson, Joan Hoff. *American Business and Foreign Policy, 1920–1933*. Lexington: University of Kentucky Press, 1971.

———. *Ideology and Economics: U.S. Relations with the Soviet Union, 1918–1933*. Columbus: University of Missouri Press, 1974.

Wood, Bryce. *The Making of the Good Neighbor Policy*. New York: Columbia University Press, 1961.

ENTERTAINMENT, SPORT, AND THE MEDIA

Barnouw, Eric. *A Tower in Babel: A History of Broadcasting in the United States*. New York: Oxford University Press, 1966.

Burk, Robert F. *Much More Than a Game: Players, Owners & American Baseball since 1921*. Chapel Hill: University of North Carolina Press, 2001.

———. *Never Just a Game: Players Owners, & American Baseball to 1920*. Chapel Hill: University of North Carolina Press, 1994.

Covert, Catherine L., and John D. Stevens. *Mass Media between the Wars: Perceptions of Cultural Tension, 1918–1941*. Syracuse: Syracuse University Press, 1984.

Gomery, Douglas. *Shared Pleasures: A History of Movie Presentations in the United States*. Madison: University of Wisconsin Press, 1992.

Gorn, Elliott, and Warren Goldstein. *A Brief History of American Sports*. New York: Hill & Wang, 1993.

Krutch, Joseph Wood. *The American Drama since 1918: An Informal History*. New York: George Braziller, 1957.

Marchand, Roland. *Advertising the American Dream: Making Way for Modernity, 1920–1940*. Berkeley: University of California Press, 1985.

May, Lary. *Screening Out the Past: The Birth of Mass Culture and the Motion Picture Industry*. New York: Oxford University Press, 1980.

Ogren, Kathy J. *The Jazz Revolution: Twenties America and the Meaning of Jazz*. New York: Oxford University Press, 1989.

Riess, Steven A. *City Games: The Evolution of American Urban Society and the Rise of Sports*. Urbana: University of Illinois Press, 1989.

Sklar, Robert. *Movie-made America: A Social History of American Movies*. New York: Random House, 1975.

Smulyan, Susan. *Selling Radio: The Commercialization of American Broadcasting, 1920–1934*. Washington, D.C.: Smithsonian Institution Press, 1994.

Stearns, Marshall W. *The Story of Jazz*. New York: Oxford University Press, 1956.

Sullivan, Dean A., ed. *Middle Innings: A Documentary History of Baseball, 1900–1948*. New York: Bison Books, 2001.

PROHIBITION

Ashbury, Herbert. *The Great Illusion: An Informal History of Prohibition*. Garden City, N.Y.: Doubleday, 1950.

Clark, Norman H. *Deliver Us from Evil: An Interpretation of American Prohibition*. New York: W. W. Norton, 1976.

———. *The Dry Years: Prohibition and Social Change in Washington*. Seattle: University of Washington Press, 1988.

Kerr, K. A. *Organized for Prohibition: A New History of the Anti-Saloon League*. New Haven, Conn.: Yale University Press, 1985.

Kobler, John. *Ardent Spirits: The Rise and Fall of Prohibition*. New York: G. P. Putnam, 1973.

Lender, Mark E., and James K. Martin. *Drinking in American History*. New York: The Free Press, 1982.

Sinclair, Andrew. *Prohibition: The Era of Excess*. Boston: Little, Brown, 1962.

Timberlake, J. H. *Prohibition and the Progressive Movement, 1900–1920*. Cambridge, Mass.: Harvard University Press, 1963.

SOCIAL CONFLICTS AND IMMIGRATION

Abrams, Douglas Carl. *Selling the Old-Time Religion: American Fundamentalism and Mass Culture, 1920–1940*. Athens: University of Georgia Press, 2001.

Blee, Kathleen M. *Women of the Klan: Racism and Gender in the 1920s*. Berkeley: University of California Press, 1991.

Bodnar, John, et al. *Lives of their Own: Blacks, Italians, and Poles in Pittsburgh, 1900–1960*. Urbana: University of Illinois Press, 1982.

Bornet, Vaughn D. *Labor Politics in a Democratic Republic*. Washington, D.C.: Spartan, 1964.

Chalmers, David M. *Hooded Americanism: The History of the Ku Klux Klan*. Garden City, N.Y.: Doubleday, 1965.

Divine, Robert. *American Immigration Policy 1924–1952*. New Haven, Conn.: Yale University Press, 1957.

Eldot, Paula. *Governor Alfred E. Smith: The Politician as Reformer*. New York: Garland, 1983.

Feldman, Glenn. *Politics, Society, and the Klan in Alabama, 1915–1949*. Tuscaloosa: University of Alabama Press, 1999.

Furniss, Norman F. *The Fundamentalist Controversy, 1918–1931*. New Haven, Conn.: Yale University Press, 1954.

Ginger, Ray. *Six Days or Forever?* Tennessee v. John Thomas Scopes. Boston: Beacon Press, 1958.

Gonzales, Manuel G. *Mexicanos: A History of Mexicans in the United States*. Bloomington: Indiana University Press, 2000.

Gonzales, Manuel G., and Cynthia M. Gonzales. *En Aquel Entonces [In Years Gone By]: Readings in Mexican-American History*. Bloomington: Indiana University Press, 2000.

Higham, John. *Strangers in the Land: The Patterns of American Nativism, 1860–1925*. New York: Atheneum, 1981.

Huthmacher, Joseph J. *Massachusetts People and Politics, 1919–1933*. Cambridge, Mass.: Belknap Press, 1959.

Jackson, Kenneth T. *The Ku Klux Klan in the City, 1915–1930*. New York: Oxford University Press, 1967.

Josephson, Matthew and Hanna Josephson. *Al Smith: Hero of the Cities*. Boston: Houghton Mifflin, 1969.

Kaiser, David E. *Postmortem: New Evidence in the Case of Sacco and Vanzetti*. Boston: University of Massachusetts, 1985.

MacLean, Nancy. *Behind the Mask of Chivalry: The Making of the Second Ku Klux Klan*. New York: Oxford University Press, 1994.

Moore, Leonard J. *Citizen Klansmen: The Ku Klux Klan in Indiana, 1921–1928.* Chapel Hill: University of North Carolina Press, 1991.

O'Connor, Richard. *The First Hurrah: A Biography of Alfred E. Smith.* New York: Putnam, 1970.

Russell, Francis. *Tragedy at Dedham: The Story of the Sacco-Vanzetti Case.* New York: McGraw-Hill, 1962.

Silva, Ruth C. *Rum, Religion, and Votes: 1928 Reexamined.* University Park: Pennsylvania State University Press, 1962.

Slayton, Robert A. *Empire Statesman: The Rise and Redemption of Al Smith.* New York: Free Press, 2001.

Takaki, Ronald T. *Strangers from a Different Shore: A History of Asian Americans.* Boston: Back Bay Books, 1998.

AFRICAN AMERICANS

Anderson, Jervis. *A. Philip Randolph: A Biographical Portrait.* Berkeley: University of California Press, 1986.

———. *This Was Harlem: A Cultural Portrait, 1900–1950.* New York: Farrar, Straus, and Giroux, 1981.

Barbeau, Arthur E., and Florettte Henri. *The Unknown Soldiers: Black American Troops in World War I.* Philadelphia: Temple University Press, 1974.

Carter, Dan T. *Scottsboro: A Tragedy of the American South.* New York: Oxford University Press, 1971.

Cronon, David. *Black Moses: The Story of Marcus Garvey and the Universal Negro Improvement Association.* Madison: University of Wisconsin Press, 1955.

Drake, St. Clair, and Horace R. Cayton. *Black Metropolis: A Study of Negro Life in a Northern City.* (2 vols.) New York: Harcourt, Brace and World, 1945.

Ellis, Mark. *Race, War, and Surveillance: African Americans and the United States Government during World War I.* Bloomington: Indiana University Press, 2001.

Ellsworth, Scott. *Death in a Promised Land: The Tulsa Race Riot of 1921.* Baton Rouge: Louisiana State University Press, 1982.

Fairclough, Adam. *Better Day Coming: Blacks and Equality, 1890–2000.* New York: Viking, 2001.

Franklin, John Hope, and Alfred A. Moss. *From Slavery to Freedom.* New York: McGraw-Hill, 1994.

Franklin, John Hope, Alfred A. Moss, and August Meier, eds. *Black Leaders of the Twentieth Century.* Urbana: University of Illinois Press, 1982.

Goodman, James. *Stories of Scottsboro: The Rape Case that Shocked 1930s America and Revived the Struggle for Equality.* New York: Pantheon Books, 1994.

Gottlieb, Peter. *Making Their Own Way: Southern Black Migration to Pittsburgh, 1916–30*. Urbana: University of Illinois State Press, 1987.

Greenberg, Cheryl Lynn. *Or Does It Explode?: Black Harlem in the Great Depression*. New York: Oxford University Press, 1991.

Griffin, Farah Jasmine. *"Who Set You Flowin'?": The African-American Migration Narrative*. New York: Oxford University Press, 1995.

Grossman, James R. *Land of Hope: Chicago, Black Southerners, and the Great Migration*. Chicago: University of Chicago Press, 1989.

Harris, William H. *Keeping the Faith: A. Philip Randolph, Milton P. Webster, and the Brotherhood of Sleeping Car Porters, 1925–1937*. Urbana: University of Illinois Press, 1977.

Harrison, Alferdteen, ed. *Black Exodus: The Great Migration from the American South*. Jackson: University Press of Mississippi, 1991.

Haynes, Robert V. *Night of Violence: The Houston Riot of 1917*. Baton Rouge: Louisiana State University Press, 1976.

Hill, Robert A., ed. *The Marcus Garvey and Universal Negro Improvement Association Papers*. Berkeley: University of California Press, 1983–1986.

Huggins, Nathan. *Harlem Renaissance*. New York: Oxford University Press, 1971.

Kellogg, Charles Flint. *NAACP: A History of the National Association for the Advancement of Colored People, Volume 1: 1909–1920*. Baltimore: Johns Hopkins University Press, 1967.

Kornweibel, Theodore, Jr. *"No Crystal Stair": Black Life and the Messenger, 1917–1928*. Westport, Conn.: Greenwood Press 1975.

———. *"Seeing Red": Federal Campaigns against Black Militancy, 1919–1925*. Bloomington: Indiana University Press, 1998.

Lamon, Lester C. *Black Tennesseans, 1900–1930*. Knoxville: University of Tennessee Press, 1977.

Levine, David Alan. *Internal Combustion: The Races in Detroit, 1915–1926*. Westport, Conn.: Greenwood Press, 1976.

Lewis, David Levering. *W. E. B. Du Bois: Biography of a Race, 1868–1919*. New York: Henry Holt, 1993.

———. *When Harlem Was in Vogue*. New York: Oxford University Press, 1981.

Little, A. W. *From Harlem to the Rhine: The Story of New York's Colored Volunteers*. New York: Covici, 1936.

Locke, Alain, ed. *The New Negro*. (1925). New York: Atheneum, 1968.

Martin, Tony. *Race First: The Ideological and Organizational Struggles of Marcus Garvey and the Universal Negro Improvement Association*. Westport, Conn.: Greenwood Press, 1976.

McMillen, Neil R. *Dark Journey: Black Mississippians in the Age of Jim Crow*. Urbana: University of Illinois Press, 1990.

Nielson, David G. *Black Ethos: Northern Urban Life and Thought, 1890–1930*. Westport, Conn.: Greenwood Press, 1977.

Osofsky, Gilbert. *Harlem: the Making of a Ghetto, 1890–1930*. New York: Harper & Row, 1966.

Phillips, Kimberley L. *Alabama North: African-American Migrants, Community and Working-Class Activism in Cleveland, 1915–1945*. Urbana: Illinois State University Press, 1999.

Rudwick, Elliott M. *Race Riot at East St. Louis, July 2, 1917*. New York: Atheneum, 1972.

Scott, Emmett J. *The American Negro in the World War*. Chicago: Homewood Press, 1919.

———. *Negro Migration during the Great War*. New York: Oxford University Press, 1920.

Spear, Allen H. *Black Chicago: The Making of a Negro Ghetto, 1890–1920*. Chicago: University of Chicago Press, 1967.

Stein, Judith. *The World of Marcus Garvey: Race and Class in Modern Society*. Baton Rouge: Louisiana State University Press, 1986.

Thomas, Richard W. *Life for Us Is What We Make It: Building Black Community in Detroit, 1915–1945*. Bloomington: Indiana University Press, 1992.

Trotter, Joe William, Jr., ed. *Black Milwaukee: The Making of an Industrial Proletariat. 1915–1945*. Urbana: University of Illinois Press, 1985.

———. *Coal, Class, and Color: Blacks in Southern West Virginia, 1915–1932*. Urbana: University of Illinois Press, 1990.

———. *The Great Migration in Historical Perspective: New Dimensions of Race, Class, and Gender*. Bloomington: Indiana University Press, 1991.

Tuttle, William M. *Race Riot: Chicago in the Red Summer of 1919*. New York: Atheneum, 1970.

Weiss, Nancy J. *The National Urban League, 1910–1940*. New York: Oxford University Press, 1974.

Williams, Lee E., and Lee E. Williams II. *Anatomy of Four Race Riots: Racial Conflict in Knoxville, Elaine, Tulsa, and Chicago, 1919–1921*. Jackson: University and College Press of Mississippi, 1972.

Williams, Lillian Serece. *The Development of a Black Community: Buffalo, New York, 1900–1940*. Bloomington: Indiana University Press, 1999.

WOMEN

Alonso, Harriet Hyman. *Peace as a Women's Issue: A History of the U.S. Movement for World Peace and Women's Rights*. Syracuse, N.Y.: Syracuse University Press, 1993.

Baker, Jean H. *Votes for Women: The Struggle for Suffrage Revisited*. New York: Oxford University Press, 2002.

Becker, Susan. *The Origins of the Equal Rights Amendment: American Feminism between the Wars*. Westport, Conn.: Garland Publishing, 1985.

Brown, Dorothy M. *Setting a Course: American Women in the 1920s*. Boston: Twayne, 1987.

Buechler, Steven M. *The Transformation of the Woman Suffrage Movement*. New Brunswick, N.J.: Rutgers University Press, 1986.

———. *Women's Movements in the United States: Woman Suffrage, Equal Rights and Beyond*. New Brunswick, N.J.: Rutgers University Press, 1990.

Chafe, William H. *The American Woman: Her Changing Economic and Political Roles, 1920–1970*. New York: Oxford University Press, 1972.

Cook, Blanche Wiesen. *Eleanor Roosevelt: A Life*. New York: Viking, 1992.

Davis, Allen F. *American Heroine: The Life and Legend of Jane Addams*. New York: Oxford University Press, 1973.

Degler, Carl. *At Odds: Women and the Family in America from the Revolution to the Present*. New York: Oxford University Press, 1980.

Elshtain, Jean Bethke. *Jane Addams and the Dream of American Democracy*. New York: Basic Books, 2001.

Finnegan, Margaret. *Selling Suffrage: Consumer Culture and Votes for Women*. New York: Columbia University Press, 1999.

Flexner, Eleanor. *A Century of Struggle: The Women's Rights Movement in the United States*. Cambridge, Mass.: Harvard University Press, 1959.

Foster, Carrie. *The Women and the Warriors: The United States Section of the Women's International League for Peace and Freedom, 1915–1946*. Syracuse, N.Y.: Syracuse University Press, 1995.

Gavin, Lettie. *American Women in World War I: They Also Served*. Boulder Springs: University Press of Colorado, 1999.

Greenwald, Maurine. *Women, War, and Work: The Impact of World War I on Women Workers in the United States*. Westport, Conn.: Greenwood, 1980.

Harvey, Anna L. *Votes without Leverage: Women in American Electoral Politics, 1920–1970*. Cambridge: Cambridge University Press, 1998.

Kennedy, Kathleen. *Disloyal Mothers and Scurrilous Citizens: Women and Subversion during World War I*. Bloomington: Indiana University Press, 1999.

Kessler-Harris, Alice. *Out to Work: A History of Wage-earning Women in the United States*. New York: Oxford University Press, 1990.

Kraditor, Aileen. *The Ideas of the Woman Suffrage Movement, 1890–1920*. New York: Columbia University Press, 1965.

Lemons, J. Stanley. *The Woman Citizen: Social Feminism in the 1920s*. Urbana: University of Illinois Press, 1975.

Lunardini, Christine A. *From Equal Suffrage to Equal Rights: Alice Paul and the National Woman's Party, 1910–1928*. New York: iUniverse, 1986.

May, Elaine Tyler. *Great Expectations: Marriage and Divorce in Post-Victorian America*. Chicago: University of Chicago Press, 1983.

O'Neill, William L. *Everyone Was Brave: A History of Feminism in America*. Chicago: Quadrangle, 1971.

Paulson, Ross Evans. *Women's Suffrage and Prohibition: A Comparative Study of Equality and Social Control*. Glenview, Ill.: Scott Foresman/Addison Wesley, 1973.

Scharf, Lois. *Eleanor Roosevelt: First Lady of American Liberalism*. Boston: Twayne, 1988.

Scharf, Lois, and Joan Jensen, eds. *Decades of Discontent: The Women's Movement, 1920–1940*. Westport, Conn.: Greenwood Press, 1983.

Schneider, Dorothy, and Carl J. Schneider. *Into the Breach: American Women Overseas in World War I*. New York: Viking, 1991.

Sprull, Marjories, ed. *One Woman One Vote: The Rediscovery of the Women's Suffrage Movement*. New York: New Sage Press, 1995.

Steinson, Barabara. *American Women's Activism in World War I*. New York: Garland, 1982.

Strom, Sharon Hartman. *Beyond the Typewriter: Gender, Class, and the Origins of Modern Office Work*. Urbana: University of Illinois Press, 1992.

Walker, Nancy A. *Shaping Our Mothers' World: American Women's Magazines*. Jackson: University Press of Mississippi, 2000.

LABOR MOVEMENTS

Barrett, James R. *William Z. Foster and the Tragedy of American Radicalism*. Urbana: University of Illinois Press, 1999.

Bernstein, Irving. *The Lean Years: A History of the American Worker, 1920–1933*. Boston: Houghton Mifflin, 1960.

Brandes, Stuart D. *American Welfare Capitalism, 1880–1940*. Chicago: University of Chicago Press, 1976.

Brody, David. *Labor in Crisis: The Steel Strike of 1919*. Philadelphia: Lippincott, 1965.

———. *Workers in Industrial America: Essays on the Twentieth Century Struggle*. New York: Oxford University Press, 1980.

Carlson, Peter. *Roughneck: The Life and Times of Big Bill Haywood*. New York: W. W. Norton, 1983.

Dubofsky, Melvyn. *"Big Bill" Haywood*. Manchester, England: Manchester University Press, 1987.

———. *Industrialism and the American Worker, 1865–1920*. Wheeling, Ill.: Harlan Davidson, 1996.

———. *We Shall Be All: A History of the Industrial Workers of the World*. New York: Quadrangle, 1969.

Foner, Philip S. *History of the Labor Movement in the United States: Volume 6: On the Eve of America's Entrance into World War I, 1915–16*. New York: International Publishers, 1982.

———. *History of the Labor Movement in the United States: Volume 7; Labor and World War I*. New York: International Publishers, 1987.

Gerstle, Gary. *Working-Class Americanism: The Politics of Labor in a Textile City, 1914–1960*. Princeton, N.J.: Princeton University Press, 2002.

Green, James R. *The World of the Worker: Labor in Twentieth Century America*. Urbana: University of Illinois Press, 1998.

Hall, Greg. *Harvest Wobblies: The Industrial Workers of the World and Agricultural Laborers in the American West, 1905–1930*. Eugene: University of Oregon Press, 2001.

Kaufman, Stuart B., et al., eds. *The Samuel Gompers Papers*. (4 vols.) Urbana: University of Illinois Press, 1986–1992.

Livesay, Harold. *Samuel Gompers and Organized Labor in America*. Boston: Little, Brown, 1978.

Montgomery, David. *The Fall of the House of Labor: The Workplace, the State, and American Labor Activism, 1865–1925*. Cambridge: Cambridge University Press, 1987.

———. *Workers' Control in America: Studies in the History of Work, Technology, and Labor Struggles*. New York: Cambridge University Press, 1979.

Renshaw, Patrick. *The Wobblies: The Story of the IWW and Syndicalism in the United States*. New York: Doubleday, 1967.

Schatz, Ronald W. *The Electrical Workers: A History of Labor at General Electric and Westinghouse, 1923–1960*. Urbana: University of Illinois Press, 1987.

Sellars, Nigel A. *Oil, Wheat, and Wobblies: The Industrial Workers of the World in Oklahoma, 1905–1930*. Norman: University of Oklahoma Press, 1998.

Shannon, David A. *The Socialist Party of America: A History*. New York: Macmillan, 1955.

Weinstein, James. *The Decline of Socialism in America, 1912–1925*. Brunswick, N.J: Rutgers University Press, 1984.

Zeiger, Robert. *American Workers, Amerian Unions*. Baltimore, Md.: Johns Hopkins University Press, 1994.

THE CRASH AND GREAT DEPRESSION

Bernstein, Michael A. *The Great Depression: Delayed Recovery and Economic Change in America, 1929–1939*. Cambridge: Cambridge University Press, 1987.

Bird, Caroline. *The Invisible Scar*. New York: McKay, 1966.

Bordo, Michael D., Claudia Goldin, and Eugene N. White, eds. *The Defining Moment: The Great Depression and the American Economy in the Twentieth Century*. Chicago: University of Chicago Press, 1998.

Chandler, Lester V. *America's Greatest Depression, 1919–1941*. New York: Harper, 1970.

Daniels, Roger. *The Bonus March: An Episode of the Great Depression*. Westport, Conn.: Greenwood Press, 1941.

Fearon, Peter. *War, Prosperity and Depression, 1919–1941*. Deddington, Oxfordshire: Philip Allan, 1987.

Friedman, Milton, and Anna Jacobson Schwartz. *The Great Contraction, 1929–1933*. Princeton, N.J.: Princeton University Press, 1965.

Galbraith, John Kenneth. *The Great Crash: 1929*. Boston: Houghton Mifflin, 1955.

Garraty, John A. *The Great Depression: An Inquiry into the Causes, Course, and Consequences of the Worldwide Depression of the Nineteen Thirties*. New York: Harcourt Brace Jovanovich, 1986.

Klingaman, William K. *1929: The Year of the Great Crash*. New York: Harper & Row, 1989.

Lowitt, Richard, and Maurine Beasley, eds. *One Third of a Nation: Lorena Hickock Reports on the Great Depression*. Urbana: University of Illinois Press, 1981.

McElvaine, Robert S. *The Great Depression: America 1929–1941*. New York: Times Books, 1984.

Rosen, Elliott. *Hoover, Roosevelt, and the Brains Trust: From Depression to New Deal*. New York: Columbia University Press, 1977.

Rothbard, Murray N. *America's Greatest Depression*. Princeton, N.J.: D. Van Nostrand, 1963.

Terkel, Studs. *Hard Times: An Oral History of the Great Depression*. New York: Pantheon, 1970.

Thomas, Gordon, and Morgan-Witts, M. *The Day the Bubble Burst: A Social History of the Wall Street Crash of 1929*. New York: Doubleday and Company.

Schlesinger, Arthur M., Jr. *The Age of Roosevelt: The Politics of Upheaval*. Boston: Houghton Mifflin, 1960.

Watkins, T. H. *The Great Depression: America in the 1930s*. Boston: Little, Brown, 1993.

FRANKLIN D. ROOSEVELT,
THE ELECTION OF 1932, AND NEW DEAL

Badger, Anthony J. *The New Deal: The Depression Years, 1933–40*. New York: Hill & Wang, 1989.

Burns, James MacGregor. *Roosevelt: The Lion and the Fox*. New York: Harcourt Brace, 1956.

———. *Roosevelt: The Soldier of Freedom*. New York: Harcourt Brace Jovanovich, 1970.

Davis, Kenneth S. *FDR*. (4 vols.) New York: Random House, 1985–1993.

Friedel, Frank. *Franklin D. Roosevelt: The Triumph*. Boston: Little, Brown, 1956.

Kennedy, David M. *Freedom from Fear: The American People in Depression and War, 1929–1945*. New York: Oxford University Press, 1999.

Leuchtenburg, William E. *Franklin D. Roosevelt and the New Deal, 1932–1940*. New York: Harper & Row, 1963.

Schlesinger, Arthur M., Jr. *The Coming of the New Deal*. Boston: Houghton Mifflin, 1958.

ABOUT THE AUTHOR

Neil A. Wynn was born in 1947 to British parents stationed in The Hague, Holland. When the family returned to Great Britain. Wynn completed his school education in Edinburgh, Scotland, where he also attended university from 1965 to 1969. Following his graduation with an M.A. in History he went to the Open University in England to undertake research for his Ph.D. After four years, including a year as a graduate assistant at State University of New York at Buffalo, Wynn was awarded the first Ph.D. in History at the Open University in 1973 for his thesis on "The Afro-American and the Second World War."

In 1973 Dr. Wynn took up an appointment as lecturer in History at what was then Glamorgan Polytechnic (later the Polytechnic of Wales and from 1989 the University of Glamorgan) to develop and teach courses in American History and American Studies. He was subsequently promoted to Senior Lecturer, Principal Lecturer, and in 1994 became Reader in History and American Studies. In 1979 Dr. Wynn was awarded a fellowship by the American Council of Learned Societies and spent a year engaged in research in Washington, D.C. In 2003, Dr. Wynn took a chair in Twentieth Century American History at the University of Gloucestershire. He has taught on international programs at Central Missouri State University and at the Maastricht Center for Transatlantic Studies in the Netherlands, of which he is a director.

Dr. Wynn is the author of *The Afro-American and the Second World War* (1976, 1993), *From Progressivism to Prosperity: World War I and American Society* (1986), chapters on "The 1940s" and "The 1960s" in Willi Paul Adams, ed., *Die Vereinigten Staaten von Amerika* (*The United States of America*) (1977), and various articles on African American and American History. He also coedited *America's Century: Perspectives on U.S. History since 1900* (1993). Since 1990 he has reported on events in the United States for the *Annual Register*.